AMERICAN BAR ASSOCIATION
Business Law Section

Guide to Representing Animal Protection Organizations

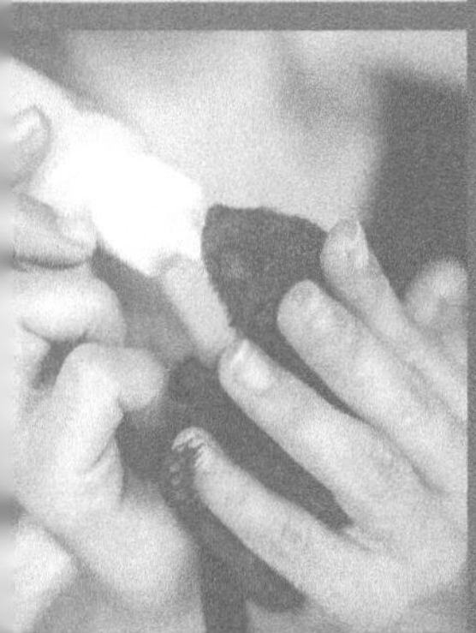

Daina Bray and Yolanda Eisenstein
EDITORS

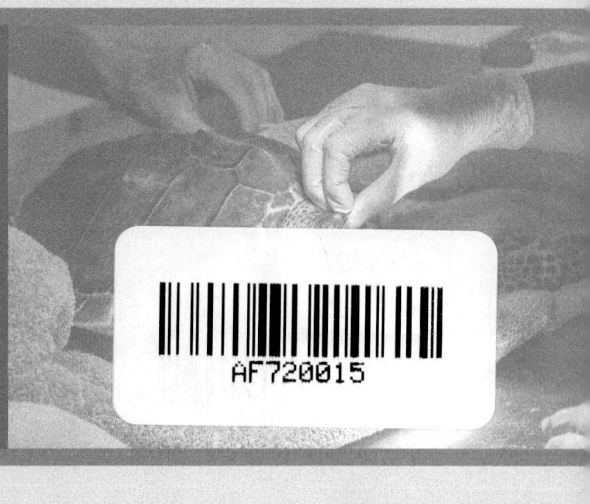

Cover design by Catherine Zaccarine.

The photographs on the back cover are provided courtesy of the editors. Photo back cover at bottom left by Kayla Forleo, photo at bottom right by Jesse Freidin.

Printed in the United States of America.

27 26 25 24 23 5 4 3 2 1

ISBN: 978-1-63905-396-4

Discounts are available for books ordered in bulk. Special consideration is given to state bars, CLE programs, and other bar-related organizations. Inquire at Book Publishing, ABA Publishing, American Bar Association, 321 N. Clark Street, Chicago, Illinois 60654-7598.

www.shopABA.org

For the Animals

Contents

Acknowledgments

We are grateful to the authors, without whom this important book would not have been possible and who took time away from their busy legal practices to contribute. We thank Rebecca Álvarez, Associate Professor at New Mexico Highlands University, who generously volunteered to assemble and format the work of seventeen authors. We also thank the Nonprofit Organizations Committee in the ABA Business Law Section for its early support of the idea for this book, and the Tort, Trial & Insurance Practice Section (TIPS) of the ABA for its longstanding support of animal law and animal lawyers—the editors and many of the authors met through the ABA TIPS Animal Law Committee.

Introduction

Daina Bray and Yolanda Eisenstein, Editors

Our understanding of the internal lives and experiences of nonhuman animals (referred to as "animals" in this volume, although of course we are animals as well) is growing at an unprecedented pace. The science of animal behavior regularly brings us information that challenges long-held beliefs. We are beginning to appreciate and understand that animal sentience—their ability to experience feelings, both pleasant and painful—is in many ways more similar than different from our own. This greater knowledge about the lives of animals and our relationship with them raises critical questions about our interactions with them.

These interactions, particularly our mistreatment of animals and the widespread destruction of the environment we share, are at the center of many of the most pressing challenges of our day. The situation of animals—whether viewed at the level of individual animals, species, or ecosystems—is dire. The Anthropocene, or this geologic epoch in which human activity is having a significant impact on climate and other natural systems, is characterized by dramatic environmental degradation, widespread and systemic cruelty to animals, and the Sixth Mass Extinction. Whether we look to the climate crisis (of which our intensive raising of animals for food is a major driver) or the COVID-19 pandemic (which likely spread from a live animal market), we cannot escape the harms that we visit on animals. It is thus nothing short of critical that our efforts to protect animals continue to grow, evolve, and become more effective. With these thoughts in mind, we present this book with the hope that it will contribute in some small way to addressing these challenges, by supporting the efforts of the animal protection organizations that are on the frontlines of these global issues.

As animal lawyers, we are thrilled to see a need for this book, which speaks volumes about the growth and progress of animal protection law and the increasing sophistication of organizations working in this area. We are honored to have worked with a group of leading experts in the field and to contribute to that progress with this essential guidebook.

Intended Audience

This book is for the growing number of lawyers who advise and support organizations working for animals. In the title and throughout the book, we refer to these groups as "animal protection organizations," to denote that the intended audience is the lawyer representing a client that is working to improve the situation of animals. Such groups may focus on animal well-being as their primary purpose or may work at the intersection of other issues, including those that benefit people or the environment. They may take approaches grounded in pursuing animal rights or improving animal welfare, and they may focus on individual animals, populations, or species. The book will be helpful to lawyers employed in-house by animal protection organizations, outside counsel who represent such groups or take pro bono matters, and lawyers and students who are considering a career path focused on advising those who work for animals.

How to Use This Book

Many of the legal matters that arise for animal-oriented groups are unique because they involve living, sentient beings who are nonetheless considered property under the law. This book is grounded in a perspective and analysis that consider both the organizations and the animals. Attorneys who represent animal protection organizations, as well as those who have not yet done so, now possess a resource that gathers a wealth of relevant legal information.

The seventeen authors of this book are legal experts and practitioners in animal law and policy who have provided excellent guidance for addressing a broad range of legal issues. The book is divided into two parts. Part I offers practical, hands-on advice for representing clients, starting with an overview of the variety of types of organizations whose missions are to promote and further the humane treatment of animals and how lawyers can support them, and then moving to formation and governance, operational topics (including staffing, finance, and liability), constitutional matters, diversity, equity, inclusion, and justice issues, and legal ethics. Part II provides an extensive, although not exhaustive, overview of the laws (including local, state, federal, and international) that are most relevant to animals and representing animal protection organizations.

We and the authors hope that this volume serves you well in advising those who work to improve our relationship with our fellow creatures, and with our world.

PART I

Representing Animal Protection Organizations

CHAPTER 1

Animal Protection Organizations and Ways to Represent Them

Margaret Robinson and Bruce Wagman

Introduction

Although there have been laws protecting animals in place for centuries, the practice of animal law has vastly expanded in the past two decades. This chapter aims to illustrate the different ways that lawyers can work on behalf of animals by representing the organizations dedicated to protecting them. We first provide some general background about the focus of these organizations' missions, their geographic reach, and their tax status. We then discuss the various types of animal protection organizations and the diverse and vital services they provide. Finally, we explore ways that lawyers can use their expertise to represent these organizations, as both in-house and outside counsel. While this chapter addresses basic considerations that arise in representing animal protection organizations, these issues are discussed more fully in other chapters.

Animal Protection Organizations' Focus, Geographic Reach, and Tax Status

The focus of animal protection organizations' missions varies. Some organizations work on behalf of a particular species or kind of animal. For instance, the Jane Goodall Institute focuses much of its efforts on promoting the understanding and protection of great apes and their habitat.[1] Similarly, some animal sanctuaries provide permanent homes for big cats, while others provide a home only for elephants. Other organizations concentrate their efforts on a

1. *About*, Jane Goodall Inst., https://janegoodall.org/about/ (last visited Aug. 13, 2022).

particular category of animals, such as wildlife, farm animals, companion animals, or animals used in research. For instance, Animal Outlook, Mercy for Animals, and Farm Sanctuary's missions center on protecting farm animals by combatting factory farming (i.e., the large-scale production of animals used for food).[2] Best Friends Animal Society is devoted to securing homes for companion animals.[3] Likewise, local shelters—such as San Francisco Society for the Prevention of Cruelty to Animals (SPCA), San Diego Humane Society, Humane Rescue Alliance, and Massachusetts SPCA—primarily work to protect companion animals. The American Anti-Vivisection Society and Rise for Animals advocate for animals used in research and are dedicated to ending animal experimentation.[4] Groups like the Center for Biological Diversity and Defenders of Wildlife work to protect wildlife (and biodiversity generally), including working to conserve wild animals and their habitat.[5] Other animal protection organizations work to improve the treatment of many types of animals. For example, Animal Legal Defense Fund (ALDF) works to protect animals used in research, animals held in captivity, companion animals, farm animals, and wildlife.[6] The Humane Society of the United States (HSUS) focuses on combatting the institutionalized and societal animal cruelty found in puppy mills, factory farms, the fur trade, trophy hunting of wildlife, and animal cosmetics testing while also providing sanctuary, care, and rescue for animals.[7]

Similar to their areas of focus, animal protection groups' geographic reach also varies. Some organizations operate internationally. For instance, the International Fund for Animal Welfare works in more than forty countries, and Humane Society International works in more than fifty countries.[8] Other organizations focus their efforts on protecting animals across the United States but may also work at the state or local level. The American Society for the Prevention of Cruelty to Animals (ASPCA), for instance, is a national organization that maintains a strong local presence in New York City, where it is headquartered.[9] The HSUS is a national organization that also has state directors who advocate for policy changes at the state and local levels.[10] Other organizations primarily focus their work at the state or local level. For example, Animal Protection New Mexico is dedicated to protecting New Mexico's

2. *About Us*, Animal Outlook, https://animaloutlook.org/about/ (last visited Aug. 13, 2022); *About Mercy for Animals*, Mercy for Animals, https://mercyforanimals.org/about/ (last visited Aug. 13, 2022); *About Us*, Farm Sanctuary, https://www.farmsanctuary.org/about-us/ (last visited Aug. 13, 2022).

3. *Who We Are*, Best Friends, https://bestfriends.org/who-we-are/our-mission (last visited Aug. 13, 2022).

4. *About AAVS*, American Anti-Vivisection Society, https://aavs.org/about/ (last visited Aug. 13, 2022); *Our Story*, Rise for Animals, https://riseforanimals.org/our-story/ (last visited Aug. 13, 2022).

5. *About the Center*, Center for Biological Diversity, https://www.biologicaldiversity.org/about/ (last visited Aug. 13, 2022); *About Us*, Defenders of Wildlife, https://defenders.org/about (last visited Aug. 13, 2022).

6. Animal Legal Def. Fund, https://aldf.org/ (last visited Aug. 13, 2022).

7. *Our Mission*, Humane Soc'y U.S., https://www.humanesociety.org/our-mission (last visited Aug. 13, 2022).

8. *About IFAW*, International Fund for Animal Welfare, https://www.ifaw.org/about (last visited Aug. 13, 2022); *About Us*, Humane Soc'y Int'l, https://www.hsi.org/about-us/ (last visited Aug. 13, 2022).

9. *About Us*, ASPCA, https://www.aspca.org/about-us (last visited Aug. 13, 2022).

10. *Our Mission*, Humane Soc'y U.S., https://www.humanesociety.org/our-mission (last visited Aug. 13, 2022).

animals.[11] And the San Diego Humane Society provides animal services for many cities in San Diego County.[12]

The tax status of animal protection organizations also varies. As discussed in chapter 2, while the majority of nonprofit organizations are formed pursuant to the parameters and rules under federal Internal Revenue Code section 501(c)(3), there are other ways to register as a nonprofit organization, under both state and federal law. On the federal law side, there are section 501(c)(4) organizations, dedicated exclusively to the promotion of social welfare.[13] The "(c)(4)" status allows organizations to engage in more extensive lobbying and even certain political activities that are limited—or in the case of political activities, prohibited—by the rules governing "(c)(3)" organizations.[14] In addition to the two most common federal nonprofit structures, each state provides for its own nonprofit structure. Rules and laws with respect to state nonprofits vary, and specifics can be found online in most situations. Even for experienced attorneys, it can be helpful to consult with attorneys who have experience with the state laws at issue when advising clients, as the various requirements can be confusing and complex.

Note that it is not mandatory for animal protection groups to register for nonprofit status under state or federal law. There are many advantages to such registration, especially in the taxation area. That is, for 501(c)(3) (but not 501(c)(4)) organizations, donors can claim those donations on their federal taxes and may be eligible to obtain tax advantages—which encourages the donations. Nonprofits are also exempt from paying a number of taxes under state and federal law, thereby saving the organizations money.

Despite the advantages of nonprofit status, a minority of animal protection groups opt to forego it. This of course means that none of the tax benefits accrue —for either donors or the organization. Groups that decide not to undertake nonprofit registration often make that decision to avoid the potential traps for the unwary involved in the nonprofit registration process, as well as the ongoing reporting requirements and potential costs involved with obtaining and maintaining nonprofit status. So, smaller groups and groups with guaranteed donors that are not concerned about receiving tax deductions for those donations may opt out of nonprofit registration. This does not relieve these organizations of all obligations under state and federal law and will have tax implications for the organizations or individuals who run them. But these organizations will not have to comply with the more complex rules for nonprofits registered under state and federal law.

---

11. *About Us*, Animal Protection New Mexico, https://apnm.org/about-us/ (last visited Aug. 13, 2022).

12. *Creating a More Humane San Diego*, San Diego Humane Soc'y, https://www.sdhumane.org/about-us/our-mission.html (last visited Aug. 13, 2022).

13. 26 U.S.C. § 501(c)(4).

14. *See, e.g.*, Exemption Requirements—501(c)(3) Organizations, IRS, https://www.irs.gov/charities-non-profits/charitable-organizations/exemption-requirements-501c3-organizations (last updated Feb. 17, 2022) (501(c)(3) organization "may not attempt to influence legislation as a substantial part of its activities and it may not participate in any campaign activity for or against political candidates").

The Different Types of Animal Protection Organizations

There is no single type of animal protection organization, and the work that these groups undertake varies greatly. Some organizations, such as sanctuaries, provide a home and direct care for animals permanently. Others, such as local animal shelters, rescue animals, provide care for them temporarily, and provide other services to their communities. Other organizations provide limited or no direct care and instead primarily work to effect change for animals through advocacy efforts. Given the richness and diversity of the animal protection field, it would be impossible to provide an exhaustive discussion of the work these organizations undertake. Instead, this section provides an overview of the most common types of animal protection organizations—advocacy groups, sanctuaries, shelters, and rescues. This section also provides examples of what these organizations' work looks like in practice, basic information about the structure of the various types of animal protection organizations, and the types of legal representation that these groups may require.

Animal Advocacy Organizations

There are numerous organizations that work to improve the treatment of animals through advocacy efforts. Such organizations work to effect change for animals in many ways, including by seeking to change consumer behavior or corporate practices and policies, investigating cruel practices, lobbying for stronger laws, undertaking strategic litigation, and promoting conservation. This section discusses those activities in more detail and provides basic information about the structure of advocacy organizations as well as the types of legal representation such organizations may require.

Advocacy Activities

Animal protection advocacy organizations engage in myriad activities to further their missions. Many organizations seek to advance animal welfare through education and advocacy campaigns to change consumer behavior. Often organizations seek to educate consumers about the cruelty associated with the many industries that produce or use animals and to promote consumer behavior that fosters the humane treatment of animals. The ASPCA, HSUS, and other organizations educate consumers about the cruelty associated with the puppy mill industry and promote the adoption of homeless animals.[15] The ASPCA, HSUS, other national organizations, and local shelters also engage in extensive spay and neuter campaigns to reduce the number of homeless animals

15. *Barred from Love,* ASPCA, https://www.aspca.org/barred-from-love (last visited Aug. 13, 2022); *Stopping Puppy Mills,* Humane Soc'y U.S., https://www.humanesociety.org/all-our-fights/stopping-puppy-mills (last visited Oct. 2, 2022).

in need of adoption.[16] Groups such as Animal Outlook and Mercy for Animals focus more singularly on educating consumers about the cruelty and environmental harms associated with the meat, egg, and dairy industries and promoting vegan diets.[17] And—recognizing that consumers wanted cruelty-free cosmetics but that companies were defining what was "animal friendly" without input from animal advocates—eight animal protection groups formed the Coalition for Consumer Information on Cosmetics.[18] That coalition operates the Leaping Bunny Program, which requires participating companies to pledge to end animal testing at every stage of product development, allowing consumers to readily identify "cruelty-free" products.[19]

Animal protection groups also work to change how industries that use animals operate. For instance, the HSUS works with retailers, designers, and clothing companies, such as Neiman Marcus and Prada, to secure their commitment to stop selling products containing animal fur.[20] Animal Outlook undertakes targeted campaigns to increase the vegan options offered by major national food brands.[21] The HSUS and other groups work with major food companies to secure commitments to eliminate the cruel confinement of animals from their supply chains.[22] And Mercy for Animals' Transfarmation Project helps farmers transition from industrial animal-agriculture operations to plant-focused farms.[23]

In addition to corporate and consumer outreach, some advocacy groups carry out undercover investigations to expose the cruelty associated with humans' use and consumption of animals and their products. Mercy for Animals, Animal Outlook, and other organizations focus on sending investigators to factory farms and slaughterhouses to expose the horrific conditions farm animals experience during their lives.[24] The HSUS and other groups undertake

---

16. *See, e.g.*, *Spay/Neuter Services*, ASPCA, https://www.aspca.org/helping-people-pets/spayneuter-services (last visited Aug. 13, 2022).

17. *Why—Animals*, Animal Outlook's TryVeg, https://tryveg.com/why-animals/ (last visited Aug. 13, 2022); CHOOSEVEG, https://chooseveg.com/ (last visited Aug. 13, 2022).

18. *About Leaping Bunny*, Leaping Bunny Program, https://www.leapingbunny.org/about/about-leaping-bunny (last visited Aug. 13, 2022).

19. *Id.*; *The Leaping Bunny Difference*, Leaping Bunny Program, https://www.leapingbunny.org/leaping-bunny-difference (last visited Aug. 13, 2022).

20. *Fur-Free Fashion*, Humane Soc'y U.S., https://www.humanesociety.org/fur-free-fashion (last visited Aug. 13, 2022); *Neiman Marcus Group Goes Fur-Free as Part of Its Forthcoming ESG Strategy: Animal Welfare Policy Is Supported by the Humane Society of the United States*, Neiman Marcus Group (June 30, 2021), https://www.neimanmarcusgroup.com/2021-06-30-Neiman-Marcus-Group-Goes-Fur-Free-as-Part-of-Its-Forthcoming-ESG-Strategy; *The Prada Group Announces Fur-Free Policy and Joins the International Fur Free Retailer Program*, PRADA Group (May 2019), https://www.pradagroup.com/en/news-media/news-section/fur-free-policy.html.

21. *Campaign Victories*, Animal Outlook, https://animaloutlook.org/campaign-victories/ (last visited Aug. 13, 2022).

22. *See, e.g.*, *Abolishing Cages and Crates*, Humane Soc'y U.S., https://www.humanesociety.org/abolishing-cages-and-crates (last visited Aug. 13, 2022).

23. *Building a Farmer-Led Movement for a Better Food System*, Transfarmation, https://the-transfarmationproject.org/#about (last visited Aug. 13, 2022).

24. *Undercover Investigations*, Mercy for Animals, https://mercyforanimals.org/investigations/ (last visited Aug. 13, 2022); *Investigations*, Animal Outlook, https://animaloutlook.org/investigations/ (last visited Aug. 13, 2022).

investigations to expose the cruel treatment of animals in a variety of industries, such as the clothing industry, the pet trade, and the animal research industry.[25] The treatment of animals documented in these types of undercover investigations is often used in conjunction with other advocacy activities, such as litigation, educational efforts, and consumer and corporate engagement campaigns.

Additionally, many animal protection organizations seek to improve the treatment of animals by advocating for new laws—or changes in existing laws—that will benefit animals. In some instances, these groups are involved in the conception and drafting of proposed legislation. In addition, advocacy groups often work closely with like-minded legislators to introduce animal-friendly bills and then work to secure support from other legislators once the bills are introduced. Advocacy groups also help garner support from voters, both for ballot initiatives and proposed legislation that afford animals greater protections.

These efforts occur at the local, state, and federal levels. For instance, animal protection organizations have played critical roles in advancing state and local laws that prohibit inhumane practices or ban the sale of products resulting from animal cruelty. States and local jurisdictions have passed laws protecting companion animals, ranging from laws that ban cat declawing to laws preventing pet stores from selling cats and dogs from breeding mills.[26] Multiple states have banned the cruel and intensive confinement of farm animals, and some states have prohibited the in-state sale of animal products that are produced using certain cruel confinement methods.[27] Several localities and the state of California have passed laws banning the sale of fur products in their jurisdictions.[28] Numerous states have banned the sale of shark fins because of the cruel treatment involved in obtaining those fins.[29] At the federal level, animal protection groups advocate for both stand-alone laws to protect animals and animal-friendly provisions in more generalized legislation, such as appropriations bills. For instance, animal advocacy groups played a key role in the passage of the Big Cats Safety Act, which prohibits private ownership and public

---

25. *See, e.g.*, *Investigations & Reports*, Humane Soc'y U.S., https://www.humanesociety.org/resources/investigations-reports (last visited Oct. 2, 2022).

26. Hilary Hanson, *Maryland Becomes 2nd U.S. State to Ban Declawing Cats*, Huff Post (Apr. 23, 2022), https://www.huffpost.com/entry/maryland-bans-declawing-cats_n_62640a1be4b07c34e9e15723; *States with Humane Pet Sales Laws*, Best Friends, https://bestfriends.org/advocacy/ending-puppy-mills/states-humane-pet-sales-laws (last visited Aug. 13, 2022).

27. *Farm Animal Confinement Bans by State*, ASPCA, https://www.aspca.org/improving-laws-animals/public-policy/farm-animal-confinement-bans (last visited Aug. 13, 2022).

28. *See, e.g.*, Jeffery Ritter, *Flager Humane Society: Hallandale Beach, Florida, Bans Sale of Furs*, Daytona Beach News-Journal (Dec. 2, 2021, 12:03 p.m.), https://www.news-journalonline.com/story/news/2021/12/02/flagler-humane-society-reports-ban-fur-sales-florida-city/8786439002/; Sophie Lewis, *California Become First State to Ban the Sale of New Fur Products*, CBS News (Oct. 12, 2019, 2:55 p.m.), https://www.cbsnews.com/news/california-becomes-first-state-to-ban-the-sale-and-manufacture-of-new-fur-products-ab44-today-2019-10-12/; Janie Har, *San Francisco Becomes Largest U.S. City to Ban Fur Sales*, USA Today (Mar. 21, 2018, 1:09 a.m.), https://www.usatoday.com/story/news/nation/2018/03/20/san-francisco-fur-sales-ban/444519002/.

29. *See, e.g.*, Cal. Fish & Game Code § 2021; Haw. Rev. Stat. § 188-40.7; 515 Ill. Comp. Stat. 5/5-30; Tex. Parks & Wild. Code Ann. § 66.2161.

handling of big cats (e.g., lions, tigers).[30] Additionally, animal advocacy groups helped secure the introduction of numerous stand-alone bills to protect animals, such as the Humane Cosmetics Act, which would prohibit animal testing for cosmetics and prohibit the sale of cosmetics developed using animal testing.[31] Animal advocacy groups also vigorously oppose proposed legislation, at all levels of government, that would be harmful to animals. As just one example, over the years, these groups have opposed many bills that would liberalize state wolf hunting laws.[32]

In addition to working with legislators, advocacy groups engage with administrative agencies in their efforts to improve the treatment of animals. In some cases, organizations file formal "rulemaking petitions" for regulatory change. For instance, several animal protection groups successfully petitioned the U.S. Fish and Wildlife Service (USFWS) to eliminate the agency's "split-listing" of wild and captive chimpanzees under the Endangered Species Act (ESA).[33] The resulting regulatory change effectively ended invasive research on chimpanzees, as well as their use in entertainment. Animal protection organizations also inform administrative agencies of potential legal violations and seek enforcement of laws meant to protect animals. The U.S. Department of Agriculture (USDA), for example, temporarily suspended inspections at a beef slaughterhouse after viewing an undercover video filmed by an animal protection group documenting the inhumane treatment of cows at the facility.[34] Animal protection organizations also regularly comment on proposed state and federal actions (such as the removal of wild horses from their home ranges) and regulations to explain how proposed agency decisions and rules will impact animals and violate the law, and to advocate for policies that afford animals the most protection possible.

In addition to seeking to change laws and regulations to improve the treatment of animals, some animal protection groups also use strategic litigation to advance their missions. Animal protection groups have brought lawsuits against private entities that the organizations believe are mistreating animals, for example, suing facilities for their treatment of animals protected under federal laws.[35] Other groups have filed consumer protection lawsuits alleging

---

30. Christine Chung, *President Biden Signs Bill Outlawing Private Ownership of Big Cats*, N.Y. Times (Dec. 21, 2022), https://www.nytimes.com/2022/12/21/us/politics/biden-tiger-king-law.html.

31. H.R.6207—Humane Cosmetics Act of 2021, Congress.gov, https://www.congress.gov/bill/117th-congress/house-bill/6207?r=9&s=1 (last visited Aug. 13, 2022).

32. *See, e.g.*, KTVB Staff, *Idaho Governor Greenlights Killing of 90% of the State's Wolf Population*, KTVB7 (May 7, 2021, 10:44 a.m.), https://www.ktvb.com/article/news/local/capitol-watch/idaho-governor-greenlights-killing-of-90-of-states-wolf-population/277-7e28dfee-c68d-4d07-b663-6d4714868ff4.

33. Endangered and Threatened Wildlife and Plants; Listing All Chimpanzees as Endangered Species, 80 Fed. Reg.34,500 (June 16, 2015).

34. CNN Wire Staff, *USDA Suspends Slaughterhouse after Video Appears to Show Animal Cruelty*, CNN (Aug. 23, 2012, 2:47 p.m.), https://www.cnn.com/2012/08/22/us/california-slaughterhouse-video/index.html.

35. *See, e.g.*, People for Ethical Treatment of Animals, Inc. v. Tri-State Zoological Park of W. Md., Inc., 424 F. Supp. 3d 404 (D. Md. 2019), *aff'd*, 843 F. App'x 493 (4th Cir. 2021); People for Ethical Treatment of Animals, Inc. v. Miami Seaquarium, 879 F.3d 1142 (11th Cir. 2018); *Challenging the Inhumane Treatment of Animals at Pymatuning Deer Park Roadside Zoo: Animal Legal Defense Fund and PETA v. Pymatuning Deer Park*, ALDF, https://aldf.org/case/challenging-the-inhumane-treatment-of-captive-wild-animals-at-pymatuning-deer-park/ (last updated Feb. 2, 2022).

that companies' statements related to their treatment of animals mislead consumers.[36] In other cases, animal protection groups have repeatedly failed when trying to bring suit on behalf of a particular animal or group of animals, with the hope of securing broader systemic changes for animals.[37]

Additionally, animal protection organizations regularly sue federal and state agencies. These lawsuits challenge regulations, specific actions, and administrative policies that are harmful to animals. For example, animal protection groups have filed multiple lawsuits challenging various USFWS regulations removing ESA protections for gray wolves.[38] As another example, groups like Front Range Equine Rescue regularly challenge decisions by the Bureau of Land Management and the U.S. Forest Service regarding those agencies' treatment of the United States' wild horses.[39] The American Anti-Vivisection Society and the Avian Welfare Coalition sued USDA for its delay in issuing standards for the humane handling of certain birds under the Animal Welfare Act.[40] In addition to challenging agency rules and policies, animal protection groups file suits against the government to obtain information under the federal Freedom of Information Act or similar state public records laws. For instance, Humane Society International successfully challenged the USFWS's refusal to release certain wildlife trade data, including information related to U.S. imports of hunting trophies of imperiled species, live animals for the pet trade, and animals used in experiments.[41]

Animal protection groups also engage in litigation to safeguard their own advocacy efforts. In some cases, animal groups bring challenges against laws or government positions that negatively impact their advocacy or humane messaging campaigns. For instance, several lawsuits have challenged state efforts to prevent food companies from using terms such as "meat," "butter," and "dairy" to describe plant-based products.[42] And groups have challenged state "ag-gag" laws, which criminalize conduct associated with undercover investigations at agricultural facilities.[43] Additionally, animal groups help to defend laws that protect animals when such laws are challenged in the courts. For instance, the

---

36. Kitty Block, *We're Suing the World's Largest Pork Producer for Misleading the Public about Animal Abuse*, Humane World: Kitty Block's Blog (Oct. 18, 2021), https://blog.humanesociety.org/2021/10/lawsuit-smithfield-foods-misleading-public-about-animal-abuse.html; *Simple Truth Chicken Labeling Lawsuit—Settlement Reached*, Animal Outlook (Oct. 13, 2014), https://animaloutlook.org/press/press-releases/simple-truth-chicken-label-removed/.

37. *See, e.g.*, Cetacean Cmty. v. Bush, 386 F.3d 1169 (9th Cir. 2004).

38. *See, e.g.*, Humane Soc'y of U.S. v. Zinke, 865 F.3d 585 (D.C. Cir. 2017); Defenders of Wildlife v. U.S. Fish & Wildlife Serv., No. 21-CV-00344-JSW, 2022 WL 499838 (N.D. Cal. Feb. 10, 2022).

39. *See, e.g.*, Colorado Wild Horse & Burro Coal., Inc. v. Salazar, 639 F. Supp. 2d 87 (D.D.C. 2009).

40. American Anti-Vivisection Soc'y v. U.S. Dep't of Agric., 946 F.3d 615 (D.C. Cir. 2020). Standards for Birds Not Bred for Use in Research under the Animal Welfare Act, 87 Fed. Reg. 9880 (Feb. 22, 2022).

41. Humane Soc'y Int'l v. U.S. Fish & Wildlife Serv., No. CV 16-720 (TJK), 2021 WL 1197726 (D.D.C. Mar. 29, 2021).

42. *See, e.g.*, Turtle Island Foods SPC v. Strain, No. CV 20-00674-BAJ-EWD, 2022 WL 909039 (M.D. La. Mar. 28, 2022); Miyoko's Kitchen v. Ross, No. 20-CV-00893-RS, 2021 WL 4497867 (N.D. Cal. Aug. 10, 2021).

43. *See, e.g.*, Animal Legal Def. Fund v. Kelly, 9 F.4th 1219 (10th Cir. 2021); Animal Legal Def. Fund v. Reynolds, 8 F.4th 781 (8th Cir. 2021); Animal Legal Def. Fund v. Reynolds, No. 4:19-CV-00124-SMR-HCA, 2022 WL 777231 (S.D. Iowa Mar. 14, 2022).

HSUS—often in coalition with other animal advocacy groups—has intervened or filed amicus briefs to defend laws that ban the sale of products resulting from animal cruelty when industry participants have filed lawsuits challenging such laws.[44]

Finally, wildlife advocacy groups often engage in conservation efforts. These efforts can employ many of the methods discussed earlier, such as petitioning the USFWS for ESA protections for imperiled species or bringing lawsuits to challenge the denial of such protections. The Center for Biological Diversity engages in such activities through its Carnivore Conservation Program, among others.[45] In addition, wildlife groups frequently work with communities living near threatened wildlife. The Jane Goodall Institute, for example, operates projects in communities living in or near chimpanzee habitat to promote sustainable livelihoods, thereby increasing income and the communities' capacity to preserve natural resources.[46] Panthera works with local communities to protect livestock from wild cats, such as leopards and jaguars, and to build sustainable ecotourism opportunities, which create jobs.[47] Groups also work with a range of country governments and communities to conserve and restore habitat for wildlife, and in some cases, they may identify and protect wildlife corridors to minimize the impacts of habitat fragmentation.[48]

Advocacy Organization Structure and Representing Advocacy Organizations

Typically, there are three basic levels in the organizational makeup of advocacy organizations—a governing body, management, and staff. These same broad categories apply to most animal protection groups discussed in this chapter. Chapter 2 contains an in-depth discussion of governance in general, including information about the governing body of the organization—usually known as a board of directors—and other relevant issues at that level of the organization. We will not duplicate that information here. It always bears repeating, however, that a board should be comprised of individuals who bring skills and experience particular to the work being done. This ranges from knowledge about running a

---

44. *See, e.g.*, *Nat'l Pork Producers Council v. Ross*, 598 U.S. 356 (2023) (rejecting industry challenge to California law prohibiting the sale of products from animals raised using cruel confinement methods). Chinatown Neighborhood Ass'n v. Harris, 794 F.3d 1136 (9th Cir. 2015) (challenging California law prohibiting the sale of shark fins); Just Puppies, Inc. v. Frosh, 565 F. Supp. 3d 665 (D. Md. 2021) (challenging Maryland law prohibiting sale of dogs and cats by retail pet stores); International Fur Trade Fed'n v. City & Cnty. of San Francisco, 472 F. Supp. 3d 696 (N.D. Cal. 2020) (challenging San Francisco ordinance prohibiting sale of fur products).

45. *Carnivore Conservation*, Center for Biological Diversity, https://www.biologicaldiversity.org/programs/carnivore-conservation/ (last visited Aug. 13, 2022).

46. *Strategy: Sustainable Livelihoods*, Jane Goodall Inst., https://janegoodall.org/our-work/our-approach/sustainable-livelihoods/ (last visited Aug. 13, 2022).

47. *The Threat: Human-Cat Conflict*, Panthera, https://panthera.org/threat-human-cat-conflict (last visited Aug. 13, 2022).

48. *See, e.g.*, *Protecting Habitat*, Defenders of Wildlife, https://defenders.org/issues/protecting-habitat (last visited Aug. 13, 2022); *The Threat: Habitat Loss and Fragmentation*, Panthera, https://panthera.org/threat-habitat-loss-and-fragmentation (last visited Aug. 13, 2022); *Strategy: Healthy Habitats*, Jane Goodall Inst., https://janegoodall.org/our-work/our-approach/healthy-habitats/ (last visited Aug. 13, 2022).

business and complying with government regulations to specific expertise (if possible) about the animals at the heart of the advocacy group's mission, human resources, and philanthropy.

Advocacy organizations typically employ both managers and staff. The roles and responsibilities for employees can vary widely among advocacy organizations, depending on the activities and size of the organization. For instance, some organizations have hundreds of employees on staff, while others have fewer than twenty. Particularly in smaller organizations, employees may assume more than one role. Generally, though, a chief executive officer (or similar role) is responsible for overseeing the programmatic and other operations of the organization, often with a team of managers dedicated to human resources, finances, programs, legal compliance, technology, fundraising, and other functions. Advocacy organization staff carry out the day-to-day work of the organization, including programmatic activities (e.g., educational efforts, corporate engagement campaigns, and strategic litigation) and activities crucial to the operation of the organization (e.g., human resources, legal compliance, information technology, and fundraising). Volunteers are often a critical component of advocacy organizations as well, supporting both programmatic and operational work.

The legal representation needs of advocacy organizations can vary and often depend on the types of advocacy activities in which the organization engages. As a general rule, animal advocacy groups require legal support for their standard operations. This can include contract review and drafting, examining legal compliance issues (including with respect to federal and state nonprofit status), protecting the organization from liability, and advising on human resources matters. In addition, legal support is often required for advocacy organizations' programmatic work. This can include the development and filing of strategic litigation, drafting legislation, interfacing with legislators or administrative agencies, drafting public records requests, and advising the organization on policy matters. Legal support of programmatic work can also include advising on risk to the organization and liability issues, for example, relating to undercover investigations or corporate campaigns.

Sanctuaries

This section discusses animal protection organizations that engage in direct and daily care of animals—groups that have animals onsite and do the day-to-day work of providing for the needs of their resident animals. The choice of the word "sanctuary" to describe the hundreds of facilities around the world that provide refuge to animals is rooted in the original meaning of the term, which had a religious connotation and refers to a sacred place that provides safety and protection in both a physical and spiritual sense. At their best, sanctuaries are indeed such places. In the context of this book, animal sanctuaries are specific physical locations—most commonly with indoor and outdoor access and facilities—where the resident animals are often provided a home for the rest of their lives. Sanctuaries are places where animals are protected from exploitation, use, or abuse of any kind (both affirmative harmful acts and neglect).

Before we talk more about animal sanctuaries, it is important to understand several points. First, there are no governing legal principles for sanctuaries, in particular. They are subject to state and federal laws in place for the keeping of animals (including limitations on types of animals that may be kept in a jurisdiction, the number of animals of a given species that are allowed, the running of nonprofit organizations, and other general business considerations under the law). But other than such laws—which apply to non-sanctuary settings as well—there is nothing specific to sanctuaries.

Second, there is no agreed-upon definition of what a sanctuary is, and so the term can be employed by any number of organizations. While all of them will likely be involved in some form of direct care of animals, simply labeling a facility as a "sanctuary" does not mean that it is providing care according to any regulated, approved, or even acceptable standard. The discussion at the beginning of this section outlines the abiding doctrine of most good sanctuaries: the provision of a permanent life of safety and protection. But, because there is no law governing sanctuaries, the definition is mutable, and every sanctuary can define itself as it pleases. As such, it behooves anyone getting involved—whether as a donor, employee, partner, or counsel—to undertake sound inquiries and investigation of any organization labeling itself a "sanctuary," to try to ascertain the organization's bona fides. There are private, independent accreditation bodies that set standards, engage in voluntary inspections, and provide certification to sanctuaries interested in participating. These can be a useful resource to gather information about sanctuaries.

Third, because of the absence of governing law and definition, there is no guarantee, simply by use of the word "sanctuary," that the resident animals are provided the level of care, and the type of protection, that the word suggests. In the vast majority of cases, it is certainly our experience that sanctuary animals are protected, sheltered, and treated with a high caliber of care, support, and enrichment. But there have also been examples of tragic conditions of neglect and abuse discovered at so-called sanctuaries. We do not discuss those in any further detail but simply provide this word of caution to readers. The following discussion is focused on sanctuaries operating at the highest degree.

We first provide a brief description of sanctuary residents and organizational structure—to offer an understanding of sanctuary needs and their daily functions—and then discuss the legal work that is required to support them.

Sanctuary Residents

There are sanctuaries for almost every type of animal you can name, and one initial way to differentiate them is that some sanctuaries focus on a particular species (e.g., dogs, cats, chimpanzees), some on a general classification (e.g., farm animals, big cats, reptiles), and others will accommodate any kind of animal they feel equipped to accept and for whom they can properly care. Perhaps the first type of sanctuaries seen in the United States were wildlife sanctuaries. Such sanctuaries take in wildlife saved or rescued from bad situations, wild animals used in entertainment who have been retired, or injured wildlife who can no longer survive in the wild but have years to live if cared for by dedicated humans. Black Beauty Ranch in Murchison, Texas is probably the most famous and certainly one of the biggest such sanctuaries, with nearly 800 residents, including domestic and exotic species.[49] To allow animals to roam as they would naturally, wildlife sanctuaries often need large tracts of land, as well as adequate shelter and housing.

There are many sanctuaries set up like Black Beauty Ranch, but there are also a fair number of sanctuaries that focus on a single species that may require highly specialized attention and knowledge to provide the highest level of care. Chimpanzees, our closest genetic relatives in terms of our shared percentage of DNA, are one species that merits a single focus and requires an intensive and highly specialized set of considerations based on expertise and training. For that reason, there are less than ten chimpanzee sanctuaries in North America.[50] The chimpanzees in the country's leading sanctuaries are generally prior biomedical research subjects, with a minority who are refugees from the entertainment business or private ownership. Although not limited to a single species, there are also a few high-quality sanctuaries for "big cats"—lions, tigers, cheetahs, leopards, as well as servals, lynx, and other wild cats—who may be cared for at the same sanctuary.[51] And, dotted around the country, there are many sanctuaries for exotic birds, which care for birds who have been abandoned by private owners or rescued from the illegal exotic pet trade.[52]

Farm animal sanctuaries are found across the United States. Perhaps the two most well-known are Farm Sanctuary, which started in Watkins Glen, New York, and Animal Place, which started in Vacaville, California.[53] Both organizations are nonprofits that are also involved in a variety of advocacy activities but are primarily focused on the care of rescued and retired animals, almost all of whom were either destined to become food (e.g., beef cows, pigs, sheep) or involved in the production of food (e.g., dairy cows, egg-laying hens). These two flagship organizations have been joined by numerous like-minded groups that obtain their animals when they are abandoned, seized in cruelty cases, "spent" from production and ready to be killed, or in rare cases, when the animals escape their circumstances and are delivered to their facilities. These specialized sanctuaries deal with the medical problems seen in these animals when they are allowed to live much longer than they ever would at food production operations. Because of their genetically altered rapid growth and their typically short lives, when these animals are allowed to live out their lives in sanctuary, they can experience unanticipated issues that the sanctuaries support as much as

49. *Black Beauty Ranch*, Humane Soc'y U.S., https://www.humanesociety.org/blackbeautyranch (last visited Aug. 13, 2022).

50. *See, e.g.*, Project Chimps, https://projectchimps.org/ (last visited Aug. 13, 2022); Save the Chimps, https://savethechimps.org/ (last visited Aug. 13, 2022); Chimp Haven, https://chimphaven.org/ (last visited Aug. 13, 2022).

51. *See, e.g.*, Wildcat Sanctuary, https://www.wildcatsanctuary.org/ (last visited Aug. 13, 2022).

52. *See, e.g.*, *Sanctuary*, Foster Parrots, https://www.fosterparrots.com/sanctuary (last visited Aug. 13, 2022).

53. *See* Farm Sanctuary, https://www.farmsanctuary.org/ (last visited Aug. 13, 2022); Animal Place, https://animalplace.org/ (last visited Aug. 13, 2022).

possible. Instead of living their lives in a rigid production schedule, the rescued animals spend their days in green fields or comfortable barns, playing with and relating to other similarly lucky animals of the same (and other compatible) species.

There are also many dog and cat sanctuaries (as opposed to animal shelters, discussed in the next section). Such sanctuaries are often limited to one species or the other, but many of the larger organizations (e.g., Best Friends Animal Society in Kanab, Utah) are able to care for both species and keep them safely apart. Many of the animals (especially dogs) who end up in sanctuary settings are ones for whom the only other option may have been euthanasia because of biting or behavioral incidents. In some situations, however, the dog and cat sanctuaries are able to adopt their residents out, which is a significant difference from the traditional sanctuary role of providing a home for the rest of an animal's life.

Sanctuary Organizational Structure

As with advocacy groups, sanctuaries' organizational makeup generally includes a governing body (usually a board of directors), management, and staff. Chapter 2 addresses the governing body's roles and responsibilities, so we will not discuss it further here.

With governance as the formative first level of the organization, the second level of the organization, then, is sanctuary management. In a sanctuary setting, this includes managers in each of the key areas—usually an executive director or chief executive officer who supervises everyone else, with managerial positions in animal care (usually an on-call or on-site veterinarian), facilities, human resources, and donor relations/development. At this level of the organization, vital involvement with the outside world is a constant. Along with line staff, managers are ultimately responsible for compliance with local, state, and federal laws (both laws governing businesses in general, as well as the specific laws that may apply to the keeping of the types of animals at the sanctuary). Especially where captive wildlife or other "exotic" animal species are involved, there are often legal requirements for importing the animals and keeping them. In addition, regular inspections by various government bodies (as well as industry groups, such as the accreditation bodies mentioned earlier) are often required to keep the facility, and the organization, functioning and accredited.

A third level that includes arguably the most important jobs at sanctuaries is occupied by those who do the day-to-day, hands-on work. Within this classification, there are usually multiple levels of staff members differentiated by training, experience, and accessibility to the resident animals. Support staff range from valuable team members who undertake sanitation and food and other preparations for the animals at various stages of the day, to "aides" who directly assist more experienced senior caregivers and may work with the animals, to the highest level of caregiver who are responsible for carrying out the overall care plans for the animals as well as ensuring the proper performance of duties by other staff members. The range and level of expertise needed for these "care staff" varies depending on the species involved, as well as other factors. But the particular species is a defining—and often limiting—factor in selecting staff. With exotic animals, a certain amount of concrete experience, and often advanced education, should be required to ensure that both the animals and the public are adequately protected and cared for.

The staff level of the organization also includes key personnel in charge of the proper functioning of the organization's infrastructure. In larger sanctuaries, a facilities department is involved in all aspects of the maintenance, repairs, and any construction work that does not require outside professional skills. When construction using external vendors is planned, facilities team members are involved, although special committees and task forces are often established for bigger projects. And, in sanctuaries that require special and extensive safety and security measures to protect the public, staff, and the animals (e.g., a chimpanzee or big cat sanctuary), facilities staff are also integrally involved with those measures.

A separate category of personnel is of course involved in medical/veterinary care. Some level of veterinary support is always necessary, but varies broadly, depending on the species and number of animals at a sanctuary. There may be a full-time veterinarian, or one who cares for the animals on a regular but intermittent basis. Some situations call for trained support staff for sanctuary veterinarians. These staff members are involved in the routine medical care of sanctuary residents, including constant monitoring of the animals for daily indicia of health (or health problems), and they also assist the veterinarians in the performance of surgical and other procedures and veterinary care, as governed by state laws with respect to the amount and scope of work that non-veterinary personnel are allowed to perform. One or more of these individuals may also be trained behaviorists: because of the range of situations—sometimes abusive or neglectful—that sanctuary residents endure before arriving at a sanctuary, extensive behavioral assessments and training are often necessary and very beneficial for the animals.

For any nonprofit, but especially a highly functioning and large sanctuary (or shelter), the volunteer pool can be one of the most valuable "departments" in the organization. Virtually every area of a sanctuary's functions—food preparation, facilities, technology, bookkeeping, veterinary support, caregiving —can benefit from well-trained, motivated volunteers. Where the volunteer program works well, a large amount of money is saved and therefore available for the operations of the sanctuary, thus allowing for expansion of other programs and a reduction in the amount that must be raised on an ongoing basis. Volunteers can also serve as important ambassadors for animal protection organizations, credibly informing the community about their good work.

Representing Sanctuaries

Given the foregoing, it is probably obvious that sanctuaries are functioning businesses with employees and human resources, benefits, and payroll issues along with government reporting and compliance requirements. Further, these entities regularly enter into agreements with vendors and other third parties. With respect to all of these areas, traditional legal assistance is always part of running a sanctuary. Although most sanctuaries are nonprofit organizations, it only makes the legal protections of dealing with their money all the more important. A complex set of rules apply to nonprofit organizations, which counsel will need to evaluate from time to time. Given the frequency of donations in the form of trusts and bequests, lawyers proficient in those areas are helpful. Providing pro bono legal services in such areas is a great way to contribute to the important work of supporting animals. When required, of course, legal bills will be part of the operational costs of running a sanctuary, but given sanctuaries' usual nonprofit nature, they generally welcome pro bono assistance.

Given the special nature of sanctuaries, animal lawyers with expertise in some areas unique to the sanctuary community can also be invaluable. Of course, it is the nature of this text that lawyers well-versed in nonprofit law—formation, operation, annual reporting, taxation issues—are at the forefront of the legal needs of sanctuaries. But there are several other situations that present themselves on a regular basis. The need for legal assistance, for example, related to the transfer of ownership of animals, is vital, so that the sanctuary has clear control, possession, and custody of the animals it is protecting.[54] It is one of the most important preventative defenses to someone coming into the picture and claiming ownership over sanctuary residents; as long as the transfer of rights was done correctly and completely, this concern should be minimal.

In connection with that need for clear ownership transfer, and often prefatory to it, is the actual means and method of obtaining the animals in the first place. The most common means by which animals are transferred to sanctuaries are through a seizure by law enforcement (where there may also be a pending criminal case), as the settlement or ruling in a lawsuit, or based on a private contract between the sanctuary and the original owner of the animals. Each of these circumstances requires a slightly different approach for counsel, and experience dealing with the special nature of animal ownership, and ensuring protection for both the animals and the sanctuaries that take them in.

As mentioned earlier, in the extralegal world of sanctuaries, there have been over the years a series of recognized accrediting bodies that set standards, engage in inspections, and provide certification to sanctuaries when requested. Lawyers may be helpful in guiding sanctuary clients through the requirements of these accreditation bodies and counseling them on the value of participation and membership.

---

54. Without that clear and legally proper establishment of ownership, animals can be taken from their protected settings years after being rescued and retired. Booee, one of the famous "signing chimps," was reclaimed by his owner and then sent back into years of research in 1982 because title had never been correctly established. Roger Fouts & Stephen Tukel Mills, NEXT OF KIN 283–285 (Quill 2003) (1998). And Tarra, an elephant who lived for decades at The Elephant Sanctuary in Tennessee, was also removed from her longtime home after a legal battle. Nick Beres, *Tarra the Elephant Leaves Hohenwald Sanctuary Following Lengthy Legal Battle*, NEWS CHANNEL 5 (Nov. 18, 2021), https://www.newschannel5.com/news/tarra-the-elephant-leaves-hohenwald-sanctuary-following-lengthy-legal-battle#::text=Tarra%20was%20the%20first%20elephant,Buckley%20won%20in%20court.

Shelters and Rescue Groups

For many Americans, the main—and maybe only—animal protection organization they deal with is the shelter or rescue group from which they adopt their pets. Likewise, it may be the most accessible entry point for lawyers interested in helping animal protection groups, and it involves opportunities within local communities, with organizations that are usually loved by the populace. There is significant variety in such organizations, first between shelters and rescues and then between the different types of shelters that engage in a sizable amount of overlapping conduct. To understand the potential opportunities for representation, and different considerations due to the different structures, we first explain what shelters and rescues do on a daily basis, then how these organizations exist as a legal and organizational matter and, finally, we provide some examples of the kind of specialized representation they may need.

Shelter Services

An animal shelter (which may be referred to as "the pound" in some areas) provides the services of receiving, holding, caring for, and transferring animals in a community. The animals come from a variety of sources, but most commonly they are (1) strays and lost pets who are found by local authorities or Good Samaritans aiming to reunify pets with their owners; (2) animals who are turned in by their owners or others when their owners cannot continue to care for them (e.g., because their owners have been hospitalized, evicted, arrested, or died, or if the animal has a health or behavioral issue that the owner is unable or unwilling to address); and (3) animals seized or rescued from animal cruelty situations or other circumstances. Shelters take these animals in and provide them with food, water, shelter, and veterinary services. Then, after whatever "holding period" is imposed by law, if the animals have not been reunited with their owners, the shelter obtains ownership and is able to provide an outcome for the animal. This means the animal may be adopted, transferred to a rescue organization, or temporarily placed with a foster family. In cases of untreatable medical or behavioral challenges and, in some situations, due to lack of space, the animal may be euthanized.

While pick-up of strays, adoption, foster care, reunification, and euthanasia are the most common types of services provided by animal shelters, the scope has been expanded far beyond that for many contemporary shelters in urban and suburban areas. Common additions to shelter services are behavior and training consultations and classes, free and low-cost veterinary care, temporary foster and boarding services, public education about companion animals, and animal advocacy. The advocacy side of shelters ranges from support of local ordinances and promotion of spay-neuter resources and microchipping services, to fully engaged advocacy departments with in-house and outside counsel involved in the drafting and active support of legislation, entry into strategic litigation or defense of adverse litigation, and engagement in big picture policy issues that have a broader impact on the community at large and companion animals throughout the jurisdiction, the state, or even the country.

Shelter Business Structure

There are three kinds of animal shelters, which we will call "municipal," "private," and "hybrid." There is generally no governing law with respect to what kind of shelter must be established in a given area, and there can be more than one shelter in a small geographic space.

Municipal shelters are, as the term suggests, run by local governments. Sometimes they serve a given city or town; sometimes a particular county; and some serve multiple towns, cities, or counties in a geographic area. Formal legal agreements outline the basic services provided by the shelter. Municipal shelters may be run by a separate "Animal Services" or "Animal Control" division of the municipality, or the shelter management and direction may be organized under the police department, the department of health, or even under a zoning department within the local government.

As part of the government, municipal shelters are subject to the laws governing any government agency, including laws like "sunshine laws" (public records laws) and other restrictions on hiring, termination, and governance that may be directed by state or local law. Additionally, municipal shelters may be mandated by local or state laws to impound certain types of animals while they will have discretion to impound others. For example, in California, municipalities are required to pick up animals who are obviously owned and are in some sort of danger, either physically or medically.[55] However, California state law does not require shelters to pick up healthy dogs and cats, and so that is a matter of local law or each shelter's policy and practice. Likewise, the law generally does not require municipal shelters to accept animals from their owners for the purposes of euthanasia when the animal suffers from untreatable medical or behavioral conditions, but this may be a valuable component of the shelter's services provided to the community.

Private shelters are typically federal nonprofit organizations under section 501(c)(3) of the Internal Revenue Code but may also be completely private organizations supported by private funding. They generally have no legal mandate to pick up animals and may decide to accept or decline animals brought to them based on their own policies, practices, and criteria. If private shelters do take in animals, however, they will typically be subject to the same laws regarding holding periods as municipal shelters and, of course, they are subject to all the general laws with respect to treatment of animals.

The third type of shelters, "hybrid shelters," are private shelters that contract with one or more municipalities and provide animal services in those areas. The services provided may be limited in nature (e.g., pick up of strays and providing a facility to hold animals) or more expanded (possibly with certified humane officers or other law enforcement personnel responsible for animal cruelty investigations and other legal violations related to the keeping of animals). Because of their connection to municipalities and their agency/

55. Cal. Penal Code § 597.1(a).

contractor relationship and agreement to carry out municipal obligations and services, the hybrid shelters must deal with both the private side of operations (in terms of donors, vendors, and other members of the public) and the public-facing community operations in which they engage (as a participant in municipal contracts, subject to restrictions on those involved with municipalities, and often running aspects of animal control services or other outsourced community functions).

Services and Structure of Rescue Organizations

The term "rescue" refers to a wide variety of groups and individuals, some of which are organized as nonprofit organizations, and others which are more loosely organized—or not really organized at all but serve the same function. As there is no formally recognized definition or legal requirement for such a group, the term generically refers to any group that receives animals from shelters or private individuals. Usually rescue groups focus on a particular species—dogs, cats, rabbits, birds—but some groups may be able to accommodate more than one species. Some rescue groups, especially for dogs, are specialized as to breed —while others may seek only dogs in need of long-term rehabilitative care. And many will take any dog in a shelter who may be subject to euthanasia because of lack of space there. Some shelters work very well with some rescues, although sometimes there may be tension between the two groups based on differences in policies or practices.

The specialized "breed rescue" groups may be utilized by breeders to dispose of puppies or older dogs who are not valuable enough to keep or sell. Some breed rescue groups, while they do not work with breeders, have connections with owners of the specific breed and may assist in placement for dogs in need. For the most part, however, rescues interact with shelters and act as a safe waystation between the shelter and an adopter. Rescues serve animals, shelters, and the community and take some of the burden of saving animal lives from shelters, which may be overextended and underfunded. Because many shelters are overwhelmed with the number of animals they take in, or because some animals require expensive or extensive veterinary care or behavioral training that shelters may not have the capacity to provide, rescues can fill those needs and add another layer of protection for animals who end up in shelters.

Representing Shelters and Rescues

There are many opportunities for lawyers interested in helping local shelters. As a general rule, shelters are filled with dedicated individuals whose focus is the intake, care, and positive outcomes of the animals who come through their doors. Shelter workers and even shelter management rarely have the funds, or the time, to focus on often-important legal issues that could impact shelter operations. And it is our experience that they may not even be aware of lurking legal issues that are better addressed before they become problems. These issues range from traditional business operations to the specific types of circumstances that come up in shelter daily work. For example, a series of agreements—adoption, foster, owner reunification, owner-surrender, owner-requested-euthanasia, surgical consent, to name the most common—are part and parcel of the shelter's daily operations. But very often these documents have been in place for years, were not prepared by lawyers, and have been working for the shelters only because no one has ever challenged them. The consequences can be dire, however, if a shelter is dragged into litigation over an inadequate contract, and the potential for liability could be significant. Animal lawyers can view these agreements through both shelter-based and liability-based lenses and help craft or revise these agreements so that they better serve all involved.

The potential for representation varies widely and depends in part on the services provided and the type of shelter. Most municipal shelters are represented by city or county counsel for the jurisdiction, although these lawyers may have no experience whatsoever with issues relating to animals in general, or shelters in particular. The value of understanding the work of shelters and their daily challenges is immeasurable, and where county or city counsel is willing to take assistance from lawyers more in tune with shelter work, the partnership provides benefits to the government, the animals, and the shelters. In the private and hybrid shelter settings, the need for counsel is even greater: "shelter law" requires consideration of compliance with state and federal laws, normal business operations, fundraising issues, and the generation of long-term gifts for the sustenance of the organization. Especially for private shelters, advocacy for companion animals is often a part of the organization's operations. While some shelters may not want to get involved in advocacy, shelters represent one of the best possible advocates to improve the lives of companion animals because shelters are generally not viewed as activists or tied to a political agenda but rather only to the best interests of the animals they serve. In addition, shelters may have inherent standing with respect to issues that impact companion animals on a policy or legal level since they deal with these animals constantly. Animal lawyers who have like interests can partner with these types of shelters to forge meaningful change at the local or even state level.

The legal needs of rescues are similar to those of animal shelters. Contracts and other legal agreements are a regular part of rescues' operations, and lawyers can assist with drafting these documents. Active rescue groups usually work with foster homes (homes where the rescued animals go, pending adoption) and adopters. One cannot underestimate the importance of carefully drafted agreements with those fosters and shelters, as well as with eventual adopters; those documents are vital to the stable and successful operation of a rescue. Decisions must be made by the rescue as to how much liability it is willing to accept, and how much it wants to pass on to those who adopt animals from the rescue. There are many variations in these contracts, and some rescues also want to have the ability to reclaim animals they have adopted out, if new owners are not treating the animal properly. This kind of arrangement must be carefully drafted in the agreements, so that ownership is successfully transferred for liability purposes, but recovery of the animals is possible.[56] Rescues may also have agreements in place with local shelters, governing the parameters of their relationship, options for claiming animals who would otherwise have a negative outcome, and other particulars. Rescue groups may also embrace some advocacy component, and have a similar, though not identical, connection to companion animals as shelters do that may provide them both the gravitas and the connection to be actively involved in changing things for the type of animals they serve. Lawyers can assist with these efforts as well.

It should be noted that some states have shelter-specific, or rescue-specific, laws. In general, though, shelters and rescues are simply subject to the state and local laws that apply to the running of a business, or the keeping of and caring for animals. So, lawyers wanting to get involved in the representation of these groups must carefully navigate the laws that will cover them and, like much of the practice of animal law, be creative in applying the law to the shelter or rescue's operations.

Opportunities to Represent Animal Protection Organizations

As discussed earlier, animal protection organizations—and the work these organizations undertake—vary significantly. Legal work, however, is a consistent part of the operation of these organizations, and so there are many opportunities for attorneys to represent them. Many animal protection groups have attorneys on staff, and these attorneys provide legal support in a variety of ways. There are also opportunities to represent animal protection organizations as outside counsel, as discussed below, including on a pro bono basis.

In-House Counsel

Many animal protection organizations, such as the HSUS and ALDF, have a team of in-house attorneys who use litigation and other legal tools to advance the organizations' goals. These in-house attorneys can support organizations' animal protection missions in many ways. In-house attorneys may develop and litigate cases in federal, state, or local courts—sometimes partnering with outside counsel to do so. As discussed previously, these cases take many forms, varying from strategic litigation designed to effect change for animals to defending laws that have been passed to increase the humane treatment of animals. In-house attorneys may also draft federal or state regulatory petitions or comments on proposed regulations. They might draft and review federal, state, and local laws to secure or increase humane treatment for animals. They

56. Often when a rescue is at the point where it is trying to reclaim an animal, the recipient of the animal may not be willing to give the animal up. A clear agreement covering the rescue's rights will be very helpful, should that situation arise.

may also support their clients' advocacy efforts by researching legal questions, drafting requests to enforce laws, drafting public records requests, or advising their internal clients on policy strategies.

There are several other ways that attorneys can work directly for animal protection organizations. For example, some in-house attorneys work to develop relationships with congressional and/or state legislative offices and advocate for laws that protect animals (and against those that would harm them). Similarly, many groups have attorneys on staff who work directly with administrative agencies to promote regulations and administrative policies that benefit animals and to oppose harmful regulations and policies. In addition, some animal protection organizations have an office of general counsel. Attorneys in these positions provide legal advice on a wide range of issues, including addressing matters that arise concerning organizations' programs, investigations, legal compliance, operations, and corporate governance.

The work that in-house attorneys conduct varies between animal protection organizations. At some organizations, attorneys may assume one or more of the roles discussed earlier. And, at some organizations—particularly larger organizations—an attorney's work may be relatively specialized. For example, larger organizations may hire some attorneys to litigate on specific issues or campaigns, some to build relationships with legislators, and others to work as general counsel. It is also worth noting that many animal protection organizations offer legal internships, so law students interested in pursuing a career in animal law should consider interning with these groups.

Outside Counsel

Many animal protection organizations have no in-house lawyers or have legal needs that exceed the capacity of their in-house legal teams. They may rely on legal assistance (pro bono or not) from a variety of outside lawyers, each one serving the organization in a specific role. Human resources, tax issues, nonprofit organization compliance, dealing with bequests and other special donations, and local, state, and federal business operation issues, are all vital to running a company and for the most part do not depend on knowledge of the particular work of the organization. Interesting, exciting, and impactful work is also done within the animal law sphere, where the groups are carrying out their missions and goals through the work they do on a daily basis, which may or may not include direct advocacy for the specific issues upon which each group focuses. The work that lawyers can do for, and with, these organizations ranges from assistance in drafting public messaging, to help in reviewing and possibly drafting new legislation (state or local), to assistance in litigation, to helping new campaigns for legal change in the organization's area of focus.

To find clients, it is very helpful—invaluable, in fact—to gain some level of expertise and knowledge about the areas of animal law and animal protection in which you are most interested. Within the field, there are already broad areas of specialization, such as farm animals, wildlife, animal research, or companion animals. Within companion animal law, specialization opportunities include focusing on the individual pet and owner/guardian relationship, or on a bigger level dealing with shelters and rescues, or even on regional and national issues such as the harms caused by puppy mills, or the challenges of managing free-roaming (community) cats. Obviously the more of these topics you can gain experience in, the larger will be the number of groups that will potentially be your clients. Animal protection organizations are best served by lawyers who understand the particulars of their operations and the strategic considerations inherent in each legal move that may be made. It is only through this comprehensive, holistic understanding of both the animal side of things and the legal implications that animal protection organizations are best represented by an outside lawyer.

Finding animal protection organizations that you might want to represent is not difficult but actually getting the work can be. This is because most of these groups do not have a large (if they have any) legal budget, and either have in-house lawyers (if they have a dedicated legal advocacy department) or have connections with lawyers and firms willing to work pro bono. But there are certainly some groups out there that will be hiring outside counsel, and once lawyers develop some animal law expertise, and have done some work for animal protection organizations, word-of-mouth referrals are as good as anything for finding new clients.

There are several options for payment of services. It is a given that all nonprofits prefer pro bono legal help, so that their funds can be used elsewhere. If you are in a position to offer such services, this may facilitate your ability to identify new clients. But lawyers may be able to find paying work in animal protection if they brainstorm helpful and creative new projects for nonprofits interested in advocacy. There are certainly animal protection organizations across the country that, if approached with the right proposal, may be willing to sign up with new counsel interested in helping the group further its mission. Animal law and animal protection organization representation generally falls to those who are particularly supportive of the work that the groups undertake—and this may be a selling point when trying to get work from some groups. That is, when a group realizes counsel is interested in furthering the group's purpose and goals, a symbiosis may develop. And if a group can be convinced of the value of paying a lawyer (rather than in some cases getting free counsel who is not as committed), the relationship can be established. Since "creative billing" is also an option at most firms, you can also consider work on a "low bono" rate, i.e., at a significantly reduced rate that is not pro bono but will not impact the animal protection organization and its bank accounts as much as normal hourly rates. Options for "low bono" include the aforementioned reduced rate, a set fee for a project, or an hourly rate with a cap on fees.

From the lawyers' side, with the payment issue resolved (through finding paying clients, providing "low bono" billing, or offering pro bono work), doors certainly open and important work that might otherwise never have been done can lead to great change for animals. It is of course important to be sure that you are committed to take a big project all the way if you are offering pro bono work, and so a careful assessment of the amount of time and length of a matter is important up front.[57]

Conclusion

As the discussion above demonstrates, the work and needs of animal protection organizations vary widely. Accordingly, there are many ways that attorneys can use their skills to assist these organizations in their efforts to improve the treatment and lives of animals. In our experience, such legal representation is both intellectually stimulating and deeply rewarding. We hope this chapter, along with others in this book, prompts additional attorneys to explore the ways they can contribute their expertise to the animal protection movement.

57. Several federal statutes allow prevailing parties to recover attorneys' fees, and those fees can often be substantial. Under the Endangered Species Act, the Equal Access to Justice Act (which allows prevailing parties in cases against the federal government to recover attorneys' fees in some circumstances), the Fair Housing Act (under which claims relating to assistance animals can be brought), and others, even if pro bono representation has been provided, there may still be options for fee recovery.

CHAPTER 2

Formation, Governance, and Related Tax-Exempt Status Issues

Rebecca J. Huss

Introduction

This chapter provides general information relating to the formation of a nonprofit entity, governance issues, and some introductory guidance on the organization and operation of a tax-exempt organization under federal law. Because meaningful resources are required to establish and maintain a new entity, it is worthwhile to consider whether there is an existing nonprofit, tax-exempt entity that could perform the type of activities envisioned. Even if the decision is made to form a new entity, it is helpful to identify what other organizations are working in the area (geographically or subject matter) for potential collaboration in the future. If it is determined that a new group is needed, it is possible to operate without establishing a separate legal entity and filing for tax-exempt status. However, as successful as an organization can be without those formalities, parties should consider making the effort to use the legal structures available.

As governmental entities at both the state and federal levels have a substantial interest in ensuring that nonprofit entities comply with the law, there is a great deal of useful information available on various states' websites and the irs.gov website. Although states (relating to the establishment of an entity) and subsequently the Internal Revenue Service (IRS) (relating to tax-exempt status) have a lot of resources available for laypersons because of the impact of mistakes, both in time lost and potential liability, it is recommended that parties work with a lawyer to assist with the process.

Formation of Animal Protection Organizations Under State Law

If it is determined that a new entity is necessary, the first step is establishment of the entity under state law. The most common type of business entity used for a nonprofit entity is a corporation, which is the focus of this chapter. Although the limited liability company (LLC) entity's flexibility has many benefits, some states either do not allow nonprofit entities to be established as LLCs or have additional provisions that may complicate their operation. In addition, 2021 guidance from the IRS reiterated that an LLC would only be recognized as tax-exempt if all of the LLC's interest holders (commonly referred to as members) were already 501(c)(3) tax-exempt organizations or governmental units.[1]

The purpose of the nonprofit animal protection corporations that are the focus of this book is to work for the public benefit, as compared to cooperative or mutual benefit corporations, which benefit a select group of people (like a social club or the American Bar Association). Public benefit entities are traditionally viewed as being for a "charitable" purpose. This chapter focuses on organizations that will apply for tax-exempt status and qualify as a "public charity."

Just as with a for-profit corporation, doing business as a nonprofit corporation provides liability protection to the directors, officers, and employees. Especially for organizations working directly with animals or engaging in animal advocacy work that could result in risk (such as corporate campaigns or exposés), liability protection is key. The corporate liability shield also protects individuals (except in certain limited circumstances) from personal responsibility for day-to-day debts or liability incurred by the organization.

The law of the state of incorporation will determine not only the incorporation process but also the obligations of the directors and the rights of any members of the corporation. This "internal affairs" doctrine also means that the law of the state of incorporation will determine, for example, whether the entity can hold directors' meetings electronically and utilize a written consent process for decision-making without convening a meeting. Another consideration in choosing where to incorporate is that an entity will be subject to state authority (e.g., to court jurisdiction and enforcement by the state charity division) in a state in which it engages in substantial activities such as having a physical office or a significant number of employees. It may therefore make sense to incorporate in a state in which a company is operating and therefore already exposed to such authority—rather than incorporating in another state that will then also have regulatory authority. On the other hand, there can be tax or other structural advantages to incorporating in a state that is friendly to business entities (such as Delaware) that may have less onerous registration and reporting processes as compared with other states.

1. For this reason, it is not uncommon for an existing 501(c)(3) organization to use the LLC form for a subsidiary. If properly structured, such a subsidiary LLC may be treated as what is known as a "disregarded entity" and not be required to file a separate federal tax return.

There are many similarities between for-profit and nonprofit corporations and their respective governing statutory provisions. For example, Delaware has one statute that applies to all corporations, whether they are for-profit or nonprofit. The primary distinction between nonprofit and for-profit corporations is that a for-profit corporation is owned by its shareholders. As discussed below, while some states allow nonprofit corporations to have members who would have the right to provide input on decisions relating to the entity, the rights of these members are distinct from those of shareholders.

Name of Corporation

An animal protection organization's corporate name should be unique and descriptive but not so specific that it is necessary to change it if the focus of the organization's activities shifts over time. The organization's name should not infringe on another person's intellectual property and should not be confusing to members of the public. If it is likely that the type of activities may change or expand over time, it may be helpful to not include "limiting" language (such as "sanctuary") in the name. Otherwise, it may become necessary to change the name (whether by a legal name change or a "doing business as" registration). In general, it is best to try to plan ahead and choose a name that can grow with the organization, so that there is no loss of any "brand value" if the name has to be changed later.

Each state has a database of the corporate entities formed under the laws of that state. If an attempt is made to incorporate using the name of an existing entity, the state will reject the application. Some states have specific rules relating to the form of the entity name, including requiring a word or designation indicating that it is a corporation at the end of the name, such as Inc., Company, Co., or Corp. Even if an entity's home state does not require such a designation, when registering as a "foreign" corporation in some other states—which is required if an entity engages in a certain minimal level of activity in another state—it may be necessary to add such a designation. Some states allow the reservation of a name for a period of time prior to incorporation and use. As discussed earlier, an entity may also register a "doing business as" name in addition to the legal name of the entity, either because the original legal name does not accurately reflect the work being done or for use with particular programs.

In addition to confirming that the preferred name is available and in the form required by state law, it is necessary to ensure that the name and any logos being used do not infringe upon another party's intellectual property rights. This should be confirmed through formal trademark searches (described below) and also by online research. The latter is important because, even if a name has not been registered for state or federal trademark protection, the common law provides a "first user" with certain protections in the event the first user can document consumer confusion.

The United States Patent and Trademark Office's (USPTO) website provides links to the various state agencies where trademark and/or service mark registration information is available.[2] If an organization is confident that it will only be doing business in one state (which is unlikely given the benefits of fundraising across state lines), registering for trademark protection using a state's process is an option. Otherwise, registration at the federal level is appropriate. Prior to settling on a name, a check should be made in at least the databases of the primary states where the organization will be doing business, along with the USPTO Trademark Electronic Search System database, to ensure that the new entity name will not be substantially similar to another entity.

Registration makes it easier to defend the trademark in future, including when demanding that others cease and desist from using the new entity's name. Trademark registration occurs using categories of activities referred to as classes. There are forty-five federal trademark classes, with each class covering a wide range of services or goods. Because organizations pay for each class registered, identifying the critical class or classes is key. In addition to determining the appropriate class or classes, registrants must develop a description of the goods or services to be provided within each class. As an example, Class 041 is Educational and Entertainment services. A description in that class might be something like "conducting seminars related to animal care; arranging and conducting conferences and workshops to assist others in establishing organizations for animal rescue and rehabilitation services." In Class 036, Insurance and Financial, a description could read: "Charitable services, namely raising money for animal welfare organizations through promotions and/or incentives" and in Class 045, Personal and Legal, "animal cruelty investigations."

Before it can apply for protection, the entity must already be in existence (or, in the case of the USPTO, there must be an intent to use such name within the following six months), as it is necessary to prove use of such name to be granted and to maintain the protection. If the USPTO's examination determines that there is a "likelihood of confusion" with a previously registered or pending application with an earlier filing date, the application will be denied. The USPTO does not use a mechanical test to determine confusion, but instead considers whether consumers are likely to assume that the activities are from a common source. The USPTO also considers whether a new request may cause confusion if a similar name is being used in the same or related activity classes—which is another reason to consider carefully (ideally with assistance from an intellectual property attorney) in which classes to apply for protection.

Once an organization has applied for trademark protection and the USPTO confirms receipt of the application, the USPTO will instruct the applicant to begin using the trademark "TM" symbol next to the trademarked name or logo wherever it appears, to serve as notice to third parties of the entity's claim to the

---

2. The term trademark is often used to reference both goods and services. Technically, though, a "trademark" is used for goods and a "service mark" for services. For example, the American Society for the Prevention of Cruelty to Animals® has registered the word mark "ASPCA®" for activities involving both goods (such as clothing) and services (such as educational services). This mark is therefore referred to both as a trademark and as a service mark.

mark. If the registration process is successfully completed, the entity should then switch to using the "®" symbol next to the trademark.

Given the similarity of areas of work across animal protection organizations, the ubiquity of certain words to describe that work (e.g., animals, protection, welfare, humane, rescue), and use of animal images as logos, an organization may sometimes learn of another group using a name or logo similar to its own. This can happen at any time during the life cycle of an organization, including when a new organization forms or because an organization has been using a name without registering it. An example of how an organization can learn of an issue like this is when a donor complains about a donation that the donor thought was going to another organization. In such a circumstance, the organization that has trademarked the name—depending on where and in which classes it is registered—may have strong grounds on which to send a cease and desist letter to urge the other organization to stop using the potentially infringing name. This approach can be uncomfortable or undesired, though, given that animal protection organizations are generally working toward the same purposes and often collaborate with each other. Provided the names, geographical use, and/or activities are sufficiently different, it may be adequate to send a letter to the other organization informing them of the registered trademark and reserving the right to object to their future use of their name or logo, should it become confusing. An organization may also request that the non-registered organization take steps to make it clearer that it is not affiliated with the registered organization, such as making changes to the non-registered organization's logo or including disclaimer language in communications to the public.

Because this is a specialized field, whenever possible, organizations should consult with an intellectual property attorney to ensure that they are sufficiently protecting their trademarks. Once an organization has determined a name, the next step is to draft articles of incorporation (known as a "certificate of incorporation" in Delaware) for filing with the relevant state agency.

Articles of Incorporation

The articles of incorporation can be viewed as the "constitution" of the organization. State law determines what must be included in this document, so it is important to start the process by reviewing the relevant statutory provisions. In addition to ensuring that the document contains the necessary provisions to support incorporation (and as discussed below, the ability to qualify as a tax-exempt organization), because articles of incorporation are easily accessed by members of the public, an entity should consider how the content of this document may be viewed by potential donors and other people interested in the organization.

In addition to stating the name of the entity (see the discussion below), common statutory requirements include listing the registered agent for purposes of service of process (which is the process by which an organization is provided effective notice that a legal action is being taken against it) and the name or names of the incorporator/s. In some states, the names of initial directors and officers must also be provided. The registered agent may be a compensated company or an individual. It is important to ensure that the registered agent is able to effectively communicate with the organization. In addition to any other types of legal notices, a nonprofit organization can be administratively dissolved if it fails to file any required annual or biennial reports to the state—and communications about such filing requirements may be sent to the registered agent. In states that allow for or require a nonprofit corporation to have members (discussed below), the articles of incorporation should designate whether there are members. It is also important to include a provision describing the process to amend the articles of incorporation.

Two specific provisions (discussed in turn below) must be included in the articles of incorporation in order for a nonprofit corporation to be eligible for federal tax-exempt status: a properly drafted purpose clause and an irrevocable dedication of assets. These clauses are also important when applying for tax relief from state authorities, and a state's nonprofit corporation act may contain other requirements for the contents of the articles of incorporation.

The purpose clause is an important part of the "story" of the organization. By providing some information about the charitable activities in the articles of incorporation, potential donors and volunteers can learn about the organization without even viewing the organization's website. Similar to the entity's name, it is important to allow for some evolution in focus by including general language such as "and any other lawful purpose" to allow for some flexibility in an organization's work before it is necessary to amend the articles of incorporation. For this reason, it is common in purpose clauses to see language such as "the Corporation is organized and operated exclusively as a nonprofit corporation for charitable, educational or scientific purposes in accordance with Section 501(c)(3) of the Internal Revenue Code," with additional language setting forth more specific information about the planned activities of the organization. In addition to samples available from the IRS and state authorities, it can be helpful to review the articles of incorporation for entities that are engaging in similar activities. Copies of articles of incorporation for entities in existence are generally accessible for a nominal fee via a "business entity" search on the Secretary of State's website in the state where the entity was incorporated.

As stated above, language prohibiting the assets of the corporation from being used to benefit individuals (rather than for the charitable purpose) and identifying the disposition of any assets upon dissolution are also required. The IRS provides example language, including language relating to ensuring that (a) no part of the net earnings of the entity will inure to the benefit of insiders or private persons (other than reasonable compensation), (b) the amount of legislative lobbying is limited and the organization does not engage in political campaign activities, and (c) there is a process for distribution of assets upon dissolution, either to another tax-exempt organization or to the government.

State law often allows for the inclusion of nonmandatory provisions in the articles of incorporation. Such provisions may include the names of the initial board of directors, the limitation of liability of directors, and indemnification language. Given the need of organizations to attract and retain qualified directors, such liability limitation and indemnification provisions are useful. They can eliminate or limit the liability of a director to the corporation or its members for money damages and/or provide for the most expansive indemnification rights available under state law, including coverage for litigation expenses and attorney's fees. As discussed later in this chapter, the laws of some states automatically provide a liability shield for directors of nonprofit corporations under certain circumstances. Some states require that the type of nonprofit entity be identified in the articles. In the context of an animal advocacy or protection organization, as discussed above, the type of entity is likely to be a public benefit rather than a mutual benefit organization.

The relevant state agencies involved in the incorporation process generally provide step-by-step instructions and template documents on their websites to assist in the preparation and filing of required documents. In some states, such as Utah, the state's platform even facilitates new entities' registration in other contexts such as for taxes. Once the articles of incorporation are properly filed (along with any required application form and the fee) and accepted by the relevant state agency, the entity will come into existence pursuant to state law.

Bylaws

In addition to the articles of incorporation, a new entity must prepare and adopt bylaws. Unlike the articles of incorporation, bylaws are not filed with the state and can be kept private (though you may find that potential donors and others ask to review them). If there is any inconsistency between provisions of an entity's articles of incorporation and bylaws, the articles will control.

The bylaws set out the day-to-day governance of the entity. Thoughtful drafting of bylaws can help avoid potential issues, such as disputes over who has the right to vote and when. Generally, if an issue is not set forth in the articles of incorporation or bylaws, the relevant state nonprofit corporation act provision will apply by default. So, it is useful to review the applicable state statute (often called the corporation code or nonprofit business corporation act) to determine whether there is anything in the applicable statute that would be counterproductive for the smooth running of the organization. The state statute will also determine whether a particular provision of state law may be overridden by a company's governing documents. In the context of nonprofit organizations, it is especially useful to ensure that these documents do not inadvertently limit the application of a state volunteer limitation of liability law (discussed below).

Members

As discussed above, some states allow or require nonprofit corporations to have members. The legal status of members of a nonprofit corporation is not the same as shareholders in for-profit corporations. Specifically, "members" in this context do not have any *ownership* rights but are individuals or entities that have the right to vote on electing directors and other significant (often articulated as "fundamental") matters impacting the organization. Having voting members adds a layer of complexity to a nonprofit entity's governance given that organizations with voting members must hold members' meetings to elect directors and conduct other significant business. Members' meetings will have notice and quorum requirements and a voting process (including for written consents). With a self-perpetuating board (no voting members), generally the sitting directors determine who will serve on the board through the process set forth in the bylaws.

Another factor that may influence the decision on whether to have members is that some state statutes allow members to bring derivative causes of action against directors of the nonprofit. A derivative cause of action is a claim on behalf of the entity, usually alleging that one or more of the directors have acted inappropriately. Although the possibility of significant money damages (and accompanying attorney's fees) is much more limited in the context of nonprofit entities (see the liability discussion below), this possible avenue for claims and litigation should be part of the analysis in determining whether members would be appropriate. From a practical perspective, it is common for people involved in animal advocacy to be passionate, and thoughtful people can disagree about how and what work should be done. Although transparency and encouraging involvement is generally a laudable goal, there are other readily available ways for interested members of the public to engage with the organization, short of formal membership. For all of these reasons, where permitted by state statute, it may be preferable not to have members, who add an additional layer of complexity to the organization's structure.

If members are appropriate or required, the articles and/or bylaws would set out the qualifications necessary to qualify as a member. For example, to maintain membership status a member may have to pay dues, volunteer a certain number of hours, or live in a particular geographic area. Members could also be representatives of other organizations. Even in states that do require nonprofit corporations to have members (such as Delaware), one possible workaround is to make the criteria for membership be that the directors are the members, thereby ensuring that the same people serve in both roles. The bylaws would also set forth the term of membership and on what topics the members would have the right to vote (subject to state law). As referenced above, the bylaws also would need to set forth the process for member meetings, including timing, who can call them, structure, quorum, etc.

If a decision is made to forgo having voting members, it should be clear in the articles of incorporation. This does not mean that a nonprofit corporation cannot have "members" in a broader sense. It is common for nonprofit organizations to have programs through which a donor or supporter can become a "member" and receive certain benefits, whether that consists of a t-shirt, invitations to member-only events, discounts, or otherwise. However, such "members" do not have any decision-making authority in connection with the running of the organization itself.

Directors

The bylaws will describe the power and duties of the board of directors. The board of directors acts as a body to make decisions for the organization. Individual directors, without either having another status (such as an employee) or having been provided specific authority (such as being appointed as an officer) do not have authority to bind an organization. The role of the board is to determine the general direction of an organization, set policies, and oversee the work of the officers (who manage the organization's daily operations).

The bylaws will set forth the number of directors, often as a range. A range provides flexibility, for example, allowing for an increase in the number of directors as an organization grows without the need to amend the bylaws. From a practical perspective, it is helpful to have an odd number of board members to avoid deadlocks in voting. When deciding an optimal size for the board, an organization's founders must balance the benefit of having a critical mass of people with different ideas and backgrounds against the unwieldiness that can come with too large a group.

Any minimum qualifications for the directors would be set forth in the bylaws. For example, an organization that provides foster home-based care for animals may require that all directors are currently or have a history of fostering animals, to ensure that they have relevant experience. Just as with for-profit corporations, a nonprofit corporation can have one or more classes of directors, for example, a certain number of directors can be required to have specific qualifications (such as active engagement with the organization, or holding a particular professional licensing status, such as veterinarians). As an example, an organization providing veterinary services as a primary part of its mission may choose to have a class of directors with a connection to the veterinary profession. Such a requirement would help to ensure that there is always someone on the board with this background to provide input on activities relating to that profession, whether for example, to assist with its relationships with for-profit veterinarians in the community or challenges associated with attracting and retaining veterinary technicians.

The term or tenure of the directors is set forth in the bylaws, usually as a single-year or multiple-year term. The advantage of multiple-year terms is that a board member can gain knowledge and experience over time. On the other hand, having single-year terms may make dealing with an underperforming director easier, as the director could just not be reelected rather than having to be terminated. If the directors have multiple-year terms, it can be useful to establish classes of directors with different start dates. This allows for institutional history to be retained while having new board members, who may bring in new ideas, join on a periodic basis.

It is important to clearly establish in the bylaws the circumstances under which a director can be terminated. Including objective criteria in the termination provision may make any necessary difficult conversation with a director who is not performing to the level needed by the organization a bit easier. For example, the termination provision can establish that a director must attend a minimum percentage of meetings. In addition to objective criteria for termination, bylaws often provide that a board member can be removed for any reason by a majority vote of the other directors, which can provide welcome flexibility in a difficult situation. It may be appropriate to make it more difficult to remove a director or directors in a particular class, for example, if there is a need to ensure that directors with certain qualifications are always on a board.

If a term limit for directors is included, it should be clearly set forth whether an individual can rejoin a board after a break in service. A risk of term limits is that an active board member who is not allowed to serve for a period of time may turn their attention to a different organization and not be available to serve once such mandated break in service ends. In addition, the possibility of founders more easily losing control over the board due to term limits can be a sensitive issue. For this reason, organizations that do not establish term limits in their initial bylaws may find it easier and important to add such a provision in future, to support the continued growth and evolution of the organization.

Although it is not uncommon to have some insiders (employees) of an organization to serve as directors, best practice is that "outsiders" or independent directors should make up a numerical majority on the board. State law may have specific requirements. For example, California has an "interested person" limitation, requiring that less than half of the nonprofit organization's board members receive compensation from the organization (other than for their board services). Having an independent board is viewed by the IRS as a helpful preventive measure to avoid issues with excessive inurement (see discussion of inurement below).

Board Meetings

The bylaws should set forth all the major aspects of how board meetings will be run, including a minimum number of regular board meetings (state law generally requires at least one), how they will be scheduled, and how a special meeting can be called. Notice and quorum requirements should also be included. Flexibility in how board meetings can be held is useful. The bylaws can provide that meetings can be held in any manner allowed by the relevant state law or can set forth the ways such meetings can be held (subject to state law). If electronic meetings are contemplated, that can be set forth in the bylaws. State statutes generally permit such meetings, if the technology allows for the members to hear each other in real time. The ability to hold a meeting via a written consent process is also useful, though it is important that for any substantive decisions, board members have the opportunity to obtain sufficient information to make decisions consistent with the fiduciary duty of care (discussed below). Some states require that decisions reached by written consent be unanimous.

Including other guidelines on how a board meeting will be run (e.g., using formal rules such as Robert's Rules of Order or a more simplified procedure) can be useful. In the absence of such rules, an individual in a particular position (such as the chair of the board) should be empowered to determine the rules to help avoid disagreements about procedure so that such issues do not make it more difficult for the board to engage in substantive decision-making.

Whether certain decisions require a super-majority vote is also something that should be set forth in the bylaws. For example, the designation of the chief executive officer or the sale of real property may be issues that rise to the level of a super-majority vote. Perhaps expenditures over a certain amount would trigger the super-majority voting provision. In the alternative, if separate classes of directors are established, the majority approval of a specific class of directors may be required for decisions that are deemed to be within the expertise or special interest of the directors in that class.

Individuals appointing an agent to vote on their behalf (referred to as a proxy), which is very common for shareholders in for-profit corporations, is generally not appropriate for board members. Many states specifically articulate that proxy voting is not permissible for board action. Even if a state allows proxy voting in particular circumstances, utilizing a proxy can raise the question of whether a board member is fulfilling the duty of care (as discussed below).

Although it may be legal for board members of nonprofit public benefit organizations to receive compensation, it is not overly common (and can result in the loss of protection from a volunteer liability statute). If compensation will be provided, it should be set forth in the bylaws. Board members can be reimbursed for their actual travel costs and other direct expenses associated with board service.

The bylaws should also set forth the standing board committees. Some states require that nonprofit organizations have specific committees, and sometimes even that the members of such committees have particular qualifications. For example, the California Nonprofit Integrity Act requires certain nonprofits that are incorporated in or have activities in California to establish an audit committee. The law sets forth specific eligibility requirements for committee service (including that employees may not serve), along with limitations on overlapping membership with the organization's finance committee. The California law also sets out five specific duties of the audit committee, including making a recommendation to the board on the retention and termination of an independent auditor and conferring with the auditor to determine that the financial affairs of the nonprofit corporation are in order.

The bylaws can name and provide a general overview of the work of each committee and how the members of any committees will be determined, with the actual description of the jurisdiction, duties, and procedures of the committees being set forth in a separate committee charter or via a board resolution (which makes these guidelines easier to amend as needed in the future).

Officers

State statutes vary on whether particular "named" officers are required. Officers, who are often among the first employees of an entity, are expected to manage the day-to-day activities of the organization and implement decisions of the board of directors. It is common to have a minimum of a president or chief executive officer, secretary, and treasurer. A general description of the responsibilities of each position should be included in the bylaws. It can also be helpful to denote which officer or officers has or have the authority to manage funds, as lenders and other third-parties may request evidence of such authority. This type of authority can also be provided via a board resolution relating to a particular transaction, such as establishing a bank account.

The bylaws should set forth how officers are appointed, commonly by vote of the board of directors. Sometimes the chief executive officer/president is granted the authority to select other officers, such as a chief financial officer or chief programs officer, and determine their duties. If it is important that an officer has a particular qualification (such as professional licensing status for a chief veterinary officer), that requirement could also be included in the bylaws.

Advisory or Honorary Boards and Councils

Although not required to be included in the bylaws and generally not addressed there, some organizations choose to establish one or more "advisory boards" or "honorary boards," sometimes also called a council or committee of advisors. The members of such groups are not subject to the fiduciary duties discussed below and do not have independent decision-making authority. Instead, they can assist with specific aspects of an organization's programming or in specialized areas such as fundraising. Just as it is necessary to have procedures and processes to ensure the effectiveness of the board of directors, any advisory board should have designated leadership, guidelines for members, clear expectations of its members, and regular meetings. These guidelines should be set out in a document approved by the board of directors, which also notes the absence of formal authority of the advisory board. Organizations should be aware that, if they will not be able to provide the necessary support for such an advisory board, it may be contraindicated. An organization will not want the members of an advisory board, who are often highly engaged volunteers and donors, to have a negative experience serving on an ineffective advisory board.

Other Bylaw Provisions

If not already included in the articles of incorporation, the bylaws should include indemnification language that can protect directors, officers, and employees with respect to claims brought against them for actions taken in good faith that they reasonably believed to be in the best interest of the organization. It is also critical for animal protection organizations to have adequate insurance coverage, which is discussed in chapter 4.

It is a best practice for a nonprofit entity to have a written conflict-of-interest policy. Indeed, one of the questions on the annual report filed by tax-exempt organizations to the IRS—the Form 990—is whether the organization has a written conflict-of-interest policy along with an annual disclosure process to ensure compliance. Such policies ensure that the organization's interests are protected any time a director, officer, or key person (generally, someone with decision-making or financial authority) has an actual or potential personal interest in a decision or transaction being considered by the organization. The conflict-of-interest policy will set forth the circumstances in which it applies and the process for determining how any potential conflicts will be handled. Often potential or actual conflicts are financial in nature, for example, relating to setting compensation or if the organization is considering doing business with another entity that is owned or controlled by the interested individual. Another example is when an individual serves as a volunteer director on the boards of two nonprofit organizations (Organization A and Organization B). If Organization A is considering providing a substantial grant to Organization B, the individual sitting on both boards should not be part of the decision-making process, even though the individual does not benefit financially from the grant. Conflict-of-interest policies generally apply to directors, officers, and other employees with certain levels of decision-making or budgetary authority. Conflict resolution processes typically require disclosure of the conflict to a particular body or individual, an investigation to determine the relevant facts and whether a conflict exists, and that the person with the conflict not be part of the decision-making. A conflict-of-interest policy may also set forth the documentation to be generated as part of the conflict review process. An organization can include its conflict-of-interest policy in the bylaws. The IRS provides lengthy sample of conflict-of-interest policy language in its Instructions for Form 1023 (Form 1023 is discussed briefly below).

Other provisions that are useful for the governance and running of the organization, such as setting the fiscal (also called tax) year, can be included in the bylaws. Just like the articles of incorporation, bylaws should set out the process by which they can be amended. In addition, state nonprofit corporation laws may have provisions allowing directors (and, if relevant, members) to access certain records of the entity. The bylaws can provide greater access than required by law or, if the relevant state law permits a reduction of such rights and the organization wants to do so, the bylaws should set forth any restriction.

Additional Steps

After establishing the entity under state law, an organization will need to apply for an Employer Identification Number (EIN). Even if the organization will initially not have any employees, most banks require an EIN to open an account, and an EIN is required as part of the process to request tax-exempt status with the IRS.

Depending on the state of incorporation and the other states where the entity will be doing business, there may be other documents that need to be filed. For example, in California, within ninety days of registering a nonprofit entity with the Secretary of State, a "Statement of Information" must be filed containing basic information such as the names and contact information for certain officers.

In addition to the filing to obtain tax-exempt status at the federal level (discussed below), it is important to check in each state where an entity is doing business to determine what filings are necessary to request exempt status for other types of taxes such as property or sales taxes. Chapter 2 of this book discusses this issue in more detail. The standards supporting such state tax exemptions vary, so if such tax exemption is key to the success of the entity, it is worthwhile to ensure that the governing documents are initially structured in a way to meet such standards.

Most states require corporations incorporated under their state statutes to file reports yearly or every other year to maintain an entity's corporate status. Failure to file such periodic reports may result in the entity being administratively dissolved by the state.

A majority of states require nonprofits to register with the state prior to soliciting donations from residents of that state—so determining any filing requirements before there are any fundraising activities should be a priority to ensure any necessary filings are completed. Fundraising is discussed in detail in chapter 3.

The next section provides an overview of the fiduciary duties applicable to nonprofit directors (and officers) and potential liability they may incur.

Governance Issues

As discussed above, the role of the board of directors is to provide oversight, planning, and guidance on the overall direction of the organization. In contrast, the officers manage the day-to-day operations, and the other employees work under the direction of the officers. It is useful to have directors who have a variety of backgrounds and skills. For example, board members with backgrounds in finance, accounting, or fundraising can provide insight when the board is considering issues in these areas. And even if the decision is made to not specifically require that board members have prior experience with an organization, a genuine interest in or experience with the work of the organization is often useful, both from the perspective of ensuring that the directors are committed to the activities of organization and also because such background can be useful when directors are making decisions that impact the organization's programs. It can be a challenging balancing act to bring in new board members who can not only bring new ideas but also agree with the "core values" of an organization. As part of the planning process for the organization, it is beneficial for the founders to attempt articulating the core values that they desire for the organization as a whole.

It is also helpful to determine early on what expectations the organization will have for its board members. Does the organization need board members with particular skills or background (organizational, visionary, industry expertise)? Is there an expectation that board members will engage in substantial fundraising activities and/or be donors themselves? How important is it that board members have demonstrated that their belief systems are consistent with the organization's mission and values? For example, a farm sanctuary may not want someone who slaughters or otherwise exploits animals as a board member. It can also be helpful for board members to be ambassadors for the organization to connect with potential donors; however, some individuals are not comfortable with that role. Any expectations should be made clear in advance of someone becoming a director.

To assist board members to be most effective and to fulfill the fiduciary duties discussed below, an orientation process for new directors is critical. Board members need to understand that their status as a board member does not provide them with an independent individual right or authority to determine a particular action, such as rescuing or treatment of a particular animal. It may also be helpful to have board development or training to assist directors in areas such as interpreting financial statements or other technical aspects of an organization. Given that it is to the advantage of states to have the nonprofit organizations operating in their jurisdictions governed in a responsible manner, many states provide helpful good-governance resources and materials on their websites.

Director Fiduciary Duties

Directors of nonprofit corporations have fiduciary duties under the law. While these legal obligations may be referenced in a state's nonprofit corporation act, their scope has developed through common law.

It is important to research the state of incorporation's laws to determine its standards. One challenge is that the law relating to nonprofit directors' fiduciary obligations is much less developed than the law applicable to for-profit corporation's directors. For this reason, the law applicable to for-profit entities is often used as an analogy. The general commonalities in most state laws are the focus of this section. The primary fiduciary duties are the duty of care and the duty of loyalty. There is a separate (but as you will see similar) duty of obedience for nonprofit corporation directors in some states.[3] If directors have met their fiduciary duties, they should not have liability based on their actions as directors.

Duty of Care

The duty of care focuses on the obligation of a director to be informed. Being informed requires obtaining sufficient facts about an issue to make a decision, including making inquiries seeking additional information if necessary. At a minimum, directors should exercise the same degree of due diligence that a reasonable person (sometimes referred to as an ordinary prudent person) would utilize in similar circumstances.

3. Occasionally judicial opinions, statutory language (and legal scholarship) articulate an independent "duty of good faith." However, generally it is possible to articulate how action or inaction under such a duty would fall within the scope of a claim that the director violated the duty of care or loyalty. By the very nature of the duty of care (acting in a conscientious manner) and duty of loyalty (acting in the interests of the entity), the director must be acting in good faith to fulfill the director's obligations.

To meet the duty of care, a director should actively participate in the work of the board. This includes preparing for and regularly attending board meetings. Directors may rely on information and reports of committees, officers, employees, and outside professionals. However, directors always remain responsible for overseeing and scrutinizing the work of others on which they rely. Directors have an affirmative obligation to investigate if incomplete or suspicious information is provided to them.

The obligation to provide oversight for the activities of the organization is inherent in the duty of care. As an example, if an animal protection organization is caring for non-human animals, it would be appropriate for a director to ask questions about the policies and procedures that have been put in place to protect human and animal health and safety. Similarly, given the possibility of tort liability in such an organization, making inquiries to the appropriate officer about insurance coverage would be an example of fulfilling a director's duty of care.

Even if directors always act in a way that meets the fiduciary duty of care, it does not mean that the directors' actions must always result in the best outcome for the entity. The "business judgement rule" applied by the courts (and used as a defense by directors) creates a rebuttable presumption that decisions made by directors are made on the basis of good judgment. This presumption is often described as applying if the director has acted in good faith, with due care (meaning on an informed basis), and in the best interest of the corporation. The purpose of the presumption is to protect directors who have "done the right thing" in the process of making the decision, even if it results in a bad outcome. This way, the nonprofit corporation is able to take reasonable risks, innovate, and engage in activities that will benefit the public, without directors being in fear of personal liability if there are issues later.

The standard for breach of the duty of care is generally articulated as "gross negligence." Because gross negligence is difficult to prove, it is unusual for allegations of breaches of duty of care to be the basis for litigation or investigation by state authorities, absent pervasive behaviors over lengthy periods of time—such as when directors have clearly not been engaged with oversight of substantial aspects of an organization's work. In addition, in some states (e.g., Delaware), an entity can choose to include in their articles (called a "certificate of incorporation" in Delaware), "exculpatory clause" language, which allows for the elimination or limitation of liability for monetary damages for breaches of the duty of care. Depending on the state, officers may also benefit from this exculpatory language. However, including this exculpatory clause language does not eliminate or limit liability for breaches of the duty of good faith or duty of loyalty. For this reason, allegations of wrongdoing generally focus on purported violations of the duties of good faith or loyalty.

Duty of Loyalty

Directors are required to always act in the best interests of the entity. The focus of the duty of loyalty is on conflicts. If a director may personally benefit by an entity's action or inaction (either directly or indirectly), steps must be taken to ensure that it is clear that a decision has been made in the best interest of the entity. There are two primary situations where conflicts occur: interested transactions and corporate opportunities.[4]

(1) Interested Transactions

State statutory provisions set forth the process to follow in order for a transaction in which a director has an interest to not be deemed voidable. These provisions generally focus on the involvement of disinterested directors and the need to establish that the transaction is "fair" to the organization.

If a director has an economic or other interest in a contract that the entity may enter into, the director should disclose the interest and be recused from any deliberations on the agreement. Essentially, the entity should not enter into the agreement unless it has the ability to prove that the transaction is in its best interest. For example, that the price to be paid is at or below fair market value, that this would be the best vendor for the service, and the like. This is necessary not only to ensure that the interested director is not breaching the director's duty of loyalty but also to protect the organization's tax-exempt status (see below). A state may also utilize extreme and pervasive self-dealing as a basis for a suit to involuntarily dissolve a nonprofit corporation.

(2) Corporate Opportunities

The corporate opportunity doctrine is the concept that a director should not take for the director's own benefit an opportunity that should be offered to the corporation. Whether an opportunity is within the scope of the corporation's interests is a factual determination. Consider the following hypothetical land purchase: landowner approaches director to see if a nonprofit organization would be interested in purchasing a piece of land for use as a farm sanctuary. Rather than providing the information about the offer to the nonprofit corporation, the director purchases the land in the director's individual capacity for the director's own personal use to build a private home. The proper way to address such a situation is for the director to bring the offer to the board of directors and have the disinterested directors determine whether the nonprofit corporation has the interest and capacity to purchase the land. Only after that process is completed would it be acceptable for the initial director to purchase the land.

Duty of Obedience

Some states also have a distinct "duty of obedience" for directors of nonprofit corporations, while in other states this duty may be incorporated into the duty

4. There are other potential ways that a director could violate the duty of loyalty, including assisting in actions that are likely to be harmful to the entity. In practical terms, interested transactions and the corporate opportunity doctrine are the primary issues that are likely to arise.

of care or loyalty. The gist of the duty of obedience is that directors must ensure that the organization's activities are consistent with its stated purpose and mission.[5] This is another reason founders should be thoughtful about setting out the entity's purpose in the articles of incorporation. This is not to say that an organization's mission may not evolve over time: but, if such change is not consistent with the purposes stated, the governing documents should be amended. The purpose of an organization may also be articulated in corporate filings (such as the application for tax exemption or ongoing filings) and in fundraising materials.

The duty of obedience overlaps with the duty of care. For example, consistent with both duties, directors must ensure that the entity is fulfilling all applicable legal requirements, such as reporting mandates under relevant tax codes. Similarly, in order to comply with the duty of obedience (as well as the duty of care), directors must ensure that donated funds are always used to fulfill the organization's mission. The duty of obedience may also be relevant in the context of an organization engaging in a substantial transaction. As an example, selling significant assets in order to engage in a "similar" or "reprioritized" mission may be viewed as violating this duty of obedience, if the new activities are viewed as a fundamental alteration in the mission of the organization.

Director Liability Issues

Overview

While it is possible for directors of a nonprofit corporations to incur personal liability for money damages, there are several structures and protections in place that mean that this occurs infrequently. First, and as discussed above, the governing documents can include (depending on the state statute) exculpatory clause language and indemnification language. Also as discussed above, the standards for nonprofit director fiduciary duties are not overly onerous, and it is recommended that all nonprofit corporations maintain director and officer liability insurance to protect their leaders.

In general, a director of a corporation (whether nonprofit or for-profit) would not incur personal liability for a tort committed by a corporation just by virtue of being a director of that corporation. However, if a director participates in the wrongful action or directs that it be done, then the director could be liable for damages under general tort and agency theories. In other words, a director will not be immune from liability for wrongdoing if the director utilized a corporation to take an action that would be tortious or illegal as an individual act. It is for this reason that it is imperative that directors fulfil their duty of care if the organization is engaging in acts that may require careful structuring to ensure that the actions of the corporation remain within the bounds of the law.

5. Given the lack of "owners" and the charitable purpose of nonprofit entities, it is logical that the duty of obedience is a concept unique to them (compared with for-profit corporations, where the shareholders' economic interests are central to their corporate purposes).

For example, if an organization is engaging in direct action activities such as protesting and the activity results in a riot, a director could be charged with inciting a riot if there was evidence that the individual director "organized, promoted or encouraged" the "riot." (Advocating ideas or expressing beliefs in speech or writing is not considered incitement in this context.) In this example, directors should make certain that they understand any applicable legal restrictions on when and where such protest can occur and make sure that the organization reiterates in all communications that it is peacefully protesting within the bounds of the law.

In addition, the circumstances in which there could be director liability may be limited by state statutes that explicitly limit money damages for directors of charitable corporations to specific circumstances. For example, a statute may limit money damages to intentional violations of law or infliction of harm on the corporation or its members. This "infliction of harm on the corporation" provision has been interpreted in cases to mean that, if there is infliction of harm on an individual (such as intentional interference with contractual relations), that is not harm to the entity. For this reason, the "day-to-day" activities of a nonprofit corporation (such as relations with employees) would generally not give rise to a director having personal liability. However, if an entity is taking actions that could result in a violation of the law, and the director's intent to use the entity for this purpose with the understanding of the illegality could be proven, the director may still have personal liability.

A state statute may also specify that money damages are limited to the monetary amount a director received as compensation if the director was not entitled to a particular financial benefit. Such statutes may set forth a burden of proof, such as the requirement that there has been actual harm to a nonprofit corporation in addition to the fact that such harm was proximately caused by the director's conduct.

Volunteer Protection Acts

In addition to statutory provisions relating to the nonprofit entity itself, many states and the federal government have passed legislation to encourage volunteer service through volunteer protection acts. These acts provide that volunteers for nonprofit charitable organizations, including volunteer directors, will not be liable for actions taken within the scope of their responsibilities and when such volunteers are acting in good faith. The state statutes also describe circumstances in which the protection does not apply, such as if volunteers engage in reckless, wanton, or intentional misconduct.

The federal Volunteer Protection Act (VPA) was enacted in 1997. The VPA will preempt state law unless such state law provides greater protection to volunteers. Under the VPA, volunteers are not liable for harm for acts or omission within the scope of the volunteers' responsibilities so long as such harm is not caused by gross negligence, reckless misconduct, conscious flagrant indifference to the rights or safety of the individual harmed, or willful or criminal misconduct. The immunity afforded may be waived to the extent a volunteer is covered by liability insurance. In addition, these laws do not protect the organization from possible liability, and there are specific exclusions from coverage, such as for crimes of violence, hate crimes, sexual offenses, violations of civil rights law, or if the volunteer was under the influence of intoxicating alcohol or drugs. In addition, the VPA's protection does not apply if a state's law does not provide liability protection for actions taken by an attorney general (or other governmental officials), and the VPA defers to some other state laws that require certain actions to be taken to receive the protection of statutes limiting liability.

An example of how these acts work in practice is as follows. An entity organizes an event in which members of the public have access to animals, and someone is injured. So long as the volunteers—whether directors or not—were not acting in a manner that was grossly negligent (or other applicable standard from the act), the individual volunteers will not have personal liability. The entity itself may still be sued by the injured person and be liable if it is found to have been negligent or if there is another applicable standard (such as strict liability for injuries caused by animals).

Who Has Standing to Bring an Action

The ability to bring an action against directors for breach of their fiduciary duties is limited to a select group. Oversight of charitable organizations is generally the responsibility of state attorneys general. The attorney general's office for the state of incorporation has jurisdiction over the entity. Additionally, organizations engaging in fundraising or other activities in other states can be subject to the oversight of the relevant regulatory authorities in those states. As discussed above, if a state statute allows for members in a nonprofit organization, and an entity has chosen that structure, a member may also be able to bring a derivative cause of action.

A recent example of the resolution of a case involving a nonprofit organization and a state attorney general's office was announced by the attorney general of the State of California in April 2022. The alleged wrongful acts by the nonprofit corporation ZeroDivide took place between 2014 and 2016, before ZeroDivide ceased operations in 2016 due to financial insolvency. The California attorney general's complaint alleged that members of ZeroDivide's board had failed to stop misconduct relating to the spending of restricted donations[6] even though they were aware of the misconduct, thus violating their fiduciary duties. The attorney general alleged that ZeroDivide had used such donations to fund programs and cover costs that were unrelated to the programs to which the donations had been restricted. The attorney general also alleged that the directors knew about the misconduct because the board had created a process to deal with financial shortfalls that allowed for the "borrowing" of restricted donations. The settlement resulted in the dissolution of ZeroDivide, the

6. Restricted donations are donations that the donor has a reasonable understanding—either due to their own communications or those of the organization—will be spent for a particular identified purpose.

prohibition of two of ZeroDivide's officers from leading charitable organizations or soliciting charitable donations in California for a specified period of time, and the payment of over $460,000 in damages and fees by directors and officers.

Although there is a relatively low number of reported cases of directors of nonprofit corporations having personal liability for monetary damages, it is obviously important (for this and many other reasons) to ensure that directors are fulfilling their fiduciary duties. Even issues that do not rise to the level of breaches of fiduciary duty for which directors could be personally liable can impede the organization's ability to fulfil its mission. The disclosure of such problems can adversely impact the ability of the organization to fundraise and damage its brand. Any investigation by state authorities or the IRS will do the same and, in a worst-case scenario, can lead to the entity's status as a nonprofit corporation or federal tax-exempt organization being brought into jeopardy.

Meeting the Criteria and Applying for Federal Tax-Exempt Status

Types of Tax-Exempt Organizations

The next logical step once an entity has been formed under state law is to apply for tax-exempt status under federal law. Section 501 of the Internal Revenue Code lists a variety of categories of organizations that are eligible for tax-exempt status. The focus of this chapter and this book is on the activities of section 501(c)(3) organizations. Organizations that desire to be more involved in political activities (given the restrictions on such activity for 501(c)(3) organizations) may opt to form a section 501(c)(4) organization (a social welfare organization).

A 501(c)(4) organization may engage in more extensive political activities, specifically engaging in lobbying as its primary activity if such lobbying is related to the organization's exempt purpose. In addition, 501(c)(4) organizations can engage in limited activities involving political campaigns, subject to such expenditures being taxed. Also outside the scope of this book are political organizations subject to section 527 of the code. A section 527 organization is organized and operated for the purpose of accepting contributions or making expenditures in connection with the selection, nomination, election, or appointment of an individual to a political office (regardless of whether such office is at the local, state, or federal level).

Organizations that qualify for tax-exempt status under section 501(c)(3) are divided into public charities or private foundations. The default classification is as a private foundation. Only if an entity is able to prove that it meets one of the exceptions in section 509(a) of the code will it be treated as a public charity. The usual way for an animal protection organization to meet this test is by showing that the organization has sufficient "public" monetary support. Unless specifically stated, all references to 501(c)(3) organizations in this chapter refer to public charities.

Basics on Restrictions on Organization and Operation

Charitable Purpose, Commerciality Test, and Private Benefit/Inurement

The IRS sets out two broad requirements for how tax-exempt organizations must be organized and operated: first, they must be formed and operated for a charitable purpose; and second, they must not be used to benefit individuals (outside of the public purpose). It does not matter whether these individuals are insiders ("inurement") or not ("private benefit" issues relate to everyone).

(a) Charitable Purpose

In addition to the general exempt purpose of "charitable," other articulated exempt purposes in section 501(c)(3) include "educational" and "preventing cruelty to children or animals." Charitable is interpreted broadly and includes lessening the burdens of government, combatting community deterioration and the advancement of science. As discussed above, when developing the purpose of the organization for the articles of incorporation, it is necessary to ensure that it is clear that the organization is being organized to fit within one or more of these exempt purposes.

Rarely, the IRS or a state agency may claim that a tax-exempt (or nonprofit) organization is engaged in activities that violate public policy, thus not meeting the charitable purpose test. One well-known example at the federal level is the *Bob Jones University v. United States* Supreme Court opinion in 1983, which reaffirmed that race-based discrimination was inconsistent with an educational institution's exempt status.[7]

More recently, in 2021 in *In re Investigation of Kahea*, the Supreme Court of Hawaii ruled on the appropriateness of the Hawaii attorney general's investigation of a nonprofit organization.[8] KAHEA The Hawaiian-Environmental Alliance had opposed the construction of an astronomical observatory on the summit of the Mauna Kea volcano, including through providing funding for "frontline logistical support for non-violent direct actions taken to protect Mauna Kea from further industrial development."[9] The Hawaii attorney general issued a subpoena to KAHEA's bank to investigate the organization, and KAHEA claimed that the purpose of the subpoena was to punish it for its activities opposing the construction.

As part of its defense to allegations that the investigation was improper, the attorney general argued that it had a responsibility to investigate to determine whether the nonprofit organization had an "illegal purpose." The attorney general questioned whether KAHEA's financial support for "direct action" was an illegal purpose that would make KAHEA ineligible for 501(c)(3) tax-exempt status. Although the Hawaii Supreme Court found that certain aspects of the

7. Bob Jones Univ. v. United States, 461 U.S. 574 (1983).
8. *In re* Investigation of Kahea, 497 P.3d 58 (Haw. 2021).
9. *Id.* at 62.

subpoena were not supported, the court determined that many of the requests in the subpoena were not unreasonable.

In its decision, the court emphasized that, even if the activities in which a nonprofit entity engages are legal, such activities could still put the organization's eligibility for 501(c)(3) status in jeopardy. The court referenced a 1975 IRS Revenue Ruling (75-384) in which the IRS determined that an anti-war organization would not qualify for an exemption under either section 501(c)(3) or 501(c)(4) because the organization encouraged the commission of criminal acts, namely, by planning and sponsoring events at which acts of civil disobedience were carried out in violation of local ordinances. The IRS articulated that the encouragement of these acts frustrated the charitable goal of relief of the burdens of government and was therefore inconsistent with charitable ends. Though this is an older revenue ruling, an animal protection organization that engages in activities that could be viewed as disruptive or potentially violating the law should be cautious in both its organization and operation to make certain that it is acting in a way consistent with a charitable purpose.

(b) "Commerciality Test"

The counterpoint to a corporation organized and operated for a charitable purpose is one that is organized and operated for a commercial purpose. It is acceptable, though, for a tax-exempt organization to engage in a trade or business so long as such activities are in furtherance of the organization's exempt purpose. It is not enough for an organization merely to allocate any profits from a trade or business to the exempt purpose. Thus, the analysis of commerciality is an aspect of the operational test (that the organization must be organized and operated for an exempt purpose).

Courts have analyzed this issue in a variety of ways, all of which are heavily fact dependent. Factors include whether the business activities in which the organization is engaging are similar to a commercial enterprise, whether the activities have a "commercial hue," and who benefits from the activities. To determine whether activities are conducted in a "commercial manner," courts have considered pricing policies, the use of commercial promotional methods, any profit-making motive, and the extent and degree to which any services are being provided below cost. If the IRS determines that an organization's primary purpose is "too commercial," it may deny an application for tax-exempt status or revoke the tax-exempt status of the entity.

Many of the activities in which animal protection organizations engage will clearly not be considered commercial. However, it is not unusual and is permissible for an organization to engage in some activities that may be commercial in nature. "Unrelated business activities" are activities that consist of (a) a trade or business, (b) regularly carried on, and (c) that are not substantially related to the organization's exempt purpose. This concept of "unrelated business activities" and proper reporting of such activities are discussed in more detail later in this book.

Finally, tax-exempt organizations should be thoughtful if they partner with for-profit entities. While ensuring effective control by the nonprofit entity over any joint activities will not change the ultimate determination of whether an activity is deemed commercial or subject to tax, such control can nonetheless be helpful because a tax-exempt organization's management is likely to be more sensitive to ways to structure the work to avoid the application of unrelated business income tax and other problems. For example, and as discussed below, such relationships should also be structured to ensure that they do not create inurement or private benefit issues for the tax-exempt organization.[10]

(c) Inurement and Private Benefit

Inurement is the concept that nonprofit organizations cannot be organized or operated for the benefit of private interests. The term "inurement" is generally used to describe situations in which insiders of the organization receive a benefit. It is imperative that a 501(c)(3) organization has a conflict-of-interest policy in place to identify such scenarios. Section 501(c)(3) tax-exempt organizations are prevented from engaging in transactions with insiders unless the entity can prove that such transactions are reasonable. There is no *de minimis* exception to the obligation of a tax-exempt organization to ensure that, among other issues, any transactions with insiders are negotiated at arms-length and for fair market value. If the IRS determines that inurement has occurred, the result can be an excess-benefit tax (intermediate sanctions) or revocation of the entity's tax-exempt status. The IRS may determine there is an excess benefits issue regardless of whether intentional wrongdoing has occurred.

The concept of "private benefit" encompasses inurement, but applies if *any* person (not within the category of people the 501(c)(3) organization is intended to assist) is in receipt of a nonincidental benefit from the organization. In analyzing whether a private benefit has occurred, it is necessary to determine whether such benefit is non-substantive (usually interpreted to mean insubstantial) in addition to being incidental. A benefit that is the mere byproduct of the public benefit would be considered incidental. In the context of the establishment of an organization, generally the smaller the group of individuals who are receiving the benefit, the more likely it is to be non-incidental (and thus an impermissible private benefit).

When the IRS is determining whether an organization meets the criteria to be granted tax-exempt status in connection with the prohibition on inurement, the IRS will consider how an entity is structured and governed. In a private letter ruling released in 2011, the IRS referenced the lack of proof that an entity's organizational structure and manner of operation did not result in inurement to a related for-profit business.[11] In a 2008 private letter ruling, the IRS factors included the lack of information about governance (including the lack of bylaws) in addition to the absence of a conflict-of-interest policy as

10. IRS Revenue Ruling 2004-51 provides a useful starting point when engaging in this analysis.
11. I.R.S. Priv. Ltr. Rul. 201108042 (2011).

factors leading to the rejection of another's entity's application for tax-exempt status.[12] Essentially, if the structure of an organization indicates that it could be used to benefit private individuals, that may be used to support an IRS determination to reject an application for tax-exempt status. The Form 990 questions relating to governance and structure, and the other disclosures on that document, mean the IRS has an annual opportunity to determine whether it appears that an organization is not being operated for a charitable purpose. If such a determination is made, the IRS may begin the process to revoke an entity's tax-exempt status.

An example of how to prevent against a future claim by the IRS of inurement (as well how to support an argument that the duty of loyalty has been met) is in connection with establishing compensation. 29 C.F.R. Section 53.4958-6 sets out the factors that can be used to support a rebuttable presumption that a compensation arrangement is not an excess benefit transaction. The first requirement is that the compensation agreement is approved in advance by board members who do not have a conflict of interest. The second requirement is that, prior to approval, the board relied upon appropriate comparable data, that is, data from other entities supporting that the compensation in its entirety is reasonable. The final requirement for the presumption to apply is that the board adequately documented the basis for its decision. The documentation must set forth the terms of the arrangement, when it was approved, the comparability data, and information about the decision-making process, including the role (and recusal) of anyone who has a conflict of interest.

An example of an interested-party transaction to which these principles can be applied would be a board member who is also a veterinarian with an ownership interest in a veterinary clinic that provides services to the organization. To obtain the benefit of the rebuttable presumption, the agreement would need to be approved by independent directors relying on information about rates charged by other veterinary clinics for similar services in the geographic area and would need to be properly documented.

Limitation on Legislative Activity and Prohibition on Political Campaign Activity

The second broad limitation for entities seeking tax-exempt status to consider are those around legislative lobbying and political activity.

(a) Legislative Activity/Lobbying

As discussed above, the IRS provides sample language for articles of incorporation that serves to restrict a 501(c)(3) entity from engaging in substantial lobbying activity. The two primary questions that arise in this analysis are (1)

12. I.R.S. Priv. Ltr. Rul. 200830028 (2008).

whether the activity fits the definition of lobbying and (2) how much activity is more than insubstantial?

Lobbying includes attempts to influence legislation either through appealing to the general public (grassroots lobbying) or through direct contact with legislators (direct lobbying). Legislation is broadly defined to apply to legislation considered at all levels of government (including, in certain circumstances, parts of foreign governments and international bodies) and ballot initiatives and referendums.[13] The IRS has also found that activities that support or oppose a nominee to the U.S. Supreme Court, specifically the process of Senate confirmation, are considered legislative lobbying.

In addition to lobbying within permissible limits, 501(c)(3) organizations can interact with governmental officials in contexts other than lobbying. Treasury regulations set forth a variety of communications that are not considered lobbying, including communicating with governmental officials if the purpose is providing technical advice to a governmental entity (if invited to do so) or providing nonpartisan analysis or research. Another example is engaging in "self-defense" communications with governmental entities, for example, when pending legislation could adversely impact the deductibility of contributions to the entity or impact the entity's tax-exempt status.

An entity engaged in lobbying must track its related expenses, including the value of the time employees are spending on such activities. The default analysis that the IRS uses to determine if an organization is engaging in more than "insubstantial" lobbying is the (no surprise) "substantial part test." This is a facts and circumstances analysis that does not set forth a particular percentage of assets or income to determine what is substantial.

Given that the IRS has not provided clear guidance on the "substantial part test," many organizations elect to report their lobbying activities under section 501(h) of the Internal Revenue Code. A 501(h) election allows for organizations to spend on activities relating to lobbying up to a threshold calculated based on its exempt purpose expenditures. Exempt purpose expenditures—which is a line on the Form 990—are the amount an organization spends on its exempt work minus certain expenses, such as those related to unrelated business income or taxes, capital improvements, and costs relating to outside fundraising. Section 501(h) election reporting requires entities to distinguish between expenditures for grassroots and direct lobbying activities.

There is no specific methodology or system that organizations are required to use to track lobbying expenditures. It is important to ensure that everyone in the organization understands the definition of lobbying and knows how to accurately report any expenditures so that the organization can defend itself if the IRS questions whether it is engaging in substantial lobbying activities or has accurately completed the schedule required as part of the annual return if the organization elects to be treated under section 501(h).

13. *See International Advocacy: What You Need to Know*, Bolder Advocacy (Apr. 2012), *available at* https://bolderadvocacy.org/wp-content/uploads/2012/04/International_Advocacy.pdf.

The IRS can revoke an entity's tax-exempt status if it fails the substantial part test or the expenditure test under section 501(h). The IRS also may choose to apply an excise tax on organizations exceeding their allowed expenditures under section 501(h). As discussed above, 501(c)(4) organizations have more flexibility in engaging in legislative lobbying, however a 501(c)(3) entity cannot "convert" to 501(c)(4) status if it fails in one of these standards on lobbying.

In addition to complying with restrictions on lobbying in order to maintain the entity's tax-exempt status, entities should proactively determine if any federal, state, or local laws require registration of contract or staff lobbyists or reporting of activities based on the actions of the entity and its employees and agents. Legislatures and their staffs are also often subject to ethics rules that govern any gifts or benefits they may accept. Although not technically the responsibility of the nonprofit entity, it is prudent for an entity to have a general awareness of when such rules would apply.

(b) Political Campaigns

The prohibition on political campaigning is focused on whether an organization's activities are viewed as intended to benefit one candidate for public office over another. Obvious prohibited actions include endorsing any candidate or making expenditures or campaign contributions on behalf of a candidate. Communications to employees or members of the public about the candidates or even about high profile "wedge" or partisan issues on which the candidates have different views can be prohibited, depending on the overall context of the communication and proximity in time to an election. If an organization allows access to its facilities (through rental or otherwise) by one candidate, all candidates must have the same access.

There are, however, many activities relating to campaigns in which 501(c)(3) organizations can engage, including conducting (always in a non-partisan manner) educational events about participating in the political process, creating voter guides, sponsoring candidate debates, and engaging in voter protection activities in addition to conducting voter registration or get out the vote drives. Each of these activities may have specific rules and guidance that apply to them, which can create pitfalls for the unwary. The Bolder Advocacy/ Alliance for Justice organization (www.bolderadvocacy.org/www.allianceforjustice.org) provides extensive information on its website to assist tax-exempt entities in navigating the limitations on lobbying and prohibition on political campaigning.

Application Process

Once an organization determines that it can comply with these restrictions on its activities and that it meets the standards for a tax-exempt organization, the next step is to apply for tax-exempt status with the IRS. The IRS website contains a substantial amount of information to assist organizations seeking recognition and maintenance of tax-exempt status. With very few exceptions (e.g., some information about contributors and payment information), all documentation and correspondence submitted to the IRS will be available to the public. Form 1023-EZ or Form 1023 are the current forms used to apply for tax-exempt status. The ability to use the shorter Form 1023-EZ is based on limits for projected gross receipts and the total assets of the organization.

An entity can begin fundraising prior to applying for or receiving notice that the IRS has granted it tax-exempt status. However, if—and only if—the entity is granted 501(c)(3) tax-exempt status will contributions made by donors during the time an application is pending be eligible to be tax-deductible at the federal level. It is important to be clear on any communication with potential donors what the status of the organization is during this time: if the IRS ultimately finds that the organization does not meet its standards for tax-exempt status, the contributions will not be tax deductible. Of course, an organization's receipt of confirmation of tax-exempt status provides an excellent opportunity to reach out to those donors to thank them again for their support.

Annual Report

A subsequent chapter of this book provides more detail on the annual tax filing that must be made by tax-exempt organizations to the IRS (i.e., the Form 990). Although it may seem counterintuitive, an organization that has applied for tax-exempt status but has not yet received confirmation from the IRS that it is recognized as a tax-exempt organization is still required to file an annual exempt organization return. The timing for the filing is based on the fiscal (tax) year-end that the organization has chosen: the fifteenth day of the fifth month following the end of the organization's tax year. As an example, if an organization's tax year end is December 31, the initial return due date is May 15. As with other IRS filings, an organization can request an extension which increases the time available to file substantially. For example, if an organization with a tax year-end of December 31 requests an extension in a timely manner, the extended due date is not until November 15. The IRS website includes a handy table to help organizations determine the date the filing is due.

It can be useful to become familiar with the questions and material that will need to be disclosed in the full Form 990 early in the life cycle of an organization, to assist in structuring governance and activities in a way to make it easier to comply with the legal standards discussed in this chapter and elsewhere in this book.

It is imperative that a tax-exempt entity has a process to ensure that it will file its annual report on time, as the IRS will impose penalties for late filing. If the annual report is not filed at all, the IRS will automatically revoke an entity's tax-exempt status. (As a reminder and as discussed above, annual or bi-annual reporting to the relevant state agency or agencies is also required to maintain the entity's status as a nonprofit corporation.)

Conclusion

The steps to establish a nonprofit organization and be granted federal tax-exempt status may initially appear daunting. However, as with the formation of any new venture, having a plan and allocating time for each step (especially for those steps as to which you will be waiting for governmental agencies to respond) will reduce the likelihood of failure and set up your organization for success in achieving its mission to protect animals.

CHAPTER 3

Financial Issues: Fundraising, Tax, Investments, and Real Estate

Beverly J. Jones and Lauren Martin

Introduction

Animal protection organizations must conduct their finances in an ethical and prudent manner, comply with applicable financial and fundraising laws, and maintain fiscal responsibility. Like all nonprofits, animal protection organizations bear a weighty responsibility as stewards of donated funds, but animal protection organizations are also the primary agents to create change for animals who are desperately in need of help. By maintaining strong financial health and engendering public trust through responsible fundraising, these charities can maximize their impact on the animals that they seek to protect.

This chapter addresses four key areas of nonprofit finances. First, the chapter discusses charitable fundraising, which is a critical element of operating a nonprofit organization—not only for the obvious benefit of raising funds to fuel its work but also because charitable fundraising is one of the primary avenues through which a not-for-profit organization connects with the general public. Next, the chapter turns to taxation at both the federal and state levels, providing practical guidance regarding tax filings, unrelated business income tax, fiscal sponsorships, and other matters. The chapter then discusses endowment funds and investments, focusing on compliance with the state laws governing the prudent management of institutional funds that apply to nearly all nonprofit organizations. Finally, the chapter considers real property issues that are of special concern for nonprofit organizations, including zoning considerations, permits needed to conduct animal protection work, and animal-related laws to keep in mind when entering a new jurisdiction.

Charitable Fundraising

Governmental Oversight

Fundraising is subject to significant state oversight and regulation. In New York, for instance, that power rests with the New York Attorney General's Office, which has established a dedicated Charities Bureau to handle this responsibility. In other states, this responsibility may be held by the Department of State, the Department of Consumer Affairs, or another agency.[1] The agency within a state that oversees fundraising may vary, but the common thread is that these agencies are tasked with ensuring that charitable fundraising is conducted in a manner that is transparent and ethical. The state stands in the shoes of donors (and potential donors) to ensure that they are protected from unscrupulous solicitation.

Registration

Most, though not all, states require that an organization seeking financial support from the general public within its borders registers for permission to fundraise, including identifying its corporate officers and an address where the organization can be reached.[2] Organizations will generally be required to register within the state where their activities are conducted. If an animal protection organization provides services across state lines, then it should consider whether its activities constitute "solicitation" such that registration in multiple states is required. While specific definitions vary, generally speaking, any request made to the general public for financial support will be considered solicitation and may trigger the registration requirement. Solicitation includes such activities as special events (from a gala dinner to a 5k Fun Run in the park), neighborhood fund drives, tabling at a local street fair, donation boxes at the supermarket checkout lane, and similar fundraising activities. Increasingly, solicitation also includes fundraising conducted on the internet, such as providing a QR code to potential donors or seeking support from donors and their friends through social media. Generally speaking, any state where fundraising activity is being coordinated or targeted will potentially require the animal protection organization to register to conduct this solicitation activity.

In addition, there may be times when the charitable organization is not conducting the solicitation directly but is engaging others to fundraise on its behalf. Many states require that professional solicitors or professional fundraisers be registered to conduct those activities, such as phone banking to raise funds in support of a specific entity or effort. Some states also require the

1. The Urban Institute's "State Regulations and Enforcement in the Charitable Sector" report is a great resource for this information: https://www.urban.org/research/publication/state-regulation-and-enforcement-charitable-sector.

2. The National Association of State Charity Officials provides a helpful guide to state registration requirements. *See State Charity Registration Provisions*, NASCO (2020), https://www.nasconet.org/wp-content/uploads/2020/05/NASCO-State-Charities-Registration-Survey-5.15.20-.pdf.

registration of fundraising counsel, who may advise a charity on how to maximize the impact of its charitable appeals. If an organization is engaging with any outside professionals to conduct fundraising activities on its behalf or to guide its fundraising campaigns and strategy, the organization should consider whether that individual, and/or the charity itself, needs to register and report that activity with any state.

Enforcement by State Attorneys General

State attorneys general are tasked with overseeing charitable organizations. An area of primary enforcement focus is charitable fundraising, including the investigation and prosecution of fraudulent charitable solicitations, registration of entities that raise funds in the state, and regulation of third parties that may assist with fundraising, such as professional fundraisers, professional solicitors, and fundraising counsel.[3] Nonprofit organizations should be sure to comply with the regulations of the state or states in which they are soliciting as well as their home state, and should ensure transparency in their fundraising materials.

Most animal protection organizations engage in online fundraising, including on social media. State regulators may view such online requests for donations as fundraising in their states even if the organization does not maintain a base of operation in that state and has not mailed any physical materials to, or made any phone solicitations of, state residents. In 2001, the National Association of State Charity Officials developed the "Charleston Principles," which evolved from discussion at the National Association of Attorneys General/National Association of State Charities Officials Conference in Charleston, South Carolina in October 1999.[4] Recognizing that the applicable statutes did not adequately contemplate online fundraising, these principles are meant to guide states "as to when charities, and their fundraisers, fundraising counsel and commercial co-venturers may be required to register, or may be subject to enforcement action, and in what jurisdictions, with regard to charitable solicitations via the Internet."[5] The Charleston Principles are nonbinding and were not broadly adopted by states. While the usage of online fundraising has evolved since these principles were issued in 2001, there are not yet updated guidelines for nonprofit organizations. As a result of this dearth of guidance, many experts in the field have advised that nonprofits take a conservative approach when engaging in broad online solicitation, by registering in all states that require charitable fundraising registration. Nonetheless, in what may mark the beginning of changes from the states to address online fundraising, California amended its charitable solicitation laws in 2021 to regulate online

3. *See, e.g.*, *The Regulatory Role of the Attorney General's Charities Bureau*, New York State Attorney General Charities Bureau (July 15, 2002), https://www.nycourts.gov/reporter/webdocs/role.pdf.

4. Nat'l Ass'n of State Charities Off., The Charleston Principles: Guidelines on Charitable Solicitations Using the Internet, Mar. 14, 2001, https://www.nasconet.org/wp-content/uploads/2018/04/Charleston-Principles.pdf.

5. *Id.* at 2.

charitable fundraising platforms and the charities hosted on those platforms;[6] however, as of the date of publication, the implementing regulations had not yet been finalized.

In 2020, New York Attorney General Letitia James announced a multi-agency settlement resulting from the investigation of a fraudulent fundraising scheme. In her comments, Attorney General James stated, "It is critically important that donors are able to trust that their contributions are being used as they intended, and not to line the pockets of individuals who exploit the generosity of others. My office will continue to . . . protect donors and legitimate charitable entities."[7]

A Word on Gaming

Another activity that is highly regulated on both the federal and state level is gaming. Again, there is huge variety among states in terms of the specific rules that apply. Generally speaking, it is not safe to assume that a raffle, bingo game, "50/50," sweepstakes, "casino night," or a similar activity involving games of chance is unregulated simply because it is conducted to raise funds for a charitable purpose. While some states do have broad carveouts for certain of these types of activities, others strictly regulate and may even prohibit them, so it is imperative that attorneys check state and local laws before their clients engage in such activities. Under some circumstances, the organization may be required to report winnings to the Internal Revenue Service (IRS), and the donor may also be required to report winnings on their personal income tax return.[8] The rules around taxation, reporting, and withholding related to gaming activities can be complex—if the client organization anticipates conducting gaming activities, then it is strongly recommended to consult with a tax professional who is well versed in this area of the law.

Clarity in Donor Communications and Restricted Funding

Nonprofit animal protection organizations should solicit funds in a clear and transparent manner in order to conduct their work ethically and professionally, reflecting sound corporate governance and a respectful organizational culture. Solicitation is broadly understood to include "oral, written, or online requests for contributions."[9] In addition to these principled rationales, many state codes

6. Cal. Gov't Code §§ 12599.9–12599.10 (West 2023).

7. Press Release, N.Y. Att'y Gen. Off., Attorney General James Shuts Down Fundraising Operation That Solicited Donations on Behalf of Sham Charities (Sept. 16, 2020) (on file with N.Y. Att'y Gen. Off.).

8. I.R.S. Pub. 3079, *Tax-Exempt Organizations and Gaming*, https://www.irs.gov/pub/irs-pdf/p3079.pdf (2018).

9. *See* Cindy Lewin et al., *Does My Nonprofit Really Have to Register Before Asking for Money? What You Need to Know About Fundraising Regulations*, National Council of Nonprofits, https://www.councilofnonprofits.org/articles/does-my-nonprofit-really-have-register-asking-money-what-you-need-know-about-fundraising (last visited Mar. 31, 2023).

explicitly require charitable solicitations to be transparent and truthful.[10] These state laws are intended to protect the public from fraudulent solicitations and ensure that donors' funds are going toward their intended use.

Fundraising Disclosure Statements

Many states require that nonprofit organizations include specific language, often in a prescribed font or font size, on all charitable solicitations sent within their state. These disclosure statements can be quite simple, such as Maine's requirement that the name and physical address of the organization be disclosed to potential donors at the time of the solicitation but prior to the request for contribution.[11] Other states may require more detailed information, such as the deductibility of the solicited donation.[12] Still other states dictate that specific language—which can be somewhat lengthy—be included on a written solicitation.[13] Moreover, additional disclosures may be required if a professional fundraiser is used, and some states require nonprofits to provide additional information upon a donor's request.

When charities distribute their fundraising materials only within their state, compliance with these requirements can be rather straightforward. For those fundraising on a national level, however, accommodating all state laws that require disclosure can be cumbersome, as the disclosures are lengthy relative to most written fundraising appeals. Many resources are available that provide sample disclosures accommodating all state requirements.[14] Of course, nonprofit organizations or their counsel should always confirm that the sample disclosures are compliant, as state laws may be updated from time to time.

Use of Images in Fundraising Materials

To avoid potentially burdensome and expensive claims, organizations must have the proper permissions to use any images in their charitable solicitations, either through direct ownership of the images or by obtaining consent of the owner of the images and the individuals featured. For example, if an organization were to use an image that it simply downloaded from the internet without first obtaining the consent of its owner, then the organization could face a copyright infringement claim, damages for failure to distribute payment for

10. *See, e.g.*, 6 Del. C. § 2595(a) (stating that "any deception, fraud, false pretense, false promise, misrepresentation or the concealment, suppression or omission of any material fact with the intent that others rely upon such [statements] in connection with a charitable solicitation" constitutes an unlawful practice); 225 Ill. Compiled Stat. § 460/15(b) (stating that if a charitable organization conducts a fundraising campaign and "engages in any public solicitation and therein purports to relate the purpose or purposes for which the funds are solicited, such shall then be fully and accurately identified to the prospective donor").

11. *See* 9 Maine Rev. Stat. § 5012 (2023).

12. *See, e.g.*, Minn. Stat. § 309.556; R.I. Gen. L. § 5-53.1-12 (2023).

13. *See, e.g.*, Miss. Code Ann. § 79-11-523(3); 10 Pa. Cons. Stat. § 162.13 (2023).

14. *See, e.g.*, *Model Disclosure Statement for Charities*, Perlman & Perlman, LLP, *available at* https://www.perlmanandperlman.com/wp-content/uploads/2021/06/MODEL-DISCLOSURE-STATEMENT-FOR-CHARITIES.pdf (last visited Mar. 31, 2023).

usage of the image, and may even face the prospect of having resulting donations clawed back. In addition, images used in fundraising solicitations should always be described accurately. For example, if an animal protection organization takes in animals from a hoarding case that is described in its fundraising materials, but it chooses to include a particularly compelling image of an animal who did *not* come from the case described in the solicitation, the caption or description of the picture should not mislead the public to believe that the animal was from that specific operation.

Finally, if a nonprofit animal protection organization supports law enforcement cases, it may have images of animals who are the victims of cruelty and who are the subject of open criminal investigations. If this is the case, the organization should receive very clear approval from law enforcement and/or the prosecutor that the images may be used in any public communications, including fundraising solicitations.

As to the content of images, nonprofits must achieve a balance between sharing their work honestly and compellingly and putting emotionally stressful images or other content in public view. Nonprofits, particularly in the animal protection field, should be mindful of including content that may make recipients disregard the materials, and it may choose to include a warning about the nature of the materials on an envelope or in the beginning of a television advertisement. Indeed, members of the public may lodge complaints online, or with state enforcement authorities over distressing or shocking fundraising materials.

Raising Funds for a Restricted Purpose

A nonprofit organization may choose to focus fundraising materials on a particular issue or event, such as support for a natural disaster deployment or for a shelter refurbishment, and the nonprofit may further choose to restrict the donations received as a result of that solicitation to support only that singular purpose. In such cases, the organization must take great care to respect the intention of donors and ensure that any donations received from that targeted campaign are used only in furtherance of the purpose described in the fundraising materials. Such donations are commonly referred to as "restricted funds." The organization may choose, for example, to direct all funds raised as a result of the solicitation to a separate account that will be spent only in furtherance of the restricted purpose.

While restricting donations in this manner is a lawful practice when done compliantly, it is critical that the language describing the usage of the funds is clear and accurate. For example, an animal protection organization may wish to renovate the cat housing area in its shelter and may choose to raise funds specifically designated for this purpose; however, the shelter must anticipate what it would do if, in response to that particular solicitation, it were to raise more than the necessary funds to satisfy that purpose. Language in the fundraising materials should anticipate this issue and advise, for example, that any donations received over the amount needed for the specified purpose will be put toward other charitable purposes of the organization.

To avoid this complexity, an animal protection organization may choose to describe a project or campaign—to celebrate its great work with potential donors—but then phrase the fundraising appeal so that it is clear that funds will support the organization's work more generally. One way for a lawyer advising an animal protection organization to think about this frequently recurring issue is by applying a commonsense test: would a reasonable donor understand how their donation would be used, or is this communication—taken in its totality—confusing? While simply including language like "funds will be used where needed most" in small print at the end of a communication that otherwise seems restricted is likely not enough, lawyers can work with fundraising staff at animal protection organizations to develop creative language that communicates the proposed use of funds in clear but simple language.

Giving careful consideration to language describing the use of donations can avoid legal and accounting complexities. When fundraising departments decide to run a restricted fundraising campaign (perhaps because it is expected to perform better), legal and financial teams should closely monitor the use of the funds raised, in order to ensure strict compliance with donor intent. Failure to honor donor intent may result in donor complaints to the attorney general, which may result in an investigation or negative publicity for the organization, and also in unfavorable comments in an audit letter issued by an independent auditor.

Donor-Imposed Restrictions on Use of Funds

In addition to the charitable organization raising funds for a particular campaign and thereby creating a charity-generated restriction, a donor may initiate a restriction by limiting the manner in which funds may be used. Restrictions may be permanent (e.g., a gift providing that the corpus of the donation be maintained in perpetuity and that only interest earned on the gift may be spent) or temporary. Temporary restrictions can include restrictions as to both time (such as specifying that the funds must be used within three years of the gift) and purpose (such as specifying that a gift may only be spent on equine rehabilitation).

Before accepting a restricted gift, it is important that the organization consider whether or not it can comply with the donor's restrictions, which are usually binding on the organization and can be quite difficult to modify.[15] For instance, a restriction that limits the use of a gift to the care of dogs may be much easier for a general admission shelter to adhere to than a restriction to dogs of a particular breed. A breed-specific dog rescue group, on the other hand, may be easily able to handle such a restriction (but might be confounded by a gift restricted to the care of cats!). Similarly, if a donor restricts a donation to a construction project and further requires that the funds must be spent within

15. *See* "*Clarity in Donor Communications and Restricted Funding*" above.

twelve months, if the project expenses will likely not be incurred for eighteen months, the organization should ask the donor to modify their restriction; if the donor declines to modify, the charity may have to decline the gift.

To remedy such issues, if the donation is to be provided pursuant to a gift instrument, the nonprofit organization should negotiate the terms of the instrument and only accept the gift if it can abide by its limitations. If the nonprofit receives a restricted testamentary gift (i.e., a gift pursuant to a will), or if the donor of a non-testamentary gift passes away before the gift is spent, and it is determined that the restriction cannot be honored, court intervention may be necessary, as described in the next section.

If the organization receives a restricted gift, it is important to note the restriction in the organization's books and records, to ensure compliance with the restriction. The charity may need to establish a separate account to make sure that donor-imposed restricted donations are not intermingled in a way that could fail to honor the donor's intent or violate additional rules under state laws modeled after the Uniform Prudent Management of Institutional Funds Act (as described below), among other laws.

Cy Pres Relief

When donors have restricted their donations but their donative intent cannot be executed, courts may provide *cy pres* relief to nonprofit organizations. *Cy pres* is a short version of the French term *cy pres comme possible*, which means as close as possible. Under the *cy pres* doctrine, courts may prevent the failure of a charitable gift by allowing the funds to be used in a manner that honors the donor's intention in circumstances when the donor is unavailable to amend the restriction (e.g., a testamentary gift when a donor is deceased). While states may differ, the Uniform Trust Code—a model law adopted by more than half of the states—provides, with certain limited exceptions, that "if a particular charitable purpose becomes unlawful, impracticable, impossible to achieve, or wasteful . . . the court may apply *cy pres* to modify or terminate the trust . . . in a manner consistent with the settlor's charitable purposes."[16] This allows courts the flexibility to allow the donation to take place even if the restriction cannot technically be carried out; courts will try to ensure that the donative intent is preserved to the greatest extent possible. For example, perhaps a donor's will provided that funds were to be left to an organization to be used only to construct stalls to house equines in Oklahoma; however, the organization subsequently decided to relocate to Oregon and cease operations in Oklahoma. The organization may seek court intervention under the *cy pres* doctrine to modify the restrictions of the gift, to allow the funds to be allocated for the benefit of equines through some other means in order to honor the intent of the original gift.

---

16. *See* Uniform Trust Code § 413(a), *available at* https://www.uniformlaws.org/viewdocument/final-act-132?CommunityKey=193ff839-7955-4846-8f3c-ce74ac23938d&tab=librarydocuments.

Donative Intent and Substantiation Requirements

Donative Intent and Donation Forms

The concept of donative intent (a necessary prerequisite for a gift to be considered a "donation") presumes that the property no longer belongs to the donor once it has been received by the charity. The most straightforward donation to an animal protection organization is a simple gift of cash or a cash equivalent (including checks, money orders, credit card donations, donations made through text message campaigns, etc.). Other donors prefer to give stocks, estate gifts, gifts of real or personal property, or gifts of supplies that the organization needs to accomplish its work. In all cases, in order to be considered a charitable gift, a gift must be made to a qualified organization, and the donor must have "donative intent" when making the gift. If either of these two elements is missing, then the donation cannot be treated as a charitable gift.

Substantiation Requirements: Cash Gifts

For gifts of cash or cash equivalents under $250, the organization is not required to provide the donor with written substantiation of the gift. In the interest of donor stewardship, however, some organizations do provide written acknowledgment of smaller gifts, as donors may appreciate having a receipt or thank you letter from the charity to assist in their recordkeeping.

For purposes of their own taxes and no matter the size of the gift, donors are required to maintain records to substantiate their contributions. Including the organization's full legal name, the date of the contribution, and the organization's Employer Identification Number (also called the Taxpayer Identification Number or TIN) may be particularly useful to assist donors in their obligation to maintain these records.

If the amount of the donation equals or exceeds $250, the charity is required to provide additional substantiation to the donor, namely, a written acknowledgment showing the amount donated and whether the organization provided any goods or services in exchange for the gift.[17] Combining this information with the information described above (name, date, and TIN) will provide the donor with all of the necessary information in one place.

Substantiation Requirements: Non-Cash Gifts

If a donor gives property to an animal protection organization, the requirements are similar, except that the donor is also required to provide the fair market value (i.e., the price to which a buyer and seller on the open market would agree) for the donated property. The charitable organization should generally not provide, in the acknowledgment, the value of the item donated. The organization should simply acknowledge that a gift was received, including again

17. See "Special Events" discussion later in this chapter.

the name, date, and TIN. Instead of showing the amount donated, the acknowledgment should include a basic description of the item(s) donated (e.g., "Thank you for your generous gift of twelve (12) twenty-pound bags of Best Cat Kitty Litter"). If the donation is valued at more than $5,000, the donor will also be required by the IRS to substantiate their gift with a qualified appraisal. Again, that should be a function performed by the donor, not by the charity. It is always best to avoid providing tax advice of any kind to the organization's donors.

A Word on Cryptocurrency

As of the date of this writing, the IRS still considers gifts of cryptocurrency to be gifts of noncash property, requiring the same type of diligence and substantiation as for other noncash gifts—namely, the donor will be required to provide a qualified appraisal if the value of the gift exceeds $5,000. Generally speaking, given the high volatility of these specific assets, it may be wise for the charity to consider liquidating any gifts of cryptocurrency into cash as soon as practicable, to avoid potential devaluation of the gift.

Gifts of Vehicles

From time to time, a donor may wish to donate a motor vehicle (or, less commonly, a boat or an airplane) to the organization. If a vehicle is in good repair, the animal protection organization may wish to use the vehicle to further its tax-exempt purposes (e.g., to use a donated vehicle to transport cats to and from the veterinarian for surgery as part of a trap-neuter-return (TNR) project). Whether the organization intends to sell or use the vehicle has a significant impact on the amount the donor can deduct, so it is important to be clear with the donor about the organization's intentions. When a charity sells a vehicle, generally the deduction is limited to the actual sales price. But if the vehicle is used in the organization's work or in certain other limited circumstances, the donor can take a deduction of the vehicle's fair market value.[18] To assist organizations that may find the administration of accepting gifts of vehicles to be too burdensome, there are organizations that will handle vehicle donations for charities for a fee or portion of the donation.

Gifts of Labor (and Accompanying Expenses)

Many animal protection organizations rely extensively on the assistance of volunteers, whether those volunteers are feeding and walking shelter dogs, fostering animals in their homes, caring for equines, or assisting with administrative work behind the scenes. The time that these volunteers spend is not considered tax deductible to the donor, but thanks to a 2011 tax court case

18. I.R.S. Notice 2006-1, Information Reporting by Organizations That Receive Charitable Contributions of Certain Motor Vehicles, Boats, and Airplanes, https://www.irs.gov/pub/irs-drop/n-06-01.pdf.

brought by an animal protection volunteer and foster caretaker, the U.S. Tax Court clarified that deductions are available when a nonprofit volunteer incurs unreimbursed expenses while performing volunteer services. To be deductible, such expenses must be incurred solely in connection with those volunteer duties (such as purchasing food for community cats).[19] Volunteers must also show that the organization is tax exempt and that the volunteer has a strong affiliation with the organization, which may be proven by factors such as the extent to which the organization affirmatively asks the volunteer to provide services and supervises the work of the volunteer, and how much the volunteer is accountable to the organization.

Special Events

Whether through an annual fundraising breakfast, a 5K dog walk in a local park, or a bingo night,[20] many animal protection organizations host special events throughout the year to ramp up their fundraising efforts. It is always a good idea to advise your client organization to confirm with its insurance broker that it is covered in the event that a person or animal gets injured, or property gets damaged, at a special event hosted by the organization. Events can also come with particular tax consequences of which the organization needs to be aware, namely, that donors who purchase event tickets should be provided with an acknowledgment that states how much value they received from the organization. For instance, if the organization hosts a fundraising luncheon and charges $30 per ticket, and in return for that ticket, the donor receives a meal worth $10, the donor would only be entitled to deduct the $20 that was given above the fair market value of the meal. In this circumstance, the organization should provide the donor with that information in its acknowledgment of the gift.

Pledges

In some cases, rather than making an immediate gift to the organization, a donor will prefer to make a pledge of a gift to be paid at some point in the future. A pledge can be unconditional (e.g., a donor who is interested in helping the organization buy a $1,200 piece of equipment might promise to give the organization a total of $1,200 over the course of a year with a monthly commitment of $100 per month) or conditional (the organization is interested in the same $1,200 piece of equipment, but this time the donor makes their pledge conditioned on the organization raising the rest of the necessary funds, i.e., I pledge $100 that I will give only if the organization raises the remaining $1,100).

Whether a pledge is binding or nonbinding is a matter of contract law, and somewhat outside the scope of this chapter. It is important, however, for the organization to give some thought as to which form of agreement might be in

19. Van Dusen v. Comm'r, 136 T.C. 515 (2011).
20. See "A Word on Gaming" above.

the organization's best interest. Similar to a binding contract with a vendor by which the organization wants to make sure that the vendor is obligated to provide certain goods or services, a binding pledge agreement may give the charitable organization more confidence that the pledge will be fulfilled. Such reliance may be critical in the case of significant gifts or gifts on which the organization is relying to complete a capital project. Or a donor might insist on having a binding pledge agreement in place to secure their desired tax treatment for the gift. Unlike other agreements (such as a more arms' length vendor agreement), though, an organization may be unlikely to ever file a lawsuit to enforce a donor pledge, in order to maintain the relationship with the donor or its reputation with other donors. In any event, attorneys should be prepared to advise an animal protection organization of the pros and cons of a binding versus a nonbinding pledge well in advance of any potential conflict.

Estate Issues and Planned Giving

Estate Gifts

Another important source of income for animal protection organizations can be gifts that are left to the organization when people pass away. Arguably the most important guiding principle related to these gifts is to ensure that the organization is acting in a manner consistent with the donor's intent, as evidenced by the language in the gift instrument and any ancillary documentation the organization may have related to that donor's intent in making the gift.

Sometimes, an individual donor may reach out to the organization in advance to plan for a gift that they intend to make from their estate upon their passing. At other times, an animal protection organization may be named as a beneficiary on an individual's retirement account or other bank account, which most times will be able to pass to the organization without going through the probate process. As with *inter vivos* gifts (those that are made during the donor's lifetime), these estate gifts may be restricted or unrestricted. There is, of course, an additional challenge when the organization determines that it cannot reasonably comply with a decedent's restrictions, in that there is no longer an opportunity to discuss a potential change to the estate gift language once the individual had passed away. This challenge makes a strong gift acceptance policy (discussed below) important, to guide decision making in a fair and objective manner.

In their estates, in addition to gifts of cash and marketable securities, individuals may leave gifts of real and/or personal property to the animal protection organization. Such gifts may be quite valuable to the organization (e.g., if a donor gifts a tract of land that borders the animal protection organization's existing shelter) or may pose a challenge (such as a donor who wishes to gift their collection of cat-related figurines that were of great sentimental value to the donor, but may not have particular utility or value to the organization going forward). Because the value and usefulness of gifts of property to the recipient organization vary greatly, it is important to know in advance the steps that the organization will take in relation to such gifts (such as obtaining a base level of insurance immediately to protect the organization if someone should slip and fall on a gifted piece of real property), and to put in place mechanisms to reduce the potential burden of such gifts where necessary (up to and including disclaiming a gift that may cost the organization more than the gift is worth, such as a piece of real estate that needs extensive renovation in order to be marketable).

Pet Trusts

It is especially important for an animal protection organization to plan, in advance, for the possibility that an individual may, as part of their plans, need to make arrangements for the ongoing care and shelter of beloved companion animals when they become unable to care for those animals, due to death or disability. While in an ideal circumstance there would be a loving family member or friend to whom ownership of the decedent's pets could be transferred, from time to time an animal protection organization may find itself fielding questions about whether it can provide care for a decedent's animal(s). Fortunately, all states now have so-called pet trust laws, which provide a mechanism by which an individual can create a trust for the care of one or more companion animals.[21] An animal protection organization may be able to provide some peace of mind by encouraging its donors to work with their advisors to create a sound plan for the care of their companion animals in their estate plans.

Donor-Advised Funds

A popular mechanism that individuals may wish to use for tax planning purposes is the Donor-Advised Fund, or DAF. By creating a DAF, the donor gets to take an immediate tax deduction for the money and securities contributed, but they can let the funds in the DAF grow on a tax-free basis and take additional time to determine where those assets should ultimately be directed.[22] The contribution the donor makes to the DAF is irrevocable, and therefore it is immediately considered tax deductible; the donor subsequently can recommend that payments be made to various charities from the DAF. When advising the charitable organization, it is important to note that the donor is restricted to some extent in terms of what the DAF may be used to fund. DAFs cannot, for instance, be used to fulfill legally binding pledges. Nor can DAF funds be used, in most cases, to pay for tickets to special events such as a charity's gala ball (or any other event wherein the donor is entitled to a substantial return benefit in exchange for the gift).

---

21. AM. SOC'Y FOR THE PREVENTION OF CRUELTY TO ANIMALS, *Pet Trust Laws*, https://www.aspca.org/pet-care/pet-planning/pet-trust-laws (last visited Mar. 31, 2023).

22. I.R.S., *Donor-Advised Funds*, https://www.irs.gov/charities-non-profits/charitable-organizations/donor-advised-funds (last visited Mar. 31, 2023).

Other Planned Giving Mechanisms: Alphabet Soup

A number of other giving vehicles may be used to provide donors with tax advantages and opportunities to leverage their charitable giving. Charitable gift annuities (CGAs), charitable remainder annuity trusts (CRATs), charitable remainder unitrusts (CRUTs), charitable lead trusts (CLTs), and pooled income funds (PIFs) are some of the mechanisms that donors can use to support the organizations they care about. While this alphabet soup of planned giving opportunities is a bit beyond the scope of this guide, it is important to be aware of these terms and to know that both the donor and the charitable organization should consult independent tax advisors to appropriately manage these instruments, which can be complex and have important tax implications. There are many informative (and free!) videos and publications designed for professionals advising donors that are useful for establishing a basic understanding of these important giving tools.[23]

Additional Income Streams

Fee for Service Income

Another important source of income for many animal protection organizations is so-called "fee for service" income, in other words, the amounts charged to individuals in return for providing services, such as adoption fees, spay/neuter fees, and the like. While in some circumstances services may be provided to animals in need for free or on a contractual reimbursement basis as part of a state or municipal voucher program, it is perfectly acceptable for animal protection organizations to generate some portion of their revenue from the sale of goods or services that are related to the organization's mission and exempt purpose.[24] The operation of an animal hospital, the rental of humane traps to neighborhood community cat rescuers for TNR, or the sale of behaviorally appropriate toys to new adopters would all fit into this category. Generally speaking, this stream of income will be considered unrestricted, so the proceeds may be used for any of the organization's charitable purposes. Under some state and local laws, fees charged in exchange for services must be returned to individuals if the services are not, in fact provided. For example, if a client of a spay/neuter clinic pays for their dog's surgery in advance, but then upon examination the veterinarian determines that surgery cannot be performed on that dog that day, the organization must have some mechanism to return the fee to the client. In certain circumstances, refunds that are not claimed by the organization's customer (such as a check that is sent for the refunded amount that is never cashed) must be given over to the state in a process known as

23. *See* https://www.youtube.com/playlist?list=PLXlw33tLHLH_ROHvdFp-QJ34rQfpXyV8d for a series of videos by tax advisor Russell James that covers a broad range of charitable giving law topics.

24. For a discussion of the appropriate tax treatment of funds raised from activities unrelated to the organization's exempt purpose, please see "Unrelated Business Taxable Income", below.

"escheatment." This topic is quite complicated and state specific, and the penalties for failure to comply may be significant, so it is important to consult local counsel to advise on specific requirements.

Cause-Related Marketing and Commercial Co-Ventures

Another popular type of fundraising on which animal protection organizations frequently need legal advice is referred to as "cause-related marketing" or "commercial co-ventures." "Cause-related marketing" is an umbrella term that includes various arrangements in which a for-profit business provides support to a nonprofit and promotes that nonprofit in their own marketing, and may include a flat donation, a "round up at the register" promotion, or other form of gift. A commercial co-venture, or CCV, is a specific type of cause-related marketing in which a percentage or flat amount of a consumer's purchase is donated to the charity. In a CCV arrangement, the nonprofit partners with the for-profit company (anything from a local pet supply store to a major big box retailer) to receive financial support through sales of specific products. For instance, perhaps a local dog treat bakery wishes to show its commitment to the community by advertising to its customers that it will donate fifty cents to an animal rescue group from the sale of every package of "Fido's Sweet Potato Treats" sold in the month of April. These types of partnerships can be a great benefit to both the nonprofit (which, of course, gets the company's donation and increased visibility within the community) and to the for-profit business (which gets to feel good about its support, potentially sell more of the featured product, and associate itself with the goodwill and warm feelings that are generated when its consumers choose to make a difference with their purchase). *It is important to realize, however, that these types of arrangements are heavily regulated.* State regulatory authorities have an interest both in protecting charities from being taken advantage of by for-profit entities that are "using" the nonprofit's goodwill to increase their sales, and in ensuring that consumers have all the right information to know exactly how much is being contributed to charity as a result of their purchase.

Several states have specific requirements to register commercial co-venture activities with a central state agency. Other states (and the Better Business Bureau) require a contract between the charity and the for-profit entity that must include specific language and be registered with the state in advance of the start of the specific fundraising campaign. Still others may dictate exactly what type of language can be used to advertise the promotion.

When advising animal protection organizations on CCVs and other cause-related marketing arrangements, it is important to keep in mind the variation in state laws and the scope of a particular proposed activity. For example, a cause-related marketing event related to in-store sales in California (a state with relatively light requirements) is much easier to structure in compliance with law than a nationwide, online promotion—which may be required to comply with the laws of multiple states. The Better Business Bureau's Wise Giving Alliance (discussed below) has additional guidelines on what it considers to be sound practices in this area.

Returning a Charitable Gift

From time to time, a donor may reach back out to an animal protection organization after having initially made a charitable gift, requesting that the gift be returned. Alternatively, an organization itself may determine that it does not want to accept a particular gift, for reasons of ethics or policy, or if the gift is restricted in such a way that the organization cannot comply with the donor's restriction. That said, there may be applicable state laws that specify circumstances in which gifts may or must be returned, and it will likely serve the organization well to determine—and set out in a written policy, which can be consistently applied—when the organization will return a gift. A well thought-out and objective written policy on returning gifts, which may exist side-by-side with the gift acceptance policy described below, will help the animal protection organization's staff to make these sometimes difficult decisions in a fair and impartial manner, without having to conduct a subjective balancing of the organization's financial and reputational needs in a moment of crisis (for the organization or for the donor). In any event, if an acknowledgment of the gift has already been issued by the organization, correcting that acknowledgment will be an important step to take if and when such gift is returned to the donor, due to the role of the acknowledgment letter as substantiation for the donor's tax purposes.

Gift Acceptance Policies

Given the complexities involved with the various forms that charitable gifts can take, it may be wise for the animal protection organization's board to formally adopt a gift acceptance policy to provide guidance to the organization to ensure sound, legal, and consistent treatment of gifts. Such a policy will designate an individual or committee charged with thinking through the ramifications of accepting certain gifts, and identify which types of gifts likely require the advice of counsel (such as gifts of closely held stock, transactions with potential conflicts of interest, complex probate matters, and gifts that require the animal protection organization to take on certain obligations). While the majority of gifts will be routine and will present little controversy, nonroutine gifts and potentially problematic gifts (such as those in which the gift itself, or the donor making the gift, might have a negative impact on the organization's mission or those that might be particularly burdensome to administer) should be carefully considered before the organization decides to accept them. The gift acceptance policy should also set forth documentation that the organization requires in order to consider specific types of gifts and may also describe the types of acknowledgments that the organization will provide to donors, so that these questions may be handled in a consistent manner.

Better Business Bureau Wise Giving Alliance: Charity Accountability Standards

The Better Business Bureau Wise Giving Alliance (BBB WGA) is a private organization that monitors charities. The BBB WGA sets forth twenty "Charity Accountability" standards, which were developed to assist donors in making sound giving decisions and to foster public confidence in charitable organizations. The standards seek to encourage fair and honest solicitation practices, promote ethical conduct by charitable organizations, and advance support of philanthropy. While the BBB WGA is a private entity—and compliance with its standards is therefore voluntary—the standards represent many best practices that can help to ensure organizational health. In addition, as a widely known entity relied on by the public, charitable organizations may benefit from complying with the standards. For organizations that choose to participate in its program, the BBB WGA produces a report based on data provided by the charity every two years to reflect information that donors may want to consider in evaluating appeals for support. Charities that meet all twenty standards are referred to as BBB Accredited Charities.

The twenty standards used to assess nonprofit organizations have four key areas of focus. The first is governance, which focuses on the board of directors, including its oversight of the organization, size, compensation, and meeting cadence and structure. The governance area also looks at conflicts of interest for both board members and employees. The second key area looks at effectiveness, focusing on whether the board has a policy that requires the organization, at least every two years, to measure its effectiveness and progress toward achieving its mission, and whether the board issues a report documenting those efforts.

The third key area of the standards is finances, the importance of which is illustrated by the fact that it is the subject of seven of the twenty standards. Here, the BBB WGA looks at, among other things, an organization's program and fundraising spending ratios and whether it produces audited financial statements and a board-approved budget. Finally, the fourth area of the standards looks at fundraising solicitations and informational materials. To accord with the standards, solicitations and informational materials must be accurate and contain the proper disclosures. Furthermore, organizations must promptly address complaints regarding their fundraising practices as well as any privacy concerns raised by donors. The standards also require that qualifying nonprofits produce an annual report that is available to the public upon request.

Data Protection

Data protection is a critical issue for nonprofit animal protection organizations just as it is for any business that holds credit card or banking information, employee information, or any other type of personally identifiable information or sensitive data. Data protection issues for nonprofit animal protection organizations extend far beyond the reach of this chapter and should be considered not only in the financial context—which is the focus of this chapter—but also at all points at which personal or sensitive data is obtained. For example, the information that most animal protection organizations collect from adopters is typically considered to be personally identifiable information that needs to be safeguarded under the laws of most states.

As nonprofit organizations, animal protection organizations regularly collect financial information, including credit card information and banking information, as well as personally identifiable information, such as names, addresses, zip codes, and dates of birth, from their individual donors. Organizations may also collect banking information from vendors, and they will maintain payroll and other records that include confidential information about their employees, contractors, and volunteers. They may even gather personally identifiable information of emergency contacts, insurance beneficiaries, and other ancillary third parties.

While comprehensive guidance for data protection is outside the scope of this chapter, attorneys should advise animal protection organizations that the consequences of data security breaches can be quite significant.[25] If possible, having expert technological and/or legal guidance on data security measures is strongly recommended; however, if resources are not available to allow an organization to take such precautions, there are free resources available to help navigate this complicated territory.[26] If an organization engages in international fundraising or transactions, particularly in the European Union, heightened data protection measures may apply.

Taxation

Federal Tax Issues

Annual Information Returns

Organizations that are exempt from taxation under Section 501(c)(3) of the Internal Revenue Code of 1986, as amended (the "Code"), are required to file an annual information return with the IRS. This filing may be required to be made electronically or on a paper form—please check the IRS website for the most up-to-date guidance, as this is an area that has been subject to rapid change over the past several years. This is similar to an individual's or a business's tax return, but generally (except as noted below) without the requirement to pay income tax. There are several different versions of Form 990, and which version an animal protection organization must file is dependent on its finances.

25. *See, e.g.*, Cal. Civ. Code §§ 1798.100 *et seq.*; Va. Code Ann. §§ 58.1-575 *et seq.*; *see also* Int'l Ass'n of Privacy Professionals (IAPP), *U.S. State Privacy Legislation Tracker*, https://iapp.org/resources/article/us-state-privacy-legislation-tracker/ (last visited Mar. 31, 2023).

26. *See, e.g.*, Cybersecurity & Infrastructure Security Agency (CISA), *CISA Cybersecurity Awareness Program*, https://www.cisa.gov/cisa-cybersecurity-awareness-program (last visited Mar. 31, 2023); Nat'l Council of Nonprofits, *Cybersecurity for Nonprofits*, https://www.councilofnonprofits.org/tools-resources/cybersecurity-nonprofits (last visited Mar. 31, 2023).

Organizations less than $50,000: Form 990-N

With some exceptions (which do not typically apply to animal protection organizations), an organization that normally has gross receipts under $50,000 is eligible to file Form 990-N (also called the "E-Postcard").[27] The E-Postcard requires the organization's legal name, any other names the organization goes by, the mailing address, and the Employer Identification Number (EIN), as well as contact information for a principal officer of the organization and the date of its tax year-end. Then, it asks only two simple questions:

a) Has your organization gone out of business?; and

b) Are your gross receipts normally $50,000 or less?

The authors have heard an IRS representative describe the Form 990-N as simply a way for an organization to raise its hand and say "yes, we're still here!" Note that an organization eligible to file Form 990-N may elect to file a Form 990-EZ or the standard Form 990 (more on why they might choose to do this below).

Organizations at or more than $50,000: Form 990-EZ

If an organization normally has gross receipts under $200,000 and total assets under $500,000, it may file a Form 990-EZ, which requires disclosure of key financial and governance information as well as descriptions of the organization's programmatic and fundraising activities. As its name suggests, the 990-EZ is a simplified version of the full Form 990 (discussed below). In addition, any organizations that generate unrelated business taxable income (UBTI, further discussed below) must also file a Form 990-T, which may require the payment of tax.

Form 990: Traps for the Unwary—Independent Directors, Compensation, and Governance

If an organization exceeds either of the 990-EZ thresholds (i.e., if gross receipts equal or exceed $200,000 or if total assets equal or exceed $500,000), it must file the full Form 990. Lawyers advising animal protection nonprofits should be aware that tax professionals who lack experience with tax exempt organization information returns may be unaware of a few aspects of the Form 990 that may trigger suspicion from the IRS, other regulators, or potential donors. The first is board member independence. Under state law, your client organization may have been able to incorporate its animal protection organization with only a small number of board members (in New York, the minimum is three), and many organizations get off the ground with a very small group of dedicated

27. *See* I.R.S. Pub. 5248, *IRS Form 990-N Electronic Filing System (e-Postcard) User Guide*, https://www.irs.gov/pub/irs-pdf/p5248.pdf (2023).

volunteers, some of whom may be related through business or family ties. The Form 990 requires the organization to disclose not only the number of members in the governing body (e.g., the board of directors) but also how many of those individuals are "independent." An independent director cannot be compensated by the organization, nor will a director who is related to another director or who is engaged in certain business relationships with another director be considered independent. It is important from a sound governance perspective to ensure that a majority of the board is independent.

Organizations that are in a position to be able to compensate their staff should also carefully consider and document on the Form 990 how compensation is set. The general rule is that individuals who are providing professional services to a tax-exempt organization may be fairly compensated for the work that they perform. Senior staff compensation should be determined by looking at comparable organizations in the area, retaining a reputable compensation consultant, or other reliable means (or by a combination of these approaches). The rules applicable to establishing executive compensation are discussed further in chapter 2.

In a recent set of revisions to the Form 990, the IRS has taken the view that the Form 990 can and should inform the general public not only about whether the organization is compliant with applicable tax law, but also about whether the organization has policies and practices in place that are likely to ensure sound governance. As a result, the Form 990 now includes questions related to management of conflicts of interest and other internal policies that speak to this issue, including whether the organization has policies related to the protection of whistleblowers and the retention of documents. Samples of all three of these policies are readily available. Adopting these key policies is a good way for an animal protection organization to signal to its external stakeholders that it is thorough, thoughtful, and aware of its compliance obligations.

Ancillary Benefits of a Thoughtful Form 990

It may be tempting for an organization to simply retain a CPA firm (or maybe your client organization has a great accountant on its board) to assemble and file the organization's Form 990. However, the organization may wish to take a more active role in contributing to and reviewing this document. The Form 990 can be a useful tool for reasons that go well beyond simple compliance with IRS regulations. Many donors, both institutional and private, look to the Form 990 to learn more about an organization. Forms 990 and 990-EZ are considered public information, and in fact, they are required to be publicly disclosed.[28] It can be a good sign of transparency for an organization to publicly post its

28. The IRS requires that an organization must make available for public inspection its annual information return for at least three years, including most schedules, its application for tax exemption, and all supporting documents (if it was filed on or after July 15, 1987), and the determination letter from the IRS showing its tax-exempt status. The IRS offers a training on public disclosure requirements which can be found at https://www.stayexempt.irs.gov/home/existing-organizations/required-disclosures.

current Form 990 on its website. In addition, the website www.Guidestar.org pulls periodically from IRS public databases and posts the Forms 990 of filers.

While it may seem counterintuitive for a tax filing, the Form 990 can be a great place to share with potential donors and the general public the most compelling details about an organization's programs and activities, fundraising priorities, and good governance practices. An organization that is able to answer the Form 990 questions comprehensively may, in so doing, show regulators and current and future donors that it has thought through these important issues and that it is run in a way that is more likely to ensure appropriate management of donor dollars.

A Word on IRS Audits

Just as it does with individual taxpayers and for-profit businesses, the IRS audits tax-exempt organizations regularly, either on the IRS's own initiative or upon receiving a complaint. For instance, several years ago, the IRS looked specifically at issues related to U.S. colleges and universities, and so notified the tax-exempt sector that these types of organization would be more likely to be subject to audit. The annual letter from the IRS's Tax Exempt and Government Entities Section can help identify whether any activity in which an organization is involved might be more likely to mean it will be subject to audit in a particular tax year.

In any event, once the IRS does select an organization for audit, it will issue requests for information to substantiate the information reported on the Form 990. Most often, an initial set of requests will be sent to the organization by the assigned auditor, with additional requests to follow as the auditor identifies issues for review. While this process can be quite time consuming, it is important to respond to the auditor as comprehensively as possible. The organization should not shy away from sharing with the auditor stories of the great work that it is doing: not only does it make everyone feel good to hear a Happy Tails adoption story about that stray who was cared for by the organization, but it also shows the auditor that the organization is doing the concrete work that is the reason the IRS granted the exemption in the first place. Above all, encourage the organization's representatives to be courteous to the auditor and to work diligently to provide them with the information they are seeking. At the end of the day, the audit process can help the organization identify areas in which governance and compliance can be improved.

Fiscal Sponsorship

It is impossible to overstate the importance of ensuring that, except in certain limited circumstances, all of the activity that takes place under the auspices of a 501(c)(3) organization is consistent with the tax-exempt purposes for which the organization was created. It is unlawful to permit another organization or an individual to "borrow" an animal protection organization's tax-exempt status, even if they are also doing very good and important work in the community. That said, there are some circumstances under which, with the right level of control or oversight (and with a sufficiently close relationship to the group's charitable purpose) an organization with 501(c)(3) status can choose to act as the so-called fiscal sponsor for another organization's or individual's activity.[29] So, for instance, say your client organization runs a limited admission shelter in its community. The exempt purposes for which the organization applied, and received, federal tax exemption include the prevention of cruelty to animals primarily through reducing intake, surrender prevention, and caring for and adopting out strays and surrendered animals. A new group is forming that will be conducting trap/neuter/return (TNR) activities in the local area, which will assist with your client organization's goal of reducing intake. That new group has not yet applied for 501(c)(3) status from the IRS, though its leaders say they intend to do so once "kitten season" slows down in the winter. In the meantime, however, they have an opportunity to secure $5,000 in grant funds from the city council to purchase supplies and subsidize some spay/neuter surgeries. They approach your client organization to see if it can help. The great news is that there are a few ways to assist them, but the mechanics can be tricky. For example, your client organization could enter into a contract with the new group under which the new group will provide the TNR as a service to the 501(c)(3) organization as a subcontractor. In this case, the 501(c)(3) organization would complete the city council application in its own name and then pay the TNR group for provision of the services. Other methods of fiscal sponsorship can be more or less complicated, depending on the circumstances of the organizations involved and the nature of the projects they intend to pursue. With any of these approaches, the key is that the organization that holds the 501(c)(3) status must exercise dominion and control over the funds that it receives. This means that it not only takes in and regrants the funds but also, at the end of the day, is responsible for ensuring that the funded work gets accomplished and the funds are used for the exempt purpose that it shares with the recipient group.

Unrelated Business Taxable Income

UBTI Generally

As discussed in chapter 2, an organization's exemption from the payment of federal income tax extends only to that income that is related to the organization's exempt purpose.[30] Income that is unrelated to that purpose may be subject to the corporate tax rate and may need to be reported on Form 990-T.

---

29. The authors highly recommend the following publication to anyone who is interested in learning more about fiscal sponsorship, as this resource is easy to digest and walks through some of the complexities involved in various methods for becoming a fiscal sponsor. Gregory L. Colvin, Fiscal Sponsorship: Six Ways To Do It Right—A Synopsis (attach. for A.B.A. Exempt Orgs. Comm. meeting, Feb. 5, 1993), https://www.adlercolvin.com/fiscal-sponsorship-six-ways-to-do-it-right-a-synopsis/.

30. 26 U.S.C. §§ 511–514 (2023).

Historically, the exemption was much broader. The general rule was that, so long as all of the funds were spent in the service of the organization's mission, federal income tax would not be assessed. In 1950, the IRS modified the rules to ensure that the nonprofit sector was not gaining an undue advantage over for-profit businesses, by undercutting prices with the benefit of their exemptions.

The rules governing UBTI and its related concept, the unrelated business income tax (UBIT), are complex with many exceptions and exclusions, such that they could be the subject of their own chapter of this text. What follows is just an overview of some of the most salient points of the applicable tax law.

The general rule for determining whether an organization must pay tax on an activity depends on whether the activity is:

a) a trade or business that is

b) regularly carried on by the organization; and

c) the business is not substantially related to the organization's exempt purpose.

If an activity meets all three criteria, then it may be subject to taxation under the UBTI rules. For sake of analysis, let us look at a couple of examples. Say you represent a client that has a group of volunteers who annually wish to raise funds by hosting a $10 car wash on a warm Saturday in the summer, and they usually raise around $300 to support the organization's farmed animal sanctuary. The car wash is arguably a "trade or business" given that the volunteers are providing a service (washing the cars) for a price, and there are other businesses out there that operate for-profit car washes that have to pay taxes on their income. This activity, however, is only a one-time event each year. Therefore, it is likely that this would not be considered "regularly carried on" and thus would not fall within the bounds of the UBTI rules.

Alternatively, consider an organization that operates an animal shelter from which it conducts a number of animal adoptions every day. In order to facilitate the best experience for the adopters and their new family members, the shelter sells pet essentials, such as small bags of pet food, litter, litter boxes, leashes, and a few chew toys, to ensure a smooth transition home. In this case, the sale of these products is certainly a trade or business carried on by many pet supply stores, and the shelter does regularly carry on this business as part of its operations. However, the activity in this case is closely related to the organization's exempt purpose of facilitating animal adoptions, and therefore this activity would also likely not be considered subject to UBIT.

Now, on the other hand, let us say that the same shelter opens a separate storefront next door where it starts selling new children's books, toys, home decor, and other items that are not themed around shelter pets and do not have any direct tie to the mission. In this example, there is a trade or business, regularly carried on, that is unrelated to the exempt purpose of the animal shelter. Thus, even if all of the funds raised from the proceeds of sales at the shop were directed toward the shelter, this activity would likely be deemed taxable and reportable on Form 990-T as UBTI.

UBTI Exceptions and Passive Activity

That said, there are exceptions to the general rule governing UBTI. The exceptions are too numerous and complicated to receive full treatment here, but generally speaking there are exemptions from UBIT for rents (so long as the underlying property is not debt-financed), royalties, and other passive income sources. Similarly, the sale or exchange of donor lists likely does not generate UBTI.[31] There is also a specific rule that permits a 501(c)(3) to operate a volunteer-run thrift store to support its operations without generating UBTI, notwithstanding the fact that this may constitute a business, regularly carried on, with no direct tie to the organization's exempt purpose.[32]

Another important distinction that the IRS has drawn is between advertisement on the one hand (the income from which would be subject to UBIT if all three criteria are met) versus acknowledgment on the other hand (which is not subject to UBIT). This distinction has particular salience when a tax-exempt organization has the opportunity to cooperate with a for-profit business that wishes to support its work. Let's say, for instance, that your client runs a bully breed rescue group that rehomes animals within a state. A local grocery store that supports that mission says they want to support the organization by hosting an adoption event in the parking lot, featuring photos of adoptable pets on in-store signage, and to give a $15,000 donation. In return, the business would like the nonprofit organization to distribute discount store coupons and fliers about weekly in-store specials to its volunteers and adopters, as well as place a link on its website to their home delivery shopping site. Unfortunately, you should advise your client that the requested activities would likely be considered "advertisement" under the UBTI rules, risking part or all of the monetary contribution being considered taxable. Both the distribution of store coupons and fliers, and potentially also adding the link to the store, would be considered advertising activities. However, more passive activities, such as providing a banner on the organization's website saying, "We Thank Ron's Grocery for Its Generous Support!" would likely be considered sufficiently passive so as to not trigger the same UBTI concern.

As noted above, these rules are very complicated, and a lawyer advising animal protection clients should consult with a knowledgeable tax advisor if they suspect their client organization's activities may be generating UBTI.

---

31. Edward Gonzalez & Charles Barrett, *UBIT: Royalty Income and Mailing Lists*, *in* CPE Technical Instruction Program Textbook 122–126 (1994), https://www.irs.gov/pub/irs-tege/eotopici94.pdf.

32. S. Rep. No. 2375, 81st Cong., 2d Sess. (1950) at 108.

State Tax Issues

As noted in chapter 2, animal protection organizations may qualify for exemption from certain state level taxes. Each state is different, and while some states will simply extend a blanket exemption to their state sales taxes (i.e., taxes imposed generally on the consumer for the sale, transfer, or exchange of a taxable item or service) and use taxes (i.e., taxes imposed on the use of a taxable item or service for which no sales tax has been paid) as a result of securing 501(c)(3) status, other states require a separate application for exemption. Yet other states do not provide sales and use tax exemptions or only offer narrow ones. Some states only recognize sales tax exemptions on a refunded basis (meaning that the organization must pay for the tax up front and then submit an annual state return seeking reimbursement). In some states, the only organizations that are permitted to seek exemption from state sales taxes are churches, (human) hospitals, and schools. Attorneys should advise their nonprofit clients to consult with a local tax advisor to determine whether there are any exemptions for which the organization might qualify. It is also important to remember that, if your nonprofit client is selling any goods or services, it may have an obligation to collect and remit sales tax to its home state.

States and municipalities also often have complex and multifaceted rules on when and whether certain types of organizations are entitled to exemption from the payment of property taxes on real property that they own or use. Here again, some states and municipalities only allow certain types of organizations to qualify for such exemptions, while others require that the property is actually being used for the exempt purpose. If the organization owns or rents property for which it is responsible for the payment of property taxes, seeking advice from an experienced tax professional is likely warranted.

Endowment Funds and Investments

Nonprofit animal protection organizations hold varying types of monetary assets. Some assets are held free and clear of any restrictions; however, certain funds may not be spent except in accordance with restrictions placed on those funds.[33] The term "endowment fund" means "an institutional fund or part thereof that, under the terms of a gift instrument, is not wholly expendable by the institution on a current basis."[34] It is imperative that organizations spend endowment funds only in a manner that respects the restrictions imposed on those funds. In addition, and as discussed below, nearly all states have laws that

33. For a discussion of how donors may restrict donations, please see "Donor-Imposed Restrictions on Use of Funds," above.

34. Uniform Prudent Management of Institutional Funds Act, § 2(2), which adds that "[t]he term does not include assets that an institution designates as an endowment fund for its own use." *See also* Office of the N.Y. State Att'y Gen. Charities Bureau, *A Practical Guide to the New York Prudent Management of Institutional Funds Act*, p. 2 (2010) (stating that endowment funds are "funds that are not fully expendable on a current basis due to donor-imposed restrictions on spending").

govern the manner in which nonprofit organizations must treat endowment funds.

Permanent endowments, also known as true endowments, are gifts to nonprofit organizations that are permanently restricted by the donor, often through a gift instrument such as a pledge agreement. Temporary endowments are gifts to nonprofit organizations that are restricted by the donor but, as the name suggests, only temporarily.

Nonprofit organizations may also hold quasi-endowment funds, which are funds upon which the organization's board of directors has imposed a restriction. Unlike donor-imposed restrictions, the organization's board can decide to lift the restriction on the funds. Boards may also choose to impose a time limitation on quasi-endowment funds. Because the restrictions on these funds are self-imposed by the organization and can therefore be lifted by the organization, these funds are generally not subject to the legal restrictions of Uniform Prudent Management of Institutional Funds Act (UPMIFA) as adopted by the states (as described in the following section).

Uniform Prudent Management of Institutional Funds Act

Background

In 1972, the National Conference of Commissioners on Uniform State Laws (also known as the Uniform Law Commission) approved the Uniform Management of Institutional Funds Act (UMIFA). UMIFA provided uniform rules for nonprofits on the investment and spending of their endowment funds. UMIFA was centered on two primary ideas: "1) that assets would be invested prudently in diversified investments that sought growth as well as income, and 2) that appreciation of assets could prudently be spent for the purposes of any endowment fund held by a charitable institution."[35]

To reflect both the growth of assets and expenditures in nonprofit institutions, as well as the increased sophistication of asset management, UMIFA was modified and the UPMIFA became the new standard in 2006.[36] Much like its predecessor, UPMIFA supports the responsible investment of assets and expenditure of a nonprofit organization's funds, particularly endowment funds. UPMIFA has been adopted in every state except for Pennsylvania, with (as is a common theme in this chapter and this book) the specific provisions of the law varying from state to state.

---

35. *Prudent Management of Institutional Funds Act—Summary*, Uniform Law Comm'n, https://www.uniformlaws.org/committees/community-home?CommunityKey=043b9067-bc2c-46b7-8436-07c9054064a3 (last visited Mar. 31, 2023).

36. *See id. See also Uniform Law Commission: An Update*, Nat'l Conference of State Legislatures (Dec. 2009), https://www.ncsl.org/legislators-staff/legislative-staff/research-editorial-legal-and-committee-staff/uniform-law-the-legislative-lawyer-december-20.aspx (last visited Mar. 31, 2023).

Investment

UPMIFA requires that nonprofit organizations invest funds in good faith and with the care an ordinarily prudent person in a like position would exercise under similar circumstances. This affects a range of investment activities, including but not limited to assessing the reasonableness of investment costs, such as fees charged by investment managers or funds; considering diversification; and ensuring that investments are made in relation to a nonprofit's overall portfolio rather than considering investments discretely.

UPMIFA requires that the following factors, if relevant, be considered in managing and investing institutional funds: (a) general economic conditions; (b) the possible effect of inflation or deflation; (c) the expected tax consequences, if any, of investment decisions or strategies; (d) the role that each investment or course of action plays within the overall investment portfolio of the fund; (e) the expected total return from income and the appreciation of investments; (f) other resources of the institution; (g) the needs of the institution and the fund to make distributions and to preserve capital; and (h) an asset's special relationship or special value, if any, to the charitable purposes of the institution.[37]

Expenditure

The expenditure provisions of UPMIFA govern the manner in which a nonprofit organization can spend its endowment assets. Originally under UMIFA, the organization was able to spend both the appreciation and income of an endowment fund; however, the endowment could not be spent below its historic dollar value, which was defined as the "aggregate fair value in dollars of (1) an endowment fund at the time it became an endowment fund, (2) each subsequent donation to the fund at the time it is made, and (3) each accumulation made pursuant to a direction in the applicable gift instrument at the time the accumulation is added to the endowment fund."[38] Critically, UPMIFA eliminated this concept of "historic dollar value." Instead, a nonprofit organization may appropriate for expenditure or accumulate so much of an endowment fund as the institution determines to be prudent for the uses, benefits, purposes, and duration for which the endowment fund is established.

In determining whether it is appropriate for a nonprofit organization to expend an endowment fund in accordance with those principles, the organization must consider seven factors: (1) duration and preservation of the endowment fund; (2) purposes of the institution and the endowment fund; (3) general economic conditions; (4) effect of inflation or deflation; (5) expected

37. UNIFORM LAW COMM'N, Prudent Management of Institutional Funds Act, § 3(e)(1), at https://www.uniformlaws.org/committees/community-home?CommunityKey=043b9067-bc2c-46b7-8436-07c9054064a3 (last visited May. 27, 2023).

38. *See* UNIF. MGMT. OF INST. FUNDS ACT § 1(5).

total return from income and appreciation of investments; (6) other resources of the institution; and (7) the investment policy of the institution.[39]

Case Study: The New York Prudent Management of Institutional Funds Act

As one of the last states to codify UPMIFA, New York enacted the New York Prudent Management of Institutional Funds Act (NYPMIFA) in September 2010 through Article 5A to the New York Not-for-Profit Corporation Law.[40] New York had previously adopted UMIFA in 1978, and the adoption of the modernized UPMIFA brought welcome changes to New York-based not-for-profit organizations by giving them the flexibility (upon careful consideration by their boards and in compliance with NYPMIFA) to spend endowment funds below their historic dollar value without first obtaining the approval of a court or the New York State Attorney General.[41] New York provides an interesting case study of the manner in which UPMIFA rules have been codified by a particular state.

Expenditure of Endowment Assets

As set forth above, while states generally adopted the provisions of UPMIFA, they retain the ability to modify the uniform law, and so the laws may vary from state to state. New York, for example, added an eighth factor to the list of seven factors that must be assessed before appropriating endowment assets. New York additionally requires nonprofit organizations to "[w]here appropriate and circumstances would otherwise warrant, [evaluate] alternatives to expenditure of the endowment fund, giving due consideration to the effect that such alternatives may have on the institution" before expending endowment funds.[42]

Moreover, unlike UPMIFA, NYPMIFA imposes a rebuttable presumption of imprudence if the nonprofit organization spends more than 7 percent of the endowment's market value in any year.[43] The fair market value is calculated "on the basis of market values determined at least quarterly and averaged over a period of not less than five years immediately preceding the year in which the appropriation for expenditure is made."[44] If the endowment was created fewer than five years prior to the calculation, the fair market value is calculated for the period when the endowment has been in existence.

39. *See id.* § 3(e)(1).

40. N.Y. Not-for-Profit Corp. Law §§ 551 *et seq.* (2022).

41. New York created a unique notification process that allowed donors who made restricted gifts to an organization prior to September 17, 2010, to opt out of the new rule that allowed for the spending of the gift below the historic dollar value. The law even included specific language for nonprofits to include when they communicated this opt-out to the donors who had made the restricted gifts. *See id.* § 553(e). This notification process was not contemplated under UPMIFA.

42. *Id.* § 553(a)(7).

43. *Id.* § 553(d).

44. *Id.* There are certain limited exceptions to this rebuttable presumption. *See id.*

Bearers of Duties and Responsibilities

Much like UPMIFA, the New York law outlines the duties and responsibilities of those who oversee institutional funds. For example, Section 552(b) of NYPMIFA provides that, in addition to the duty of loyalty imposed on not-for-profit directors (and other duties, such as duty of care and duty of obedience that may be imposed under the common law), each person "responsible for managing and investing an institutional fund shall manage and invest the fund in good faith and with the care an ordinarily prudent person in a like position would exercise under similar circumstances."[45] Thus, directors and other key persons should abide by this standard in exercising discretion over institutional funds. In addition, the nonprofit organization may, in compliance with other sections of the New York Not-for-Profit Corporation Law, delegate management and investment of assets to its committees, officers, or employees.[46] For example, the board of directors of an animal protection organization may delegate these responsibilities to a finance or investment committee under the organization's bylaws.

Section 554 of NYPMIFA further provides that the nonprofit institution may delegate the management and investment of an institutional fund to a third party, if that may be done prudently and provided such delegation is not prohibited in the gift instrument.[47] NYPMIFA further imposes certain specific requirements on the not-for-profit in selecting, terminating, compensating, and monitoring investment advisors.[48] If the management and investment of an institutional fund is appropriately delegated, the institution is not liable for the actions of the agent to which these responsibilities were delegated.[49]

Moreover, NYPMIFA imposes duties on the investment advisor to which the duty of managing the investments has been delegated. Specifically, the agent must use "reasonable care, skill and caution to comply with the scope and terms of the delegation."[50] The agent also submits to the jurisdiction of the New York courts in any proceedings arising from the delegation or the performance of the functions under the delegation.[51] The designated agent must also agree in the engagement contract to allow the nonprofit organization to terminate the agreement on not more than sixty-days' notice, without penalty, at any time.[52]

Written Investment Policy Statements

Section 552(f) of NYPMIFA requires each nonprofit organization to adopt a written investment policy statement. The investment policy statement must identify guidelines for investments as well as the delegation of management and

45. *Id.* § 552(b).
46. *Id.* § 552(f).
47. *Id.* § 554(a).
48. *See id.*
49. *See id.* § 554(c).
50. *See id.* § 554(b).
51. *See id.* § 554(d).
52. *See id.* § 554(e).

investment functions. This requirement for a written policy does not contain exceptions for smaller institutions or institutions with limited (or no) endowment funds. While larger nonprofit organizations may adopt investment policies reflective of the level of sophistication of their investments, smaller nonprofit organizations may elect to adopt simpler investment policy statements.[53]

Real Property

Engaging in real property transactions, whether through purchasing or leasing property, is legally complicated. A full review of the legal considerations of real estate projects is outside the scope of this chapter, and attorneys for nonprofit animal protection organizations should advise their clients to strongly consider engaging specialized experts, such as architects and engineers, licensed in the jurisdiction where the real property transaction will take place when entering into any material real property transaction.[54] There are, however, many issues specific to not-for-profit animal protection organizations that should be considered when buying or leasing property.

Zoning

When not-for-profit animal protection organizations seek to move to a new location, whether by purchasing or leasing property, there are many zoning considerations specific to animal protection work that the organization may need to consider. Zoning laws and ordinances govern the manner in which parcels in particular geographic areas can be used. For example, if a zoning ordinance designates a certain area as strictly a residential zone, only residential usage—as defined in that locality's zoning laws—is permitted in that zone. Accordingly, some zoning areas may permit animals to be on site, but the zoning may limit the type or number of animals or the nature of animal-related activities. For example, an agricultural zone may permit individuals to maintain farm animals outdoors but may not permit indoor kennels.

When it comes to animal-related activities, the zoning regulations are often quite specific in governing which activities are permitted in each zone; therefore, attorneys should ensure that animal protection organizations closely consider the types of activities in which they may engage when selecting property. For instance, many nonprofit animal protection organizations may engage in on-site veterinary services for the animals in their care; however, some jurisdictions

53. Many excellent online tools are also available to provide guidance for those entities needing assistance. *See, e.g.*, Weil, Gotshal & Manges LLP, *Guide to Nonprofit Governance 2022*, at 160, *available at* https://www.weil.com/-/media/files/pdfs/2022/november/2022-guide-to-not-for-profit-governance.pdf. As noted by Weil, "[e]ach not-for-profit organization will need to consider factors including the extent of the financial resources of the institution, the type of investments it holds, the charitable purposes of the institution, and the nature and scope of the institution's activities or programs." *Id.*

54. Depending on the nature of the issue or transaction, these experts may include non-legal experts such as architects, engineers, and/or surveyors. In addition, attorneys who do not specialize in real estate and/or land use matters in that locality should consider engaging specialized counsel.

are rather granular in detailing which types of veterinary activities are permitted in which zones. Certain locations may, for example, distinguish between veterinary facilities that allow animals to stay overnight (often referred to as "veterinary hospitals") and veterinary facilities that do not allow animals to stay overnight (often referred to as "veterinary clinics"). Localities may permit animal shelters or veterinary facilities in a geographic area, but they may nonetheless prohibit outdoor kenneling of animals or limit the number of animals who can be housed outdoors at any particular time.

While shelters may be able to procure special use permits, variances, or other accommodations to address these issues, it is critical for the nonprofit animal protection organization to ensure that its activities are permitted in the location. If there is any ambiguity when reviewing the zoning law, attorneys advising nonprofit organizations may either engage specialized local land use counsel or simply reach out to the local land use committee or planning board for confirmation. This type of diligence can prevent a very expensive mistake. Similarly, organizations should ensure that their certificates of occupancy permit the proposed activities of the organization.

As with any other type of business, animal protection organizations should review the zoning laws to ensure that they do not restrict the number of buildings or types of buildings in a manner that could limit the plans the organization has for the location. Zoning laws, or other local land use laws, may also impact things like visible signage, number of parking spots, building height, and other matters, so comprehensive review of these types of laws is critical.

Permits

Once the threshold question of appropriate zoning has been addressed and the nonprofit animal protection organization has purchased or leased its property, the organization must obtain the proper permits to conduct the work in that jurisdiction. While they are critically important, this section does not address construction-related permits or certificates of occupancy. Rather, there are several types of operating permits that are specifically relevant to animal protection organizations:

- *Shelter permits:* Most jurisdictions require animal shelters to operate pursuant to a permit. Permitting may be required at the state level, the local level, or both.
- *For organizations that have veterinary operations:*
    - *Veterinary Clinic Permits*: In states where it is required,[55] facilities where veterinary medicine is practiced must be licensed by the state's veterinary board. This often includes mobile clinics as well as

55. *See, e.g.*, Code of Ala. § 34-29-88. ("Any facility, including mobile clinics or any other premises where a licensed veterinarian practices shall have a premise permit issued by the board."); *see also* Ohio Admin. Code § 4741-2-01(A).

stationary veterinary clinics.[56] Such permits must be obtained prior to practicing veterinary medicine at the facility.

- *Controlled substance registrations and/or prescription drug registrations*: Federal and state laws regulate the purchasing, distribution, storing, and administration of certain substances. Upon entering a new location, organizations must ensure that they are acquiring, maintaining, prescribing, and administering controlled substances only after the proper registrations are implemented. In addition, certain states may require supplemental licensure prior to ordering prescription drugs. For example, Florida requires many veterinary clinics to obtain a Health Care Clinic Establishment permit through the Florida Division of Drugs, Devices, and Cosmetics before purchasing prescription drugs.[57] These types of controlled substance and other drug-related permits and registrations are typically specific to an address, and so new permits or registrations must be obtained, or existing permits or registrations must be modified, upon moving to a new location.
- *Radiology and Radiation Permits*: Not only must radiology and radiation veterinary equipment be operated pursuant to a permit, state and local laws also require that employers monitor exposure to radiation and/or that written documentation related to radiology equipment is maintained, among other requirements.
- *Waste disposal permits*: Organizations that dispose of sharps or biological waste may need to obtain a permit at their new location to allow for such disposal.

Animal-Related Laws to Consider When Entering a New Jurisdiction

Like any other business, when engaging in work at a new location, nonprofit animal protection organizations must ensure that they are legally compliant by following all local laws and regulations. The following areas of law represent just a sampling of considerations that are specific to animal protection organizations when purchasing or leasing property in a new jurisdiction where they have not previously conducted business.[58] Written protocols memorializing best practices based on the laws in the organization's new jurisdiction should be implemented in each of these areas prior to entering the new jurisdiction to ensure compliance with law and to minimize legal risk. Relevant laws may include:

- *Stray-Hold and Microchip/Reunification Laws:* Stray-hold laws differ among localities, and organizations should be familiar with the local law. In addition, certain jurisdictions may require animal protection

56. *See, e.g.*, Code of Ala. § 34-29-88.

57. *See* Fla. Drug & Cosmetic Act § 499.01(r).

58. There are many other legal considerations when purchasing or leasing real property in a new jurisdiction. This list is meant to highlight certain areas that are of specific concern for animal protection organizations.

organizations to scan animals for microchips and/or attempt to reach potential owners.[59] Other jurisdictions require shelters to keep photographs of animals who have been placed in foster homes available in a conspicuous place viewable to the general public.[60]

- *Animal Bite Protocols:* In the case of an animal bite, localities vary in their holding requirements and the duration of holds.
- *Mandatory Spay/Neuter Laws:* When entering a new jurisdiction, animal protection organizations should familiarize themselves with state and local requirements to spay or neuter animals before adopting animals out to the public. Some states allow for the matter to be addressed contractually under certain circumstances.
- *Animal Importation and Transport Laws:* States differ in their health-related requirements when animals are brought into the state. Most states require that animals are only brought into the state pursuant to a health certificate issued by a duly accredited veterinarian.
- *Civil Abandonment Laws:* Many states and municipalities have laws governing cases of civil abandonment (i.e., when an animal is left in the care of a veterinarian and the owner never returns). There are often detailed processes to follow in these circumstances, and lawyers advising shelters—particularly those with veterinary practices—should familiarize themselves with these laws.
- *Other Legal Considerations:* While not always applicable, the following should be considered if advising organizations looking to buy or lease property in a new jurisdiction:
    - *Limitations on Nonprofits' Ability to Employ Veterinarians:* Certain states prohibit the corporate practice of veterinary medicine, meaning that a non-veterinarian or an entity not owned by veterinarians may not employ veterinarians for the purpose of practicing veterinary medicine. While there may be exceptions for practicing solely on an entity's own animals[61] (which would often cover animal protection organizations' treatment of their owned animals in their facilities), organizations may wish to provide veterinary support to the public or may house animals that are not owned by the shelter, such as animals being held in criminal investigations. Such organizations may need to consider alternative corporate structures to ensure legal compliance.
    - *Breed Discrimination Laws:* Animal protection organizations working with dogs should be aware of any applicable state or local breed discrimination laws, which can impose requirements on or ban certain dog breeds.[62]
    - *Dangerous Dog Laws:* Animal protection organizations should be aware of the so-called dangerous dog laws in their jurisdiction, including what could cause a dog to be designated "dangerous,"

59. *See, e.g.*, N.Y. AGRIC. & MKTS. LAW § 380.
60. *See, e.g.*, N.C. GEN. STAT. § 19A-32.1.
61. *See, e.g.*, TENN. CODE ANN. § 63-12-137(c)(1).
62. A more comprehensive review of breed discrimination laws is provided in chapter 7.

"vicious," or a similar categorization, the legal process governing those designations, and the restrictions (if any) placed on dogs who are so designated. Those groups that assist the animal victims of dog fighting, in particular, should be aware that certain laws deem animals to be dangerous if they have been seized in relation to dog fighting, even if there are no known incidents of the animal acting in a dangerous manner.[63]

Conclusion

Sound and effective fundraising and financial management are key to ensuring that nonprofit organizations can continue to grow, innovate, and thrive. By advising animal protection organization clients to conduct the organization's fundraising in a manner that comports with sound legal and ethical principles, the legal advisor assists in keeping the vital "engine" of fundraising humming along smoothly, enabling the animal protection organization to devote those funds to the animals that need their assistance the most. By ensuring that the organization is responsive to the tax authorities and other regulatory oversight bodies, the advisor can keep the organization focused on its essential mission, rather than being distracted, or having its operations suspended, by an enforcement action that might otherwise have been avoided. By thinking strategically about the organization's investments (including its real estate), an organization can ensure that its mission and purpose can thrive to the benefit of future generations of individuals who are committed to protecting animals.

---

63. *See, e.g.*, S.C. Code Ann. § 47-3-710. A more comprehensive review of dangerous dog laws is provided in chapter 7.

CHAPTER 4

Employees, Volunteers, Liability, and Insurance

Abbey Jay and John Seber

EMPLOYEE AND VOLUNTEER ISSUES

The risks associated with employees and volunteers can be significant, especially in the animal protection movement, where organizations often have limited human resources capacity, are unable to pay employees as much as for-profit companies, have large volumes of work, sometimes have workers completing a variety of tasks without clearly delineated individual job responsibilities, depend on volunteers to support their mission, and may have employees and volunteers working with animals who could cause injuries.

Employees

Animal protection organizations must comply with a variety of federal, state, and local employment laws. Although it is not possible to analyze here every potential employment law that may impact the operations of an animal protection organization, several key federal and state laws will have a significant impact on the organization's relationship with its employees.

Wage and Hour Laws

Both federal and state laws can affect the minimum pay and overtime requirements that apply to an animal protection organization. The Fair Labor Standards Act (FLSA) establishes federal minimum wage, overtime, record-keeping, and child labor standards. It will apply to an animal protection organization if it has at least two employees, engages in commercial activity (e.g., selling goods or charging fees for services), and has gross annual revenue exceeding $500,000.[1] Even if the organization does not meet this minimum threshold, its employees will be covered by the FLSA if they engage in interstate commerce (e.g., making or receiving interstate telephone calls, or shipping materials to another state).[2]

The FLSA sets the federal minimum wage, which is currently $7.25 per hour,[3] and provides that an employer must pay an employee at least 1.5 times the employee's regular rate of pay for all hours worked over forty hours in a work week, unless the employee can be classified as exempt from overtime pay requirements.[4] Determining whether an employee is exempt from overtime pay requirements is a complex process, but the most common exemptions relate to executives, administrative personnel, and professional employees.[5] It is important to note that states, cities, and counties may have their own wage and hour laws, which could affect both minimum wage and overtime compensation. For example, in 2022, the minimum wage in California was $15.00/hour for employers with at least twenty-six employees, and $14.00/hour for employers with twenty-five employees or less,[6] while the minimum wage for all employers in San Francisco was $16.99 per hour.[7] Similarly, California has unique provisions relating to overtime, requiring the employer to pay twice the employee's regular rate of pay for any work in excess of twelve hours in one day and any work in excess of eight hours on any seventh day of a work week.[8]

Although federal law does not require employers to provide paid leave for holidays, vacation, or illness, states and local jurisdictions may have their own requirements for sick leave,[9] while state law may affect how an employer must administer any accrued vacation.[10] Moreover, organizations with at least fifty employees must comply with the federal Family and Medical Leave Act (FMLA).[11] Under FMLA, an organization must give an unpaid, job-protected leave of up to twelve weeks to a qualifying employee under certain circumstances, including birth or adoption of a child, caring for a relative, or due to a serious health condition that makes the employee unable to perform their work.[12] To be eligible for leave, the employee must have worked for the organization for at least twelve months and 1,250 hours during the twelve months

1. 29 U.S.C. § 203(s).

2. *See* U.S. Dep't of Labor Fact Sheet #14A: Non-Profit Organizations and the Fair Labor Standards Act (FLSA), *available at* https://www.dol.gov/sites/dolgov/files/WHD/legacy/files/whdfs14a.pdf.

3. 29 U.S.C. § 206.

4. 29 U.S.C. § 207.

5. 29 U.S.C. § 213(a)(1).

6. *See* Cal. Lab. Code § 1182.12; *see also Minimum Wage*, California Department of Industrial Relations, *available at* https://www.dir.ca.gov/dlse/faq_minimumwage.htm.

7. *See San Francisco Minimum Wage Poster*, City & County of San Francisco, *available at* https://sfgov.org/olse/sites/default/files/minimum%20wage%20poster%202022_2.pdf.

8. Cal. Lab. Code § 510(a).

9. *See, e.g.*, N.Y. Lab. Law § 196-b.

10. *See, e.g.*, Cal. Lab. Code § 227.3.

11. 29 U.S.C. §§ 2601–2654.

12. 29 U.S.C. § 2612(1).

immediately preceding their request for leave.[13] The organization may request certification from a healthcare provider to confirm that the employee is eligible for leave.[14] In addition, an increasing number of states and cities are going beyond FMLA to require that employers offer paid leave to eligible employees in other circumstances. For example, California requires that employees receive up to eight weeks of wage replacement benefits if they take time off work to care for a seriously ill family member, to bond with a new child, or if due to a qualifying exigency related to a family member's active duty in the armed forces.[15]

Hiring and Firing

When preparing to hire employees, animal protection organizations should understand that there are a variety of legal requirements associated with the hiring process, including job posts, applications, and interviews. Some of the requirements are relatively well known or easy to find, such as the Colorado requirement that all employers with at least one employee in the state must include salary ranges and benefits information with all job postings for remote positions or positions located in Colorado.[16] Other states have rather unique requirements that may be less known, such as being required to include in an application document that the employer cannot require candidates to take polygraph tests[17] or, where an employee must list work history in an application, the section must include a statement that the applicant may include volunteer work in that history.[18] Moreover, to the extent that an animal protection organization would like to express a preference for candidates who do not engage in certain behaviors relating to animals or the use or consumption of products derived from animals, it should research and understand state laws relating to employee off-duty conduct and the consumption of lawful products[19] to determine whether—and if so, how—this might be legally permissible.

When hiring a new employee, the organization should memorialize the employment offer in a written letter that identifies the position, whether it is exempt from overtime requirements, start date, rate and frequency of pay, working hours, whether the employee will work on an at-will basis, benefits available, the employee's supervisor, and any possible conditions of employment (e.g., completing a background check). Similarly, if employees or volunteers will have access to sensitive donor or financial information, they should also sign a nondisclosure agreement that requires them to keep this information confidential. Organization should be aware that federal or state law may affect the extent to which nondisclosure agreements can restrict the disclosure of

13. 29 U.S.C. § 2611(2).

14. 29 U.S.C. § 2613.

15. Cal. Unemp. Ins. Code § 3301.

16. Colo. Rev. Stat. §§ 8-5-101(5); 8-5-201(2).

17. *E.g.*, Md. Code, Lab. & Empl. § 3-702 (d)(1).

18. Mass. Gen. Laws ch. 149, § 52B.

19. *See, e.g.*, Colo. Rev. Stat. § 24-34-402.5(1); Minn. Stat. § 181.938.

information relating to certain employment disputes—especially claims involving allegations of sexual harassment or assault.[20]

Animal protection organizations may have specific confidentiality concerns that can be memorialized in confidentiality agreements. For example, an organization that houses companion animals from domestic violence situations should impose requirements to protect the person subject to the abuse as well as the animal. In some situations, employees with knowledge of the location of threatened or endangered wildlife should keep that information confidential to protect the animals, and shelters that house animals that are the subject of criminal animal cruelty proceedings may have court-imposed confidentiality regimes.

Some states may find that the prospect of continued employment after an employee has been working at the organization will not be sufficient consideration for signing one of these agreements,[21] so the organization should include these agreements within the onboarding process. States may also have unique requirements relating to the onboarding process. For example, New York requires that every employer provide "a notice containing such employer's sexual harassment prevention policy and the information presented at such employer's sexual harassment prevention training program" at the time of hiring.[22]

The organization should also develop a comprehensive set of employment policies and use its employee handbook as an opportunity for the organization to reaffirm compliance with governing laws, general best practices, and its organizational values. For example, the handbook may reinforce the at-will nature of employment, detail policies to avoid conflicts of interest and the inurement of private benefits, articulate the organization's commitment to providing equal opportunity and a discrimination-free work environment, and provide employees with a clear pathway for reporting potential violations of law or organizational policy.

Although discrimination can be an area of potential legal exposure for all employers, including nonprofits, it is not possible to discuss all of the federal and state discrimination laws within this chapter. At a minimum, however, an animal protection organization should understand the various laws relating to employment discrimination on the basis of an employee's membership in a protected class, including race, ethnicity, national origin, citizenship, sex, gender, pregnancy, sexual orientation, religion, disability, veteran status, genetic information, and age. An organization with at least fifteen employees will be covered under Title VII of the Civil Rights Act of 1994,[23] which prohibits discrimination against race, color, religion, sex, gender, sexual orientation,

---

20. *See, e.g.*, Cal. Civ. Proc. Code § 1001(a) (prohibiting the use of a nondisclosure agreement to limit the disclosure of factual information relating to a sexual assault, harassment, discrimination, or retaliation claim); *e.g.*, 42 U.S.C.A. § 19403(a) ("With respect to a sexual assault dispute or sexual harassment dispute, no nondisclosure clause or nondisparagement clause agreed to before the dispute arises shall be judicially enforceable in instances in which conduct is alleged to have violated Federal, Tribal, or State law.").

21. *See, e.g.*, Cost Mgmt. Incentives, Inc. v. London-Osborne, No. CV02-0463081, 2002 WL 31886860, at *7 (Conn. Super. Ct. Dec. 5, 2002) ("It is well settled law in Connecticut that continued employment is not consideration for a covenant not to compete entered into after the beginning of the employment.").

22. N.Y. Lab. Law § 201-g(2-a)(a).

23. 42 U.S.C. §§ 2000e–2000e17.

gender identity, national origin, and requires employers to provide reasonable accommodation for a sincerely held religious belief, the Americans with Disabilities Act,[24] which prohibits discrimination against individuals with physical or mental disabilities and requires employers to offer reasonable accommodation for a disability, and the Genetic Information Nondiscrimination Act,[25] which prohibits discrimination based on genetic information (e.g., genetic tests or the manifestation of diseases or disorders in the individual's family). An organization with at least twenty employees will also be subject to the Age Discrimination in Employment Act, which protects individuals aged 40 and older from discrimination based on age.[26] The Immigration Reform and Control Act also prohibits employers with at least four employees from discriminating in hiring based on national origin or citizenship.[27] The Uniformed Services Employment and Reemployment Rights Act, which prohibits discrimination based on military service, applies to all employers.[28]

These federal discrimination laws generally prohibit the employer from taking an adverse employment action against an employee on the basis of the protected characteristic. Adverse actions can include refusing to hire, discharging, depriving the employee of opportunities, harassing, or otherwise affecting the employee's status as an employee or their compensation, terms, conditions, or privileges of employment.[29] They also generally prohibit retaliation against an employee who has filed or supported a complaint or otherwise opposed a prohibited discrimination practice.[30] States may also have their own anti-discrimination and harassment laws, which can expand the scope of these federal laws. For example, the California Fair Employment and Housing Act covers many of the same classes referenced in the federal laws discussed above but adds additional protections and applies to employers who may otherwise be too small to be subject to several federal anti-discrimination laws.[31] Similarly, some states and municipalities have mandatory harassment training and education programs, which may require an organization to ensure that its employees receive state-compliant harassment training.[32]

Volunteers

Many animal protection organizations rely on committed volunteers to help further the organization's mission. Although animal protection organizations can maximize limited resources and develop strong community engagement

24. 42 U.S.C. §§ 12101–12213.

25. 42 U.S.C. §§ 2000ff–2000ff11.

26. 29 U.S.C. §§ 621–634.

27. 8 U.S.C. § 1324b(a).

28. 38 U.S.C. § 4303(4)(A).

29. *See* 42 U.S.C. § 2000e-2(a) (Title VII); 29 U.S.C. § 623(a) (ADEA); 29 C.F.R. § 1630.4(a) (ADA).

30. *See* 42 U.S.C. § 2000e-3(a) (Title VII); 29 U.S.C. § 623(d) (ADEA); 42 U.S.C.A. § 12203(a) (ADA).

31. *See, e.g.*, Cal. Gov't Code § 12926 (applying to employers with 5 or more employees, protecting against discrimination on the basis of marital status).

32. *See, e.g.*, Cal. Gov't Code § 12950; Conn. Gen. Stat. § 46a-54(15).

through the use of volunteers in certain contexts, it is important to manage these relationships appropriately to avoid potential legal pitfalls. Both federal and state laws can affect the organization's relationship with its volunteers.

Volunteer Classification

It is critical for an animal protection organization to understand how federal and state wage and hour laws define the term "volunteer," to ensure that a volunteer worker is not inadvertently treated as an employee under federal or state law. For example, the U.S. Department of Labor (DOL) has provided specific guidance on criteria for volunteers at nonprofit organizations to be exempted from the FLSA:

> Individuals may volunteer time to religious, charitable, civic, humanitarian, or similar nonprofit organizations as a public service and not be covered by the FLSA. Individuals generally may not, however, volunteer in commercial activities run by a non-profit organization such as a gift shop. A volunteer generally will not be considered an employee for FLSA purposes if the individual volunteers freely for public service, religious or humanitarian objectives, and without contemplation or receipt of compensation. Typically, such volunteers serve on a part-time basis and do not displace regular employed workers or perform work that would otherwise be performed by regular employees. In addition, paid employees of a non-profit organization cannot volunteer to provide the same type of services to their non-profit organization that they are employed to provide.[33]

Thus, in order to comply with federal law, an animal protection organization should not depend on unpaid volunteers to do work that otherwise would be done by employees. An animal protection organization should also develop a clear onboarding process and job description for the volunteer that documents the limited scope of the volunteer's engagement, to ensure that the volunteer engagement remains consistent with the FLSA by not displacing the work of employees.[34] If it is found that an individual was misclassified as a volunteer instead of an employee, the misclassified individual could seek the remedies otherwise available under wage and hour laws. Under the FLSA, for example, this could include back pay, liquidated damages, and attorney's fees.[35]

States also distinguish between employees and volunteers under their respective wage and hour laws. For example, California excludes volunteers from its wage and hour requirements, defining a "volunteer" as "an individual who performs work for civic, charitable, or humanitarian reasons for a public agency or corporation qualified under Section 501(c)(3) of the Internal Revenue Code as a tax-exempt organization, without promise, expectation, or receipt of any compensation for work performed."[36]

---

33. DOL Fact Sheet #14A: Non-Profit Organizations and the Fair Labor Standards Act.
34. *See* DOL Fact Sheet #14A: Non-Profit Organizations and the Fair Labor Standards Act.
35. 29 U.S.C. § 216(b).
36. Cal. Lab. Code § 1720.4.

Animal protection organizations can also offer paid or unpaid internships to recent graduates, students, or others who seek to gain practical experience in a particular job, potentially gaining helpful insights and contacts while improving their chances of obtaining a permanent position in the field. Although the DOL has developed guidance that for-profit organizations must comply with in order for interns to be exempt from minimum wage and overtime requirements found in the FLSA, it recognizes that "[u]npaid internships for public sector and non-profit charitable organizations, where the intern volunteers without expectation of compensation, are generally permissible."[37] That said, many animal protection organizations are recognizing that internships, which are gateway opportunities for obtaining paid employment within the animal protection movement, should be paid so that candidates from diverse socioeconomic backgrounds can afford to pursue these opportunities.[38]

Volunteer Liability

At the federal level, the Volunteer Protection Act (VPA) provides protections for individual volunteers, though it does not "affect the liability of any nonprofit organization or governmental entity with respect to harm caused to any person."[39] Thus, these protections shield the individual volunteer only—not the organization itself, which can still be liable for the volunteer's acts. Under the VPA, a volunteer is defined as "an individual performing services for a nonprofit organization or a governmental entity who does not receive—(A) compensation (other than reasonable reimbursement or allowance for expenses actually incurred); or (B) any other thing of value in lieu of compensation, in excess of $500 per year. . . ."[40]

Under the VPA, a volunteer generally will not be liable for harm caused by the volunteer on behalf of the organization as long as the "volunteer was acting within the scope of the volunteer's responsibilities in the nonprofit organization or governmental entity at the time of the act or omission" and "the harm was not caused by willful or criminal misconduct, gross negligence, reckless misconduct, or a conscious, flagrant indifference to the rights or safety of the individual harmed by the volunteer."[41] If the volunteer is engaging in an activity that requires a license, certification, or authorization, then the volunteer must have obtained the applicable credential to be protected under this provision.[42]

The VPA contains several other exclusions and limitations. Most importantly for the organization, the VPA does not "affect any civil action brought by

37. *See* U.S. DOL Fact Sheet #71: Internship Programs Under the Fair Labor Standards Act, *available at* https://www.dol.gov/sites/dolgov/files/WHD/legacy/files/whdfs71.pdf.

38. *See, e.g., Why Mercy for Animals Must Mean Mercy for Everyone: Our Commitment to Fighting Racial Injustice*, Mercy For Animals, https://mercyforanimals.org/blog/why-mercy-for-animals-must-mean-mercy-for/.

39. 42 U.S.C. § 14503(d).

40. 42 U.S.C. § 14505(6).

41. 42 U.S.C. § 14503(a).

42. 42 U.S.C. § 14503(a)(2).

any nonprofit organization or any governmental entity against any volunteer of such organization or entity."[43] Thus, an organization may still take action against a volunteer for wrongdoing. The VPA also does not protect a volunteer if the volunteer caused the harm while operating a motor vehicle, vessel, aircraft, or other vehicle for which the state requires the operator or the owner of the vehicle, craft, or vessel to possess an operator's license or maintain insurance.[44] Finally, the VPA does not apply to volunteer misconduct that constitutes a crime of violence, international terrorism, a hate crime, a sexual offense, a civil rights violation, or a crime committed while the volunteer was under the influence of alcohol or a drug.[45]

Notably, the VPA allows states to limit volunteer liability subject to certain conditions, such as, inter alia, requiring organizational risk management procedures, volunteer training, or maintaining an insurance policy or other arrangements, ensuring that the organization will be able to pay for losses up to a specified amount.[46] Moreover, each state may have its own laws protecting volunteers, such as additional protections for volunteer directors or executive officers of nonprofit organizations.[47]

Safe Workplaces

Animal protection organizations may present unique workplace risks for employees and volunteers. Organizations that work directly with animals, such as shelters, sanctuaries, and wildlife rescuers, should be especially careful with workplace health and safety requirements, as even large zoos with ample resources can fail to manage risks related to employee interactions with animals and face costly fines as a result.[48] Moreover, employees and volunteers of animal protection organizations can experience all of the less unique risks of any workplace, such as repetitive use injuries or slip and fall incidents.

The Occupational Safety and Health Act, which created the Occupational Safety and Health Administration (OSHA), applies to all organizations that have employees and engage in interstate commerce.[49] OSHA can impose civil and criminal penalties, depending on the nature of the violation.[50] Although most OSHA sanctions are limited to fines, imprisonment is possible if the employer makes false statements or representations to OSHA, an employee dies

43. 42 U.S.C. § 14503(c).

44. 42 U.S.C. § 14503(a)(4).

45. 42 U.S.C.A. § 14503(g)(1).

46. 42 U.S.C. § 14503(e).

47. *E.g.*, Cal. Corp. Code § 5047.5.

48. *See U.S. Department of Labor Cites Jacksonville Zoo After Rhinoceros Injures Zookeeper*, OSHA News Release—Region 4, U.S. Dep't of Labor, *available at* https://www.osha.gov/news/newsreleases/region4/06252019; *OSHA Fines Fort Worth Zoo After Elephant Injures Zookeeper*, NBC DFW (Mar. 18, 2016), *available at* https://www.nbcdfw.com/news/local/osha-fines-fort-worth-zoo-after-elephant-injures-zookeeper/147168/.

49. *See* 29 U.S.C. § 652(4)-(5).

50. 29 U.S.C. § 666.

as a result of a willful violation, or unauthorized advance notice of inspection is given.[51] States are permitted to develop their own state plans to regulate workplace health and safety, if those plans are approved by OSHA.[52] Under federal law, organizations have a general duty to protect their employees from recognized workplace hazards.[53] Commonly referred to as the "general duty clause," this provision requires employers to "furnish to each of his employees . . . a place of employment . . . free from recognized hazards that are causing or are likely to cause death or serious physical harm to his employees."[54] The Secretary of Labor also issues specific safety standards pursuant to their statutory authority.[55]

Employers are required to post OSHA informational materials in a conspicuous place where employees can see them, with many states having their own materials that must also be posted.[56] Employers are also subject to various recording and reporting requirements for workplace illnesses and injuries.[57] Employees may file complaints with OSHA if they believe that they are being exposed to workplace hazards, and employers are prohibited from retaliating against employees for filing such complaints.[58]

Aside from potential OSHA liability, animal protection organizations can be liable to employees and volunteers for workplace injuries. To address these risks, employees and volunteers should be required to sign waivers upon onboarding, to ensure that the individual understands the potential risks associated with working at an animal protection organization (e.g., potential injury caused by an animal at a shelter or sanctuary) and releases the organization from potential liability. For example, in *Brown v. Northwoods Animal Shelter*, a volunteer who sued an animal shelter for an injury she sustained while volunteering could not recover damages because she had signed a waiver when she first started volunteering.[59] Similarly, in *Biscamp v. Special Pals, Inc.*, a signed written waiver compelled a similar result where the volunteer developed a subsequent bacterial infection.[60]

Most animal protection organizations with employees will be required to obtain workers' compensation insurance, and workers' compensation benefits are typically the employee's exclusive remedy against the employer when the employee is injured on the job, thus limiting the employer's liability. Employers may still be liable for tort claims if the employer acted intentionally, deliberately

---

51. *Id.*

52. 29 U.S.C. § 667.

53. 29 U.S.C. § 654(a)(1).

54. *Id.*

55. 29 U.S.C. § 655.

56. *See Job Safety and Health: It's the Law Workplace Poster*, U.S. Dep't of Labor, *available at* https://www.osha.gov/publications/poster; *see also State Plan Version of Job Safety and Health Poster*, U.S. Dep't of Labor, *available at* https://www.osha.gov/publications/poster#modal-state-poster.

57. *See, e.g.*, 29 C.F.R. §§ 1904.29, 1904.35, 1904.39, 1904.41.

58. 29 U.S.C. § 660.

59. *See* Brown v. Northwoods Animal Shelter, 2011 WL 5072600 (Mich. Ct. App. Oct. 25, 2011).

60. Biscamp v. Special Pals, Inc., No. 01-19-00005-CV, 2020 WL 716739, (Tex. App. Feb. 13, 2020), *rev. denied* (May 7, 2021).

put the employee in danger, or violated provisions of the Occupational Safety and Health Act.[61]

Organizations working directly with animals should also understand the unique disease risks posed by those animals and provide relevant training to their employees and volunteers. For example, many types of animals can spread dangerous pathogens, such as *E. coli* and *Salmonella*,[62] and particular types of animals, such as marine mammals can pose more unique zoonotic disease risk for rescuers.[63] Serious zoonotic diseases like rabies will merit specific organizational policies around vaccination, prevention, and response to possible exposure, if employees are interacting with animals who may be infected.[64] In general, courts recognize that organizations cannot be required to completely eliminate the risk of zoonotic disease transmission but will look to the facts of the situation, including the level of care and precautions adopted by the organization, to determine whether the organization can be held liable for zoonotic disease transmission.[65]

Compassion Fatigue and Burnout

Burnout and compassion fatigue are occupational conditions that can negatively impact a person's health, relationships, productivity, job performance, and career success. Lawyers representing animal protection organizations may be at risk for both conditions due to workplace stress and indirect exposure to the suffering of animals. This section helps readers to gain an understanding of the symptoms and preventive measures associated with these conditions.

Definitions

Burnout is "a syndrome conceptualized as resulting from chronic workplace stress that has not been successfully managed."[66] Burnout is not a medical condition, though it has been recognized by the World Health Organization as

---

61. *See, e.g.*, Salazar v. Torres, 141 N.M. 559, 564 (2007) ("The injury, if determined to be intentional, would fall well outside the bounds of the [Workers' Compensation] Act."). Workers' compensation insurance is discussed further in the section of this chapter on insurance.

62. *See E. coli Infection—Healthy Pets, Healthy People, Centers for Disease Control and Prevention*, *available at* https://www.cdc.gov/healthypets/diseases/ecoli.html; *see, e.g.*, *North Carolina E Coli Outbreak Traced to Petting Zoo*, Center for Infectious Disease Research & Policy (Dec. 23, 2004), *available at* https://www.cidrap.umn.edu/news-perspective/2004/12/north-carolina-e-coli-outbreak-traced-petting-zoo; *Toddler Dies from E. Coli Infection After Visit to Petting Zoo at County Fair*, Food Safety News (July 1, 2019), *available at* https://www.foodsafetynews.com/2019/07/toddler-dies-from-e-coli-infection-after-visit-to-petting-zoo-at-county-fair/.

63. Tania D. Hunt, et al., *Health Risks for Marine Mammal Workers*, 81 Diseases of Aquatic Organisms 81 (2008), *available at* https://www.int-res.com/articles/dao_oa/d081p081.pdf.

64. *See, e.g.*, The Fund for Animals, Rural Areas Veterinary Services Safety Policy, *available at* https://www.ruralareavet.org/info_safety.php.

65. *See* Rolan v. N.C. Dep't of Agric. & Consumer Servs., 233 N.C. App. 371, 385 (N.C. Ct. App. 2014).

66. *Burn-Out an "occupational phenomenon": International Classification of Diseases*, World Health Org. (May 28, 2019).

an "occupational phenomenon."[67] Burnout can apply to anyone exposed to chronically stressful workplace conditions, and it is not limited to professionals in a specific type of role. Burnout is not a sudden onset condition, but it rather progresses through stages, potentially worsening over time unless stress is properly managed.[68]

Compassion fatigue has been defined as "the cumulative physical, emotional and psychological effect of exposure to traumatic stories or events when working in a helping capacity, combined with the strain and stress of everyday life."[69] Like burnout, compassion fatigue is not considered a medical condition. Unlike burnout, compassion fatigue is most closely linked to certain types of professions, namely those that involve helping or caring for people or animals while indirectly being exposed to their trauma or significant suffering. Treating or caring for a suffering animal, or witnessing animal abuse, may constitute indirect exposure to trauma in this context. Even lawyers who do not work directly with animals or witness animal abuse can be indirectly exposed to trauma, for example, through studying the details of animal abuse or reviewing images or videos of animal suffering. Other terms for compassion fatigue include "vicarious trauma, secondary traumatic stress, second hand shock and secondary stress reaction."[70]

Symptoms

While burnout and compassion fatigue are distinct phenomena, many of their symptoms can overlap. For example, both are associated with a variety of mental and physical health consequences that may include headaches, migraines, insomnia, nausea, anxiety, depression, mental health problems, alcohol and substance misuse, chest pain, heart disease, high blood pressure, diabetes, and increased susceptibility to illness.[71] Both syndromes can also cause sufferers to experience a variety of negative emotions about themselves, their careers, their relationships, and the world at large, such as irritability, anger, detachment, numbness, fear, sadness, cynicism, and despair.

Moreover, burnout and compassion fatigue can negatively impact relationships, both professionally and personally. Given the stress and negative emotions associated with these conditions, sufferers can experience tension in interpersonal relationships. Moreover, both syndromes are associated with

67. *Id.*

68. *E.g.*, *id.*

69. *Compassion Fatigue*, AM. BAR ASS'N, *available at* https://www.americanbar.org/groups/lawyer_assistance/resources/compassion_fatigue/.

70. *Id.*

71. *See, e.g.*, Michael Precker, *How Job Burnout Can Hurt Your Health—And What to Do About It*, AMERICAN HEART ASSOCIATION NEWS (Oct. 12, 2022), https://www.heart.org/en/news/2022/10/12/how-job-burnout-can-hurt-your-health-and-what-to-do-about-it.

social withdrawal, isolation, and an unhealthy work life balance, which can lower one's wellbeing and worsen relationships.[72]

Burnout and compassion fatigue may also negatively impact professional success. Both conditions have been found to be associated with lower employee productivity, reduced job satisfaction, and increased thoughts of leaving one's job, all of which can significantly disrupt a person's career trajectory.[73] Both conditions can also lead to self-criticism and doubts about one's own professional competence, which may decrease motivation and hinder professional success. Moreover, people suffering from these syndromes may experience reductions in their ability to think clearly, work efficiently, exercise sound judgment, and concentrate on tasks.[74]

Those suffering from compassion fatigue may develop additional distressing symptoms stemming from their indirect exposure to suffering or trauma. For example, they may become distressed by their inability to erase others' trauma or suffering. Some people suffering from compassion fatigue may be "harmed by the work they do, experiencing intrusive imagery and a change in world-view."[75] This has been referred to as "[t]he 'double-edged sword' phenomenon of working in the animal care industry—you've dedicated your life to making a positive difference for animals, but the emotional stress is draining, exhausting and taking a toll on you."[76]

Prevention and Reversal

While workplace stress is pervasive and indirect exposure to trauma may be unavoidable depending on one's role, burnout and compassion fatigue can be both prevented and reversed. Many of the same preventive or remedial measures apply to both conditions.

Healthy habits and stress-reduction techniques are associated with a reduced risk of burnout and compassion fatigue. For example, healthy behaviors that can improve wellbeing and counteract both conditions include exercising regularly, eating a balanced diet, treating underlying health conditions, remaining hydrated, and getting enough sleep. Practicing self-care and seeking support during times of high stress or emotional difficulty are other worthwhile steps. There are a variety of compassion fatigue and burnout resources that focus on animal activism, which may be particularly helpful.[77]

---

72. *E.g.*, *id.*; Susan B. Haas, *Teetering on the Edge of Burnout? Don't Avoid People*, Psychology Today, Dec. 29, 2016, *available at* https://www.psychologytoday.com/us/blog/prescriptions-life/201612/teetering-the-edge-burnout-dont-avoid-people.

73. *See, e.g.*, Ben Wigert, *How to Eliminate Burnout and Retain Top Talent*, Gallup (Aug. 25, 2021), *available at* https://www.gallup.com/workplace/353831/eliminate-burnout-retain-top-talent.aspx.

74. *See, e.g.*, Sandee Lamotte, *Burnout May Be Changing Your Brain. Here's What to Do*, CNN (Mar. 10, 2022), *available at* https://www.cnn.com/2022/03/10/health/burnout-changing-brain-wellness.

75. *Compassion Fatigue*, *supra* note 69.

76. Colleen Mehelich, *Compassion Fatigue: Emotional Burnout in the Animal Care Field*, BellaDOG (Sept. 2011), *available at* http://compassionfatigue.org/pages/belladog.pdf.

77. *E.g.*, *Compassion Fatigue Resources for Animal Activists*, IDAUSA, *available at* https://www.idausa.org/campaign/sustainable-activism/compassion-fatigue/; Mckenzee Griffler, *Recognizing and Managing*

Positive mindset shifts can also help counteract the negative emotions associated with both conditions. Unfortunately, both conditions can create a vicious cycle in which the conditions themselves intensify one's stress and negative emotions, and the stress and negative emotions then serve to worsen the severity of the conditions.[78] For example, those suffering from burnout and compassion fatigue may be more likely than those not suffering to obsess over negative thoughts, such as their own imperfections or failures or the scale of animal suffering, or to ruminate on negative emotions, such as resentment or hopelessness. This can exacerbate their already-heightened levels of stress and negativity, making the severity of their conditions worse. It can be difficult to break this cycle, but experimenting with different ways to achieve a positive mindset shift may help. Examples include reframing or reevaluating negative thoughts, actively concentrating on positive thoughts or emotions, practicing mindfulness, reflecting on the meaning of one's work, and focusing on digestible solutions within one's control.[79] For animal advocates, reflecting on past successes for animals or spending time with animals in high-welfare settings such as sanctuaries may be helpful.

Developing and maintaining a healthy work-life balance is also crucial. A healthy work-life balance is linked not only to lower stress and greater wellbeing but also to increased productivity, lower turnover, and greater employee morale.[80] Therefore, maintaining reasonable professional boundaries and learning to say no when appropriate can, perhaps unintuitively, boost one's efficacy, productivity, and professional success.

LIABILITY

Contract Liability

An animal protection organization will enter into various contracts throughout the year relating to services, goods, donations, and other arrangements. To ensure that the organization protects its interests and clearly defines its relationships with other parties, such as donors or vendors, it is important for the organization to have clear policies or procedures identifying who can enter into contracts on behalf of the organization (and up to what dollar amount), how contracts are reviewed or drafted, and whether any key terms must be included.

Compassion Fatigue at Your Animal Sanctuary, Open Sanctuary (Nov. 13, 2018), *available at* https://open-sanctuary.org/recognizing-and-managing-compassion-fatigue-at-your-animal-sanctuary/; *Compassion Fatigue*, Humane Pro, *available at* https://humanepro.org/topics/compassion-fatigue.

78. *See, e.g.*, Bryan Robinson, *Burnout Can Intensify Your Job Stress and Throw You into a Vicious Circle*, Forbes (Nov. 14, 2020), *available at* https://www.forbes.com/sites/bryanrobinson/2020/11/14/burnout-can-intensify-your-job-stress-and-throw-you-into-a-vicious-circle/.

79. *See, e.g.*, Kandi Wiens & Annie McKee, *Why Some People Get Burned Out and Others Don't*, Harvard Business Rev. (Nov. 23, 2016), *available at* https://hbr.org/2016/11/why-some-people-get-burned-out-and-others-dont.

80. *See, e.g.*, Wigert, *supra* note 73.

The organization should also have clarity on where contracts will be stored and how important dates identified in the contract (e.g., automatic renewal deadlines or donor reporting deadlines) will be tracked. For organizations with limited resources, online resources may provide helpful contract templates.[81]

Overview of Key Considerations and Provisions

Before executing a contract, it is important to understand the key provisions including who will be a party to the agreement, the length of the agreement, the rights and responsibilities of each party, and how the agreement can be terminated. For example, in analyzing the duration of the agreement, the organization should pay close attention to whether or how the contract can be renewed. Service providers may include auto-renewal provisions, which provide that the contract will be renewed before it expires unless the organization contacts the service provider in writing before a specific date. The organization should take note of these provisions and ensure that it does not inadvertently renew a contract.

The organization should also assess what will be required of each party under the agreement. For example, if a payment is being made, the organization should understand who is paying, when, and how—including, for example, whether an organization will be able to withhold payment if goods or services are inadequate. The organization should ensure that its expectations for any services being provided are accurately represented in the text of the agreement and, if a transfer in ownership is occurring (e.g., of animals, property, or inventory), then the terms of this transfer are clear. If the organization is making any representations or warranties to another party in the contract, it should ensure that these representations and warranties are accurate, sufficiently limited in scope, and that any representations or warranties not included in the written contract are expressly disclaimed. If the organization is relying on representations or warranties of the other party, it should ensure that these statements are memorialized in the contract and not so limited or qualified that they are effectively meaningless. Finally, the organization should pay close attention to indemnification—whether one party will compensate the other for certain costs or liabilities arising from the subject matter of the contract.

Although an organization generally does not want to dwell on the various ways in which a relationship could deteriorate or go wrong, it is important to assess these considerations before signing a significant agreement: arguably, the termination provision of a contract is its most important section. Many contracts will set forth the conditions that are necessary to terminate a contract before the end of its term. One or both of the parties may be able to terminate for any reason or only under specified circumstances. If the ability to terminate is restricted to circumstances in which the other party has breached the agreement, then the organization should ensure that the events giving rise to a

81. *See, e.g.*, *Nonprofit Corporations Form and Sample Documents*, Stanford Law School Mills Legal Clinic, *available at* https://nonprofitdocuments.law.stanford.edu/documents.

breach are sufficiently clear and broad enough to capture the circumstances that would make the organization want to end the contract. The organization should also understand its payment obligations when a breach occurs (e.g., whether any payments are due, suspended, or refunded), as well as the termination process, since some contracts may include procedural requirements like providing written notice to a specific individual or allowing a certain period of time for a party to cure a breach.

Ultimately, every contract is unique, and there are many other important provisions that the organization should understand before executing a contract, including what jurisdiction's law applies to the contract, how disputes are resolved, whether and how terms can be modified or waived, how confidential information is treated, what remedies and damages are available, whether the contract can be assigned to another party, what happens if part of the contract is deemed invalid or illegal, and whether any understandings, agreements, or representations other than those set out in the agreement are superseded by the contract.

Adoption and Foster Contracts

Animal shelters and organizations involved in facilitating the rescue and adoption of animals should exercise particular care in preparing adoption and foster contracts. An organization that adopts out animals should ensure that its adoption contracts clearly transfer ownership of the animal and limit the organization's liability, so that the organization is not liable if the animal subsequently injures other (e.g., by biting someone).[82] Organizations should also be aware that provisions of adoption contracts that purport to allow the organization to take an animal back from the adopter in the case of inadequate care may not be enforceable (at least without a trip to court) and in some cases can undermine the critically important transfer of ownership.[83] Moreover, the organization should be careful about the disclosures associated with an adoption. Even if the organization includes a full release in an adoption contract, it could still be liable for injuries caused by the animal if the organization knew or should have known about an animal's propensity to cause injury and failed to disclose this to the adopter;[84] however, whether the organization knew or should have known that an animal could cause injury is likely to depend on the unique circumstances of each case.[85] Thus, organizations should ensure that they are providing comprehensive disclosures about any behavioral or medical

82. *See, e.g.*, Frank v. Animal Haven, Inc., 107 A.D.3d 574, 574 (N.Y. App. 2013) (shelter was no longer owner of animal after adoption occurred and therefore could not be liable for injury from bite).

83. *See*, *One Size Does Not Fit All When It Comes to Animal Welfare Agreements*, Best Friends, *available at* https://network.bestfriends.org/proven-strategies/editorials/animal-welfare-agreements (recommendations on best practices relating to adoption contracts).

84. *E.g.*, Brown by Brown v. Southside Animal Shelter, Inc., 158 N.E.3d 401, 403 (Ind. Ct. App. 2020).

85. *See, e.g.*, Blake v. Cnty. of Wyo., 147 A.D.3d 1365, 1366 (N.Y. App. 2017) ("Contrary to plaintiff's contention, the fact that shelter personnel may have been informed at the time of the dog's surrender that the dog had previously knocked over a child is insufficient to raise an issue of fact as to the dog's vicious propensities to bite.").

issues relating to the animal and not making any express or implied warranties about the way the animal may behave.

Like adoption contracts, foster agreements can also give rise to a number of complicated issues and should clearly identify the rights and responsibilities of each party.[86] To limit potential liability in a foster situation, the organization may want to include a waiver of liability and indemnification provision within the foster agreement, in addition to disclosing any significant behavioral or medical issues, and identifying any specific conditions that the foster must agree to follow (e.g., taking the animal to foster events, keeping the animal away from other animals). The ABA Animal Law Committee offers resources for foster programs, including a template foster agreement, template foster application, and a compendium of state foster laws and regulations.[87]

Contract Signing Authority

As 501(c)(3) organizations, animal protection charities are required to exercise responsible financial oversight, avoid conflicts of interest, and ensure that documents are stored appropriately. For example, the IRS's Governance Check Sheet, which is used in the course of examining a 501(c)(3) organization, inquires whether there are systems or procedures in place to make sure that assets are properly used, whether the organization has and follows a conflict of interest policy, and whether documents are retained pursuant to a written policy.[88] Thus, aside from analyzing the terms of the contracts themselves, the organization should also have clarity on who within the organization can enter into contracts, where they are kept (and for how long), and how they are created or negotiated, as well as how to identify and manage potential conflicts of interest if they arise. All of these procedures can be incorporated into a standard operating procedure, to ensure that the organization exercises appropriate oversight of its transactions.

Criminal Liability

Criminal law is a branch of law concerned with governmental prosecution of crimes for the purposes of deterrence, retribution, and rehabilitation.[89] While the individual victims of criminal violations are often private persons or entities,

86. *See, e.g.*, Take Me Home Rescue v. Luri, 208 Cal. App. 4th 1342, 1346 (Cal. App. 2012) (dispute between nonprofit organization and individual providing foster care over individual's failure to have animal spayed).

87. ABA Animal Law Committee, *Resources to Help Animal Shelters Build Foster Programs*, American Bar Association, *available at* https://www.americanbar.org/groups/tort_trial_insurance_practice/committees/animal-law/pro_bono_opport/.

88. *See* Governance Check Sheet, IRS, *available at* https://www.irs.gov/pub/irs-tege/governance_check_sheet.pdf.

89. *E.g.*, Harmelin v. Michigan, 501 U.S. 957, 959, 111 S. Ct. 2680, 2683 (1991).

crimes are construed as wrongs against society or the state and as such are prosecuted by governmental authorities. Criminal law is primarily a body of state and federal statutory law, made up of the federal criminal code[90] and the criminal codes of each state. The body of criminal law thus contains a vast number of jurisdictional variations. This section provides a brief overview of the principles of corporate criminal liability, including vicarious criminal liability, potential corporate penalties, and the effect of criminal conduct on 501(c)(3) tax exemption.

Corporate Criminal Liability of Nonprofit Organizations

Nonprofit organizations today often operate or carry out activities in more than one jurisdiction and may therefore be subject to the criminal laws of multiple states as well as the federal criminal code. As a result, lawyers advising nonprofits likely need to understand the criminal laws of multiple jurisdictions with potentially significant variations. Practitioners should analyze all potentially applicable criminal laws to ensure that the conduct of the organization does not create criminal liability. For example, crimes such as harassment or failure to disperse may be relevant if an organization engages in protests or other demonstrations. Organizations that deal directly with animals may need to consider property crimes, such as theft or conversion, as animals are generally considered property under the law.

Nonprofits and other corporate entities are generally subject to the entire body of state and federal criminal law in modern jurisprudence, though this was not always the case. Under an early doctrine of common law, corporate entities were considered incapable of criminal culpability.[91] This doctrine was based on the theory that corporations had no mind with which to exhibit the requisite mens rea for criminal liability. The element of mens rea, which describes the mental state the actor must have at the time of the act in order to be considered criminally culpable, is a necessary element of most state and federal crimes.[92]

It is of course true that corporations do not have minds or mental states in the same sense as natural persons. Nonetheless, the early criminal law approach to corporate entities has eroded over time as criminal laws and regulations expressly applying to corporations were passed into law, and the Supreme Court held in the early twentieth century that a corporation may be held criminally liable for the acts of its agents through a theory of vicarious liability.[93] As the Supreme Court explained, imposing criminal liability on corporations enables

90. *See* 18 U.S.C. §§ 1–6005.

91. *E.g.*, People v. Rochester Ry. & Light Co., 195 N.Y. 102, 104 (1909) (citing Blackstone Commentaries on the Laws of England, c. 18, § 12) (Noting that under the early common law doctrine, it was said that "a corporation cannot commit treason, or felony, or other crime, in its corporate capacity: though its members may, in their distinct individual capacities.").

92. While strict liability crimes, or public welfare offenses, do not have a mens rea element, "[t]he existence of a mens rea is the rule of, rather than the exception to, the principles of Anglo-American criminal jurisprudence." *Dennis v. United States*, 341 U.S. 494, 500 (1951).

93. New York Cent. & H.R.R. Co. v. United States, 212 U.S. 481, 495–496 (1909).

the criminal law system to more effectively deter corporate entities from engaging in criminal conduct.[94] Corporate criminal liability may also have a retributive and rehabilitative effect.

With some jurisdictional variation, a corporation generally faces vicarious criminal liability for its agent's conduct if such conduct falls within the scope of the agent's authority and is undertaken at least in part for the benefit of the corporation.[95] Authority may be actual or apparent, so the corporation need not actually authorize the relevant conduct. In fact, corporate liability may apply in some situations even when the agent's conduct is "against corporate policy or express instructions."[96]

In modern jurisprudence, corporations and other business entities are largely subject to the entire body of criminal law, including state and federal misdemeanors and felonies. Many modern criminal statutes apply to corporate entities expressly, so the legislative intent to create corporate criminal liability is generally clear on its face. This is true even when criminal statutes use terms such as "person" to describe those to whom the law applies, as such terms are typically defined by statute to include corporations and other legal entities.[97]

With respect to criminal penalties, corporations cannot be imprisoned, distinguishing them from natural persons. Nonetheless, corporations are subject to essentially all other penalties as set forth by statute, which generally include fines and sometimes additional penalties, such as injunctions, restitution, and other civil remedies. Some state and federal statutes impose larger fines on organizations than they do on natural persons. For example, a federal felony is generally punishable by a fine of up to $250,000 for individuals and up to $500,000 for organizations.[98]

501(c)(3) Status and Criminal Liability

In addition to the criminal penalties set forth by statute, nonprofits can also face the loss of their tax-exempt status as a result of criminal activity. As a general matter, and as discussed in chapter 2, nonprofit entities in the United States are

94. *See id.*; United States v. Hilton Hotels Corp., 467 F.2d 1000, 1006 (9th Cir. 1972) (noting that the criminal prosecution of corporate agents is not an effective enough deterrent for corporations).

95. *See, e.g., In re* Hellenic, Inc., 252 F.3d 391, 395 (5th Cir. 2001); Corporate criminal liability, 17 Ind. Prac., Business Organizations § 9.6; New York Cent. & H.R.R. Co. v. United States, 212 U.S. 481, 495–496 (1909).

96. United States v. Basic Constr. Co., 711 F.2d 570, 573 (4th Cir. 1983) (citations omitted) ("[A] corporation may be held criminally responsible for antitrust violations committed by its employees . . . even if, as in *Hilton Hotels* and *American Radiator,* such acts were against corporate policy or express instructions.").

97. For example, the federal criminal code defines the terms "person" and "whoever" to "include corporations, companies, associations, firms, partnerships, societies, and joint stock companies, as well as individuals." 1 U.S.C. § 1. *See also* Wash. Rev. Code Ann. § 9A.04.110(17) ("'Person,' 'he or she,' and 'actor' include any natural person and, where relevant, a corporation, joint stock association, or an unincorporated association"); N.C. Gen. Stat. Ann. § 12-3(6) (The word "person" shall extend and be applied to bodies politic and corporate, as well as to individuals, unless the context clearly shows to the contrary."); Ind. Code Ann. § 35-41-2-3.

98. 18 U.S.C. § 3571(b)(3), (c)(3).

those that are exempt from federal income tax pursuant to section 501(c) of the Internal Revenue Code, which sets forth distinct classifications of nonprofit organizations. Each classification has its own criteria for eligibility as well as its own rules relating to matters such as lobbying, tax-deductible contributions, and permissible activities.[99]

Organizations that are exempt from federal income tax pursuant to section 501(c)(3) of the Internal Revenue Code make up a large portion of the nation's more than 1.5 million nonprofits.[100] To qualify for tax exemption under section 501(c)(3), an organization must meet several eligibility requirements, including that the organization must be organized and operated "exclusively" for exempt purposes, such as charitable purposes, educational purposes, and the prevention of cruelty to animals.[101] Many nonprofit organizations that work to protect, shelter, advocate for, or provide care for animals are set up as 501(c)(3) nonprofits.

An organization is not deemed to be operated "exclusively" for exempt purposes, as required, if "non-exempt" purposes make up more than an "insubstantial part of its activities."[102] As applied to section 501(c)(3), "non-exempt" purposes include conduct that is illegal or otherwise at odds with the public good or public policy.[103] This definition is guided by the rationale that tax exemption under section 501(c)(3) is grounded in charity law, under which there is a general principle that charitable purposes do not include acts that are unlawful or against the public good.[104] A 501(c)(3) nonprofit therefore risks losing its tax-exempt status if a substantial part of the organization's activities involve engaging in conduct (or even planning or encouraging others to engage in such conduct) that is illegal or otherwise against public policy or the public good.[105]

In determining substantiality, the quantity or ratio of the nonprofit's conduct that is undertaken for non-exempt purposes is one factor, but it is not the only consideration.[106] The analysis is multifactorial and includes both quantitative and qualitative factors. One important qualitative factor is the seriousness of the illegality or wrongfulness of the conduct. For example, "[a] great many violations of local pollution regulations amounting to a sizable percentage of an organization's operations" may be required in order to disqualify the organization from its 501(c)(3) tax-exempt status.[107] On the other hand, even a single serious wrong or illegal act, such as robbing a bank or committing an act of "planned violence or terrorism," can disqualify an organization, even if its activities are otherwise carried out lawfully and for

99. 26 U.S.C. § 501. See discussion *supra* chapter 2.

100. *The Nonprofit Sector in Brief*, NAT'L. CTR. FOR CHARITABLE STATISTICS, June 8, 2022, *available at* https://nccs.urban.org/project/nonprofit-sector-brief.

101. 26 U.S.C. § 501(c)(3).

102. 26 C.F.R. § 1.501(c)(3)–1(c)(1).

103. *E.g.*, I.R.S. G.C.M 34631 (Oct. 4, 1971); Rev. Rul. 71-447, 1971-2 C.B. 230 (1971).

104. *E.g.*, I.R.S. G.C.M 39862 (Nov. 22, 1991).

105. *E.g.*, I.R.S. G.C.M. 36153 (Jan. 31, 1975).

106. *E.g.*, I.R.S. G.C.M 34631, *supra* note 103.

107. *Id.*

exempt purposes.[108] Other considerations include the quantity of resources devoted to the non-exempt conduct and the connection between such conduct to the nonprofit's primary or regular activities.[109]

Tort Liability

A tort is a civil wrong characterized by the commission of an "act or omission that is unauthorized by law and independent . . . of contract, trust, or other fiduciary duty. . . . "[110] In tort law, "both natural persons and corporations have legal obligations to refrain from causing harm to another person and if harm is done to repair or compensate for it."[111] While tort law originated in common law, modern tort law is a body of both common law and statutory law.

Penalties vary by tort and jurisdiction but generally include compensatory damages for all types of provable losses, such as lost wages and indirect costs. Punitive damages are often permitted for tortious conduct that is deemed particularly wrongful, such as the commission of a tort with malice.[112]

This section provides a brief overview of the application of tort law to nonprofit organizations, including corporate liability via respondeat superior and direct liability; as well as a survey of some common torts in the employment and commercial contexts, including defamation and negligent hiring, training, and retention.

Application of Tort Law to Animal Protection Organizations

Tort law generally applies to nonprofit organizations just as it would to any other business entity. While the doctrine of charitable immunity historically exempted charitable nonprofit organizations from tort liability, this doctrine has since been abolished in the vast majority of U.S. jurisdictions.[113] In a few states, charitable nonprofit organizations maintain some degree of immunity from tort liability,[114] but these exceptions are rare and have limited practical application.

---

108. *Id.*

109. *E.g.*, Rev. Rul. 75-384, 1975-2 C.B. 204 (1975).

110. § 2. Nature of Tort, Int'l Ency. Cyber Law 13883467.

111. *Id.*

112. *See, e.g.*, Cal. Civ. Code § 3294; S.D. Codified Laws § 21-3-2; Tex. Civ. Prac. & Rem. Code Ann. § 41.003.

113. *See, e.g.*, 2 Nonprofit Organizations: Law and Taxation § 14:7 (2d) ("Nonprofit corporations generally are held to the same standards of legal liability for negligence and other torts as are other business enterprises.").

114. *See, e.g.*, S.C. Code Ann. § 15-74-30 ("A bona fide charitable or nonprofit organization or food bank or prepared and perishable food program which in good faith receives distressed food apparently fit for human consumption is not subject to criminal penalty or civil damages arising from the condition of the food unless an injury results from the gross negligence, recklessness, or intentional misconduct of the organization."); N.J. Stat. Ann. § 2A:53A-7 (providing charitable immunity in the context of claims brought by beneficiaries of nonprofit organizations).

Today, nonprofit organizations generally face the same tort liability as any other business entity.[115]

Nonprofit attorneys should be aware that there are significant jurisdictional differences within the body of tort law. Moreover, a nonprofit organization may face potential tort liability in numerous jurisdictions, depending on where the organization operates and where its acts or omissions may hypothetically cause harm to others. Counsel for nonprofit organizations should analyze and gain expertise on the tort laws of all applicable jurisdictions in order to effectively advise on tort liability.

Respondeat Superior Liability

Respondeat superior is a legal doctrine of vicarious liability under which an employer or principal may be held legally responsible for the tortious acts of its employees or agents.[116] Like other corporate entities, nonprofit organizations may face tort liability under the theory of respondeat superior.[117]

With some jurisdictional variation, respondeat superior liability generally applies when at least two elements are established: (1) there was an employment or agency relationship between the tortfeasor and the purported employer or principal, and (2) the tortious conduct fell within the scope of the tortfeasor's employment.[118] Both elements hinge on questions of fact.

The first element imposes respondeat superior liability for torts committed by employees or agents but generally not those committed by independent contractors, with certain exceptions.[119] The rationale underlying this distinction is based on the notion that an independent contractor's work processes, methods, and conduct are not subject to the same degree of control as those of an employee or agent.[120] When analyzing this element, courts look to a number of factors (which vary somewhat by jurisdiction) to assess the purported employer's degree of control over the tortfeasor; the contractual designation of a person as an independent contractor is not dispositive.[121]

115. *See, e.g.*, 2 Nonprofit Organizations: Law and Taxation § 14:7, *supra* note 113.

116. *E.g.*, Judith M. v. Sisters of Charity Hosp., 93 N.Y.2d 932, 933 (1999).

117. *E.g.*, Goldman v. Winkelstein, 263 A.D. 958, 32 N.Y.S.2d 949, 949 (App. Div. 1942) (citations omitted) ("The recognized rule of law now is that a charitable institution is not exempt from the rule of respondeat superior in the event of injury to a beneficiary occasioned by the negligence of its servants or employees."); *Klema v. St. Elizabeth's Hosp. of Youngstown*, 170 Ohio St. 519, 527, 166 N.E.2d 765, 771 (1960) (citation omitted) (holding that a not-for-profit hospital may face tort liability under a theory of respondeat superior).

118. *E.g.*, McDaniel v. Peterborough Cablevision, Ltd., 206 Ga. App. 437 (1992).

119. *See, e.g.*, Zirkle v. Winkler, 214 W. Va. 19, 22, 585 S.E.2d 19, 22 (2003) (citing Walton v. Cherokee Colliery Co., 70 W.Va. 48, 73 S.E. 63 (1911)).

120. *See, e.g.*, *id.* (citing Sanders v. Georgia-Pacific Corp., 159 W.Va. 621, 627 (1976); Clark v. Southview Hosp. & Family Health Ctr., 68 Ohio St.3d 435, 438 (1994) (citation omitted) ("Generally, an employer or principal is vicariously liable for the torts of its employees or agents under the doctrine of respondeat superior, but not for the negligence of an independent contractor over whom it retained no right to control the mode and manner of doing the contracted-for work.").

121. *E.g.*, Stanley v. Ameren Illinois Co., 982 F. Supp. 2d 844, 853 (N.D. Ill. 2013) ("[T]he contractual language is not dispositive if the facts show that in practice the employer nevertheless exercised control."),

With respect to whether the tortious conduct was within the scope of employment, relevant factors may include the motivation of the employee, the connection between the tort and the type of work the employee was hired to perform, the employer's actual or apparent authorization of the conduct, the foreseeability of the conduct, and the time and place at which the conduct occurred.[122]

Under respondeat superior, only the provable tortious acts of an employee or agent can create vicarious liability for an employer or principal.[123] This does not, however, mean that a plaintiff is required to sue the employee or agent in their individual capacity to bring a respondeat superior case against the employer or principal: a plaintiff may sue the employer without suing the employee, may join the employer and employee as codefendants, or may sue the employer and employee separately.[124]

Direct Tort Liability

Business entities, including nonprofit organizations, may also face direct tort liability in some contexts. Whereas the doctrine of respondeat superior holds an employer vicariously liable for the tortious conduct of its agents, direct liability holds an employer liable for its own tortious conduct. Therefore, unlike respondeat superior liability, direct liability does not require the plaintiff to prove that an employee or agent was tortiously liable.

An organization may face direct liability when it directs others to engage in tortious conduct, ratifies an agent's tortious conduct, or owes a duty of care that it fails to perform.[125] For example, an organization may face direct tort liability if it is negligent in hiring, training, supervising, or retaining its employees, as discussed further in the following section.

Common Torts

Negligent Hiring, Supervision, and Retention

Common torts in the employment context include negligent hiring, supervision, and retention. Employers face direct, rather than vicarious, liability for these

---

Stewart v. Lofton Timber Co., LLC, 943 So. 2d 729, 733 (Miss. Ct. App. 2006) (citing Richardson v. APAC–Mississippi, Inc., 631 So.2d 143, 147 (Miss.1994)).

122. *See, e.g.*, Halliburton Energy Servs., Inc. v. Dep't of Transp., 220 Cal. App. 4th 87, 95 (2013) (citations omitted); Walsh v. United States, 31 F.3d 696, 699 (8th Cir. 1994); Sparks v. Jay's A.C. & Refrigeration, Inc., 971 F. Supp. 1433, 1435 (M.D. Fla. 1997); Park v. Southeast Serv. Corp., 771 F. Supp. 2d 588 (D.S.C. 2011).

123. Therefore, "[o]ne of the limitations of the doctrine [of respondeat superior] is that the employer has no liability unless the employee is liable." Dickens v. Associated Anesthesiologists, P.C., 709 N.W.2d 122, 125 (Iowa 2006) (citations omitted).

124. *E.g.*, Walker v. Choudhary, 425 N.J. Super. 135, 148, 40 A.3d 63, 71 (App. Div. 2012) (citations omitted); *See also* Horras v. Leavitt, 495 F.3d 894, 904 (8th Cir. 2007) (citations omitted).

125. *E.g.*, Restatement (Third) Of Agency § 7.03 (2006).

torts because employers generally have a duty to exercise reasonable care in hiring, supervising, and retaining their employees.[126] While these are distinct torts, their elements overlap significantly. The elements vary by jurisdiction but generally require a showing that (1) the employer's decision to hire or to retain a particular employee, or the employer's failure to properly supervise the employee, rose to the level of negligence; (2) such negligence breached a duty care owed by the employer; and (3) such negligence proximately caused harm to the plaintiff.[127]

Negligence in this context generally means that the employer knew or should have known that the employee was not fit or competent for the role.[128] Thus, negligence can be demonstrated either by showing that the employer was not but should have been aware of the employee's unfitness or incompetence for the role pursuant to the employer's duty of reasonable care, or by showing that the employer did have actual notice but failed to properly respond. For example, negligent retention claims can be brought in situations in which an employer fails to appropriately investigate or take corrective measures in response to reports of employee misconduct.[129] In such cases, employers may be liable for claims arising from the employee's misconduct, such as sexual harassment or assault.[130]

This area of tort liability highlights the importance of developing and consistently enforcing strong internal policies regarding hiring, training, supervision, retention, and termination processes; employee conduct requirements and assessments; and investigations into claims of employee misconduct.

Defamation

Defamation is another commonly litigated tort in both employment and commercial contexts. The elements of defamation vary somewhat from state to state, but generally require: (1) a false and defamatory statement of fact; (2) an unprivileged communication of the statement to a third party other than the plaintiff; (3) reference to the plaintiff, or context sufficient for the plaintiff's identity to be understood; (4) fault amounting to at least negligence; and (5) resulting harm to the plaintiff.[131] Corporations may face either direct or vicarious liability for defamation.

---

126. *E.g.*, Sandage v. Bd. of Comm'rs of Vanderburgh Cnty., 897 N.E.2d 507, 511 (Ind. Ct. App. 2008) (citing the Restatement (Second) of Torts § 317 (1965)) ("[T]o determine whether an employer is liable for negligent hiring or retention of an employee, the court must determine if the employer exercised reasonable care.").

127. *See, e.g.*, Bryant v. Better Bus. Bureau of Greater Md., Inc., 923 F. Supp. 720, 751 (D. Md. 1996) (citation omitted).

128. *E.g.*, Shanks v. Walker, 116 F. Supp. 2d 311, 314 (D. Conn. 2000) (citations omitted).

129. *See, e.g.*, Ashmore v. J.P. Thayer Co., 303 F. Supp. 2d 1359, 1375 (M.D. Ga. 2004).

130. *See, e.g.*, Mandy v. Minnesota Min. & Mfg., 940 F. Supp. 1463, 1471 (D. Minn. 1996); T.W. v. City of New York, 286 A.D.2d 243, 246, 729 N.Y.S.2d 96, 98 (2001).

131. *E.g.*, Hoffman v. Bailey, 257 F. Supp. 3d 801, 819 (E.D. La. 2017); Crain v. Lightner, 178 W. Va. 765, 772, 364 S.E.2d 778, 785 (1987).

Although courts' interpretations of these elements also vary by jurisdiction, a "defamatory" statement is generally one that harms the plaintiff's reputation or deters others from associating or dealing with them.[132] A "false" statement may be technically true but misleading given the implications of the statement or the surrounding context.[133] Courts generally look to how a reasonable person would interpret the statement in context to determine its meaning, with words and phrases given their ordinarily understood meaning.[134] A "statement" can include ideas communicated by means other than written or spoken word, such as pictures or other visual representations.[135] Moreover, a "statement of fact" can include a statement of opinion that a reasonable person would interpret as being based on unstated facts.[136]

Practitioners should familiarize themselves with the defamation laws of relevant jurisdictions, as defamation may be relevant to a nonprofit's conduct or rights in various contexts. For example, nonprofits that care for abused animals or advocate against animal abuse may wish to speak publicly, or to like-minded people or groups, about acts of animal abuse that were perpetrated by specific people, companies, or industries. Such statements can create defamation liability in some contexts. In one relevant case, an animal nonprofit was sued for defamation based on its assertion that a kennel was a "puppy mill" and its inclusion of the kennel in a report on the "worst puppy mills in Missouri"; the court, however, found that these were not statements of fact capable of supporting a defamation claim.[137]

In the employment context, nonprofits and other employers can also face defamation liability for making negative statements about an employee, including in situations involving employee references and evaluations. A nonprofit may also be the subject of defamatory statements made by third parties. In such cases, a nonprofit may wish to consider the legal steps it can take to protect itself from resulting harm.

Disaster Response

Many animal protection organizations respond in the wake of natural disasters to help animals in need. Importantly, many states have adopted the Uniform Emergency Volunteer Health Practitioners Act (UEVHPA), which provides protections for health professionals who provide volunteer services as part of a disaster relief effort.[138] The UEVHPA expressly includes veterinary

---

132. *E.g.*, Dossett v. Ho-Chunk, Inc., 472 F. Supp. 3d 900, 910 (D. Or. 2020) (citations omitted).

133. *See, e.g.*, Corp. Training Unlimited, Inc. v. Nat'l Broad. Co., 868 F. Supp. 501, 511 (E.D.N.Y. 1994) (holding that statements could be actionable despite not expressly stating untrue facts as a result of their reasonable implications).

134. *E.g.*, Conroy v. Kilzer, 789 F. Supp. 1457, 1462 (D. Minn. 1992).

135. *E.g.*, Bierman v. Weier, 826 N.W.2d 436, 451 (Iowa 2013) (citation omitted).

136. *E.g.*, Baker v. Galusha, 114 A.D.3d 1124, 1125 (2014) (citation omitted); Reesman v. Highfill, 327 Or. 597, 604, 965 P.2d 1030, 1034 (1998) (citation omitted).

137. Smith v. Humane Soc'y of United States, 519 S.W.3d 789 (Mo. 2017).

138. The American College of Surgeons maintains a list of states that have adopted the UEVHPA on its website at https://www.facs.org/advocacy/state-legislation/uniform-emergency-volunteer-health-practitioners-act/.

services[139] and generally protects a volunteer veterinarian who provides veterinary services from personal liability as long as the volunteer does not engage in any of the following: willful misconduct or wanton, grossly negligent, reckless, or criminal conduct; an intentional tort; breach of contract; a claim asserted by a host entity or by an entity located in this or another state which employs or uses the services of the practitioner; or an act or omission relating to the operation of a motor vehicle, vessel, aircraft, or other vehicle.[140] It also allows a volunteer veterinarian who is not licensed in the jurisdiction where the emergency occurred to practice veterinary medicine there during the emergency, so long as the volunteer is properly licensed in a different jurisdiction.[141] Aside from providing veterinary care, some animal protection organizations will take custody of animals if their owners abandon or are otherwise unable to care for them during a disaster. The Humane Society of the United States has developed a template surrender-to-foster agreement that can be used to memorialize such arrangements in the course of an organization's disaster relief effort.[142]

Intellectual Property

Intellectual property law protects and enforces the rights of the creators and owners of many types of works and creations, such as inventions, literary and artistic works, logos, business techniques, websites, and software. Owners of most types of intellectual property can choose to license their works to others. Intellectual property law can be broken down into the categories of copyrights, trademarks, patents, and trade secrets, each of which is covered by a distinct set of laws that protect specific types of intellectual property. This section covers basic principles of intellectual property of relevance to nonprofit organizations, including copyright, fair use, trademarks, and license agreements.

Copyright

Copyright law, which is governed by federal law,[143] generally protects creative or artistic expressions, such as literary works, music, art, software, and others. To qualify for copyright protection, a work must be "independently created by

139. *See* Uniform Emergency Volunteer Health Practitioners Act, § 2, para. (14), *available at* https://www.uniformlaws.org/HigherLogic/System/DownloadDocumentFile.ashx?DocumentFileKey=632ad7d2-8b4c-eecf-c61e-912840ac3a0e&forceDialog=0.

140. *See* Uniform Emergency Volunteer Health Practitioners Act, § 11, *available at* https://www.uniformlaws.org/HigherLogic/System/DownloadDocumentFile.ashx?DocumentFileKey=632ad7d2-8b4c-eecf-c61e-912840ac3a0e&forceDialog=0.

141. *See* Uniform Emergency Volunteer Health Practitioners Act, § 6, *available at* https://www.uniformlaws.org/HigherLogic/System/DownloadDocumentFile.ashx?DocumentFileKey=632ad7d2-8b4c-eecf-c61e-912840ac3a0e&forceDialog=0.

142. *Foster Care Agreement Between Pet Owner and Foster Care Provider*, *available at* https://www.petfinder.com/docs/disaster/foster-care-agreement.pdf.

143. *See* 17 U.S.C. §§ 1–15.

the author" and must demonstrate at least minimal creativity.[144] Expressions of ideas are subject to copyright protection, but ideas themselves are not.[145] Moreover, facts are not subject to copyright protection because they lack any minimal level of creativity,[146] but compilations of facts may be subject to copyright protection depending on the context.[147]

Works need not be registered with the U.S. Copyright Office, the federal government body that maintains copyright registrations, to qualify for protection.[148] Registration can be worthwhile because it affords practical and procedural advantages to the copyright owner. For example, registration enables copyright owners to bring copyright infringement actions in federal court,[149] and it can entitle copyright owners to additional damages.[150] Moreover, copyright registration, along with publication and a copyright notice, can help deter and protect against a third party's copyright infringement.

A copyright owner can bring a claim for copyright infringement if, without proper license, another person or legal entity violates the owner's exclusive rights under federal law, which include reproducing, copying, or distributing the work; making derivatives of the work; and displaying the work publicly.[151] With regard to digital acts, downloading, uploading, or sharing electronic copies of the work without authority also constitute copyright violations.[152]

One exception to liability for copyright infringement is the defense of fair use. Under the fair use doctrine, copyrighted works may be used for "purposes such as criticism, comment, news reporting, teaching (including multiple copies for classroom use), scholarship, or research. . . . "[153] In determining whether a use qualifies as fair use, a court will consider whether the use is "of a commercial nature or is for nonprofit educational purposes," how much of the copyrighted work is used, and whether the purported fair use will impact the "market for or value of the copyrighted work."[154] A use is more likely to be deemed fair use if it is for nonprofit educational purposes, uses only a small portion of the copyrighted work, and does not impact the copyrighted work's value. In determining fair use, courts look to the nature of the use itself rather

---

144. Feist Publ'ns, Inc. v. Rural Tel. Serv. Co., 499 U.S. 340 (1991) (citing 1 M. Nimmer & D. Nimmer, Copyright §§ 2.01[A], [B] (1990)).

145. *E.g.*, 17 U.S.C. § 102(b); Golan v. Holder, 565 U.S. 302, 328 (2012) (explaining the "idea/expression distinction").

146. *E.g.*, Experian Info. Sols., Inc. v. Nationwide Mktg. Servs. Inc., 893 F.3d 1176, 1181 (9th Cir. 2018) (citation omitted).

147. *Feist Publ'ns, Inc.*, 499 U.S. 340.

148. 17 U.S.C. § 408(a) ("Such registration is not a condition of copyright protection.").

149. 17 U.S.C.A. § 411.

150. *E.g.*, 17 U.S.C. § 412.

151. 17 U.S.C. § 106.

152. *E.g.*, Warner Bros. Recs. Inc. v. Walker, 704 F. Supp. 2d 460, 465 (W.D. Pa. 2010) ("Courts have uniformly held that downloading sound recordings on a peer-to-peer network without the authorization of the copyright holder constitutes an unlawful reproduction of the work in violation of § 106(1) of the Copyright Act.").

153. 17 U.S.C.A. § 107.

154. *Id.*

than the nature of the defendant, and the defendant's status as a nonprofit organization is not dispositive.[155]

Trademarks

A trademark can be a word, phrase, symbol, design, or combination of these things that identifies one's services or goods.[156] In order for a trademark to be registered, it must be distinctive—capable of distinguishing the applicant's goods or services from those of others.[157] For most animal protection organizations, their primary trademark concerns will relate to the organization's name and logo.

Federal trademark law is governed by the Lanham Act,[158] which addresses registration, maintenance, and protection of trademarks used in interstate commerce, though states may also have statutes for registering trademarks used within the state. Before filing a federal registration application with the United States Patent and Trademark Office (USPTO), an organization can search the USPTO websites to determine whether any trademarks have been registered or applied for that are similar and relate to the same services or products.[159] An initial trademark registration is effective for ten years before it needs to be renewed, though periodic filings are required to maintain the registration.[160]

Organizations should take steps to protect their trademarks, since the trademark can be deemed to have lost its distinctiveness if the holder fails to take action against infringers; however, an owner is not required to act immediately against every possibly infringing use to preserve its mark.[161] One potential pitfall for an animal protection organization is failing to control the quality of its trademarks by, for example, allowing licensees to use the organization's trademark without exercising any quality control over the use of its trademark.[162] Thus, the organization should regularly monitor the use of its trademarks, taking action when necessary.

Unfortunately, animal protection organizations sometimes need to take legal action to prevent trademark infringement that confuses donors, supporters, or members of the public. For example, People for the Ethical Treatment of Animals, holder of the PETA trademark, had to pursue legal action to secure rights to the PETA.org website.[163] More recently, a prominent sanctuary in Colorado sued an organization that was using a similar name, URL, and

155. *E.g.*, Harper & Row Publishers, Inc. v. Nation Enters., 471 U.S. 539 (1985) ("The crux of the profit/nonprofit distinction is not whether the sole motive of the use is monetary gain but whether the user stands to profit from exploitation of the copyrighted material without paying the customary price.").

156. *See* 15 U.S.C. § 1127 (defining the term "trademark").

157. Two Pesos, Inc. v. Taco Cabana, Inc., 505 U.S. 763, 768 (1992).

158. 15 U.S.C. §§ 1051–1141n.

159. *See* United States Patent and Trademark Office, *Search Trademark Database, available at* https://www.uspto.gov/trademarks/search.

160. *See* 15 U.S.C. § 1058.

161. Wallpaper Mfrs., Ltd. v. Crown Wallcovering Corp., 680 F.2d 755, 766 (Fed. Cir. 1982).

162. *See* FreecycleSunnyvale v. Freecycle Network, 626 F.3d 509, 515–516 (9th Cir. 2010).

163. *See* People for Ethical Treatment of Animals v. Doughney, 263 F.3d 359 (4th Cir. 2001).

website design after the sanctuary's donors began donating to this other organization.[164]

License Agreements

Intellectual property licenses can be an important tool for a nonprofit organization to ensure that its intellectual property is protected and to demonstrate that the organization is exercising sufficient control when allowing others to use its intellectual property. A license is a contract between the intellectual property owner, the licensor, and a third party, the licensee. The agreement grants the licensee the right to a limited use of the work in exchange for consideration, which is commonly a licensing fee.

A license agreement does not give the licensee ownership of the work or the right to use the work beyond the agreed-upon use.[165] For example, if a license agreement permits the limited use of an image in a particular publication, the licensee does not thereby obtain the right to use, distribute, copy, download, or make derivative works of the image beyond its use in the publication.

The terms of a licensing agreement, like the terms of other contracts, are negotiated by the parties. Therefore, as a practical matter, the ease of obtaining a license can vary significantly depending on the context. Some works can be licensed easily, quickly, and for a fixed fee. On the other hand, some owners of intellectual property may require lengthy negotiations of terms or may only permit very limited use of their works in exchange for hefty fees. Still others may never permit their works to be licensed.

In some situations, nonprofit organizations may wish to license their own works to third parties. Depending on the context, doing so can provide the organization the opportunity to have its works reach new and helpful audiences. Licensing can also afford the organization the opportunity to develop or strengthen collaborative relationships with likeminded organizations. Nonprofit organizations that regularly license works of a particular type (such as images of animals) may find it convenient to use a license subscription service that provides access to a bundle of many works for a fixed fee.

INSURANCE

Overview

Like any business, an animal protection organization can experience a wide variety of losses in the course of its normal operations. Nonprofit organizations

---

164. *See Animal Sanctuary Settles Trademark Case*, Daily Camera (July 6, 2022), *available at* https://www.dailycamera.com/2022/07/06/animal-sanctuary-settles-trademark-case/.

165. *E.g.*, Design Basics, LLC v. Chelsea Lumber Co., 977 F. Supp. 2d 714, 729 (E.D. Mich. 2013) (citing M. Nimmer & D. Nimmer, 3 Nimmer on Copyright § 10.15[A][2]).

typically maintain a variety of insurance policies to protect them from significant unanticipated losses and to help manage their overall risk. Depending on the size of the nonprofit organization, both in-house and outside lawyers can play a variety of roles in the insurance process—ranging from simply reviewing policies to working closely with an outside broker to secure quotes, determine coverage levels, and bind coverage.

Insurance policies are contracts that shift the risk of specified activities from a policyholder to an insurer. Typically, although an insurance policy is a contract, a nonprofit organization may not have sufficient bargaining power to negotiate specific policy terms with the insurer—although sometimes an insurer will accommodate requests. Insurance policies can be long and complex, but animal protection organizations should invest in understanding the contours of their insurance coverage. At a minimum, lawyers advising on insurance should have sufficient command of the level of coverage provided by the organization's insurance policies and the organization's responsibilities and rights when a covered loss occurs.

Although the definitions, conditions, exclusions, and endorsements (i.e., amendments to the standard policy form) in an insurance policy should be reviewed to fully comprehend the coverage provided, the declarations section at the beginning of the policy will be helpful in identifying many key items such as the policy number, the insurer who issued the policy, the named insured or policyholder, the nature of the coverage provided, the premiums to be paid to the insurer, and important terms, such as policy limits, deductibles (often referred to as "retentions"), and endorsements.

If the organization experiences a significant event and needs to notify the insurer of an event that may subsequently give rise to a claim or submit an insurance claim, it is likely to be a stressful time for the lawyer, who may also be determining whether they need to institute a litigation hold or take other legal action while assisting organizational leadership in managing the situation. Thus, to ensure that the lawyer is prepared for these situations, it is prudent to store insurance policies together in a well-organized and easily accessible location, work with a broker around renewal time to review the organization's needs and coverages, and understand when the insurer must be notified of certain events and how to submit a claim when necessary.

Types of Insurance

Although it is not possible to provide an overview of all of the different coverages available to an animal protection organization, there are several types of coverage that may be most relevant.

Commercial General Liability

Commercial general liability (CGL) is the most common type of corporate insurance. It protects an organization from losses associated with third-party claims arising out of a company's business operations. A CGL policy can cover losses arising from bodily injury or property damage (commonly referred to as "Coverage A"), as well as personal and advertising injury ("Coverage B"). Personal and advertising injury includes injuries arising from violating the rights of another, such as defamation, infringement of intellectual property, or invasion of privacy. If an organization creates and distributes a large of amount of content, such as online advocacy videos in connection with public campaigns, it should pay close attention to the personal and advertising injury coverage available under the policy or obtain a separate medial liability policy if needed. These policies will generally contain exclusions for claims that arise from knowing violations of another's rights, publication of statements with knowledge that they were false, and prior publication (i.e., statements made over a period of time if the first publication occurred before the policy went into effect).

Directors and Officers Liability

In certain circumstances and as discussed in chapter 2, a nonprofit organization's directors and officers can face liability for decisions and actions they take within the scope of their duties. Like most for-profit companies, nonprofit organizations can protect their directors and officers from the legal expense of defending these claims by including indemnification provisions in their organizational charter and bylaws and by securing ample coverage under directors & officers (D&O) liability insurance coverage. As a nonprofit seeks to recruit an effective and diverse board of directors, it will be important to potential director candidates that the organization maintains an adequate D&O policy to protect directors from personal liability that could arise in connection with serving on the board.

A nonprofit D&O policy will generally include coverage for directors and officers who face personal liability for conduct arising out of their duties to the company when the organization cannot or will not reimburse them—commonly referred to as "Side A" coverage—as well as reimbursement for the nonprofit when it incurs costs in the course of indemnifying directors and officers for claims made against them—commonly referred to as "Side B" coverage.[166]

Notably, most D&O policies are claims-made policies, meaning that they provide coverage for lawsuits that third parties file against the company, its directors, or its officers during the policy period, regardless of whether the conduct giving rise to the claim occurred during the policy period. In contrast, many other policies are occurrence-based, meaning that they can provide coverage for losses that occur during the policy period, regardless whether a claim is filed during the policy period.

166. Although there are other coverages available under a D&O policy, such as "Side C" coverage that applies to securities claims and "Side D" coverage that applies to investigations of shareholder derivative claims, these coverages will likely have little value to nonprofit corporations.

Property

An animal protection organization with significant real or personal property should also secure property insurance, which covers losses related to physical damage to equipment, land, buildings, or inventory (if the organization sells any products). Property insurance policies will contain many important provisions worth studying, including the valuation clause, which determines how much the insurer will pay if covered property is destroyed or damaged. The organization should also understand whether the property insurance policy can apply to important data, software, or other nonphysical forms of property. If not, many insurers offer separate policies that are specifically focused on issues relating to data loss or cyber security.

Other Common Policies

Aside from these general policies, there are a variety of other specific policies that can prove useful to an animal protection organization depending on the nature of its operations. For example, if the organization depends on vehicles to do work in the field or transport animals, it should consider commercial auto insurance. If the organization relies on employees or volunteers to use their own cars or rents, leases, or borrows cars, it should consider hired and non-owned auto (HNOA) coverage. Likewise, an organization with a large number of employees may want to consider purchasing Employment Practices Liability Insurance (EPLI), which may cover liabilities relating to wrongful acts arising from the employment relationship, such as discrimination, harassment, retaliation, or other employment-based claims. Moreover, if the organization produces a substantial amount of content in connection with its advocacy activities, it may want to secure a media liability policy that provides enhanced coverage for third-party advertising injury claims—including defamation, plagiarism, infringement, or invasion of privacy—beyond the more limited coverage typically included within a CGL policy.

Animal protection organizations can gather an extensive amount of data in the course of their operations, including information about their donors, supporters, employees, and volunteers. As data breach incidents become more common and jurisdictions seek to regulate the responsibilities of companies who experience a data breach,[167] an organization may want to consider cyber insurance coverage, which may offer coverage for expenses relating to business interruption, data breach notification, data restoration, ransomware payments, public relations or crisis management costs, and attorneys' fees. Finally, it may be appropriate for certain employees within an animal protection organization to be covered for potential liabilities associated with their provision of services. For example, the in-house lawyer at an animal protection organization may want to request that the organization obtain employed lawyers professional liability insurance to cover any potential claims against in-house counsel

167. *See, e.g.*, Cal. Civ. Code § 1798.82.

relating to the advice they provide in the course of their job to the company, its employees, or external clients. Likewise, if the animal protection organization employs veterinarians who provide services, the organization may secure a professional liability policy that is specifically tailored to veterinary services.

State Insurance Requirements

Most organizations with employees will be required under state law to obtain workers' compensation insurance, which provides employee compensation and benefits for workplace injuries or illness, though there are some notable differences among the states. For example, workers' compensation insurance is optional in Texas.[168] Although workers' compensation benefits can vary by state, they may include medical expenses, lost wages, and survivor benefits if an employee passes away,[169] as well as disability benefits or vocational retraining benefits.[170] Animal organizations who temporarily deploy employees outside of their home states, for example, for disaster response, should check into workers' compensation insurance requirements in the state to which employees are deployed: some states require that employers obtain workers' compensation insurance even if employees are present in the state for relatively short periods.

Animal protection organizations should also be conscious of state unemployment insurance requirements. Animal protection organizations with a 501(c)(3) exemption are also exempt from the Federal Unemployment Tax Act,[171] but states have their own unemployment insurance requirements. States generally offer nonprofit organizations the option either to pay state unemployment insurance taxes or to reimburse the state for benefits paid to the organization's former employees.[172] If an animal protection organization elects to pay the tax, it will have greater budgetary certainty, through paying a regular tax to the state rather than having to reimburse the state when a former employee makes an unemployment claim. If, however, the organization has a fairly stable workforce, it may be prudent to forgo the tax and elect to reimburse the state for claims actually paid. If no claims are paid, then the organization will not face any cost.

---

168. *See* Tex. Lab. Code § 406.002(a).

169. *See, e.g.*, N.Y. Workers' Comp. Bens., *available at* http://www.wcb.ny.gov/content/main/Workers/lp_benefits.jsp.

170. *See, e.g.*, Cal. Lab. Code §§ 4650, 4658.7, 4660.

171. 26 U.S.C. § 3309(a)(1)(A).

172. *See, e.g.*, *Selection of Financing Method by a Nonprofit Organization Described in Section 501(c)(3) of the Internal Revenue Code*, California Employment Development Department, *available at* https://edd.ca.gov/siteassets/files/pdf_pub_ctr/de1snp.pdf.

CHAPTER 5

The First Amendment: Key Issues for Animal Lawyers

Cheryl Leahy

Introduction

There are a wide variety of constitutional issues that arise in the course of the work of animal protection organizations, in terms of both protection of the organization's impactful advocacy work and finding meaningful opportunities to increase the protection of animals through the law. Many of these involve the First Amendment, which can play out in a variety of ways. This chapter focuses on recurring issues relating to freedom of speech, defamation, and ritual slaughter. It certainly does not constitute an exhaustive tutorial on constitutional and animal law, or even on how the First Amendment may be relevant for lawyers representing animal protection organizations. Rather, this discussion is meant to give a taste of both the breadth of these issues and some insights into how they can arise in practice. The author's aim is to present something of a picture of the real-life practice of animal law in the nonprofit context. The goal is to trigger thoughts and ideas for how to address and reform some areas of law for the benefit of the nonprofit clients, to identify opportunities to use constitutional law to advance and support societal progress for animals, and ultimately to make lasting change to remedy the systemic harms that animals suffer.

Freedom of Speech and Defamation

The Importance of First Amendment Protections in Animal Law

Since the idea of "animal law" is not conceptualized along a particular established doctrine or set of doctrines, it may be better understood as a survey of different areas of law and how they might intersect, or have intersected, with animal protection-related quandaries. Animal law issues can and do come up in every substantive area of law and in every type of courtroom, administrative office, corporate board room, and legislature. Constitutional law, however, may be the single most important area of the law relating to animals, even if the frequency of its use in animal law practice is low relative to other areas. The constitutional protections—or the existential questions of whether and to what extent such protections exist—for both animals and the humans who advocate for them are central questions. The answers may determine who has basic access and visibility under our legal system, and how harms are conceptualized or acknowledged. Connecting the harm to an animal to a constitutionally protected right may be the difference between being able to argue against the assumption that corporate profit is a worthwhile justification for mistreatment or slaughter of animals and not being able to be heard at all.[1] It may also be the difference between the criminalization of activist activity that disrupts or exposes harms to animals and the protection of that activity under the First Amendment.

Advocacy Methods to Increase Transparency

First Amendment issues are particularly important in the context of the widespread institutional cruelty to and killing of animals in corporate settings, such as agriculture, vivisection, and captive animal-based entertainment. Animal cruelty is inherent in the business models and operation of these and many other industries. The sheer size and scope of institutionalized cruelty is massive, dwarfing all other forms of human-inflicted abuse and killing of animals. However, the realities of these industries are nearly impenetrable to the average person. This opacity has been shaped by these industries with protections built into law and regulation. Creative and effective activism is needed to provide even a sliver of transparency in an otherwise opaque system. As has been the case in other social movements, the status quo lacks meaningful transparency and rights of access to information about these exploitative institutions and their practices. Industry interests have used the law and their lobbying power to target speech acts—including filming conditions inside these industries—when they pose a threat to their bottom line. The First Amendment functions as a vital tool for gathering information as a way to bring some transparency into the system, protecting expressive speech and conduct about what is happening and why it matters. Generally, lawyers looking to advise their animal advocacy organization clients on activities meant to uncover or reveal corporate abuses should understand the scope of the First Amendment, whether the activity at hand is within the scope of its protections at all, if any exceptions apply, and if there are additional torts or crimes at issue.

---

1. *See* Nonhuman Rights Project v. Breheny, 38 N.Y.3d 555 (N.Y. 2022) (analyzing habeas corpus claim made on behalf of Happy the Elephant).

False Advertising

The cost to society of opaque industries and hidden harmful practices is a legal system that does not function openly or accurately reflect the will of the people. The marketplace of ideas is not meaningfully operating, and greater concepts of justice and governance cannot be developed around these industries. This is evidenced both by the public being ill-informed on basic factual issues of animal industry practice and by the disparate levels of power and influence in speech by animal industries—mainly in the form of paid advertising—as compared to counterpoint speech.[2] As a practical matter, we are all surrounded by speech about the human relationship with animals from speakers who are trying to sell us the products of the exploitation of animals.

Advertising speech is less protected by the First Amendment than other types of speech. Restrictions are subject to a lower level of judicial scrutiny than non-commercial speech, and with no protections at all for false and misleading advertising. Animal law practitioners have made this a major area of litigation, successfully bringing lawsuits under false advertising and unfair business practices laws challenging labels using terms like "humane." This kind of litigation is especially powerful when the corporate entity claims to care for its animals, which can be an attempt both to protect itself from scrutiny and regulation and to make an increased profit on products consumers will perceive to be higher welfare.

Lawsuits that juxtapose misleading advertising against undercover footage revealing the actual conditions of animals in a company's supply chains are particularly powerful. For example, in 2004 and 2005, Animal Outlook[3] filed litigation, complaints to attorneys general, and a complaint with the Federal Trade Commission (FTC) over use of the phrase "Animal Care Certified" (ACC) on egg cartons nationwide, which was used by the industry trade group United Egg Producers (UEP) to indicate that the producer was a paid member of UEP.[4] UEP had developed a private set of standards for animal welfare that applied to its members, notably including requiring a stocking density standard of 67 square inches of cage floor space per hen: significantly less space than the size of a laptop computer. Animal Outlook conducted investigations of battery egg facilities to illustrate the realities of ACC production.[5] In addition to the crowding itself—a major issue—the investigations documented a number of other categories of mistreatment, including live hens forced to live in cages with their dead and decomposing cage mates, birds stuck in the metal cages, injured birds, and ineffectual or improper euthanasia methods.[6]

---

2. Any speech made from a different point of view or with a different purpose is infinitesimally small by comparison. *See, e.g.*, Harish, *Meat Industry Advertising*, Counting Animals (May 7, 2012), *available at* https://countinganimals.com/meat-industry-advertising/.

3. Formerly known as Compassion Over Killing.

4. "*Animal Care Certified*" *Eggs Exposed*, Animal Outlook, https://animaloutlook.org/animal-care-certified-eggs-exposed/.

5. *See, e.g.*, *Investigation of ISE America in New Jersey*, Animal Outlook (Mar. 7, 2008), https://www.youtube.com/watch?v=CZvFD6VM9yA&t=2s.

6. *See, e.g.*, *Esbenshade Factory Farm Cruelty Investigation*, Animal Outlook (2007), https://animaloutlook.org/investigations/esbenshade-farms/; Press Release, *Video Exposes Cruelty at Dunkin' Egg Supplier*, Animal Outlook (2009) (on file with Animal Outlook).

As evidence in support of its complaints, Animal Outlook provided survey results showing that consumers took the phrase "Animal Care Certified" to indicate a greater-than-standard level of care. Yet, with 90 percent of the industry being members of UEP at the time, the ACC program was definitionally the standard of care in the industry.[7] Ultimately, the FTC and the UEP entered into a voluntary agreement under which UEP agreed to remove the ACC claim and replace it with the phrase "United Egg Producers Certified," with clarifying information underneath stating that the eggs were "produced in compliance with United Egg Producers Animal Husbandry Guidelines."[8]

In a more recent case, the animal protection organization Animal Recovery Mission (ARM) conducted an investigation of Fair Oaks Farm, which operates as a public theme-park style tourist destination for Fairlife dairy.[9] Fairlife is Coca-Cola's specialized dairy brand. The ARM investigation revealed widespread abuse and neglect in the non-public areas of the theme park as well as evidence of misrepresentation by the company regarding the sale of male calves for veal.[10] The investigation garnered significant media coverage, and in 2019, four separate class actions were filed on behalf of consumers under state false advertising statutes.[11] In May 2022, Fairlife announced its intent to make changes to its animal welfare monitoring and to pay $21 million to settle the cases.[12] Prior to the settlement, Animal Outlook and the Animal Legal Defense Fund (ALDF), which had been acting as co-counsel in the case, withdrew because they found the non-monetary provisions of the settlement to be inadequate for improving animal welfare.

Such cases show the limits of constitutional protections: they do not provide a safe harbor for false or misleading commercial speech. Attorneys with clients doing false advertising work should be aware of the role of the First Amendment, as well as understanding which federal and state false advertising and unfair competition laws might apply. There are federal agencies that play a role in the drafting, definition, review, and approval of a given label, and federal and state entities with additional jurisdiction over a claim of false or misleading labeling. Lawyers need to understand and address preemption issues and be

---

7. Interestingly, the UEP's own public relations firm used a marketing presentation touting the strength of the ACC claim and accompanying check mark logo using similar logic, basing its pitch on the level of trust and (lack of) knowledge the public had in the egg industry and government regulators. *See* Press Release, *Laying Out the Facts,* Golin/Harris (2004) (on file with author).

8. Mary Engle, letter "Re: Complaint seeking action against the United Egg Producers for Deceptive Action in Connection with the 'Animal Care Certified' Program," to Erica Meier and Carter Dillard, Sept. 30, 2005, https://www.ftc.gov/sites/default/files/documents/closing_letters/united-egg-producers-uep/uepstaffopinionlettercok.pdf.

9. *Operation Fairlife,* Animal Recovery Mission (2019), https://animalrecoverymission.org/operations/factory-farm-division/operation-fairlife/.

10. ARM alleged that the company had publicly stated that its calves were not going into veal production, but the investigation showed calves being trucked to veal raising facilities. *Operation Strauss Veal Feeds,* Animal Recovery Mission (2019), https://animalrecoverymission.org/operations/factory-farm-division/operation-strauss-veal-feeds/.

11. Alexia Elejalde-Ruiz, *Alleged Animal Abuse at Fair Oaks Farms Under Investigation After Activists Release Graphic Video,* Chicago Tribune (June 6, 2019).

12. Christopher Doering, *Coca-Cola and Others Agree to $21M Settlement for Fairlife Animal Abuse Lawsuits,* FOOD DIVE (May 3, 2022).

familiar with the specific facts of the process and the roles of the relevant agencies.

Defamation

Animal exploitative industries sometimes utilize defamation laws and so-called food disparagement or veggie libel laws against nonprofits and other advocates. Perhaps the most famous of these suits was brought against Oprah Winfrey in 1996.[13] In an episode of her talk show called "Dangerous Food," Oprah interviewed a representative from the beef industry's National Cattleman's Beef Association, a U.S. Department of Agriculture (USDA) official, and a former cattle rancher who is now an outspoken critic of the industry, Howard Lyman. In a segment of the show captioned "Could it happen here?," Lyman discussed the practice of feeding dead cattle to live cattle and called for a ban on the practice in the context of the spread of Creutzfeldt-Jakob Disease or "mad cow" disease.[14] Oprah responded that the discussion "just stopped me cold from eating another burger. I'm stopped."[15] Beef industry trade organizations and cattle companies sued under Texas' law prohibiting disparagement of a perishable food product.[16] Ultimately, Oprah and her co-defendants won the case because the industry plaintiffs could not establish the statutory requirement of knowing falsity. Nonetheless, the suit was a long and expensive battle, even for a highly resourced set of defendants like Oprah and her production companies. The litigation had a chilling effect on mainstream media outlets' willingness to cover stories about the harms of animal agriculture and on taking critical positions on these issues.[17]

In another food safety-focused defamation lawsuit, Beef Products Inc. (BPI) sued ABC News in 2012. The case focused on what the industry called "lean finely textured beef," more widely known as "pink slime."[18] BPI alleged ABC's reporting was defamatory, falsely indicating that pink slime posed a food safety risk, had low nutritional value, and was not in fact beef. The plaintiffs sought approximately $2 billion. ABC entered into a partial settlement for $177 million in 2017 and did not disclose the additional amount.[19]

It is against this backdrop of powerful companies and trade groups suing over who has the right to say what about a product or industry practice that nonprofit animal protection organizations must operate and may find themselves subjects of defamation lawsuits. In 2014, a pet store sued a small animal

13. *Texas Beef Grp. v. Winfrey*, 11 F. Supp. 2d 858 (N.D. Tex. 1998).

14. *Texas Beef Group v. Winfrey*, 11 F. Supp. 2d 858.

15. Aman Batheja, *The Time Oprah Winfrey Beefed with the Texas Cattle Industry*, The Texas Tribune (Jan. 10, 2018), https://www.texastribune.org/2018/01/10/time-oprah-winfrey-beefed-texas-cattle-industry/.

16. *Id.*

17. Diana Knott, *Having a Cow: Reactions to "Veggie Libel" Laws and the Oprah Trials*, *in* Citizenship and Participation in the Information Age 183–195 (Manjunath Pendakur & Roma Harris eds., 2002).

18. James Nord, *ABC Settled "Pink Slime" Defamation Suit for More Than $177 Million*, Chicago Tribune (Aug. 10, 2017), https://www.chicagotribune.com/business/ct-pink-slime-defamation-suit-20170810-story.html.

19. *Id.*

protection organization called Puppy Mill Awareness of Southeast Michigan for defamation and other claims. The organization had demonstrated outside of pet stores and engaged in other activism against puppy mills. The American Civil Liberties Union came to the aid of the nonprofit, characterizing the pet store's lawsuit as a Strategic Lawsuit Against Public Participation (SLAPP) suit.[20] SLAPP suits are those filed in retaliation against a party for first amendment protected action about a matter of public concern. A number of states have banned SLAPP suits, and lawyers should be current on the laws in their states.

Similarly, in 2016, ALDF was sued by Landry's, which owns the Houston aquarium, for defamation based on claims it had made about the treatment of tigers at the aquarium.[21] A local radio station host had made a tour of the tiger enclosure and contacted ALDF about her concerns over the tigers' conditions. ALDF filed a notice of intended suit under the Endangered Species Act and published an accompanying press release and social media posts describing the case and allegations, garnering media coverage. Landry's sued ALDF for defamation and other torts based on this, with the Supreme Court of Texas ultimately dismissing the tortious interference and business disparagement claims because Landry's was unable to make a prima facie case showing its alleged damages were caused by ALDF, but allowing the defamation case to advance, finding that ALDF's public statements were not shielded from liability by judicial proceedings privilege or attorney immunity.[22] The parties settled shortly thereafter.[23]

Cases like these can have significant chilling effects on First Amendment-protected activities, far beyond the specific facts or parties of a given case. Nonprofit animal protection organizations of every size and capacity need competent legal guidance to ensure that the threat of defamation suits does not cause them to minimize or stop constitutionally protected advocacy out of fear.

News media coverage plays a major role in advocacy speech impact and reach and can be protective against retaliation: animal use industries may be less likely to seek to chill activist speech that has already garnered significant media attention. But news media outlets themselves are not immune from the chilling effect of defamation claims. It may be defamation concerns that are driving a relatively recent policy change by newswires, which now often refuse to carry press releases containing "accusation" material unless a lawsuit has been filed.[24] Such policies can affect the ability of animal advocacy organizations to garner media coverage of undercover investigations. Moreover, this policy appears to be disproportionately applied to animal activist speech like investigations. In other subject matter areas

---

20. Press Release, ACLU, *Pet Store Can't Silence Activists Through Defamation Lawsuit, ACLU Tells Court* (Mar. 25, 2014) (on file with the ACLU).

21. Kim McGuire, *Landry's Files Defamation Suit Against Animal Rights Group*, The Houston Chronicle (Dec. 28, 2016), https://www.houstonchronicle.com/news/houston-texas/houston/article/Landry-s-files-defamation-suit-against-animal-10822612.php.

22. Landry's Inc. v. Animal Legal Def. Fund, 631 S.W.3d 40 (Tex. 2021).

23. Landry's Inc. v. Animal Legal Def. Fund, Memorandum Opinion No. 14-17-00207-CV (Texas Ct. App. Oct. 12, 2021), *available at* https://thebrooksinstitute.org/sites/default/files/article/2021-10/Landry%27s%20v.%20ALDF%20and%20Nasser%20-%20To%20Accompany%202021-10-25%20Weekly%20Digest%20No%20109.pdf.

24. Emails on file with author.

outside of the activist context, media outlets seem more willing to publish accusation material (even without corroborating video evidence).[25]

Press releases regarding investigations typically describe: the content of the undercover video; the name and location of the company or companies investigated; any action the nonprofit is taking (such as a legal complaint or a call to action to the company to make a change in its practices); and analysis from organization leaders reflecting the organization's opinion on the investigation, its importance, and implications for the public. On multiple occasions, newswire services have rejected this kind of press release, agreeing to reverse their position only if a lawsuit is filed and the complaint and filing number are shared with the wire service. It is a unique challenge of animal protection law to raise the public consciousness around these issues. With the difficulty of obtaining investigation videos, the often-hostile relationship between the industry and its critics, animal protection laws that are often inadequate, and sketchy enforcement by a small number of oft-unwilling government entities, the newswire policy restriction becomes a Catch-22. Animal groups create these rare and difficult-to-obtain videos to highlight the injustice of the system and bring them into the public discourse but then are increasingly hindered in these efforts because there is no lawsuit filed. This lack of meaningful access to the information and public education channels are additional reasons why it is worthwhile for lawyers and their nonprofit clients to find ways to creatively break new ground in terms of their litigation and enforcement strategies to address systemic harms to animals.

While it is important to understand the boundaries of defamation and advise clients of attendant risks, it is also crucial for attorneys to avoid being cautious to the point of self-censorship of their organizational clients. Constitutionally protected speech that is critical of powerful interests is a crucial part of effective advocacy. Attorneys should have a clear understanding of First Amendment protections and their exemptions (including defamation) and related state and federal statutes regarding harm arising wholly or partly from speech and expressive conduct. In addition, attorneys should advise their organizational clients on best practices vis-à-vis news media communications, both to minimize risk to the organization from a badly quoted or out-of-context statement and to ensure that truthful and impactful messages can be distributed as widely as possible.

Undercover Investigations

Undercover investigations are a key First Amendment issue for the animal protection organizations that conduct them. Indeed, the whole animal protection

25. *See, e.g.*, Press Release, Glancy Prongay & Murray LLP, *A Leading Securities Fraud Law Firm, Announces Investigation of Gaotu Techedu Inc. f/k/a GSX Techedu Inc. (GOTU) on Behalf of Investors*, BUSINESSWIRE (Jan. 4, 2023) (on file at Businesswire); Lauren Feiner, *Facebook Whistleblower Frances Haugen Launches Nonprofit to Make Social Media Healthier*, CNBC (Sept. 22, 2022), https://www.cnbc.com/2022/09/22/facebook-whistleblower-haugen-launches-nonprofit-for-healthier-social-media.html.

movement relies on them to educate the public, courts, and policymakers on animal suffering. By way of background, animal protection organizations conduct investigations in one of three ways: (1) as witnesses recording activities that can be observed from a public place, such as a street where animals are being transported to a slaughterhouse; (2) when the investigator has permission to be in a non-public place (e.g., as an employee) and records with a hidden camera; and (3) open rescues, during which activists enter an area or facility without permission and record video and may also rescue animals who are near death. In the latter category, these activities also raise questions of potential violations of criminal laws, such as trespass and larceny. In all three categories, however, the act of taking the video recording is a speech act, protected by the First Amendment.[26] In order to remove the First Amendment protection, the speech must fit into one of the narrow list of categories of unprotected speech (e.g., defamation, incitement, fraud, or true threats) and must meet all elements of the exception. For example, a false statement or omission of a material fact alone is still protected speech. It would not rise to the level of fraud unless it meets the other statutory or common law elements of fraud.

Prior to employment-based investigations, the open rescue model was more commonly used (and still is, by a small but impactful group of activists), but two federal laws and a number of state-level analogs were passed to crack down on this so-called direct action activism. The Animal Enterprise Protection Act (AEPA) was first passed in 1992 and then amended in 2006 to become the Animal Enterprise Terrorism Act (AETA).[27] A number of state-level analog bills were introduced during this time period and thereafter as well, many of which followed model language from the same conservative group behind the federal AEPA and then AETA.[28] The wording and scope of the state laws vary, but ultimately approximately twenty-eight states, many of which are in the South and the Midwest, passed versions of these laws.[29] They enhanced the penalties for otherwise minor legal violations when they occurred as part of activism against "animal enterprises." In the federal context, acts fall under the purview of the statutes if they are done "for the purpose of damaging or interfering with the operations of an animal enterprise."[30] One way to interpret these laws is that because the underlying protected speech—the heart of the activism—could not be criminalized, the strategy is to discredit and chill that speech by imposing penalties for speech-adjacent actions. The AETA is particularly damaging to speech because it has the potential to brand activism as "terrorism" and can be the basis for long prison sentences for the activist and

26. *See, e.g.*, Marceau & Chen, *Free Speech and Democracy in the Video Age*, 116 Colum. L. Rev. 991 (2016).

27. 18 U.S.C. § 43.

28. *See* Andy Parker, *Beyond AETA: How Corporate-Crafted Legislation Brands Activists as Terrorists*, Nat'l Lawyers Guild.

29. *See* Cynthia F. Hodges, *Detailed Discussion of State Animal "Terrorism"/Animal Enterprise Interference Laws, Animal Legal & Historical Center*, Michigan State University College of Law (2011), https://www.animallaw.info/article/detailed-discussion-state-animal-terrorismanimal-enterprise-interference-laws#::text=The%20laws%20prohibit%20acts%20that,be%20required%20to%20pay%20restitution.

30. 18 U.S.C. § 43(a)(1).

those meeting the law's definition of "co-conspirators." The AETA also brought increased monetary penalties, a restitution remedy for the animal enterprises, and an expanded definition of "animal enterprise." After the AETA's passage, there was significant concern among animal protection groups and activists, with many afraid to engage in what had formerly been pillar social movement activities, such as protests, corporate pressure campaigns, and other speech and expressive conduct. Changing the format of activism to avoid the reach of the AETA (and related state laws) is a rational adaptation to the text of the law as well as the fuzzy scope of what might be included or targeted by it. One downstream effect may have been the decrease in open rescue-style investigations and increase in employment-based investigations in the animal protection movement in the late 2000s and into the 2010s.

Many of the same government entities and industry groups responsible for AEPA and AETA were responsible for the introduction of a number of the so-called ag-gag bills in the early 2010s that targeted investigations by animal protection groups. The impetus for ag-gag laws was the success of employment-based investigations at driving widespread negative media coverage and the attendant outrage and public pressure. Rather than addressing the harms of industrialized animal cruelty, ag-gag laws worked to prevent those harms from coming to light by criminalizing or civilly penalizing otherwise legal activity, including First Amendment protected expression. There were a number of iterations of ag-gag legislation, some of which were clearer on their face about their intention to target investigations, but all of which had the same effect: chilling investigations. Following multiple constitutional challenges, courts have repeatedly found the laws to be viewpoint- and content-discriminatory, for example, with legislative history showing clear animus against "the vegetarian people" and other indications of anti-animal protection bias and intent.[31]

It is against this presumptively strong backdrop of constitutional protection of investigations that we must consider ag-gag and other legal threats that currently exist. Lawyers representing groups that do or are considering doing investigations must take care to understand the risks under state and federal laws and the scope and nature of the constitutionally protected activity. Although many of these laws have been found to be unconstitutional (as discussed above), it is still important to identify whether the state at issue has an ag-gag law and if so, its legal status. Likewise, the AETA is still on the books, as are a number of state-level analog laws. Organizational clients deserve thorough advice and understanding of these risks and analysis of the scope of these laws, with the goal of avoiding excessively chilling conduct without under-assessing risk. Attorneys should also be cognizant of any legal ethics issues that may come into play in this context.

---

31. *See, e.g.*, Lex Burko, *"The Vegetarian People" File the First Lawsuit for the Right to Whistleblow on Farms*, Vice (July 25, 2013), https://www.vice.com/en/article/nzzaww/first-ag-gag-lawsuit-utah-industrial-farms.

Corporate Pressure Campaigns

Another type of expressive activity that is central to social movements generally and to the animal protection movement, in particular, is targeted campaigns against corporations, or individuals associated with corporations, based on their treatment of animals. By their nature, these campaigns identify the corporate or individual targets, the practice at issue, and the recommended "call to action" for the public to take (e.g., writing to the company about cruel practices in its supply chain). These campaigns are often supported by other tactics including undercover investigations, protests, litigation, and legislative proposals. Such campaigns, which are crucial to advocacy and often obtain tangible results, are the sort of expressive speech activity that voices opposition to harmful practices as a way to seek a resolution in the public interest and is traditionally considered presumptively protected by the First Amendment.

For example, following long-term pressure campaigns against Ringling Brothers Circus over its mistreatment of animals—paired with litigation, legislative reforms, and whistleblower activism—Ringling Brothers ultimately shut down, citing "prolonged" decline in demand.[32] Corporate campaigns following investigations have resulted in changes in specific practices, and corporations often drop suppliers after public revelations of animal mistreatment. For example, Nestle dropped the dairy that was the subject of a 2018 Animal Outlook investigation and also expanded its vegan offerings.[33] A Mercy For Animals investigation of a battery-cage egg facility in 2009 paired with a corporate campaign resulted in a first-of-its-kind commitment from the major egg company Radlo Foods to phase out battery cages.[34] Animal Outlook's investigation of Tyson Foods in 2017 revealed the painful practice of shoving small plastic "nose bones" through the nostrils of male broiler breeders (i.e., the parent flocks of chickens raised and killed for their meat), and this video was used as the basis of a campaign that resulted in Tyson's prompt agreement to end the practice. Subsequent campaign efforts resulted in seventeen of the top twenty U.S. poultry companies committing to either ceasing the use of nose bones or stating that they did not use them.[35]

Such pressure campaigns can attract retaliation and have serious implications for nonprofit animal protection groups and the people who work with them. The "SHAC 7" case is the most vivid example. Stop Huntingdon Animal Cruelty (SHAC) was a grassroots animal advocacy organization with the somewhat unusual characteristic of being single-target campaign focused. As is

32. *See* Sarah Maslin Nir & Nate Schweber, *Ringling Bros. Circus Takes Final Bow*, N.Y. Times (May 21, 2017), https://www.nytimes.com/2017/05/21/nyregion/ringling-brothers-circus-takes-final-bow.html#::text=-After%20146%20years%2C%20Ringling%20Brothers%20and%20Barnum%20%26%20Bailey%20is%20closing,to%20its%20operator%2C%20Feld%20Entertainment.

33. *Nestle to Add Vegan Cheese and Bacon to Plant-Based Offerings*, Animal Outlook, Oct. 10, 2019, https://animaloutlook.org/nestle-to-add-vegan-cheese-and-bacon-to-plant-based-offerings/.

34. *Mass.-Based Egg Producer Vows to Go Cage-Free*, Foster's Daily Democrat (Apr. 6, 2009), https://www.fosters.com/story/news/local/2009/04/06/mass-based-egg-producer-vows/52038497007/.

35. *Tyson, Others to End Cruel Practice of Nose Boning*, Animal Outlook, https://chickenindustry.com/timeline/boning-gets-boot/.

evident by its name, its mission was to stop major pharmaceutical testing contractor Huntingdon Life Sciences (HLS) from conducting cruel animal tests and otherwise mistreating the animals in its care. SHAC used a number of typical—and traditionally constitutionally protected—tactics, including protests, media strategy, and investigations. Footage from inside the HLS labs showed cruel experiments on beagles and monkeys, and violent and mocking behavior of the researchers toward the animals.[36] SHAC also used tertiary targeting, that is, applying pressure campaigns not only to HLS itself but also to companies that did business with HLS, such as their insurance providers. In addition, SHAC used loud and strongly worded critiques and tactics, such as demonstrating near the homes of individuals associated with HLS. There were also allegations of property damage linked to the SHAC campaign, but none directly implicating the SHAC group itself.[37] Nonetheless, six SHAC members and the nonprofit organization itself were charged with a federal crime for conspiracy to violate the AEPA, with some of the defendants also being charged with stalking, harassment, and related conspiracy offenses.[38] The core factual focus of the case was on SHAC's website and other public statements, in which SHAC stated that it operated within the bounds of the law but that it supported and recognized those who chose not to. SHAC described both legal and illegal activity (such as taking dogs from HLS facilities and property damage) and included names and addresses of HLS affiliates in its public statements.[39] Ultimately, the SHAC individuals lost their constitutional challenge to the AEPA and were given prison sentences ranging from one to six years, held liable for fines and restitution, and served significant prison time for their activism.[40] HLS itself was acquired and still conducts animal tests.

There are torts and statutory causes of action attorneys should be aware of in corporate pressure campaign contexts, such as those protecting trade secrets. However, the legal risks and issues that come up in these cases are not much different than those that arise in other types of advocacy. These cases may generate pushback because of the influence and power of the corporate targets, so it is important to be cognizant of that. There is also an important role that attorneys can play on the advocacy side in corporate pressure campaigns. At their core, these campaigns are about negotiating agreements in a private law context where the public law is absent or inadequate. Attorneys should bring strong negotiation and transactional skills to their clients who are engaged in these kinds of campaigns.

---

36. Footage included in The Animal People (Dennis Henry Hennelly & Casey Suchan dirs., 2019).

37. *See U.S. v. SHAC*, Ctr. for Constitutional Rights, Aug. 3, 2016, https://ccrjustice.org/home/what-we-do/our-cases/us-v-shac-7.

38. United States v. Fullmer, 584 F.3d 132 (3d Cir. 2009).

39. *Id.* at 139.

40. *See* Lauren Gazzola, *Bad Things Happened: Metaphorical Fingerprints, Constellations of Evidence, and "Guilt for Association,"* 40 Vt. L. Rev. 813, 2016.

The Establishment Clause

Ritual Slaughter

The First Amendment also addresses freedom of religion and the relationship between religion and the state. A key animal-related area of intersection between religion and state action is federal regulation of ritual livestock slaughter. One of the very few federal legal protections for farmed animals is the Humane Methods of Slaughter Act (HMSA), which is enforced by the Food Safety and Inspection Service (FSIS) of the USDA and sets requirements for "humane" slaughter for livestock (excluding birds and fishes). The law identifies two separate ways a slaughter method can meet the statutory definition of "humane." The first is "conventional slaughter," which requires insensibility by a single blow or shot.[41] The other way a slaughter method can qualify as humane under the HMSA is by meeting the requirements of its ritual slaughter provision, which allows for a religious or ritual method to render an animal insensible via exsanguination, that is, by the simultaneous and instantaneous severing of the carotid arteries.[42] The key distinction between conventional and ritual slaughter is that there is no stunning requirement under the latter. Religions that have ritual slaughter method rules—namely Judaism and Islam—created these rules to minimize slaughter-related suffering through rapid bleed-out, long before other options (like pneumatic captive bolt pistols or guns) existed. The purpose of the ritual slaughter provision is to accommodate the religious interpretations and traditions that prohibit stunning or rendering the animal unconscious before slaughter. If a slaughterhouse performing ritual slaughter elects to use stunning (which it does have the option to do under the law), then that stunning must comply with the HMSA and its regulations. Namely, it needs to be quick and effective in rendering the animal insensible.[43] In both ritual and non-ritual slaughter plants, FSIS inspectors are charged with and have the authority to issue enforcement actions relating to animal handling.

The religious authorities who certify the ritual slaughter process are granted significant deference in determining compliance, inspections, and enforcement.

---

41. 7 U.S.C. § 1902(a), "in the case of cattle, calves, horses, mules, sheep, swine, and other livestock, all animals are rendered insensible to pain by a single blow or gunshot or an electrical, chemical or other means that is rapid and effective, before being shackled, hoisted, thrown, cast, or cut." Most commonly, a captive bolt pistol is used to shoot a bolt through the animal's forehead, penetrating the skull and then the brain. This method is notoriously prone to user error, and prolonged pain and suffering are commonplace occurrences at slaughterhouses. *See, e.g.*, *Central Valley Meat Investigation*, Animal Outlook (2012), https://animaloutlook.org/investigations/central-valley-meat/; Lukas Jasiunas, *How Effective Is Captive Bolt Stunning?*, Faunalytics (May 2, 2017), https://faunalytics.org/effective-captive-bolt-stunning/.

42. "Either of the following two methods of slaughtering and handling are hereby found to be humane: [conventional slaughter under (a)] . . . or (b) by slaughtering in accordance with the ritual requirements of the Jewish faith or any other religious faith that prescribes a method of slaughter whereby the animal suffers loss of consciousness by anemia of the brain caused by the simultaneous and instantaneous severance of the carotid arteries with a sharp instrument and handling in connection with such slaughtering." 7 U.S.C. § 1902(b).

43. 9 C.F.R. § 313; *Humane Handling of Livestock and Good Commercial Practices in Poultry*, Food Safety and Inspection Service, Oct. 1, 2021 at https://www.fsis.usda.gov/sites/default/files/media_file/2021-11/21_IM_Humane-Handling-GCP-10012021.pdf.

The process has given rise to constitutional critiques based on the Establishment clause, which prohibits the government from "establishing" a religion.[44] FSIS removes itself from the inspection of the crucial slaughter moment, deferring to the private religious body that a given facility hires to review the slaughter method.[45] This removal reflects the intention of the statute to defer to religious authorities and to acknowledge that religious laws are complex, with religious authorities alone qualifying as the experts on compliance. As a result, FSIS created what it terms the "ritual bubble":[46] that portion of the slaughter process (including the moment of slaughter when the animal is cut and bled out) that FSIS intentionally removes from the scope of its inspections.

There are unique issues raised by the ritual slaughter process and the ritual bubble that seem to be a direct result of the attempt to accommodate First Amendment free exercise of religion concerns. Agency failure to analyze a ritual method of slaughter—even whether it is a violation of the statutory language—and to instead defer to religious authority can have major implications for animal suffering.

Animal Outlook v. Superior Farms

This problem is illustrated by the 2017 Animal Outlook investigation of the Superior Farms lamb slaughterhouse in California.[47] The facility is the largest U.S. lamb slaughterhouse supplying meat and skin to major corporations, such as Wal-Mart, Kroger, and Ugg Boots. Importantly for the eventual lawsuit (discussed below), it also supplied meat to the USDA for food aid programs like the National School Lunch Program and to the Department of Defense for military commissary products. The slaughterhouse represented itself as engaging in ritual slaughter using halal methods.[48] As a part of its ritual slaughter process, Superior Farms elected to engage in pre-slaughter stunning using a "head and body" stunner, which is placed on the head and torso of the lamb and delivers an electrical shock with the intent to render them insensible.[49] Animal

44. *See, e.g.*, Bruce Friedrich, *Ritual Slaughter in the "Ritual Bubble": Restoring the Wall of Separation Between Church and State*, 17 Vt. J. Env't L. 222 (2015–2016).

45. There are a number of concerns about the inadequacy of private oversight of halal compliance. *See, e.g.*, *Why the U.S. Halal Food Industry Needs Better Oversight*, The Week (Jan. 8, 2015), https://theweek.com/articles/441549/why-halal-food-industry-needs-better-oversight.

46. *Id.*

47. *Horror at Superior Farms—Lamb Slaughter Exposed*, Animal Outlook (2017), https://animaloutlook.org/investigations/superior-farms/.

48. Notably, many of Superior Farms' products were not labeled halal, presumably because a significant portion of the customer base was not seeking halal products. This appears to be commonplace in ritual slaughter, despite the public perception that ritual slaughter is small, niche, and only for the relevant observant religious consumers. *See, e.g.*, Esther Honig, *You Might Be Eating Halal Meat and Not Even Know It*, NPR (Apr. 5, 2018), https://www.npr.org/sections/thesalt/2018/04/05/599520906/you-might-be-eating-halal-meat-and-not-even-know-it.

49. This implicates both religious and federal law: in many schools of thought in Islamic law, stunning prior to slaughter is not permissible. *See, e.g.*, *Stunning Animals Prior to Slaughter*, Halal Food Standards Alliance of America, https://www.hfsaa.org/stunning-animals-prior-to-slaughter/.

Outlook's investigation found a number of humane handling concerns, both inside and outside of the ritual bubble.

There are specific signs of sensibility FSIS inspectors are trained to look for, including rhythmic breathing, eye blinking, and "righting" attempts to bring their body upright.[50] This evaluation for signs of sensibility by FSIS inspectors would happen after the throat is cut, placing it outside of the ritual bubble, and therefore within FSIS's scope of responsibility to detect. Thus, for a ritual slaughterhouse that chooses to stun animals, the stunning itself must comply with both religious law (which requires a weak enough electrical current so it does not cause death) and with federal law (which requires it to be a strong enough electrical current so that the animal is rendered insensible to pain). The stunning method, its execution, and the machinery must be calibrated precisely and consistently to render the animal reliably insensible to pain for long enough that the animal does not regain sensibility before or after the throat cut but not to cause cardiac arrest. This is a very difficult balance to strike in practice and seems an impractical structure to yield effective stunning.

At the Superior Farms slaughterhouse, Animal Outlook's investigation documented signs of sensibility after the lambs' throats and tails had been cut. In 89 percent of the cases depicted on video, the animals moved at the moment of tail cut (which happened after the throat cut).[51] Assuming *arguendo* that this movement indicated sensibility, the fault in the stunning process could have happened inside or outside the ritual bubble. The short time between the two steps (with the throat cut happening inside the ritual bubble and the tail cut outside of it) complicates enforcement potential. No one inspector oversees the whole process, or at least enough of it to determine compliance with either secular or religious law. If the two authorities disagreed, which would govern?

Looking inside the ritual bubble, the slaughter method used at Superior Farms at the time of Animal Outlook's investigation involved two cuts across the underside of the animal's neck. The slaughterer would slice the neck open on one side, cutting one carotid artery, lift the knife, and cut the other carotid artery on the other side with a second slice, thereby preserving the esophagus.[52] As per the HMSA, the ritual method must meet a number of requirements to be deemed "humane," including (1) compliance with the rules of a religious method, (2) with the killing done via exsanguination of the brain, and (3) accomplished by *simultaneous and instantaneous* severing of the carotid arteries.[53] Even leaving aside (1) and (2) for the purposes of this discussion (even though they both raise major questions), the two-cut slaughter method used by Superior Farms appears to be a clear violation of part (3) because the carotids are not severed simultaneously. If it turns out the slaughterhouse is in fact not compliant with ritual methods, per deference to religious authorities, then no meaningful inspection is taking place within the ritual bubble. Slaughtering

50. *Id.*

51. Complaint, United States v. Transhumance Holding Co., U.S. Dist. Ct. Est. Cal., May 21, 2019, https://cok.net/wp-content/uploads/2019/06/complaint-1.pdf.

52. This method may have been used in order to sell the esophagi as dog treats. *Id.*

53. 7 U.S.C. § 1902(b).

without inspection is prohibited under FSIS rules and cannot take place where the meat is to be sold for human consumption.

Based on Superior Farms' sale of products to federal government agencies, Animal Outlook initiated a False Claims Act (FCA) lawsuit, arguing that Superior Farms was in violation of the underlying terms of a purchase contract that required compliance with the HMSA.[54] Ultimately, the Department of Justice (DOJ) intervened in the case. The DOJ rarely intervenes in FCA lawsuits, and its involvement suggested a strong case.[55] The dispute was eventually resolved through a settlement and consent decree, which required the appointment of a humane handling coordinator to oversee compliance with the HMSA, including the effectiveness of the stunning process and evaluation for sensibility after slaughter.[56] Notably, the agreement did not address the two-cut method, nor did Superior admit to any wrongdoing.

This case illustrates some of the difficulties with the First Amendment's religion provisions in the context of animal slaughter. The free exercise clause itself and the jurisprudence interpreting it do not seem to require categorical deference to the religious authorities.[57] If an organizational client is interested in engaging in this issue, a lawyer's familiarity with the federal law governing slaughter, the constitutional background and context, and real-life practices could help the organization develop an effective approach in this area.

54. *Id.*

55. Dave Nadler, *The False Claims Act: A Novel Tool for Enforcing Federal Animal Welfare Laws*, ABA TIPS, *available at* https://www.americanbar.org/groups/tort_trial_insurance_practice/committees/animal-law/fal-cla/.

56. *Consent Decree Between the United States Department of Agriculture Food Safety and Inspection Service and Defendant Transhumance Holding Company, Inc.* (2019), https://cok.net/wp-content/uploads/2019/06/consent-decree-1.pdf and corresponding *Settlement Agreement*, https://cok.net/wp-content/uploads/2019/06/settlement-1.pdf.

57. Jones v. Butz, 374 F.Supp. 1284 (D.C.N.Y. 1974) (substantively evaluating ritual slaughter and whether it meets the definition of humane as Congress intended: "Plaintiffs [who argue ritual slaughter is inhumane] assert that such legislative inconsistency [allowing shackling and hoisting animals while conscious for ritual slaughter but not for conventional slaughter] can be explained only as so clear a piece of deference to the tenets of one religious group as to violate the First Amendment. . . . Accepting, arguendo, that this constitutes an inconsistency in the statute, the question remains as to whether that inconsistency in any way violates the plaintiffs' rights under the Establishment Clause of the Free Exercise Clause of the First Amendment. Since Congress has determined that the Jewish ritual method is humane under the Act . . . if there is inconsistency in the statute the plaintiffs have not persuaded us that they have suffered a deprivation of rights under the First Amendment.").

CHAPTER 6

DEIJ in the Practice of Animal Law

Akisha Townsend Eaton and Michael Swistara

Introduction

Few would dispute that the horrific, video-captured police murder of George Floyd, and numerous other racially motivated killings and hate crimes, have significantly amplified the national discourse on race. Overnight, millions of activists around the world took to the streets in protest. A seismic wave of corporations and organizations released statements and campaigns committing themselves to internal and external practices that advanced racial justice.[1] The American Bar Association[2] and other bar associations[3] responded with their own statements recognizing the need to address police brutality through reforms and renewed efforts to build public trust. Businesses and nonprofit organizations, including animal nonprofits, responded in myriad ways as well. Some released statements in solidarity with racial justice movements, while others created diversity-focused workgroups, toolkits, and resources. Still others would view themselves as taking a "neutral" stance, opting to make no public statements. And, at least internally, some would disavow altogether the connection of racial justice to their animal advocacy group. Regardless of the response chosen, a common theme emerged in the animal protection movement: almost all major organizations acknowledged that diversity (specifically, racial diversity) within the animal advocacy movement was important but largely lacking.

1. Alex Altman, *Why the Killing of George Floyd Sparked an American Uprising*, TIME (2020), https://time.com/5847967/george-floyd-protests-trump/.

2. *ABA President Judy Perry Martinez Statement Re: Events in Minneapolis, Elsewhere and Equal Justice* American Bar Association (May 29, 2020), https://www.americanbar.org/news/abanews/aba-news-archives/2020/05/aba-president-judy-perry-martinez-statement-re–events-in-minnea/.

3. *Statements on George Floyd Death and Protests*, American Bar Association, https://www.americanbar.org/groups/bar_services/resources/resourcepages/floydstatements/.

In the absence of a conversation on broader principles of equity, inclusion, and justice, tensions and lack of clarity can arise when organizations and those representing them struggle to articulate the ways in which diversity is critical to achieving organization missions. This chapter is dedicated to the exploration of issues in Diversity, Equity, Inclusion and Justice (DEIJ) as they apply to attorneys representing animal protection organizations. As there is no universal definition of DEIJ and its applications vary,[4] we consider many of the unique ways that it is most applicable to animal protection organizations. As leaders continue to explore ways to increase diversity in their organizations, seldom do these efforts extend to broader principles of equity, inclusion, and justice. Only by understanding the evolving nature and complexity of these concepts can they effectively be applied in practice. Attorneys representing animal protection organizations are in the position to have tremendous positive influence on the organization's operations, ethics, governance, reputation, and even public policy as these areas apply to the advancement of DEIJ for the benefit of animals and those who advocate for them.

Though the authors understand that a wide variety of views exist in our movement on this topic and that avoiding liability is often a top concern, this chapter is especially written for attorneys who wish to advance DEIJ principles, supporting organizations in developing intentional and effective DEIJ practices. Even though it is encouraging to cover this frequently overlooked topic, we caution readers not to accept the myth that DEIJ is a tangential add-on to this important and continuing evolving field. Indeed, the more DEIJ is examined in the broader context of animal law and advocacy, the easier it becomes to understand the important ways in which it has been and continues to be integral to the very existence of the movement as well as essential for its continued success and sustainability. There is likely not a topic in this book that does not somehow touch upon matters of DEIJ.

A number of misperceptions exist around DEIJ in animal advocacy that this chapter hopes to dismantle. One of the most common misconceptions is that a focus on DEIJ somehow takes away from animal advocacy rather than informing and strengthening it. For those who have never and will never have to face bias on the basis of belonging to an underrepresented group, it may even become tempting to silo DEIJ into an "other social justice" issue bucket that is either entirely irrelevant or only minimally applicable to the larger field of animal advocacy. At best, organizations and their attorneys that adopt this view, risk working with an incomplete toolset in which solutions become more complicated and far more prolonged than they need to be. At worst, such a view may lead to detrimental outcomes for animals, animal advocates, and communities.[5] Where diversity is implemented to the exclusion of equity and

---

4. *Lawyers' Toolkit for Diversity & Inclusion, Report of the DC Bar Communities Diversity & Inclusion Working Group Best Practices Subcommittee*, DC Bar, https://www.dcbar.org/getmedia/c10cfbb4-3ccb-4d33-82c4-f481d7b83ea0/Lawyers-Toolkit-for-Diversity-Inclusion.

5. *How Is Your Community Doing When It Comes to Lifesaving: National Overview*, Best Friends Animal Society, https://bestfriends.org/no-kill-2025/animal-shelter-statistics?_ga=2.46951200.600336608.1675214738-1680718345.1673147528.

inclusion, advocates from diverse backgrounds experiencing daily lived experiences that inform matters of DEIJ may feel isolated and minimized in their roles. These feelings ultimately lead to the suppression of solutions for some of the most pressing issues facing animals in an increasingly diverse society.

The breadth of DEIJ can never adequately be condensed to a single chapter, book, or toolkit. We cannot possibly address every single scenario, question, conflict, or opportunity that may arise within animal law as it intersects with DEIJ. Instead, we believe it would be most useful to cover topics within DEIJ that resonate to our own professional and personal experiences and interests as diverse professionals, as those experiences relate to animal law and, by extension, to lawyers representing animal protection organizations. Below, we offer a brief introduction and summary of our backgrounds. At first glance, our co-authorship of this chapter may seem unusual to some, given our different backgrounds. Yet, our collaboration highlights the dedication and interest of a larger group of advocates, bringing a variety of perspectives and experiences to a shared goal of advancing the status of animals.

Akisha Townsend Eaton

I am an African American woman and attorney who has practiced in the field of animal law for more than a decade. I am a descendant of enslaved people and daughter of parents who grew up under and broke barriers during the Jim Crow segregation era. I am seen as and come to my professional and personal work as a Black woman. In my work and contributions to the field, my personal identity and experiences have never allowed me the privilege of seeing racial and social justice as "other" movements. Rather, I have always viewed animal justice as part of a spectrum of the larger movement for justice. From this lens, I have also been able to examine the ways in which many of the successes and failures within the animal advocacy movement have hinged upon the ways racial justice has been embraced or ignored, and whether critical opportunities have been embraced or missed. Moreover, I have always viewed the animal protection movement as "my" movement, and often use this terminology when presenting at professional conferences and engaging in dialogue. Though I know it is well-meaning, I always pause whenever I hear colleagues state that "we" need to make "our" movement more inclusive by opening it up to "people from diverse backgrounds," as though people like myself (whether visible or invisible) are not already an important part of the movement. I envision a movement in which people automatically believe that "our" movement is "my" movement, too.

I have worked at a number of small and large animal protection organizations throughout my career. I currently work at a nonprofit, Companions and Animals for Reform and Equity (CARE), a Black, Indigenous, People of Color (BIPOC)-led nonprofit seeking to advance human and animal well-being. Outside of work, I am active in my local National Association for the Advancement of Colored People (NAACP), having served in leadership and chair roles in the environmental, economic development, and legal redress sections.

Michael Swistara

I am a lawyer, scholar, and activist fighting for animal liberation and against all forms of oppression. Professionally, I work as a civil litigator to advance the interests of nonhuman animals. I have prior experience at nonprofits both large and small, working on litigation and policy across a range of subjects that includes worker protection and Fair Workweek laws, environmental justice, animal advocacy, and consumer protection. My academic work has primarily focused on the intersection between animal law and other areas of social justice, including work on applying abolitionist and transformative justice approaches to situations where animals are harmed. As a cis-gendered non-disabled White man in the animal movement, I understand that I come at this work with a tremendous amount of privilege. This privilege has insulated me, and coming to understand liberation as one collective movement for justice will continue to be a lifelong journey.

I am also an active member of the American Bar Association in the Animal Law Committee and International Animal Law Committee, as well as an engaged member of my local community. I have written animal protection statutes and worked with community members and legislators to get them passed, including a recent win to consider the interests of companion animals during divorce proceedings in Washington, DC. I served as a consultant to the DC Police Reform Commission, where I advocated for getting police out of traffic enforcement, and as an organizer I have been part of a larger movement to pressure the city council to invest in transformative approaches to public safety. I am deeply honored to have collaborated with Akisha on this chapter. She is a mentor and friend whose work I deeply admire.

Our contributions were produced on our own time, and solely reflect our personal opinions and not those of any organization with which we are or have been affiliated.

What is DEIJ?

Diversity

Diversity, Equity, Inclusion, and Justice, or DEIJ, takes on many forms, but the starting point for many organizations that find they are lacking in diversity is to seek to increase the numbers of board members, staff, and volunteers from underrepresented backgrounds. While such an effort can be well-meaning, diversity initiatives that address equity, inclusion, and justice at the beginning are more likely to be successful. Moreover, a focus on equity, inclusion, and justice can improve diversity initiatives when those from underrepresented backgrounds can see that these efforts are genuine rather than performative. Some non-exhaustive questions that might be helpful in assessing and improving diversity in animal protection organizations include:

- Are the board, leadership, staff, and volunteers reflective of a diverse society?
- Is diversity required in the pool of talent for hiring decisions?
- Does the organization make an effort to partner with diverse vendors and suppliers?
- Do the recipients of outward-facing programs and services reflect the diversity of the larger community?
- Does the organization actively recruit and partner with diverse institutions and organizations?
- Does the organization include the importance of diversity in its mission/vision statement?
- Does the organization partner with diversity pipeline programs?

Equity

Being committed to equity means pursuing effective ways to address and eliminate bias. Animal protection organizations that prioritize equity will seek to do the same in the environments in which they operate. Achieving equity often begins by being able to identify what it looks like in the first place. One step toward this end is to dedicate a meaningful amount of time toward developing one's own understanding and education around perspectives of equity in the animal advocacy movement. In the resources section at the end of this chapter, there are a plethora of books, journal articles, blogs, podcasts, and other resources around issues of equity, inclusion, and justice in the animal advocacy movement that can help lay a foundation for understanding. In turn, this foundation will facilitate an easier process of crafting policies and procedures that support fruitful dialogue around topics of equity, creating frameworks for assessment in which feedback by those who are most likely to be impacted by bias is welcomed, and creating meaningful steps to address situations of inequity. Some questions that an attorney representing an animal protection organization might consider in assessing matters of equity at an organization:

- Are principles of equity reflected in organizational core values, mission statements, policies, and procedures and review metrics? Is there a clear connection made as to how these principles directly apply to the organization's goals and objectives?
- Does the organization offer equitable advancement and professional development opportunities (including DEIJ professional development opportunities)?
- Are mentorship opportunities offered for those from underrepresented groups?
- Are outward-facing services and programs equally accessible to those from underrepresented backgrounds and communities?
- Does the organization have self-assessment policies in place to promote and encourage equity?

- How is the organization generally perceived by underrepresented board members, staff, volunteers, and community members?
- What policies are in place for investigating and handling matters of discrimination?
- Do nondisclosure agreements discourage or prevent employees from discussing matters of discrimination?[6]
- Does the organization have a process for 360-degree reviews?[7]
- Does the organization encourage, prioritize, and reward staff and volunteer involvement and engagement on external DEIJ initiatives, or does it create barriers to participation?

Inclusion

Inclusive animal protection organizations will ensure that everyone who interfaces with them can meaningfully contribute to their important work. One common pitfall for organizations that have traditionally lacked in diversity is to rely upon one or a handful of staff to help teach and inform other leadership and staff about the myriad of issues impacting them and others who share their identity. Not only does this reliance incorrectly presume that a single person or a small group can adequately represent the experiences of a whole population of people, but this work is frequently requested to be completed without compensation or recognition, alongside the ordinary tasks that are being considered in performance evaluations. While some staff from underrepresented backgrounds may enthusiastically volunteer to advance DEIJ initiatives based on personal experiences, not everyone will feel comfortable or able to do so. Some may feel pressured to participate when encouraged to engage in these efforts by peers and superiors, to the extent that they sacrifice time for other work-related matters on which they will be evaluated, for the benefit of others who may have never directly experienced discrimination. Especially for underrepresented employees, when participation in DEIJ activities is not tied to performance indicators, such circumstances may lead to the unintended consequence of fewer opportunities for advancement. Fortunately, there are now organizations that offer extensive trainings around matters of DEIJ, specially developed for animal protection organizations.[8]

Ultimately, an inclusive culture will value and welcome the sharing of lived experiences to inform mission-oriented work, while respecting that not everyone will feel comfortable or able to share. It will include and reward work on DEIJ by allowing those working on it adequate time, resources, and recognition,

6. *See, e.g.*, 2021 Legis. Bill Hist. CA S.B. 331. California is one state that has recently passed legislation to prevent confidentiality and nondisclosure agreements from restricting the disclosure of any claim of harassment, discrimination, or retaliation under the California Fair Employment and Housing Act.

7. *See, e.g.*, The Management Center, *360 Feedback—A Field Guide for Managers*, https://www.managementcenter.org/wp-content/uploads/2018/09/TMC-360-Feedback-Field-Guide.pdf.

8. *See, e.g.*, Companions and Animals for Reform and Equity, *https://careawo.org/* (last visited May 23, 2023). CARE, which offers a Racial Equity, Diversity and Inclusion (REDI) course, is one such organization.

through key performance indicators or other means. Other examples of questions to consider around inclusion include but are not limited to:

- Does the mission statement, training materials, and other promotions inadvertently exclude or minimize certain groups?
- Do those from underrepresented backgrounds enjoy equitable decision-making power?
- Does the organization host employee resource groups or encourage staff to attend outside resource groups geared toward providing resources for advocates from underrepresented backgrounds?

Justice

While diversity, equity, and inclusion are commonly known and accepted concepts in organizations, including those focused on animal protection, whether and how to prioritize other forms of justice can be more controversial. Animal protection organizations that are hesitant to publicly highlight and advance aspects of justice for people may justify this reluctance by emphasizing that far fewer organizations dedicated to protecting animals exist. While true in theory, this line of thinking fails to acknowledge that those from underrepresented backgrounds—including diverse staff, volunteers, supporters, and other stakeholders—by virtue of their lived experiences often have no choice but to be involved in matters of justice. For many, the connections of these lived injustices are precisely the reason why they decide to become involved in the animal advocacy movement.[9] Finally, because animal issues so frequently intersect with other issues impacting people and the environment, there are certainly an untold number of organizations working indirectly on issues significantly impacting animals to which the mainstream animal protection movement—particularly if it is not building bridges to those other movements—may never be privy.

Occasionally, when there is a clear intersection between animal advocacy and the broader justice movement, animal protection organizations will try to form diverse coalitions. Yet, if the organization has been openly indifferent to, or worse, vocally opposed to matters impacting members of those coalitions, such relationships will either never happen or be at risk of breaking down due to what may be perceived as an exploitative relationship. It is also not uncommon for decision makers in the broader justice movements, who are increasingly as diverse as the communities they represent, to criticize the animal advocacy movement for being insensitive to these issues.[10]

Organizations committed to justice in the DEIJ context will acknowledge that animal justice advocacy intersects with many other areas of justice impacting people and their environment. Moreover, rather than simply

---

9. Jasmin Singer, Aryenish Birdie & Michelle Rojas-Soto, Antiracism in Animal Advocacy: Igniting the Cultural Transformation (2021).

10. *See, e.g.*, Alison Dirr, *Meatpacker Strauss Brands' Move to Century City Draws Protests over Animal Slaughter*, Milwaukee J. Sentinel (Oct. 15, 2019), https://www.jsonline.com/story/news/local/milwaukee/2019/10/15/strauss-brands-move-milwaukee-draws-protests-over-animal-slaughter/3975449002/.

engaging with individuals and organizations outside of animal advocacy when there is an obvious connection or benefit to doing so, they will find ways to at least acknowledge the importance of dismantling injustice in a variety of contexts and offer support where feasible.

Examples of the incorporation of justice into an animal protection organization's work include:

- Demonstrating sensitivity to staff, volunteers, and other stakeholders of diverse backgrounds when discussing controversial topics internally or to a public audience.
- Using cases and other real-life examples that promote or pertain to DEIJ to inform work to promote justice for animals and the communities to which they are connected.
- Collaborating with a variety of justice-focused stakeholders beyond targeted campaigns.
- Communicating with supporters around the importance of DEIJ, especially as it relates to the mission of the organization.

DEIJ, Organizational Culture, and Anti-Discrimination Laws

Attorneys representing animal protection organizations often wear multiple hats. When it comes to DEIJ, they may on occasion feel as though they are walking a tightrope of potential conflicts. On the one hand, they are likely to be supporting organizations in their missions to advance elements of DEIJ by drafting and reviewing policies and procedures, developing and conducting trainings, and making and approving recommendations that enhance DEIJ. On the other hand, they may also represent the organization at times when elements of DEIJ are called into question, such as when complaints of discrimination arise. In addition, they should be knowledgeable about the ever-evolving landscape of federal and state statutes, rules, and executive orders pertaining to civil rights and labor laws. Key statutes enforced by the Equal Employment Opportunity Commission include the following:

- Title VII of the Civil Rights Act of 1964, which prohibits discrimination in employment on the basis of race, color, religion, sex, or national origin.[11]
- The Equal Pay Act of 1963, which prohibits sex-based wage discrimination.[12]
- Title I[13] and Title V[14] of the Americans with Disabilities Act (ADA), which prohibits employment-based discrimination against qualified individuals with disabilities.

11. 42 U.S.C. § 2000e *et seq.*
12. 29 U.S.C. § 206(d) *et seq.*
13. 42 U.S.C. §§ 12101–12213.
14. 42 U.S.C. § 12203 *et seq.*

- The Age Discrimination Employment Act of 1967, which prohibits discrimination against individuals who are 40 years of age or older.[15]

Outside of the employment context, additional anti-discrimination laws apply to animal protection organizations, especially to the extent that they work as state actors or agents (e.g., municipal animal shelters). Examples of such statutes include the following:

- Title VI of the Civil Rights Act of 1964, which prohibits discrimination on the basis of race, color, religion, sex, or national origin in any program that receives federal funds or other federal financial assistance.[16]
- Title II of the Americans with Disabilities Act, which extends protection from discrimination against individuals with qualified disabilities to all activities of state and local governments, whether these entities receive federal funding or not.[17]
- 42 U.S.C. § 1983, which creates a cause of action for monetary or injunctive relief for violations of constitutional or federal law by state or local officials, or local governments.

Animal law attorneys who represent the interests of their organizations receive directives and objectives from leadership. They are often tasked with providing the mechanisms by which to achieve them but may feel constrained to the extent that they feel they lack decision-making power. However, it is important that these attorneys feel empowered to help establish a culture that values DEIJ principles such that those principles are reflected in all ethics, compliance, and governance decisions.

Attorneys representing animal protection organizations will be most successful in advancing DEIJ when they are supported in being able to do the following:

- Prevent discrimination claims before they arise by proactively identifying and proactively mitigating instances of bias and discrimination.
- Review past and present adverse employment actions and associated demographic data for the purpose of developing the most equitable policies and practices.
- Assume an active role in developing metrics and key performance indicators that support DEIJ principles.
- Report directly to the CEO or executive director on matters relating to DEIJ.
- Regularly meet with the board of directors and include DEIJ-related updates along with other important matters impacting the organization.[18]

15. 29 U.S.C. §§ 621–634.

16. 42 U.S.C. § 2000d.

17. 42 U.S.C. § 12131.

18. Toni Hoy, *What Is General Counsel and How Does This Role Help Your Board?*, Board Effect (Feb. 8, 2023), *available at* https://www.boardeffect.com/blog/role-general-counsel-governance/#::text=In%20addition%20to%20supporting%20the,of%20guardians%20over%20an%20organization.

- Prioritize collaboration with diverse outside counsel and outside firms with strong commitments to DEIJ.

Practical Applications of DEIJ in Animal Protection Organizations

Thus far, we have presented a number of indicators for attorneys representing animal protection organizations to assess at various stages of their efforts to promote DEIJ. Below are some practical applications and examples of how these principles may be applied in day-to-day work. Attorneys representing animal protection organizations should consider:

Developing Procedures for the Comprehensive Review of Internal and External Communication for Indicators of Implicit or Explicit Bias or Potential Discrimination

Such communication includes but is not limited to social media, email and postal mail marketing, donor communications, branding material, websites, and staff material.

Scenario example: Tamara, one of two African American employees at an animal shelter, is upset that some of her colleagues routinely wear Confederate flag t-shirts and insignia at work, which began to increase after recent Black Lives Matter protests in the community. She also noticed that the shelter posts prominent photos of community members wearing the same on their social media pages after they have adopted a companion animal. When sharing her feeling that she was working in a hostile and exclusive environment, a supervisor responded that the priority was to save animal lives, not focus on "other social justice issues."

Potential impact: In addition to potential legal exposure,[19] such an environment would not feel like a welcoming or inclusive place of employment for African American employees or other racially diverse employees. Moreover, potential racially diverse adopters could be deterred from visiting or adopting animals from the shelter, thereby reducing overall adoption rates and positive community perceptions.

---

19. Moore v. Conn. Dep't of Corr., 3:19-cv-1063 (MPS) (D. Conn. Sept. 24, 2021) at 18; https://casetext.com/case/moore-v-conn-dept-of-corr-3; Jonathan Marshall, *Home News DeSoto County NAACP Wants Termination After Controversial Facebook Post*, Fox 13 (Sept. 18, 2020), *available at https://www.fox13memphis.com/news/desoto-county-naacp-wants-termination-after-controversial-facebook-post/article_078b0f0e-f293-5016-a046-9ac9bdd1c521.html.*

Developing Accountability Procedures for Ensuring that DEIJ Practices Are Being Followed

Many organizations include diversity statements on their websites and strive to communicate a welcoming message to prospective staff and stakeholders that diversity is valued. Too often, however, this is where efforts to ensure that organizations are truly diverse, equitable and inclusive places to work, volunteer, patronize or donate to, cease—this is detrimental, even if done unintentionally. Attorneys representing animal protection organizations can help by developing simple accountability checkpoints.

Scenario example: A nonprofit animal protection organization recently decided to prioritize increasing diversity, starting with increasing the number of employees from diverse backgrounds. The organization posted the commitment on its website and attended diversity fairs with the intention of increasing interest among traditionally underrepresented employees. But it failed to look at current and past departmental trends, such as applicants with ethnic-sounding names or other indicators of racial or ethnic groups being least likely to have their resumes viewed.[20]

Potential impact: According to the most recent U.S. Census, more than 40 percent of Americans identify as belonging to one or more racial or ethnic groups.[21] While there is often a perception that a lack of racial diversity exists in animal advocacy, chances are that a higher number of racially diverse job applicants, volunteers, donors, and supporters exist than what is believed. Practices to identify these stakeholders and eliminate barriers to entry will save animal protection organizations resources and allow more equal access to those who may currently be seeking opportunities to get involved. An essential part of removing barriers is identifying the root causes why they exist in the first place.

Developing Training Based upon Real-life Scenarios Pertaining to Bias and Discrimination in the Animal Advocacy Movement

As referenced elsewhere in this chapter, there are numerous resources for developing literacy around DEIJ issues. However, without a clear understanding of how these issues apply directly to the work of a particular animal protection organization, meaningful progress may never occur.

Scenario example: In part out of a desire to appeal to grant funders seeking DEIJ involvement, a farmed animal rescue organization hired an outside DEIJ consultant to present a one-time workshop to employees. While many

20. Bertrand Marianne & Mullainathan Sendhil, *Are Emily and Greg More Employable Than Lakisha and Jamal? A Field Experiment on Labor Market Discrimination*, 94 Am. Econ. Rev. (2004).

21. William H. Frey, *New 2020 Census Results Show Increased Diversity Countering Decade-Long Declines in America's White and Youth Populations*, Brookings (Aug. 13, 2021), https://www.brookings.edu/research/new-2020-census-results-show-increased-diversity-countering-decade-long-declines-in-americas-white-and-youth-populations/.

employees thought that the content was informative and useful, others complained that such training was only a distraction that took away from their ability to help animals. They could see no "real" application to their day-to-day work, especially since the organization had a very small number of employees from underrepresented backgrounds. Beyond the one-time workshop, discussion of social justice issues impacting people was discouraged as being "irrelevant" or "too political," unless there was a clear and direct connection to animal exploitation. For example, a proposal to include a guest speaker from an economic justice organization at a staff retreat was not approved on the basis that the topic appeared to be unrelated to animal advocacy.

The next month, staff learned of a large factory farming operation with a significant history of animal welfare and environmental violations, wished to locate in a community of color. For decades prior, community leaders had worked tirelessly to attract economic development opportunities, and this seemed to be the greatest of them all. When animal advocates from the farmed animal rescue group visited the community to protest the factory farming operation based on animal cruelty, community leaders found themselves at odds with a group that they felt knew or cared little about them or their interests. In approving a zoning permit, the local government body—which included a substantial number of representatives of color—found the advocates to be disingenuous to the extent they had been expressing a newly formed concern about environmental justice and the effects of the factory farm on the community.

Potential impact: While successful partnerships and collaborations between animal advocacy groups and non-animal advocacy groups have led to substantial victories for animals, there are countless other stories of missed opportunities between such groups. The intersections between animal advocacy and issues of broader justice are as plentiful as the issues themselves.

DEIJ in the Animal Protection Movement: Contemporary Approaches and Issues

As we have previously discussed, no one chapter or book can cover the true breadth of DEIJ as it applies to animal law. Instead of attempting to address every issue or scenario that may come up in the day-to-day work of an animal lawyer, we have chosen here to focus on three particularly important current issues: anti-carceral veganism, worker justice, and environmental justice. Taken together, these three examples hopefully provide a picture of the kinds of evolving conversations that are happening within organizations, at conferences, and between colleagues and allies in the broader movement. We also provide some useful highlights of cases, papers, or other resources to further explore these approaches.

Anti-Carceral Veganism and Restorative Justice

At the time of writing, approximately two million people are incarcerated in prisons and jails across the United States.[22] That represents a 500 percent increase from just forty years ago.[23] The United States locks up its own citizens at a rate that is unprecedented around the world. El Salvador, the country with the second highest incarceration rate, locks up more than 100 fewer people per 100,000 than the United States. Even Massachusetts, the U.S. state with the lowest incarceration rate, still imprisons more of its citizens than almost any other country on the planet, including authoritarian regimes like Iran.[24]

This ballooning of the American prison population was not an accident, nor was it the result of increases in criminal conduct. Over the last four decades, crime has dropped substantially across the country–yet prison populations have more than quintupled. Policy is to blame for the mass incarceration crisis.[25] Beginning in the late 1970s, states and the federal government passed a number of "tough on crime" laws that made it far easier to incarcerate people. This included "three strikes" laws, mandatory minimums, the "War on Drugs," and the broader criminalization of poverty.[26] Community demands for more investment in housing, education, and job training were ignored, as funding for more law enforcement was prioritized.[27]

As scholars Justin Marceau and Lori Gruen have documented, the "carceral logics" that drove the tough on crime narrative includes both the narrower internal logic of prisons and the legal system as well as the broader analytical framework that constrains our thinking of social problems and possible solutions.[28] Individual responsibility and accountability through punishment are prime examples of carceral logic at work. Social ills are to be punished away, rather than preemptively solved—as doing so would require systemic conceptualizations of harm and would cut against the learned instinct toward retribution.

Activists and scholars within the animal protection movement, particularly Black vegans and other people of the global majority, have long since been critical of the mainstream animal protection movement for its carceral approach

22. Wendy Sawyer & Peter Wagner, *Mass Incarceration: The Whole Pie 2022*, Prison Policy Initiative (Mar. 14, 2022), https://www.prisonpolicy.org/reports/pie2022.html.

23. *Criminal Justice Facts*, The Sentencing Project, https://www.sentencingproject.org/criminal-justice-facts/.

24. Emily Widra & Tiana Herring, *States of Incarceration: The Global Context 2021*, Prison Policy Initiative (Sept. 2021), https://www.prisonpolicy.org/global/2021.html.

25. *See Criminal Justice Facts*, *supra* note 23.

26. *See* James Cullen, *The History of Mass Incarceration*, The Brennan Center for Justice (July 20, 2018), https://www.brennancenter.org/our-work/analysis-opinion/history-mass-incarceration; *see also* Michelle Alexander, The New Jim Crow (2010).

27. *See* James Forman Jr., Locking Up Our Own: Crime and Punishment in Black America, 76 (2017) (chronicling the response by D.C.'s Black community to the rise in crime during the 1970s, with particular emphasis on demands for more investment in education, housing, and job training that fell on deaf ears. Forman writes that by 1975, such efforts to improve people's lives were seen as "a symbol of the hopeless naïveté of 1960s liberalism").

28. Carceral Logics: Human Incarceration and Animal Captivity 4 (Lori Gruen, Justin Marceau eds., 2022).

to dealing with harm to animals. Within the academic animal law community, the current conversation was largely framed by the 2019 publication of Professor Justin Marceau's book *Beyond Cages* and the 2020 racial justice uprising and international protests following the murder of George Floyd by police in Minneapolis.[29]

The feedback and criticisms that Marceau and others (including one of the authors of this chapter)[30] offer to the animal protection movement is that an emphasis on carceral solutions may be ineffective at reducing harm to nonhuman animals—and in many cases can further perpetuate harm. Laws criminalizing certain acts of cruelty to animals have been shown to be correlated with the creation of greater legal exemptions for the cruelty that occurs in our agriculture system every day.[31] A rhetorical alignment[32] of the animal protection movement with "tough on crime" politics can alienate many prospective allies of the movement[33] and act to bolster the same racist[34] state apparatus that then can target animal rights activists and whistleblowers.[35]

Many animal protection lawyers are beginning to acknowledge the drawbacks and downsides to a carceral approach. This leaves us with the question: where do we go instead? A promising place to start is learning from the restorative justice movement.

A restorative justice approach to harm asks "what should be done *for* the victim?" rather than "what should be done *to* the perpetrator?"[36] Such an approach focuses the experience of the victim of harm, seeking to have the

29. *See generally* Justin Marceau, Beyond Cages: Animal Law and Criminal Punishment (2019); *see also* Jamelle Bouie, *The Police Are Rioting. We Need to Talk About It.*, N.Y. Times (June 5, 2020), https://www.nytimes.com/2020/06/05/opinion/sunday/police-riots.html; Matthew Dessem, *Police Erupt in Violence Nationwide*, SLATE (May 31, 2020), https://slate.com/news-and-politics/2020/05/george-floyd-protests-police-violence.html.

30. *See* Michael Swistara, *Mutual Liberation: The Use and Abuse of Non-Human Animals by the Carceral State and the Shared Roots of Oppression*, 12 U. Miami Race & Social Just. L. Rev. 312 (2022); Michael Swistara, *What Comes After Defund?: Lessons from Police and Prison Abolition for the Animal Movement*, 28 Animal L. 89 (2022).

31. *See* Beyond Cages, *supra note* 391, at 98–109.

32. As just one example of rhetorical and practical support for further incarceration, consider the self-stylized "Desmond's Army" group in Connecticut. A coalition of citizens dedicated to increasing criminal penalties for those accused of animal abuse, members often protest outside of court houses. In the group's own words, it has been effective—the president has said that "[s]ince Desmond's Law, we have seen a significant increase in jail time." Carceral Logics, *supra* note 28, at 402.

33. *See* Swistara, *What Comes After Defund*, *supra* note 30, at 98–100; *see also* Charlie Mitchell, *Is the Vegan Movement Ready to Reckon With Racism?*, Civil Eats (Aug. 26, 2020), https://civileats.com/2020/08/26/is-the-vegan-movement-ready-to-reckon-with-racism/.

34. As abolitionist writer and activist Mariame Kaba has made clear: "[T]here is not a single era in United States history in which police were not a force of violence against [B]lack people." Mariame Kaba, *Yes, We Mean Literally Abolish the Police*, N.Y. Times (June 12, 2020), https://www.nytimes.com/2020/06/12/opinion/sunday/floyd-abolish-defund-police.html. The history of animal cruelty laws and their disparate enforcement further bears this out. *See* BEYOND CAGES, *supra* note 29, at 166–172 (discussing the racial disparity in prosecutions and police use of force while enforcing animal cruelty laws).

35. *See* Alleen Brown, *The Green Scare: How a Movement That Never Killed Anyone Became the FBI's No. 1 Domestic Terrorism Threat*, Intercept (Mar. 23, 2019), https://theintercept.com/2019/03/23/ecoterrorism-fbi-animal-rights/;*Ag-Gag Across America: Corporate Backed Attacks on Activists and Whistleblowers*, Ctr. for Constitutional Rights (2017).

36. *See* Gerry Johnstone, Restorative Justice: Ideas, Values, Debates 11 (Taylor & Francis 2d ed. 2011).

perpetrator take accountability for their action and using the process to restore or repair (to the extent possible) the harm.[37] A related concept, transformative justice, seeks to respond to harm without creating further cycles of trauma or violence and by using specific conflicts to address broader socioeconomic injustices.[38]

There are several organizations already putting these lessons into practice on the ground to help humans and nonhuman animals alike. Companions and Animals for Reform and Equity (C.A.R.E.) takes a holistic approach, creating community relationships through supporting companion animal owners and by partnering with social service agencies, legal aid, faith-based groups, and veteran-serving organizations. This approach means that C.A.R.E. is able to put people back on their feet again, setting both them and their companion animals up for long-term success.

Another example is Beyond Fences, an organization that builds fences for previously chained dogs to run free—as well as providing straw for warmth, tarps for shade, and free spay/neuter procedures.[39] The vast majority of animal abuse charges are for neglect or abandonment. By directly providing pet owners with the resources and tools to provide for their companions, animals are able to thrive in their homes, preempting any need for a subsequent carceral response.

Worker Protection and Safety for Farmworkers and Animal Advocates

In early 2020, as the first wave of the COVID-19 global pandemic swept across the United States, two places were hit hardest: prisons and slaughterhouses.[40] When slaughterhouse workers began testing positive for the virus by the thousands, companies like Tyson and JBS lobbied the Trump Administration to keep the facilities open. They were rewarded with an Executive Order that sought to provide the meatpacking companies a legal defense to liability claims by workers who fell ill—or by their families when workers died.[41] As a direct result of slaughterhouses remaining open, hundreds of workers died and many thousands became sick early on in the pandemic.[42]

---

37. *See* Brittany Hill, *Restoring Justice for Animal Victims*, 17 Animal & Nat. Resource L. Rev. 217, 219–221 (2021); *Lesson 1: What Is Restorative Justice?*, Ctr. for Just. & Reconciliation, https://perma.cc/8PGZ-43A7.

38. *See* Anthony J. Nocella II, *An Overview of the History and Theory of Transformative Justice*, 6 Peace & Conflict Rev. 1, 4 (2011); Mia Mingus, *Transformative Justice: A Brief Description*, Transform Harm, https://perma.cc/PQ7C-ETYM.

39. *Fence Program*, Beyond Fences, https://www.beyondfences.org/fence-program/.

40. *See* Eric Schlosser, *America's Slaughterhouses Aren't Just Killing Animals*, Atlantic (May 12, 2020), https://www.theatlantic.com/ideas/archive/2020/05/essentials-meatpeacking-coronavirus/611437/.

41. *See id.*

42. *See* Sky Chadde, *COVID-19 Cases, Deaths in Meatpacking Industry Were Much higher Than Previously Known, Congressional Investigation Shows*, Midwest Ctr. for Investigative Reporting (Oct. 28, 2021), https://investigatemidwest.org/2021/10/28/covid-19-cases-deaths-in-meatpacking-industry-were-much-higher-than-previously-known-congressional-investigation-shows/.

The pandemic only highlighted what worker safety advocates have long pointed out: slaughterhouse workers, farm workers, and other laborers in our food system are among the least protected, most at risk, and most taken advantage of workers in our economy. Slaughterhouse workers routinely suffer from repetitive stress injuries, PTSD, and other job-related injuries, as well as frequently being subjected to sexual harassment while at work.[43] While slaughter-based agriculture may be particularly dangerous, working conditions are notably poor for other farm and food workers as well.[44]

Organizations like Food Empowerment Project and Farm Sanctuary, in partnership with the Coalition of Immokalee Workers, have highlighted the fight for a more just and equitable food system—including for the exploited workers within that system—as rooted in a vegan ethos. In particular, these campaigns ask the vegan movement to apply its compassionate outlook as broadly as possible, incorporating workers at plant-based food companies and non-animal agricultural farm workers into the movement.[45]

As lawyers representing animal protection organizations, we can learn from and integrate the interests of farmworkers into our daily practice and guidance to our clients. This will differ organization-to-organization, but for farmed animal advocacy organizations, this can begin with asking serious and often difficult questions about organizational objections and campaigns. For example: Who are we targeting with this lawsuit? Will this improve circumstances for animals and workers alike? How does this campaign frame the issue of violence against farmed animals? Are there possibilities for partnering with worker organizations on this issue?

One positive trend in the farmed animal protection movement has been a shift away from focusing campaigns on specific harm inflicted by a single worker on an animal toward challenging standard industry practices that cause untold suffering. Targeting lawsuits or communications campaigns at the actions of a single "bad apple" actor on a farm or in a slaughterhouse allows the company to deflect blame onto that worker, merely replacing them with someone else. That approach can position the animal protection movement as counter to the interests of workers, undocumented individuals, and others also struggling under the same industrial agricultural system as the animals whose exploitation and suffering we seek to end.

---

43. Oscar Heanue, *For Slaughterhouse Workers, Physical Injuries Are Only the Beginning*, OnLabor (Jan. 17, 2022), https://onlabor.org/for-slaughterhouse-workers-physical-injuries-are-only-the-beginning/; Michael Lebwohl, *A Call to Action: Psychological Harm in Slaughterhouse Workers*, Yale Global Health Rev. (Jan. 25, 2016), https://yaleglobalhealthreview.com/2016/01/25/a-call-to-action-psychological-harm-in-slaughterhouse-workers/; *see also Confessions of a Slaughterhouse Worker*, BBC (Jan. 6, 2020), https://www.bbc.com/news/stories-50986683.

44. *E.g.*, American Public Health Association, *Improving Working Conditions for U.S. Farmworkers and Food Production Workers* (Policy No. 20177, Nov. 7, 2017), https://www.apha.org/policies-and-advocacy/public-health-policy-statements/policy-database/2018/01/18/improving-working-conditions.

45. *See, e.g.*, *What's Going on at Amy's Kitchen?*, Food Empowerment Project, https://foodispower.org/human-labor-slavery/whats-going-on-at-amys-kitchen/; *Farmworker Justice: In Solidarity & Deep Appreciation*, Farm Sanctuary, https://www.farmsanctuary.org/news-stories/farmworker-justice-solidarity-appreciation/.

An example of coalition building across the animal and worker protection movements was in response to the U.S. Department of Agriculture's (USDA) increase in slaughter line speeds. In 2019, unions and animal protection organizations filed a series of lawsuits against the Trump Administration for its decision to remove or significantly raise minimum line speeds at chicken and pig slaughterhouses, which hurt animals and workers alike.[46] Line speeds as fast as 175 birds per minute increase the risk of injury to workers and also heighten the odds that animals will be injured or not rendered unconscious before being slaughtered. Lawyers representing animal protection organizations should continue wherever possible to seek out and pursue coalitional litigation and legislation that align with labor interests.

In addition to better incorporating the interests of farm workers into an animal law practice, lawyers can also strive to ensure that workplaces represent and reflect the values of empathy and equity espoused as central to the animal protection movement. Mission-driven organizations are not immune from the misogyny, racism, ableism, and other forms of discrimination that are frequent across workplaces. Combating these forces starts within the animal protection movement, which should be a safe work environment for everyone.

One way in which the animal protection movement has improved, but still has ways to go, is in taking a strong stand against sex and gender discrimination. In 2018, male executives at both the Humane Society of the United States (HSUS) and Mercy for Animals (MFA) were ousted after dozens of sexual harassment complaints.[47] Both organizations are now led by women.[48] Yet, for a movement that is overwhelmingly female,[49] there remains a dearth of women in leadership positions at the largest animal rights organizations.

Similarly, BIPOC employees at animal protection organizations have publicly shared negative experiences—from being pushed into less influential

---

46. *E.g.*, United Food & Commercial Workers Union, Local No. 663 v. U.S. Dep't of Agric., 532 F. Supp. 3d 741 (D. Minn. 2021); Complaint, Farm Sanctuary v. U.S. Dep't of Agric., No. 6:19-cv-06910 (W.D.N.Y. 2019).

47. Ian Kullgren, *Female Employees Allege Culture of Sexual Harassment at Humane Society*, POLITICO (Jan. 30, 2018), https://www.politico.com/magazine/story/2018/01/30/humane-society-sexual-harassment-allegations-investigation-216553/; Danielle Paquette, *Humane Society CEO Is Subject of Sexual Harassment Complaints From Three Women, According to Internal Investigation*, WASH. POST (Jan. 29, 2018), https://www.washingtonpost.com/business/economy/humane-society-ceo-is-subject-of-sexual-harassment-complaints-from-three-women-according-to-internal-investigation/2018/01/29/12c8961e-053b-11e8-94e8-e8b8600ade23_story.html; Marc Gunther, *The Animal Welfare Movement's #MeToo Problem*, NONPROFIT CHRONICLES (Jan. 26, 2018), https://nonprofitchronicles.com/2018/01/26/the-animal-welfare-movements-metoo-problem/.

48. *Leadership*, HUMANE SOC'Y U.S., https://www.humanesociety.org/leadership; *About*, MERCY FOR ANIMALS, https://mercyforanimals.org/about/.

49. *See* Emily Gaarder, *Where the Boys Aren't: The Predominance of Women in Animal Rights Activism*, 23 FEMINIST FORMATIONS 54 (2011) (qualitative study of women in the animal rights movement); Farha Khalidi, *Why Are More Women Vegan Than Men?*, WOMEN'S MEDIA CTR. (Jan. 13, 2020), https://womensmediacenter.com/fbomb/why-are-more-women-vegan-than-men (quoting a statistic that seventy-nine percent of vegans are women); *Who Runs the (Animal Welfare) World? Girls.*, HUMANEPRO (2017), https://humanepro.org/magazine/articles/who-runs-animal-welfare-world-girls (noting that "[t]he animal protection field has been predominantly female since its inception").

roles[50] to hostile remarks in the office.[51] Employees and volunteers should be able to be their whole, authentic selves at work. Attorneys should go beyond the minimum requirements of the law to ensure that workers are protected and supported.

Organizational messaging is a big part of this, too. Veganism is more common in communities of color,[52] and yet because the best funded organizations are almost all White-led, the animal protection movement sometimes puts out messaging that ostracizes BIPOC audiences.[53] Messages crafted by White-led organizations and intended for White audiences can end up reproducing the language of White supremacy. For example, surface-level comparisons that focus on the aesthetics of oppression (such as directly analogizing the experiences of chattel slavery to factory farming) fail to consider the different ways in which oppressive hierarchies can manifest themselves in different populations—and as a result often appear shallow and tone-deaf. This can turn people off of vegan messaging[54] and makes the harmful assumption that being oppressed is a groups' entire history. In a similar vein, animal rights campaigns have sometimes focused disproportionately on already marginalized communities[55]—reinforcing the Eurocentric view that certain kinds of animal suffering are more or less justifiable.

Funders and donors also have an influence on messaging. Activists have called out "white philanthropy" for supporting White-led animal protection organizations at the expense of groups with a more explicit racial justice focus.[56] As one vegan fundraiser put it, a lot of funders "simply do not want to see anything about Black Lives Matter" because "they think it takes away from animals."[57] Some White vegans have even co-opted and manipulated the language of Black Lives Matter into an "all lives matter" message allegedly on behalf of nonhuman animals[58]—a tactic that has repeatedly been used by the political right to silence Black and brown activists.

---

50. Marc Gunther, *Alex Hershaft: An Animal Rights Pioneer, With a #MeToo Problem*, Nonprofit Chronicles (Feb. 16, 2018), https://nonprofitchronicles.com/2018/02/16/alex-hershaft-an-animal-rights-pioneer-with-a-metoo-problem/.

51. *E.g.*, Complaint, Byrne v. ASPCA (E.D.N.Y. 2022) (No. 1:22-cv-07062-BMC); Eshe Kiama Zuri, *Resignation Letter* (July 2021), https://vegan4themany.com/who/eshe-kiama-zuri (announcing resignation from The Vegan Society); *Best Friends Staff Open Up About Their Experiences with Racism in Animal Welfare*, Best Friends, https://network.bestfriends.org/proven-strategies/program-spotlights/staff-experiences-racism-animal-welfare.

52. *See Why Black Americans Are More Likely to be Vegan*, BBC (Sept. 11, 2020), https://www.bbc.com/news/world-us-canada-53787329.

53. Mitchell, *supra* note 33.

54. *See Privilege: The U.S. Vegan Movement, Whiteness, and Race Relations*, H.E.A.L.T.H. (Apr. 7, 2009), http://eco-health.blogspot.com/2009/03/privilege-us-vegan-movement-whiteness_8877.html.

55. For example, campaigns against Indigenous hunting practices, the Chinese dog meat trade, or Caribbean sacrificial religious rituals have all garnered criticism for disproportionately drawing resources from animal rights groups compared to the much larger scale White-coded (i.e., associated with Whiteness and thus frequently perceived to be more "normal" or socially accepted in countries like the United States) forms of oppression such as modern-day factory farming.

56. Mitchell, *supra* note 33.

57. *Id.*

58. *See* Marla Rose, *Attention White Animal-Rights Activists: "Black Lives Matter" Is Not Ours for the Taking*, VegNews (June 4, 2020), https://vegnews.com/vegan-news/opinion/attention-white-animal-rights-activists-black-lives-matter-is-not-ours-for-the-taking.

A unified animal protection movement is one that acknowledges the interconnected struggles for liberation across race, gender, class, and species. Incorporating a worker-focused ethos rooted in gender, ability, and racial justice will lead to a stronger movement. Animal lawyers play a pivotal role here by ensuring that AR organizations are safe workplaces for all, and that the campaigns and lawsuits we pursue work to further these strategic goals.

Environmental Justice

Animal protection organizations can help draw the connections between large-scale animal agriculture and harms to communities. Animal agriculture is the second largest contributor to anthropogenic greenhouse gas (GHG) emissions, surpassing the entire global transit sector, and is a leading cause of deforestation, water and air pollution, and biodiversity loss.[59] Yet, this enormous cost is not borne equally. The Global South eats fewer animal products and has caused only a small fraction of anthropogenic GHG emissions, but it is already bearing the brunt of the climate crisis as exemplified by heat waves, droughts, floods, rising sea levels, ocean acidification, and more frequent storms.[60] Within the Global North, economic and racial disparities exist in access to healthy environments and healthy foods.

In the United States, concentrated animal feeding operations (CAFOs, or factory farms) are disproportionately sited in minority communities.[61] The siting of these facilities in historically disenfranchised communities is no mistake, and it has serious negative ramifications for the health of those who are forced to live near CAFOs. One study by researchers at Duke University found that those who live near CAFOs experienced higher infant and overall death rates, higher rates of death from anemia, tuberculosis, kidney disease, and septicemia, among other health problems.[62]

In addition to disproportionately suffering the effects of living near industrial animal agricultural operations, Black and brown communities are also the most likely to live under food apartheid—meaning in communities with no grocery store and/or little to no access to affordable, healthy food.[63]

---

59. *Animal Agriculture's Impact on Climate Change*, Climate Nexus, https://climatenexus.org/climate-issues/food/animal-agricultures-impact-on-climate-change/.

60. *See* Saleemul Haq & Mohamed Adow, *Climate Change Is Devastating the Global South*, Al Jazeera (May 11, 2022), https://www.aljazeera.com/opinions/2022/5/11/climate-change-is-devastating-the-global-south.

61. *See* Ji-Young Son et al., *Distribution of Environmental Justice Metrics for Exposure to CAFOs in North Carolina, USA*, 195 Envtl. Res. 110862 (2021) (finding that "CAFOs in [North Carolina] are located disproportionately in minorities and low SES communities"); Arbor J.L. Quist et al., *Disparities of Industrial Animal Operations in California, Iowa, and North Carolina*, https://earthjustice.org/wp-content/uploads/quistreport_cafopetition_oct2022.pdf (finding the proportion of BIPOC residents is significantly higher than that of non-Hispanic White residents within three miles of CAFOs).

62. Julia Kravchenko et al., *Mortality and Health Outcomes in North Carolina Communities Located in Close Proximity to Hog Concentrated Animal Feeding Operations*, 79 N. C. Med. J. 278 (2018).

63. *See also Reframing Food Access Disparities as Food Apartheid*, Stray Dog Inst. (2022), https://straydoginstitute.org/food-apartheid/.

Lawyers representing animal protection organizations can encourage the incorporation of considerations of environmental justice into messaging, strategies, and coalition work when challenging industrial animal agriculture. Several of the largest animal protection organizations are already working in this space alongside rural and environmental advocacy groups.

For example, the Animal Legal Defense Fund has used environmental laws to challenge local pollution and water use by CAFOs as well as the lax enforcement of environmental laws. This includes a 2020 lawsuit against Foster Farms, a slaughterhouse in California, for its illegal water use,[64] as well as another suit filed the same year alongside coalition partners against the Council on Environmental Quality challenging regulations that would shield CAFOs and slaughterhouses from federal environmental review and "limit the ability of the public to know about and challenge the harms caused by these facilities."[65]

Another lawsuit, brought by HSUS, MFA, and Farm Sanctuary, highlights problems of environmental injustice via a challenge to the USDA inadequate avian flu response plan.[66] In that lawsuit, along with other criticisms, plaintiffs argued that USDA had failed to adequately address the environmental impacts of its avian flu response plan on low-income and BIPOC communities in the vicinity of CAFOs.

Strategic impact lawsuits like these, which can be brought in partnership with local community members and organizations, are prime examples of how the animal protection movement can collaborate and ally with environmental justice issues and organizations. Beyond factory farm work, animal lawyers can support local vegan food banks working to combat food injustice, engage in legislative and regulatory work that highlights the climate cost of animal agriculture, and work to incorporate an environmental justice lens into other areas of animal protection work.

DEIJ Resources for Attorneys in the Animal Protection Movement

Organizations:

- Apex Advocacy
  - An organization aiming "to increase the number of BIPOC individuals who participate in animal activism by advocating for collective

64. Complaint, Animal Legal Def. Fund v. Foster Poultry Farms, *available at* http://climatecasechart.com/wp-content/uploads/sites/16/case-documents/2020/20200902_docket-na_complaint.pdf.

65. *Challenging CEQ's CAFO Exemptions Under NEPA*, ALDF (Sept. 23, 2020), https://aldf.org/case/challenging-ceqs-cafo-exemptions-under-nepa/; *see* Complaint, Iowa Citizens for Cmty. Improvement v. Council on Envtl. Quality, No. 20-cv-2715, *available at* http://climatecasechart.com/wp-content/uploads/sites/16/case-documents/2020/20200923_docket-120-cv-02715_complaint.pdf.

66. First Amended Complaint, Humane Soc'y of the U.S. v. U.S. Dep't of Agric., No. 2:20-CV-03258-AB-GJS (W.D. Cal. 2020), *available at* https://blog.humanesociety.org/wp-content/uploads/2021/03/2020-07-27-First-Amended-Complaint-dckt-42_0.pdf.

liberation through animal rights, particularly in marginalized areas and communities that are disproportionately affected by the animal industrial complex."[67]
    - Runs the "Global Majority Caucus" (previously organized by Encompass Movement), a resource and space for community and professional development for BIPOC animal protection activists.[68]
- Food Empowerment Project
- C.A.R.E.
- Maddie's Candid Conversations
- HSUS "Pets for Life" Program
    - Provides free and direct medical care for companion animals whose owners would not otherwise be able to access or afford such services.[69]
- Food Not Bombs

Books:

- Carol J. Adams, *The Sexual Politics of Meat* (1990).
- *Sistah Vegan: Black Female Vegans Speak on Food, Identity, Health, and Society* (A. Breeze Harper ed., 2009).
- Claire Jean Kim, *Dangerous Crossings: Race, Species, and Nature in a Multicultural Age* (2015).
- Aph Ko & Syl Ko, *Aphro-ism: Essays on Pop Culture, Feminism, and Black Veganism from Two Sisters* (2017).
- Aph Ko, *Racism as Zoological Witchcraft: A Guide to Getting Out* (2019).
- Justin Marceau, *Beyond Cages* (2019).
- *Antiracism in Animal Advocacy: Igniting Cultural Transformation* (Jasmine Singer ed., 2021)
- Sunaura Taylor, *Beasts of Burden: Animal and Disability Liberation* (2017).

Articles:

- Sarah Mayorga-Gallo, *Whose Best Friend? Dogs and Racial Boundary Maintenance in a Multiracial Neighborhood*, 33 Soc. Forum 505 (2018).
- Kelsey Goldman, *Letting the Cat out of the Bag: How Lack of Access to Animal Companionship and Husbandry Fosters Inequality for Black Americans*, 12 UCILR 693 (2022).
- Courtney G. Lee, *Racist Animal Agriculture*, 25 CUNY L. Rev. 199 (2022).
- Ann Linder, *The Black Man's Dog: The Social Context of Breed Specific Legislation*, 25 Animal Law 51 (2018).

67. *Our Mission*, Apex Advocacy, https://www.apexadvocacy.org/about.

68. *Global Majority Caucus*, Apex Advocacy, https://www.apexadvocacy.org/globalmajoritycaucus.

69. *See Pets for Life*, The Humane Soc'y of the U.S.: HUMANEPRO, https://perma.cc/KE63-DGAZ.

- Shontel Stewart, *Man's Best Friend? How Dogs Have Been Used to Oppress African Americans*, 25 U. Mich. J. Race & Law 183 (2020).

Films:

- *Mine*, dir. Geralyn Pezanoski (2009).
- *The Smell of Money*, dir. Shawn Bannon (2022).
- *They're Trying to Kill Us*, dir. Keegan Kuhn (2021).
- *What the Health*, dirs. Kip Andersen & Keegan Kuhn (2017).

CHAPTER 7

Ethics

Russ Mead

Introduction

Attorneys who work with animal protection organizations face unique legal and ethical issues throughout their work. This is true whether the lawyer is being paid or is volunteering. The best way to recognize and handle such issues is to follow a jurisdiction's rules of professional conduct (also commonly called "rules of professional responsibility" or "professional ethics" or just "ethics"). These are ethics rules modeled off of the American Bar Association (ABA) "Model Rules of Professional Conduct," which were first drafted by the ABA Center for Professional Responsibility in 1983.[1] The 1983 rules replaced the ABA "Canons of Professional Ethics," first published in 1908.[2] These codes from the ABA set professional standards for the legal profession and system. An official comment accompanies each model rule. The comments expand on the meaning of the rule, often with illuminating examples. Jurisdictions are free to adopt, modify, and even reject any part of the model rules, though most states adhere closely to them.

While the model rules are frequently used as a resource to teach practicing lawyers about the rules of professional conduct, this is simply out of convenience. Discussing one set of model rules is more manageable than discussing any one state's official rules. It is best practice for attorneys in the field to learn the rules in their jurisdictions.

Lawyers find themselves in two entirely different situations when working in animal protection. The first is when the animal protection organization hires the lawyer to take on general counsel duties or to handle a particular legal matter or matters. The lawyer's client is the organization. Most lawyers

1. *Model Rules of Professional Conduct*, AM. BAR ASS'N, americanbar.org, https://www.americanbar.org/groups/professional_responsibility/publications/model_rules_of_professional_conduct/.

2. *Id.*

recognize that this relationship carries the duties of the rules of professional responsibility. The obligations of professional responsibility are apparent.

But there is a second situation where lawyers often find themselves in trouble. That is the case where the lawyer works as a volunteer for an organization. Then when volunteering to do nonlegal tasks, the lawyer slips into providing a legal service. But the lawyer is not thinking of this as an attorney-client relationship. The lawyers think that they are volunteering to help the animals, not representing the organization.

The issue that arises is that, as soon as the lawyer performs legal duties for the organization, the lawyer represents that organization. And it follows that all the rules of professional responsibility attach.

Attorneys should not follow the rules mechanically, however. The preamble to the model rules suggests that the rules are just a starting point:

> Compliance with the Rules, as with all law in an open society, depends primarily upon understanding and voluntary compliance, secondarily upon reinforcement by peer and public opinion and finally, when necessary, upon enforcement through disciplinary proceedings. The Rules do not, however, exhaust the moral and ethical considerations that should inform a lawyer, for no worthwhile human activity can be completely defined by legal rules. The Rules simply provide a framework for the ethical practice of law.[3]

The preamble to the model rules reminds lawyers to be ethical in their practice of the law regardless of what the rules proscribe in a given situation. Lawyers must think broadly about what each rule demands, even in the most complex cases.

Against this background, this chapter discusses the unique legal issues that can arise in the representation of animal protection organizations. Though this chapter discusses issues related to animal law, the best practice is usually the same for all practicing attorneys: to recognize, understand, and follow the relevant ethics rules.

The Issue of Whether a Client-Attorney Relationship Exists

Picture a lawyer who is helping a busy animal protection organization. Imagine the lawyer specializes in family law but is volunteering because they care about animal rights and advocacy. The organization deals with animal-related issues. Specifically, issues such as helping elephants confined in small zoo enclosures, hogs confined in gestation crates, dogs left in hot cars, and cats held at shelters. The lawyer often participates in meetings where the organization's directors discuss these issues and pose questions to people in the room.

---

3. *Model Rules of Professional Conduct: Preamble & Scope*, Am. Bar Ass'n, https://www.americanbar.org/groups/professional_responsibility/publications/model_rules_of_professional_conduct/model_rules_of_professional_conduct_preamble_scope/.

Imagine, next, that someone in the room asks the group a legal question. The lawyer is the only legal expert in the room and, without hesitating, starts to provide an answer to the question. Like many practitioners, the lawyer feels a duty to carry out their role as an expert in the room with grace, even though they have had little to no time to ask questions or research the topic. In the heat of the moment, the lawyer does not think that answering the question will create a client-lawyer relationship. Thus, the lawyer answers the question and continues contributing to the discussion. At this point, the lawyer may have unwittingly gotten a new client.

Preamble and Scope

"Preamble and Scope" of the model rules explain when a client-lawyer relationship has formed. The scope states in part:

> Furthermore, for determining the lawyer's authority and responsibility, principles of substantive law external to these Rules determine whether a client-lawyer relationship exists. Most of the duties flowing from the client-lawyer relationship only attach after the client has requested the lawyer to render legal services and the lawyer has agreed to do so.[4]

Substantive law determines whether a client-lawyer relationship has formed. In other words, it is ultimately a matter exceeding the scope of the model rules. Still, the scope establishes that most duties begin to flow following a request from a prospective client for legal services and an agreement from the lawyer to render those services. Lawyers answer legal questions frequently as part of their representation. The question on which this issue hangs is whether answering legal questions in this meeting would constitute legal services.

Lawyers may assume their participation resembles that of the other people at the meeting—active and helpful—but not tied to more significant legal obligations. However, it is essential to note that the potential client's perspective on the relationship also affects how this situation shakes out ethically.

It does not take much to create a client-lawyer relationship when viewed from the potential client's perspective. For instance, the interaction likely has a different feel to the potential client than it does to the lawyer. Even though it is part of the lawyer's everyday life, asking legal questions may be rare in the potential client's life. Indeed, it is easy to imagine the potential client walking away from the interaction thinking they just received solid legal advice and even telling other people that they have already talked to their attorney about their legal issues. This difference in perception can create ethical problems for the lawyer.

Once a client-lawyer relationship is established, the lawyer owes the client a full range of duties. These duties include being competent (Rule 1.1), diligent (Rule 1.3), and, if the issue goes to court, fair (Rule 3.4), impartial (Rule 3.5), and so on.

4. *Id.*

Best Practice: The Issue of Whether a Client-Attorney Relationship Exists

The best practice is for lawyers to refrain from answering legal questions in these settings unless they are willing to establish a client-lawyer relationship.

The Issue of Providing Competent Representation

Answering legal questions off-hand is also problematic if the lawyer is guessing the answer to the question. Lawyers, and especially those who are not at the time acting within their official capacity as counsel to a client, may not have sufficient knowledge of the specific topic, just like many of the other people present. Indeed, in the field of animal law, many diverse issues implicate federal and state laws, directly or tangentially.

For example, the organization must transport three dogs to another rescue in a neighboring state. The question of whether the organization needs to pay the driver of the dogs overtime pay comes up in a casual conversation. Many volunteer lawyers would not know about the motor carriers' exemption to the fair labor standards act. Even lawyers familiar with an exemption might not know if the exemption applied in this situation.

This kind of setting does not allow a lawyer to carry out the usual procedure for giving quality legal advice, which involves asking questions, looking things up on a legal database, or otherwise getting updated on the current state of the law. Even if a lawyer has a general understanding of a topic, the best lawyers often take the time to double-check their grasp on the material.

Picture again a scenario in which a lawyer is in a room full of people asking unconventional legal questions. The lawyer answers any legal question the best they can and moves on, assuming that their best guess is good enough. As discussed, however, this level of response is hardly adequate compared to the usual process of giving legal advice.

At this point, the lawyer may not only be newly representing a client but also—should a complaint arise—subject to disciplinary action for providing their new client with incompetent representation.

Rule 1.1: Competence

Model Rule 1.1 "Competence" warns against this kind of predicament. Rule 1.1 states, "A lawyer shall provide competent representation to a client. Competent representation requires the legal knowledge, skill, thoroughness, and preparation reasonably necessary for the representation."[5] Whether a lawyer is providing competent representation depends on the kind of representation the client needs and the ability of the lawyer to meet those needs. A lawyer is not

5. *Rule 1.1: Competence*, Am. Bar Ass'n, https://www.americanbar.org/groups/professional_responsibility/publications/model_rules_of_professional_conduct/rule_1_1_competence/.

only expected but also required to meet the representational needs of their client following the formation of a client-lawyer relationship. This duty is not boundless, of course. The accompanying comment to the rule states, among other things:

> In an emergency, a lawyer may give advice or assistance in a matter in which the lawyer does not have the skill ordinarily required where referral to or consultation or association with another lawyer would be impractical. Even in an emergency, however, assistance should be limited to that reasonably necessary in the circumstances, for ill-considered action under emergency conditions can jeopardize the client's interests.[6]

The accompanying comment to Rule 1.1, in other words, lowers the standard for the quality of advice a lawyer is expected to give in the case of emergency while still complying with the rules of professional ethics. It discourages laxity under all circumstances with a reasonableness standard, however: even in emergencies, lawyers are required to give only such advice as reasonably accords with their client's interests.

The hypothetical situation described earlier (of answering questions offhand during a meeting) was not an emergency and would not be held to a more lenient standard than the one described in Rule 1.1, requiring knowledge, thoroughness, and preparation.

The comment to Rule 1.1 also states, "Competent handling of a particular matter includes inquiry into and analysis of the factual and legal elements of the problem, and use of methods and procedures meeting the standards of competent practitioners."[7] Exempting narrow circumstances in which the lawyer is an expert in the issue and is already familiar with the facts, off-the-cuff answers are unacceptable.

How does a lawyer know if they are competent to even give advice to an organization? The first question is what is in the field of nonprofit animal law? Nonprofit animal law is any legal topic that an animal protection organization may face. That is a mind-boggling array of topics. Start with general business legal topics: employment law, wage and hour laws, disability law, nonprofit tax law, insurance law, negligence law, intellectual property law, tort law, contract law, landlord tenant law, privacy laws, land use, and so on. Then add all the specific animal-oriented laws, relating to animal cruelty, veterinarians, environmental protection, endangered species, dangerous dogs and animal bite liability, breed specific legislation, pet regulation, ag gag, rodeos, first amendment protections, and so on.

If you are looking for a best practice, try this. Assume you are not competent to give any advice without doing two things. First, stop and ask all the questions you would ask a potential client if they walked into your office with a new legal matter. Then before giving any advice, research the topic. The only

6. *Rule 1.1: Competence—Comment*, Am. Bar Ass'n, https://www.americanbar.org/groups/professional_responsibility/publications/model_rules_of_professional_conduct/rule_1_1_competence/comment_on_rule_1_1/.

7. *Id.*

exception would be on legal questions you routinely handle in your existing practice. In other words, if you are not already a general counsel for an animal-oriented organization, you probably are not competent to give advice. Keep in mind that, if you are already a general counsel for an animal nonprofit, you may have a potential conflict that you need to clear before saying anything.

Finally, the comment to Rule 1.1 mentions: "An agreement between the lawyer and the client regarding the scope of the representation may limit the matters for which the lawyer is responsible."[8] This recognizes that an agreement between the lawyer and the client regarding the scope of the lawyer's work is a reasonable means of limiting the lawyer's obligations to a client. However, it does not suggest that the scope can be drawn to allow the lawyer to provide the client with incompetent advice. Rule 1.1 imposes a duty to be competent, and an arrangement that allows a lawyer to provide their client with subpar advice is also unacceptable.

Best Practice: The Issue of Providing Competent Representation

The best practice is to take the time to ask whatever questions are necessary to understand the facts of the situation thoroughly before answering any legal questions. As in the hypothetical described above, a lawyer may not have time to ask background questions. In that case, the best practice is stating the professional need to understand the situation better and arranging to ask the person more questions after the meeting.

The Issue of Representing Clients with Conflicting Interests

Animal advocates work on various issues in tandem with many other animal activists. Picture a scenario in which some animal advocates want to move Joey, an elephant at a local zoo, out of his enclosure and into a nearby sanctuary. As the issue gets increasing media coverage, a lawyer becomes more interested in helping Joey. The lawyer notices that one animal welfare group, "Alliance for Elephants," has traction on the issue. The lawyer reaches out to them, offering them the lawyer's legal services. Alliance for Elephants is grateful for the lawyer's support during a hectic time and includes the lawyer straightaway in meetings on the organization's legal strategy. The lawyer becomes steeped in contract drafting to transfer ownership of Joey to Alliance for Elephants. However, just as the lawyer's work starts to take off, the campaign shifts focus: a 10,000-acre wildfire breaks out, and the people at Alliance for Elephants start helping relocate wildlife into a nature preserve area.

8. *Id.*

Even though the lawyer is devastated about the wildfire, the lawyer prioritizes Joey's cause and looks for other groups to work with who also prioritize it. The lawyer joins forces with a group named "Friends of Joey." The lawyer is happy to have found a group that shares an interest in Joey, but quickly learns that this group does not want Joey to go to a sanctuary. Instead, Friends of Joey wants to widen Joey's enclosure at the zoo fourfold by removing the entire penguin exhibit. The lawyer likes the idea of giving Joey four times the living space, so the lawyer abandons the contract that they had been drafting for the other client. The lawyer starts drafting a different contract to transfer the zoo's ownership of the penguins to a zoo in an adjacent state. At this point, the lawyer is representing two entities (namely, Alliance for Elephants and for Friends of Joey) that have an actual conflict of interest.

Rule 1.7 Conflict of Interest: Current Clients

Model Rule 1.7 "Conflict of Interest: Current Clients" is one of the longer rules, replete with separate parts and subparts, and helps lawyers prioritize clients and parse through interests. It states,

> (a) Except as provided in paragraph (b), a lawyer shall not represent a client if the representation involves a concurrent conflict of interest. A concurrent conflict of interest exists if:
> (1) the representation of one client will be directly adverse to another client; or
> (2) there is a significant risk that the representation of one or more clients will be materially limited by the lawyer's responsibilities to another client, a former client or a third person or by a personal interest of the lawyer.
> (b) Notwithstanding the existence of a concurrent conflict of interest under paragraph (a), a lawyer may represent a client if:
> (1) the lawyer reasonably believes that the lawyer will be able to provide competent and diligent representation to each affected client;
> (2) the representation is not prohibited by law;
> (3) the representation does not involve the assertion of a claim by one client against another client represented by the lawyer in the same litigation or other proceeding before a tribunal; and
> (4) each affected client gives informed consent, confirmed in writing.[9]

According to Rule 1.7(a), whether a concurrent conflict of interests exists depends in part on whether the representation of one client is directly averse to the other. The nonprofits in the hypothetical scenario described above have directly adverse interests: Alliance for Elephants wants Joey to roam free at a

9. *Rule 1.7: Conflict of Interest: Current Clients*, AM. BAR ASS'N, https://www.americanbar.org/groups/professional_responsibility/publications/model_rules_of_professional_conduct/rule_1_7_conflict_of_interest_current_clients/.

sanctuary, while Friends of Joey wants Joey to enjoy more space at the zoo. If one nonprofit achieves its desired outcome, the other one does not.[10]

The lawyer may still be able to represent both organizations according to Rule 1.7(b)(1) if "the lawyer reasonably believes that the lawyer will be able to provide competent and diligent representation to each affected client."[11] To provide competent representation, as discussed earlier, a lawyer must possess the legal knowledge, skill, thoroughness, and preparation to meet their client's needs.[12] To provide diligent representation, according to the official comment to Rule 1.3 "Diligence," a lawyer must engage in means reasonably likely to further their client's interests.[13] Any lawyer may struggle to meet this standard if they have two clients with concurrently conflicting interests. To be sure, the lawyer would have to perform legal work to advance a case or strategy most favorable to each respective side, an exercise that would stretch the bounds of any professional role.

In the scenario described above, for example, Friends of Joey may ask the lawyer to develop an argument in favor of the zoo. It would likely rely on the idea that the zoo would be an excellent place for Joey if Joey had more space. The lawyer would draw on facts to support this idea, including that the zoo has a large endowment, reliable long-term funding, in-house veterinarians, and elephant specialists. At the same time, Alliance for Elephants could ask the lawyer to continue drafting a contract to support their goal of transferring ownership of Joey to a sanctuary. The lawyer may then need to rely on facts to show that the sanctuary is a better place where Joey can engage in more natural elephant activities in a communal setting. If the lawyer does feel comfortable representing both clients, the lawyer would still need to obtain written consent from both clients under Rule 1.7(b)(4) ("each affected client gives informed consent, confirmed in writing").

It is doubtful, however, that the clients would consent to allow the lawyer to continue representing them both, knowing that their respective goals are at odds. If this occurs, the lawyer could pick one nonprofit for which to work or volunteer their legal services. This could be difficult if the lawyer is unsure which organization has the better approach or greater promise in achieving change on the issue. In many cases, there is no way to know which animal nonprofit will make the headway expected. Nevertheless, if the lawyer takes the route of representing a single organization, the lawyer should stick with the chosen client, even if their approach ultimately fails.

---

10. It is not uncommon to see this play out in animal protection campaigns. Two nonprofits who want to help the same animals may have wildly different ideas on how best to help them. The movement sees significant fights between animal nonprofits over the appropriate way to help the same species of animals or even the same individual animals.

11. Rule 1.7, *supra* note 9.

12. Rule 1.1, *supra* note 5.

13. *Rule 1.3: Diligence*, Am. Bar Ass'n, https://www.americanbar.org/groups/professional_responsibility/publications/model_rules_of_professional_conduct/rule_1_3_diligence/.

Another approach is to formally end a client-lawyer relationship with one client and then shift to forming a client-lawyer relationship with a second client. Rule 1.16 "Declining or Terminating Representation," subsection (b) conditions voluntary withdrawal from representation. It states in part, "a lawyer may withdraw from representing a client if: (1) withdrawal can be accomplished without material adverse effect on the interest of the clients." Thus, even if the lawyer is volunteering their legal services, the lawyer cannot suddenly withdraw their representation following the formation of a client-lawyer relationship. The lawyer must preserve the client's interests throughout the transition.

Best Practice: The Issue of Representing Clients with Conflicting Interests

The best practice for navigating the representation of clients with concurrent conflicting interests is to assess all possible options and give due consideration to the client's interests at stake. One option for the lawyer is to only represent a single nonprofit with the lawyer's same or similar views. If the lawyer finds fault with a nonprofit's approach, the lawyer can establish their own nonprofit and attack the problem as they see fit. Many lawyers have founded animal nonprofits and hold executive director and general counsel positions. This route provides the lawyer with the flexibility to work on the issues they like while also shielding themselves from ethical issues related to representing clients with conflicting interests. If an issue related to representing clients with conflicting interests has already emerged, the best practice is to terminate the representation consistent with Rule 1.16(b).

The Issue of Being Less Than Diligent About Pro Bono Work

Imagine a lawyer runs a bustling law practice all by themselves. Imagine they also have a family for which they provide and a well-rounded social life to boot. Notwithstanding what sounds like a full and busy life, imagine that the lawyer still has a desire to help their local community. The lawyer may also feel compelled as a member of the legal profession to make up for social inequalities by engaging in pro bono representation. The lawyer may be especially concerned about animal cruelty issues, for example, and decide to donate some of their free time toward bettering the lives of animals. When the lawyer starts volunteering, they commit to several legal tasks, some of which involve court filings and pending negotiations. Though the lawyer intends to follow up on their new work, life suddenly gets busy (e.g., they buy a new home). The lawyer loses touch with the organization, failing not only to do what they promised, but also to give the organization any notice that they will be unable to get it done after all. At this point, the lawyer may have failed to be diligent and subject to disciplinary action.

Rule 1.3 Diligence

Model Rule 1.3 "Diligence" is one of the shortest rules of professional responsibility. It reads: "A lawyer shall act with reasonable diligence and promptness in representing a client."[14] The official comment to Rule 1.3 expands on this sentiment, explaining, among other things, that "a lawyer should pursue a matter on behalf of a client despite opposition, obstruction or personal inconvenience."[15] Rule 1.3 applies in all cases of legal representation, even for pro bono clients. Pro bono clients are entitled to the same quality of representation as paying clients, including time spent with the client, researching, and writing.

Volunteering, in other words, takes on a different meaning in the legal profession than in other contexts. It is considered regular work and cannot be organized loosely to fit the lawyer's other personal commitments. This is due to the technical, confidential, and often time-pressured nature of legal work; once a lawyer is involved in their client's legal minutiae, the client expects the lawyer to handle it fully. Moreover, the client is subject to legal ramifications if the lawyer fails to do so. If the client needs documents filed with the court or to close a pending negotiation, for example, the lawyer must promptly and diligently carry out those tasks or risk harming the client's interests.

Best Practice: The Issue of Being Less Than Diligent About Pro Bono Work

The best practice to be diligent about pro bono work is to treat pro bono clients the same as regular clients: open a case file for the pro bono client; schedule work time for the pro bono client, and set reminders and deadlines; and conduct legal research on agreed upon legal questions and communicate in a timely and professional manner.

The Issue of the Scope of Representation of a Client

When a lawyer volunteers their legal services on a free ("non-paid" or "pro bono") basis, the issue of limiting the scope of the pro bono client's representation may arise. Picture a scenario in which an animal protection organization hires a lawyer to complete a specific task, like writing a legal research memo on cost-effective alternatives to dehorning. The lawyer completes the task promptly and diligently. The organization then pays the lawyer to complete a different task: a legal research memo on cost-effective alternatives to castration. The lawyer also completes this task in a timely and professional manner. The

14. Rule 1.3, *supra* note 13.

15. *Rule 1.3: Diligence—Comment*, Am. Bar Ass'n, https://www.americanbar.org/groups/professional_responsibility/publications/model_rules_of_professional_conduct/rule_1_3_diligence/comment_on_rule_1_3/.

organization, pleased with the lawyer's work, gives the lawyer another assignment, one that is open-ended and more complex than the prior assignments. The organization asks the lawyer to review one of their boilerplate contracts, noting that this contract is important for the organization's work, and that it will be used for a multitude of future legal projects. Unless the lawyer states otherwise, the client may think that the lawyer is agreeing to advise on all of these future projects.

Rule 1.2 Scope of Representation and Allocation of Authority Between Client and Lawyer

Model Rule 1.2 "Scope of Representation . . . " explains the scope of representation following the formation of a client-lawyer relationship and helps lawyers avoid scope-related misunderstandings. Rule 1.2(c) states, "A lawyer may limit the scope of the representation if the limitation is reasonable under the circumstances and the client gives informed consent."[16] The official comment to Rule 1.2(c) expands on what "reasonable under the circumstances" means in this context. It states that though it provides the client and lawyer with "substantial latitude to limit the representation,"[17] limitations must be reasonable and afford the client the competent representation needed to handle their legal issue.[18] The option to limit the scope, thus, does not exempt the lawyer from their duty of providing competent representation under Rule 1.1. The client must also give their "informed consent" to any limitations the lawyer wants to place on their representation before becoming legally binding.

The flip side is also proper: if the lawyer does not place any limitations on the scope of the representation, then the representation exists without legal limits. This opens the lawyer up to more legal responsibilities than they may be expecting or capable of handling.

Best Practice: The Issue of the Scope of Representation of a Client

The best practice for avoiding scope-related misunderstandings is for lawyers to put their understanding of the scope of the representation in writing. This simple step can be even more important to the volunteer lawyer. It helps avoid the situation where you have agreed to take on a single task, but someone in the

16. *Rule 1.2: Scope of Representation & Allocation of Authority Between Client & Lawyer*, AM. BAR ASS'N, https://www.americanbar.org/groups/professional_responsibility/publications/model_rules_of_professional_conduct/rule_1_2_scope_of_representation_allocation_of_authority_between_client_lawyer/.

17. *Rule 1.2: Scope of Representation & Allocation of Authority Between Client & Lawyer—Comment*, AM. BAR ASS'N, https://www.americanbar.org/groups/professional_responsibility/publications/model_rules_of_professional_conduct/rule_1_2_scope_of_representation_allocation_of_authority_between_client_lawyer/comment_on_rule_1_2/.

18. *Id.*

organization believes that you have taken on legal tasks that you did not even know existed.

In addition to clearly stating the scope of the lawyer's work, the engagement letter can also include a brief description of the facts as presented by the client. By taking the time to describe what you have been told are the relevant facts, you do two things. First, this is an invitation for the client to let you know about additional relevant facts or correct any incorrect information you have. Second, a single additional fact can totally change your legal analysis. If this does happen, you have a clear record of what the client relayed as the relevant facts that you based your legal work.

Including a time estimate in the engagement letter is just as important for a pro bono lawyer as for a paid lawyer. Clients often have no idea about how long legal task and legal proceedings take. This step is also important if existing obligations in your practice are going to delay your ability to deliver this work.

The lawyer can specify the client's needs and how the lawyer plans to meet those needs. The lawyer should explain that the lawyer's communication of the scope is the extent of the lawyer's commitment to the client. The lawyer should keep a record of the understanding, whether in a communication as formal as a contract or as informal as an email.

The Issue of Talking About Clients

Consider a typical scenario in which a lawyer attends an after-hours social gathering for the local section of their State Bar. The lawyers who attend these events expect to enjoy their postprandial downtime by networking with other practitioners in their field. The other lawyers begin the evening discussing local politics, sports, and breaking news, but as the evening progresses, the lawyers begin to trade work stories, such as the most exciting cases on which they have worked. The lawyer who is speaking starts their story with, "I had a case once where. . . . " By the end of the evening, dozens of stories have been offered up as insight into unusual clients, unique legal problems, and bizarre fact patterns. At this point, a few lawyers may have violated Rule 1.6 "Confidentiality of Information" and shared information relating to their past client's representation without that client's permission.

Rule 1.6 Confidentiality of Information

Model Rule 1.6 "Confidentiality of Information" is one of the more misunderstood model rules because it is somewhat of a misnomer ("confidentiality of information" brings to mind a slightly different concept, "confidential information"), and it also has tedium of subparts. Even so, it governs the disclosure of all information relating to the representation of a client and is therefore integral to the profession. It states,

> (a) A lawyer shall not reveal information relating to the representation of a client unless the client gives informed consent, the disclosure is impliedly authorized in order to carry out the representation or the disclosure is permitted by paragraph (b).
> (b) A lawyer may reveal information relating to the representation of a client to the extent the lawyer reasonably believes necessary:
> (1) to prevent reasonably certain death or substantial bodily harm;
> (2) to prevent the client from committing a crime or fraud that is reasonably certain to result in substantial injury to the financial interests or property of another and in furtherance of which the client has used or is using the lawyer's services;
> (3) to prevent, mitigate or rectify substantial injury to the financial interests or property of another that is reasonably certain to result or has resulted from the client's commission of a crime or fraud in furtherance of which the client has used the lawyer's services;
> (4) to secure legal advice about the lawyer's compliance with these Rules;
> (5) to establish a claim or defense on behalf of the lawyer in a controversy between the lawyer and the client, to establish a defense to a criminal charge or civil claim against the lawyer based upon conduct in which the client was involved, or to respond to allegations in any proceeding concerning the lawyer's representation of the client;
> (6) to comply with other law or a court order; or
> (7) to detect and resolve conflicts of interest arising from the lawyer's change of employment or from changes in the composition or ownership of a firm, but only if the revealed information would not compromise the attorney-client privilege or otherwise prejudice the client.
> (c) A lawyer shall make reasonable efforts to prevent the inadvertent or unauthorized disclosure of, or unauthorized access to, information relating to the representation of a client.[19]

Rule 1.6 regulates all information "relating to the representation of a client."[20] This includes not only confidential information, of course, but also more banal information, like the terms or even the existence of the client-lawyer relationship, as well as publicly known information, like the client's views on a legal matter (even if the client already shared those views publicly, such as in a televised interview).

Information that a client tells a lawyer in private, which may be detrimental to the client's interest, is an example of confidential information. If the client confesses to participating in a crime (e.g., the client tells their lawyer that their dog was participating in an illegal dog fight at the time that a neighbor is mistakenly accusing the client's dog of having bitten the neighbor's child), the lawyer may not disclose that information, even if it would help to resolve the client's legal issues with their neighbor.

---

19. *Rule 1.6: Confidentiality of Information*, Am. Bar Ass'n, https://www.americanbar.org/groups/professional_responsibility/publications/model_rules_of_professional_conduct/rule_1_6_confidentiality_of_information/.

20. *Id.*

Publicly known information can also fall into the category of "confidential information." Imagine a well-known local community member hires a lawyer to draft a donor agreement for a significant donation to a controversial cause. If, in this scenario, the client decides to mention to the locally nightly news that they donated one million dollars to a controversial cause, all information about that donation is still covered by Rule 1.6. The lawyer may not discuss the donation without violating Rule 1.6. This is true even though it is publicly known (i.e., publicly available, e.g., on the internet) information unless the lawyer has their client's informed consent to talk about the donation.

Rule 1.6 could be seen as including even the most basic information and is therefore described in the comment to the rule as "extremely broad, covering information received from the client or any other source, even public sources."[21] Thus, Rule 1.6 governs a large swath of information, not just confidential information. The lawyer must obtain the client's informed consent beforehand if the lawyer wishes to disclose such information.

The lawyer is allowed under Rule 1.6 to disclose information about the client unrelated to their representation. If the lawyer knows that the client collects vintage enamelware, for example, and describes an unusual platter in that collection to members at a dinner party one evening, the lawyer will not run afoul of Rule 1.6.

Best Practice: The Issue of Talking About Clients

The best practice when talking about clients is to use Rule 1.6's exemption, which allows lawyers to discuss the relevant information with the client's informed consent. At the outset of the client-lawyer relationship, a lawyer should meaningfully discuss Rule 1.6 and how they would be able to comply with confidentiality requirements during the client's representation.

The lawyer should then get their client's views on sharing information. The client may not, for example, have qualms about their lawyer discussing information about them that is already public or otherwise accessible online. Alternatively, the client may not want certain public information repeated, for the sake of the case, though they would not mind if their lawyer discussed the nuances of their case with other lawyers after the matter is concluded. In other words, the client and lawyer should agree on when and how the lawyer will share any information about the representation with others. Finally, although Rule 1.6 only requires the client's informed consent, it is best practice for the lawyer to put the tailored agreement into the written engagement contract.

---

21. *Rule 1.6: Confidentiality of Information—Comment*, AM. BAR ASS'N, https://www.americanbar.org/groups/professional_responsibility/publications/model_rules_of_professional_conduct/rule_1_6_confidentiality_of_information/comment_on_rule_1_6/.

The Issue of Embarrassing (or Otherwise Burdening) Third Persons

When animal lawyers work on cases involving horrific animal cruelty and suffering, the issue of embarrassing third persons may arise. Imagine a scenario where a lawyer gets a job in a nonprofit's animal cruelty unit. The lawyer takes calls reporting animal cruelty and starts investigating alleged crimes against animals. Soon after starting their job, the lawyer gets a call about an animal hoarding case. While learning more about the case, the lawyer meets the person who has been charged with animal cruelty. The lawyer perceives that the accused cares little about the animals and faults the accused for refusing to acknowledge the harm they caused. When the lawyer returns to their office, the lawyer decides the nonprofit should pressure the accused to relinquish the animals. The lawyer decides to speak to the local paper to discredit and embarrass the accused. The lawyer describes the gruesome living conditions at the home and the accused's delinquency on their property taxes. At this point, the lawyer may be violating Rule 4.4.

Rule 4.4 Respect for Rights of Third Persons

Model Rule 4.4 "Respect for Rights of Third Persons" dictates how attorneys should treat third persons (i.e., all persons other than their clients) when they act within their professional capacity as the client's representative and interact with others. Rule 4.4(a) states, "In representing a client, a lawyer shall not use means that have no substantial purpose other than to embarrass, delay, or burden a third person, or use methods of obtaining evidence that violate the legal rights of such a person."[22]

Rule 4.4(a) requires lawyers to respect the dignity and rights of third persons, even if their clients choose to behave differently. Rule 4.4(a) aims to clear the legal profession and system from moral failings like purposefully or unduly denigrating persons.

The term "third person" is a term of art under Rule 44(a). It includes everyone other than the litigants. Thus, Rule 4.4(a) covers an extensive range of conduct, including a lawyer's treatment of members of the court, the jury, witnesses, bystanders and, of course, the opponents, the opponent's family members, and opposing counsel, among others. For those animal lawyers working on farm animal protection cases, third persons may also include factory farm workers, producers, or large corporations that contract with the producers. For those animal lawyers involved in ending animal cruelty, third persons may include the abusers or hoarders of animals.

22. *Rule 4.4: Respect for Rights of Third Persons*, AM. BAR ASS'N, https://www.americanbar.org/groups/professional_responsibility/publications/model_rules_of_professional_conduct/rule_4_4_respect_for_rights_of_third_persons/.

Best Practice: The Issue of Embarrassing (or Otherwise Burdening) Third Persons

The best practice to avoid embarrassing (or otherwise burdening) third persons is for lawyers to maintain their professional composure throughout the representation. Saying little will ensure that the lawyer does not find themselves in violation of Rule 4.4.

The Issue of Researching Adversaries

When lawyers try to learn information about their client's adversaries, the issue of communicating with persons (represented or unrepresented) may arise. Picture a lawyer working with local property owners to bring a nuisance suit against a hog producer. The hog producer is incorporating a defense of being a good citizen to minimize punitive damages. The lawyer researches their client's adversary to better understand the adversary's character before going to trial. The lawyer believes that seeing the adversary's social media profiles could help the lawyer develop their theory of the case.

The lawyer cannot access any of the adversary's social media profiles, including their Twitter, Facebook, or Instagram accounts, because the adversary keeps all their social media profiles on a "private" setting. The lawyer can only access the adversary's content if the lawyer sends the adversary a friend request. The lawyer did not consult anyone before sending the request. The lawyer bets that the adversary will accept the friend request automatically, without checking from whom the request came. At this point, the lawyer may be violating Rule 4.2 or Rule 4.3, rules governing a lawyer's communications with other persons.

Rule 4.2 Communication with Person Represented by Counsel

Model Rule 4.2 "Communication with Person Represented by Counsel" applies if the person is represented by counsel. It states,

> In representing a client, a lawyer shall not communicate about the subject of the representation with a person the lawyer knows to be represented by another lawyer in the matter unless the lawyer has the other lawyer's consent or is authorized to do so by law or court order.[23]

Lawyers are bound by Rule 4.2 only if the lawyer knew before the communication took place that the person was represented by counsel. The answer to whether a person is represented by counsel may be based on actual

23. *Rule 4.2: Communication with Person Represented by Counsel*, Am. Bar Ass'n, https://www.americanbar.org/groups/professional_responsibility/publications/model_rules_of_professional_conduct/rule_4_2_communication_with_person_represented_by_counsel/.

knowledge but also inferences based on the circumstances, according to the comment to Rule 4.2.[24] It is insufficient, in other words, for a lawyer to rely on their ignorance as to that specific question of fact (i.e., whether the person is represented by counsel) to avoid having to request the represented person's lawyer's permission to communicate. Thus, the lawyer cannot evade the requirement of obtaining the consent of counsel by closing their eyes to what is otherwise apparent.

Once in effect, Rule 4.2 stands as a gatekeeper to represented persons, permitting other lawyers to communicate with them about matters to which the representation relates only after the other lawyers get permission from their lawyer, the law, or the court. The rule stands even if the represented person initiates or consents to the communication.[25] The purpose of Rule 4.2, in part, is to "protec[t] a person who has chosen to be represented by a lawyer in a matter against possible overreaching by other lawyers who are participating in the matter."[26]

In the scenario described above, if the lawyer knew the adversary was already represented by counsel, then the lawyer knowingly violated Rule 4.2, given that the lawyer did not consult with the person's lawyer before sending the requests. Of course, the represented person's lawyer would have likely refused any requests to speak to their client because the lawyer is trying to obtain information about the adversary to use against the adversary.

Significantly, the lawyer's friend request counts as a communication relating to the representation because the lawyer made the gesture to access information that could bolster their client's case against the adversary later on.

Rule 4.3 Dealing with Unrepresented Person

Model Rule 4.3 "Dealing with Unrepresented Person" applies if the person is not represented by counsel. It states,

> In dealing on behalf of a client with a person who is not represented by counsel, a lawyer shall not state or imply that the lawyer is disinterested. When the lawyer knows or reasonably should know that the unrepresented person misunderstands the lawyer's role in the matter, the lawyer shall make reasonable efforts to correct the misunderstanding. The lawyer shall not give legal advice to an unrepresented person, other than the advice to secure counsel, if the lawyer knows or reasonably should know that the interests of such a person are or have a reasonable possibility of being in conflict with the interests of the client.[27]

24. *Rule 4.2: Communication with Person Represented by Counsel—Comment*, Am. Bar Ass'n, https://www.americanbar.org/groups/professional_responsibility/publications/model_rules_of_professional_conduct/rule_4_2_communication_with_person_represented_by_counsel/comment_on_rule_4_2.

25. *Id.*

26. *Id.*

27. *Rule 4.3: Dealing with Unrepresented Person*, Am. Bar Ass'n, https://www.americanbar.org/groups/professional_responsibility/publications/model_rules_of_professional_conduct/rule_4_3_dealing_with_unrepresented_person/.

Lawyers are bound by Rule 4.3 if the lawyer knew before the communication took place that the person was unrepresented by counsel. As with Rule 4.2, however, whether the lawyer knows that the person is unrepresented may be based on actual knowledge or inferences based on circumstances.

Once in effect, Rule 4.3 protects unrepresented persons from communicating with lawyers whose client's interests are averse to the unrepresented person's. Thus, Rule 4.3 prohibits lawyers from implying impartiality or objectivity in matters relating to the representation. In the scenario described above, if the lawyer knew the person was unrepresented, then the lawyer knowingly violated Rule 4.3, given that the lawyer considers the unrepresented person their client's adversary. Notably, the lawyer's friend requests are thinly veiled attempts to communicate with the unrepresented person in a disinterested manner, given that the lawyer hoped the unrepresented person would accept the request without checking from whom the request came.

Best Practice: The Issue of Researching Adversaries

The best practice for researching adversaries is for lawyers to be honest with opposing counsel about their actions. Lawyers may make inquiries about the other party openly and confidently since they are entitled to certain information.

The Issue of Bringing Impact Litigation

When lawyers bring impact litigation (e.g., innovative litigation designed to end animal cruelty, directly or indirectly), issues related to bringing frivolous lawsuits may arise.

Rule 3.1 Meritorious Claims & Contentions

Rule 3.1 "Meritorious Claims & Contentions" warns against bringing frivolous lawsuits. It states,

> A lawyer shall not bring or defend a proceeding, or assert or controvert an issue therein, unless there is a basis in law and fact for doing so that is not frivolous, which includes a good faith argument for an extension, modification or reversal of existing law. . . .[28]

To bring a case, in other words, lawyers must have a nonfrivolous "basis in law and fact" to support suing the opposing party. There are many recent advances in our understanding of the emotional and cognitive ability of animals.

28. *Rule 3.1: Meritorious Claims & Contentions*, Am. Bar Ass'n, https://www.americanbar.org/groups/professional_responsibility/publications/model_rules_of_professional_conduct/rule_3_1_meritorious_claims_contentions/.

This provides a natural opportunity to expand the application of animal laws to fit science's new understanding of the animal world. There is also a global trend to expand the rights of animals. Rule 3.1 is built to handle situations exactly like this.

Best Practice: The Issue of Bringing Impact Litigation

Understand and use Rule 3.1. When using impact litigation to expand the reach of existing laws to aid animals, highlight that your suit is an extension of existing law. This should help avoid running afoul of Rule 3.1. It can also be an effective litigation strategy.

The Issue of Being Counsel and Advisor to Clients

When lawyers use their legal skills to help animals, issues related to being counsel and advisor to clients may arise. Imagine a lawyer practices animal law because they are motivated to help animals. The lawyer realizes that in most cases, the lawyer cannot represent the animals directly, so the lawyer gets a job at a nonprofit organization that arranges rescue, foster, and adoption efforts for free-roaming dogs and cats.

One day, the director of the nonprofit consults the lawyer about an opportunity to rescue ten dogs from a hoarding situation. The lawyer informs the director about the legal process for transferring ownership of the dogs. Then, the lawyer provides the client with the insight that it is expensive to care for the animals before they are adopted, including due to the costs of veterinary care. The lawyer advises the client to evaluate their economic standing to see whether the client would be able to afford those extra expenses before proceeding to take the dogs. At this point, the lawyer has given the client nonlegal advice in compliance with Rule 2.1 on advising clients.

Rule 2.1 Advisor

Model Rule 2.1 "Advisor" formally recognizes lawyers as advisors. It states, "In representing a client, a lawyer shall exercise independent professional judgment and render candid advice. In rendering advice, a lawyer may refer not only to law but to other considerations such as moral, economic, social, and political factors, that may be relevant to the client's situation."[29]

Rule 2.1 permits lawyers to offer their clients advice, even extralegal advice, but only when the client prompts the lawyer to give advice or the circumstances warrant it (e.g., the lawyer wants to advise the client on how to handle problems

29. *Rule 2.1: Advisor*, AM. BAR ASS'N, https://www.americanbar.org/groups/professional_responsibility/publications/model_rules_of_professional_conduct/rule_2_1_advisor/.

related to the representation).[30] In the scenario described above, the lawyer provided a client with advice after the client sought the lawyer's opinion directly. In addition, the lawyer gave the client advice regarding their economic situation as per their particular legal transaction. The lawyer did so even though it may have delayed or impeded the adoption process altogether in that case. Notably, the lawyer's advice aligned with the nonprofit's mission of placing animals into good homes. In this scenario, the lawyer anticipated the fundamental issues related to pet ownership.

Best Practice: The Issue of Being Counsel and Advisor to Clients

The best practice for being counsel and advisor to clients is to give clients candid advice. Lawyers are more valuable to their clients when they can shed light on their client's legal and nonlegal issues. Thus, lawyers should feel free to discuss the implications of a given course of action if the lawyer judges the discussion will further the client's interests.

The Ethics of Representing Organizations

When lawyers represent an organization, it is essential to establish who the client is. Rule 1.13(a) states, "A lawyer employed or retained by an organization represents the organization acting through its duly authorized constituents."[31]

This can be a problem particularly when dealing with small organizations and when the lawyer's primary contact is the organization's founder and executive director. These individuals may blur the lines between their interests and the organization's interests. But usually, the lawyer represents the organization, not the founder as an individual. The lawyer should always be mindful of who they are representing.

Rule 1.13 Organization as Client

Rule 1.13(f) states, "In dealing with an organization's directors, officers, employees, members, shareholders or other constituents, a lawyer shall explain the identity of the client when the lawyer knows or reasonably should know that the organization's interests are averse to those of the constituents with whom the lawyer is dealing."[32]

---

30. *Rule 2.1: Advisor—Comment*, AM. BAR ASS'N, https://www.americanbar.org/groups/professional_responsibility/publications/model_rules_of_professional_conduct/rule_2_1_advisor/comment_on_rule_2_1_advisor/.

31. *Rule 1.13(a) Organization as Client*, AM. BAR ASS'N, https://www.americanbar.org/groups/professional_responsibility/publications/model_rules_of_professional_conduct/rule_1_13_organization_as_client/.

32. *Rule 1.13(f) Organization as Client*, AM. BAR ASS'N, https://www.americanbar.org/groups/professional_responsibility/publications/model_rules_of_professional_conduct/rule_1_13_organization_as_client.

If lawyers find themselves in situations in which an individual within the organization, such as an executive director, starts asking questions about personal representation, stop the conversation immediately. An obvious sign that a matter is personal is when the individual's interests are not aligned with those of the organization. Handle the interaction according to Rule 4.3, "Dealing with Unrepresented Person". Also keep in mind Rule 1.7 "Conflict of Interest: Current Clients" as well as Rule 1.13(f) "Organization as Client".

Best Practice When Representing an Organization

Be quick to remind everyone you deal with in an organization that you represent the organization and not any one individual. Remind them in particular that any attorney-client privilege and confidentiality obligations that you have as the organization's lawyer are held by or owed to the organization, so you cannot guarantee the individual that you will not share the content of your communications with the organization.

Organizations and Criminal or Fraudulent Conduct

Lawyers representing organizations have unique access to activities conducted in the name of the organization. Lawyers often talk to middle managers and even line workers to effectively represent the organization. It is not uncommon for lawyers to uncover something troublesome in these conversations. It could be an illegal or potentially illegal activity. The organization might not know that its employees or board members have taken these actions. Examples could be endless, but let us look at the case of a board member seeing a dog tied to a short chain without any shelter in someone's backyard. In the normal course, the organization would work through animal control to help the dog. But the board member is so appalled at the situation that they tell the lawyer of a plan to unchain the dog, put the dog in their car, and bring the animal to the client's facility.

Rule 1.2 Scope of Representation & Allocation of Authority Between Client & Lawyer

When becoming aware of discussions of illegal activity, the lawyer needs to be keenly aware of Rule 1.2. Rule 1.2(d) states, "A lawyer shall not counsel a client to engage, or assist a client, in conduct that the lawyer knows is criminal or fraudulent, but a lawyer may discuss the legal consequences of any proposed course of conduct with a client and may counsel or assist a client to make a good faith effort to determine the validity, scope, meaning or application of the law."

This is a situation in which the lawyer can unwittingly violate the rules of professional responsibility. In this difficult situation, the lawyer will need to have a clear understanding of the factual situation. The lawyer may need to engage in a lengthy interview process for the lawyer to have sufficient understanding of the situation to give competent legal advice. It could be a better course of action to not give on-the-spot advice, and it will be important for the lawyer to ensure that they are not assisting in lawful conduct, but rather—in any advice given—that they are advising on legal consequences or on the validity or interpretation of the law.

If a lawyer uncovers that people related to the organization are engaged in or are considering engaging in illegal activities, that lawyer should immediately take a close look at Rule 1.13(b), which—depending on the lawyer's assessment of the risk to the organization and the organization's best interests—may require action from the lawyer in the form of reporting to higher organizational authorities. Rule 1.13(b) states,

> If a lawyer for an organization knows that an officer, employee or other person associated with the organization is engaged in action, intends to act or refuses to act in a matter related to the representation that is a violation of a legal obligation to the organization, or a violation of law that reasonably might be imputed to the organization, and that is likely to result in substantial injury to the organization, then the lawyer shall proceed as is reasonably necessary in the best interest of the organization. Unless the lawyer reasonably believes that it is not necessary in the best interest of the organization to do so, the lawyer shall refer the matter to higher authority in the organization, including, if warranted by the circumstances to the highest authority that can act on behalf of the organization as determined by applicable law.

Best Practice: Discovering Illegal Activity by Those Associated with an Organizational Client

These are intensely fact-specific situations. A proper response can range from doing nothing, reporting what was learned to the client's management, or reporting to higher authorities. The lawyer needs to undertake a serious analysis of what course of action is required under Rule 1.13(b).

Issues Relating to Animal Hoarding

Animal hoarding takes many forms. There is the individual who is constantly "rescuing" additional animals. Then there are animal hoarders who hide behind the structure of nonprofit rescues and animal sanctuaries. The real problem for animal lawyers is that it is easy to get deceived into "helping" these animal hoarders.

Ethical Rules Related to Animal Hoarding

All animal lawyers must be keenly aware of the duties attached when talking with animal hoarders. Rule 4.4 controls dealing with third parties. Rule 1.18 covers duties to prospective clients. Rule 4.3 explains a lawyer's duties to the unrepresented. Rule 1.9 has a listing of duties to former clients. Remember that animal hoarding can be a mental illness triggering Rule 1.14, which applies to interactions with clients with diminished capacity.

But perhaps most troubling for animal lawyers is Rule 1.7, "Conflicts of Interest with Current Clients. Rule 1.7 says in part, "a lawyer shall not represent a client if the representation involves a concurrent conflict of interest."

Let us look at how this might play out. An animal hoarder is operating as a 501(c)3 "animal rescue." This hoarding operation approaches a lawyer for legal help. The lawyer meets with the hoarder, and answers enough basic legal questions to establish an attorney-client relationship. Then the lawyer discovers that this new client is an animal hoarder. The new client has hundreds of animals being kept in filthy cages, often does not feed the animals, and the building where the animals live has no heat. The lawyer has no desire to help the animal hoarder continue in the mistreatment of the animals.

Assume that the lawyer has a long-standing animal rescue client. This long-standing client wants the lawyer's help in gaining ownership of these neglected animals to provide medical treatment and find adoptive homes. Because the two clients will be adversarial in the same matter, the lawyer is conflicted out. The lawyer cannot represent either organization without written consent from both affected clients.

Best Practice: Animal Hoarders

Lawyers must do their due diligence when taking on new clients working in animal protection. At a minimum, visit the facility before agreeing to represent the person. The lawyer should monitor their existing clients for any signs that the nature of the business has changed.

Learn the signs that may indicate that a person is an animal hoarder, not a sanctuary or rescue, and do not interact with any individual or organization with the slightest hint of being an animal hoarder. This will help preserve the lawyers' ability to continue working for the lawyers' existing clients who might want to help remove animals from the hoarder.

PART II

Key Laws for Animals and Animal Protection Organizations

CHAPTER 8

State and Local Law

Tamara Feliciano, Robert Hensley, and Meredith Beach

Introduction

Numerous state and local laws directly impact the care, protection, use, and management of animals. These laws often fill a gap left by a lack of congressional action, as discussed in chapter 9. However, in some cases, federal laws preempt state and local legislation of various animal related issues. Even the most well-drafted animal protection laws still may not address the universe of scenarios that animals and the people who seek to care for or protect them may face. Furthermore, while some areas of animal law are well established, others are evolving and ripe for debate and improvement.

This chapter examines the most common types of state and local laws that impact animals, including animal cruelty laws and laws that regulate or protect different types of animals, such as companion animals, exotic animals, farmed animals, and wildlife. Each section discusses the issues broadly and draws examples from across the country to illustrate how state and local governments have approached animal welfare issues and how these approaches vary by jurisdiction. Where applicable, this chapter also identifies challenges associated with enforcing animal laws and helps identify drafting considerations for those seeking to improve the law.[1]

1. Federal laws impacting animal welfare are discussed in chapter 9.

Animal Cruelty Laws

Overview

Every state prohibits animal cruelty.[2] While there are often variations in the statutory language, state animal cruelty laws generally include four main components: (1) a definition of "animal," (2) a description of the acts that constitute animal cruelty, (3) a description of the intent necessary to constitute a violation, and (4) consideration of the severity of the injury suffered by the animal.

While state cruelty laws typically cover many types of animals, animals deemed "companion animals" often receive heightened protections. A "companion animal" may be generally defined as any dog or cat as well as any other domesticated animal that is kept as a pet such as birds, horses, rabbits, hamsters, etc. The definition of "companion animal," as set forth in animal cruelty laws, typically excludes livestock, wildlife, and marine life.[3] For example, in New York, torturing and killing a companion animal is a felony that carries a potential sentence of up to two years' incarceration, whereas torturing and killing a farmed animal or wildlife is a misdemeanor with a possible sentence of up to one year incarceration.[4]

As to farmed animals specifically, many state cruelty laws either exclude them expressly or allow what might otherwise be considered cruelty if it is carried out as part of "normal" farming practices.[5] For example, Georgia law exempts actions taken in connection with "agricultural," "animal husbandry," "butchering," and "food processing" practices from its cruelty law.[6] Indeed, even where protections are afforded to farm animals under state anti-cruelty laws, these laws may be difficult to enforce against individuals suspected of farm animal abuse, in part because the conduct occurs at private facilities away from oversight and because certain farming practices may be customarily accepted.[7]

In general, prohibited acts of animal cruelty tend to fall into the following categories: (1) overt acts, (2) neglect and failure to provide care, (3) abandonment, (4) animal fighting, and (5) sexual abuse.[8] Overt acts are acts that are intentionally inflicted or directed, such as kicking, punching, throwing, stabbing, or shooting. While the act itself may be intentional, the effect the act may have on the animal does not necessarily have to be intended.[9] For example, shooting into a car and hitting a dog in that car is an overt act regardless of whether the shooter knew a dog was in the car prior to firing the gun. Crimes of neglect and failure to

2. *Legal Protections for Animals on Farms*, Animal Welfare Inst., https://awionline.org/sites/default/files/uploads/documents/FA-AWI-LegalProtections-AnimalsonFarms-110714.pdf.

3. *Id.*

4. N.Y. Agric. & Mkts. Law § 353-353-a.

5. Lindsey Walton & Kristen King Jaiven, *Regulating CAFOS for the Well-Being of Farm Animals, Consumers, and the Environment*, Env'l L. Rep. (June 2020), 50.10485.pdf.

6. O.C.G.A. § 4-1-7(2021).

7. Walton & Jaiven, *supra* note 5.

8. Elizabeth Brandler, *What Is Animal Cruelty and How Is It Investigated?*, PowerPoint Presentation, Topics In Biology: Forensic and Legal Aspects of Animal Cruelty Investigations for the Veterinary Professional, Florida International University (Fall 2022) (available from authors upon request).

9. *Id.*

provide care include acts, or failures to act, by which an animal fails to receive appropriate care or shelter. Examples include failure to provide sufficient food, water, appropriate shelter, or necessary veterinary care.[10] Abandonment occurs when an animal is abandoned or intentionally left without care, such as when an animal's owner moves out of their home and leaves their animal behind or "releases" the animal into the community.[11] Laws prohibiting animal fighting most commonly address dog and cockfighting, and generally prohibit the intentional fighting, training, and/or breeding of these animals for purposes of having them engage in fighting.[12] Laws against the sexual abuse of animals, commonly known as "bestiality," prohibit sexual conduct with an animal.[13]

Penalties for committing acts of animal cruelty typically become more severe based on the intent of the actor and the level of injury suffered by the animal.[14] For example, in Texas it is a misdemeanor to fail to provide necessary food, water, or shelter for an animal.[15] By contrast, it is a felony to torture an animal or, in a cruel manner, to kill or cause serious bodily injury to an animal. "Cruel manner" is defined as an action that causes or permits unjustified or unwarranted pain or suffering.[16]

There may also be circumstances in which acts that harm an animal may not be considered illegal. For instance, where the act was justified because the animal was attacking a person or animal or where a religious exemption exists in the law, such as an exemption for animal sacrifice.[17] Activities such as hunting, fishing, rodeos, research, and veterinary medicine are also typically exempted from animal cruelty laws, provided they are done in compliance with the laws regulating them.[18]

Forfeiture, Bonding, Cost of Care, and Responsible Owner Laws

Cruelty laws addressing animal victims are unique in several ways, most notably in that the victims of the crime cannot speak for themselves.[19] When violence is

10. *Id.*

11. *Id.*

12. Dogfighting is a felony in all fifty states and in the District of Columbia. Being a spectator at a dogfight is illegal in all states, and the possession of dogs for the purpose of fighting is a felony offense in most states. Cockfighting is illegal in all fifty states and is a felony offense in forty-two states. The possession of birds for fighting purposes is prohibited in thirty-nine states and the District of Columbia; being a spectator at a cockfighting event is illegal in forty-three states and the District of Columbia. National Sheriff's Association, *Animal Fighting*, https://www.sheriffs.org/animal-fighting.

13. Legal Information Institute, *Bestiality*, Cornell Law School, https://www.law.cornell.edu/wex/bestiality#::text=These%20statutes%20make%20those%20convicted,not%20have%20laws%20against%20bestiality.

14. Brandler, *supra* note 8.

15. Tex. Pen. Code § 42.092 (2023).

16. *Id.*

17. Brandler, *supra* note 8.

18. *Id.*

19. *Position Statement on Protection of Animal Cruelty Victims*, ASPCA, https://www.aspca.org/about-us/aspca-policy-and-position-statements/position-statement-protection-animal-cruelty-victims [hereinafter "ASPCA Animal Cruelty Victims"].

committed against a human being, the victim—so long as they are not a minor or otherwise prevented from doing so—can decide for themselves whether to report that abuse.[20] Upon doing so, the victim's statements regarding what occurred and who did it, as well as any associated medical records, become evidence used to help investigate and prosecute the alleged offense.[21] However, in animal cruelty cases, the animal cannot seek out help or tell a story. As such, when the victim is an animal, the legal process can look considerably different. Indeed, because animals are property under the law, whether they will even be removed from a dangerous situation is less than certain.[22]

An animal can generally be seized from its owner or caregiver via a search warrant if there is probable cause that a crime has been committed or, in many jurisdictions, without a warrant if there is an exigent need to render immediate lifesaving emergency aid. Once the animal is lawfully seized, the animal is typically provided necessary care and housed by a law enforcement agency or by a third party, such as a humane society or shelter, while the criminal case proceeds.[23] Sometimes, if the owner of the animal surrenders ownership or if the court orders forfeiture prior to a conviction, the animal may be released early in the case and made available for adoption, transferred to another organization from which adoption is more likely, or humanely euthanized if deemed necessary due to serious behavioral or medical conditions.[24]

Unfortunately for the animals, though, in many jurisdictions across the country, animals seized in cruelty cases can be held for months or even years while criminal charges are resolved.[25] The reasons for these lengthy hold periods vary. Animals remain the defendant's legal property unless the defendant relinquishes ownership rights or those rights are terminated by a court, either pre- or post-conviction. Even when ownership rights have been relinquished or terminated, animals are sometimes held as evidence in the criminal case.[26] This can result in animals being held longer than necessary for evidentiary purposes and without proper regard for the animal's well-being.

Housing and caring for animals that have been victims of cruelty can be extremely costly, especially when animals suffer significant injuries or illnesses, or when there are large numbers of animal victims in a single case. Law enforcement agencies may not have adequate resources to shoulder this cost and often turn to other agencies, such as public or private shelters, to assist them with animal care and housing. The burden on all agencies involved can be substantial.

In response to these concerns, many state and local governments have enacted various laws that are designed to help defray the cost of housing and caring for animal victims of cruelty, to shorten hold times, and to speed up

20. *Id.*
21. *Id.*
22. *Id.*
23. *Id.*
24. *Id.*
25. *Id.*
26. *Id.*

rehoming of animals whenever possible. However, these laws may not be well understood or effectively used. The resources needed to care for and house animal victims of cruelty can be significant obstacles and disincentives to enforcement of anti-cruelty laws. As a result, animals that should be protected under the law may not always receive the protection they are due.

Providing an effective and clear legal process that appropriately allocates costs and considers the welfare of animals seized in cruelty cases is essential. Such legal mechanisms may take several forms, including forfeiture, bonding, and responsible owner laws. Forfeiture laws may require proof that a particular law has been violated and, upon such a finding, either permit or require the court to order that the defendant relinquish ownership of the animal.[27]

Like forfeiture laws, bonding laws typically require proof of a violation of a cruelty statute.[28] If the burden of proof is met, the defendant is given the opportunity to post a bond or a security to pay for the cost of caring for the animals while the criminal charges are resolved. Failure to post the bond triggers either permissive or mandatory forfeiture of the animals.[29] If the defendant posts the bond and is later acquitted, they are entitled to a refund and the return of the animals. Bonding provisions represent an attempt to balance the interests of both the animal owner and the organization providing care, by preserving the defendant's ownership rights until judgment is rendered while at the same time protecting the agency from accumulating excessive costs of care.[30]

Rather than turning on a defendant's ability to pay, "responsible owner" laws focus on whether the owner or caregiver is willing and able to care for the seized animals and any other animals in their care.[31] A finding that an owner is unwilling or unable to care for the animals can result in court ordered forfeiture of the animals.[32] This approach typically considers evidence of a number of factors, including: past and present care of animals; past injuries or illnesses suffered, as documented by a veterinarian; the prevailing community standard of care for animals; and past violations by the defendant of cruelty laws or other applicable animal welfare laws.[33] "Responsible owner" laws may apply to all animals in the defendant's care as opposed to only the animals seized in a criminal case.[34]

In most states, if the defendant is found guilty after trial or pursuant to a plea agreement and still owns the animals that are the subject of that conviction, the defendant can be ordered to forfeit the animals as part of the sentence (though this result is far from universal and is not mandated in many jurisdictions). Restitution is a mechanism by which a person convicted of animal cruelty can be required, as part of a sentence, to repay the cost of caring for the animals seized in the case or who were victims of the criminal acts. The

---

27. *E.g.*, Nev. Rev. Stat. Ann. § 574.055.
28. ASPCA Animal Cruelty Victims, *supra* note 19.
29. *Id.*
30. *Id.*
31. *E.g.*, Fla. Stat. Ann. § 828.073 (West).
32. ASPCA Animal Cruelty Victims, *supra* note 19.
33. *Id.*
34. *Id.*

sentencing court typically has continuing jurisdiction over the period during which the restitution payments are to be made and can invoke additional penalties, including contempt of court, for failure to abide by the restitution order.[35]

Robust laws may be crafted to reduce hold times by allowing proceedings to be brought as quickly as possible, so that animal cruelty cases affecting living animals can be heard and resolved without lengthy delays occasioned by court calendar congestion.[36] Such laws also should: (1) provide due process (i.e., notice and a right to be heard) to the defendant, (2) authorize both prosecutors and organizations, such as shelters that house seized animals, to initiate or—at a minimum—be parties to the proceedings, (3) provide for humane methods of disposition of animals forfeited or surrendered, including via adoption, transfer to other shelters or rescue groups, and humane euthanasia where necessary due to serious medical or behavioral problems, and (4) not require euthanasia of animals that are adoptable merely because of breed type, because they were seized as part of an animal fighting case, or for other arbitrary reasons.[37] These laws can also allow for judgments in absentia when defendants or other interested parties have received adequate notice but have chosen not to respond or attend court proceedings. Moreover, appeals from proceedings may be expedited so that animals are not held for unduly long periods.[38] "No animal" orders may also be allowed—i.e., giving the sentencing judge authority to order the convicted party not to own or have contact with animals for a time the court deems reasonable.[39]

Animal Advocate Laws

Two states have enacted—and a number of state legislators have introduced proposals for—what have become known as "courtroom advocate laws." These laws allow courts to appoint legal advocates to "represent the interests of justice" in cruelty cases involving dogs and cats.[40] Advocates, who may be lawyers or law students in a clinic environment, may present the court with information relating to the alleged offense, including the defendant's conduct, planning, provocation, justification, and mitigation. Connecticut enacted the first courtroom advocate law of its kind, Desmond's Law, named after an animal cruelty victim who was violently killed by his owner.[41] Desmond's owner admitted to the crime but was spared jail time. Since the enactment of Desmond's Law, courtroom advocates in Connecticut have assisted with dozens of cases.[42]

35. *Id.*
36. *Id.*
37. *Id.*
38. *Id.*
39. *Id.*
40. Jessica Rubin et al., *Desmond's Law: Early Impressions of Connecticut's Court Advocate Program for Animal Cruelty Cases*, Harvard L. Rev. (2023), *available at:*https://harvardlawreview.org/forum/vol-134/desmonds-law-early-impressions-of-connecticutrsquos-court-advocate-program-for-animal-cruelty-cases/.
41. *Id.*
42. *Id.*

Proponents of courtroom advocate laws argue that these laws ensure that victims of animal cruelty are protected and that their interests are presented to the court, and that these laws prevent cruelty and advance justice by ensuring that well-founded cases are not dismissed and offenders are held accountable.[43] However, other animal welfare advocates have expressed skepticism over whether these laws actually result in better animal welfare outcomes or "merely a greater likelihood of incarceration" and harsher punishments for defendants in a system marred by racial injustice.[44] Furthermore, these laws may create new grounds for appeal of convictions, as they allow advocates to take on tasks and responsibilities that are traditionally carried out by prosecutors bound by ethical rules specific to their positions.

Companion Animals

A number of animal species are typically bred for companionship such as, dogs, cats, horses, rabbits, ferrets, birds, guinea pigs and so on. Indeed, where they may be housed legally and responsibly, some domestic-bred farm animals may also be maintained as companions.[45] This section discusses laws relating to such "companion animals."

Dog and Cat Breeding

Some animal welfare organizations oppose breeding in any form, including based on concerns about companion animal homelessness, the killing of adoptable animals for space in shelters, and health concerns associated with selective breeding and "purebred" animals. Others acknowledge or support responsible breeding.[46] While views differ regarding what constitutes responsible breeding, responsible breeders may be viewed as those who, at minimum, prioritize animal welfare, ensure that the animals they breed become happy and healthy pets and are provided a good home, demonstrate a commitment to transparency in the process by encouraging prospective owners to visit where the animal is bred and raised, provide accurate and reliable health records, and do not sell via third parties such as brokers or pet stores.[47]

Laws governing breeders typically apply to dogs and cats bred for commercial purposes. Although there is no uniform definition, the common statutory or regulatory definition of commercial breeding includes the breeding of numerous dogs or cats for profit and/or wholesaling, with puppies and kittens

---

43. *Id.*

44. Justin Marceau, Beyond Cages: Animal Law and Criminal Punishment 79 (2019).

45. *Species Suitable to Be Companion Animals*, ASPCA, https://www.aspca.org/about-us/aspca-policy-and-position-statements/species-suitable-be-companion-animals.

46. *Position Statement on Criteria for Responsible Breeding*, ASPCA, https://www.aspca.org/about-us/aspca-policy-and-position-statements/position-statement-criteria-responsible-breeding#::text=Responsible%20breeders%20strive%20to%20breed,sound%20and%20behaviorally%20stable%20dogs.

47. *Id.*

sold to pet stores, to brokers or middlemen, or through the Internet.[48] Because of the tendency to emphasize profit over the welfare of the animals, many commercial dog and cat breeding operations are commonly referred to as "puppy mills" or "kitten mills."[49]

State laws may require a person who meets the definition of a commercial breeder to obtain a license, pay a fee, maintain certain minimum standards of care, or have their breeding facilities inspected for compliance. In these regulatory systems, a state government agency—typically a state department of agriculture—is responsible for issuing breeder licenses and conducting inspections.[50] Commercial breeders that violate these regulatory laws may have their licenses terminated or face other criminal or civil penalties. For example, under the State of Indiana "Animal Welfare Act," dog and cat breeders harboring five or more dogs or cats are required to have a license and are prohibited from separating puppies or kittens from their mothers for the purpose of sale until they have attained the age of eight weeks.[51]

Other states do not have licensing or permitting programs but establish minimum standards of care for dogs generally in civil or criminal law and, in some instances, provide law enforcement with the right of inspection to ensure compliance. For example, California's commercial dog breeding law applies to a person or business that has sold or transferred three or more litters, or twenty or more dogs, in the preceding year. These breeders are required to maintain clean and sanitary conditions and provide veterinary care, in addition to other minimum humane care requirements.[52] California also requires dog breeders to provide written disclosures upon sale of any dog with information, including the breeder's name, address, dog's birthday, breed, sex, color, veterinary records, and a signed statement from the breeder that the dog has no known diseases. Violations of the law are subject to a civil penalty.[53]

Except where preempted by state law, local governments may impose additional restrictions on commercial dog breeding, such as limits on the number of dogs an owner may possess (discussed further below) and other minimum care standards or may prohibit commercial dog breeding outright through local ordinances, such as zoning laws. Despite the existence of state and local dog breeding laws and regulations, commercial dog breeding continues to threaten the welfare of dogs throughout the United States. Many states laws are silent on commercial breeding, while others exempt certain breeders from oversight, making it difficult to know how many commercial breeders operate in the United States, how many are subject to laws and regulations, and how many evade oversight.

---

48. *Id.*

49. *More Puppies, More Profits*, ASPCA, https://www.aspca.org/barred-from-love/puppy-mills-101/more-puppies-more-profits [hereinafter "ASPCA More Puppies"].

50. License duration and the frequency of these inspections vary by state. *Id.*

51. 225 ILC. 605/2.2 (2010).

52. Cal. Health & Safety Code § 122045–122315 (2010).

53. *Id.*

Even where commercial dog breeders are subject to legal oversight, enforcement is often lacking. There are numerous reasons dog breeding laws and regulations may not be enforced in a particular jurisdiction. Two common reasons are jurisdictional confusion and resource constraints. Questions regarding which agency is empowered to oversee and take enforcement action against a commercial breeder can result in inaction. For example, a commercial dog breeder could, through the same act or inaction, violate a state's animal welfare regulations, a state's animal cruelty laws, and/or local ordinances. In this scenario, a state's department of agriculture could be responsible for addressing the regulatory violations, a state or other local law enforcement agency could be responsible for enforcing the cruelty law, and other local law enforcement could be responsible for enforcing the local ordinance. While jurisdiction is almost always concurrent, it is often not immediately clear to law enforcement whether they may act independently of another agency if they believe that agency is already tasked with ensuring compliance with the law. As a result, law enforcement agencies may be unwilling to pursue violations of laws and regulations impacting commercial dog breeders, despite having the legal authority to do so.[54]

Resource constraints can also weigh into a law enforcement agency's decision to decline enforcement. Most commercial dog breeding laws and regulations do not limit the total number of dogs a commercial breeder may house at a facility. It is, therefore, not uncommon for a commercial dog breeder to house hundreds—or even thousands—of dogs at any given time. Even when law enforcement agencies enforce the law or regulations, they may ultimately need to take custody and house the dogs—a complicated and expensive undertaking for even the most experienced and well-funded law enforcement agency. While animal protection organizations can, and often are, enlisted to assist law enforcement, these cases often require specific expertise as well as extensive coordination and coalition building, and are taxing on the already limited resources of nonprofit organizations.

More recently, state and local governments have opted to address the welfare and enforcement problems associated with commercial breeding, as well as pet homelessness, by enacting laws restricting the sale of animals at pet stores. The reasoning behind such restrictions is that many commercial breeding facilities that violate laws and regulations or otherwise breed dogs in inhumane conditions rely on pet stores to buy their "inventory." Dog brokers and transporters create a pipeline from the commercial dog breeding facility to the pet store that can obscure a dog's origins.[55] For example, a recent survey showed that more than 53 percent (6,500) of all puppies shipped into Florida over the course of a year were from commercial puppy brokers who function as

54. ASPCA More Puppies, *supra* note 49.

55. Pet stores are typically not located near the commercial breeders that supply them with puppies. Puppy brokers arrange for transport between the commercial dog dealer and the pet store. In transport, very young puppies from several different commercial breeding facilities located in different states can be commingled in one transport vehicle and delivered to a single pet store. It is not uncommon for disease to spread and for animals to suffer during long-haul trips. *Id.*

"middlemen." Two of these major suppliers were sued by the Iowa Attorney General for illegally transferring hundreds of designer puppies through sham Iowa nonprofit "rescues" to out-of-state pet shops.[56] Once on the sales floor of the pet store, consumers can be met with high pressure sales tactics that befuddle emotionally involved buyers and obfuscate the source of the puppy. Pet store laws that aim to address both the animal welfare and consumer protection issues that arise from these transactions fall into two main categories: (1) prohibitions on the sale of dogs and cats, and (2) prohibitions on certain financial transactions.[57]

The most straightforward of these laws is an outright prohibition on the sale of dogs and cats. Such laws prohibit the sale of these animals in pet stores—cutting out the middleman broker and breaking the pipeline. Under these laws, prospective buyers may purchase directly from a breeder and observe the conditions in the facility themselves. Meanwhile, pet stores may continue to sell dog food and supplies and may host adoption events for rescues and shelters.[58]

Rather than prohibit the sale of dogs at pet stores outright, other lawmakers have sought to place restrictions on sales. For example, most pet stores offer some form of financing with associated rates and charges that may be exorbitantly high or hidden at the time of purchase, and they even offer lease transactions disguised as traditional financing. Many borrowers are not only unaware that they are entering into a lease, but they may also not realize that the terms allow for repossession of the dog in the event of default. Some borrowers report signing their lease agreement under high pressure sales tactics and in the presence of their new puppy. In some states, lawmakers have responded to purchaser complaints by enacting an outright prohibition on lease transactions for the sale of dogs or prohibiting any finance transaction for the sale of dogs.[59]

---

56. *Florida's Puppy Mill Pipeline: Tracing the Source of Pet Store Puppies*, ASPCA, https://www.aspca.org/sites/default/files/floridas_puppy_mill_pipeline-tracing_the_source_of_pet_store_puppies-06082021-final-r1.pdf.

57. Prior to the enactment of laws prohibiting the retail sale of dogs at pet stores and finance transactions, some states, such as California, enacted "puppy lemon laws" requiring sellers to provide certain health guarantees and remedies. Cal. Health & Safety Code § 122045–122315 (West). Other states, such as Maryland, enacted "source restrictions" requiring pet stores to purchase from commercial breeders licensed by the United States Department of Agriculture (USDA) with a certain types of license class and inspection history. Unfortunately, these laws fell short of ensuring animal welfare, in part due to impracticalities in enforcement and mismanagement of the USDA's Animal Care Program, which has eroded confidence in the agency's ability to ensure the humane care and treatment of commercially bred dogs under its oversight. Just Puppies, Inc. v. Brian E. Frosh, 565 F. Supp. 3d 665 (D. Md. 2021).

58. As of the date of this publication, California, Illinois, Maine (new pet stores only), Maryland, New York, and Washington (new pet stores only) have enacted state-wide prohibitions on the sale of dogs at pet stores. Hundreds of local governments in other state have enacted similar prohibitions. *States with Retail Pet Sale Bans*, Best Friends Animal Soc'y, https://bestfriends.org/advocacy/ending-puppy-mills/states-humane-pet-sales-laws.

59. As of the date of this publication, seven states have enacted state-wide prohibitions on pet leasing including, California, Connecticut, Nevada, New Jersey, New York, Washington, and Indiana. Illinois has prohibited any finance transaction for the sale of dogs. Cal. Civ. Code § 2670.10 (2018); Conn. Gen. Stat. Ann. § 22-354a (2019); Nev. Rev. Stat. § 597.997 (2017); N.J. Stat. Ann. § 56:8-211 (2019); N.Y. Gen. Bus. Law § 753-3 (2018); RCW § 63.10.070 (2019); IC § 24-4.5-2-407.5 (2019); Ill. 205 ILCS 660/10.6 (2022).

Exotic Animals as Pets

Each year millions of exotic animals are also bred and sold as pets. Although the legal definition of "exotic" animal may vary, most state laws consider non-native and/or wild animals to be "exotic."[60] Exotic animals range from small animals, such as guinea pigs and reptiles, to large animals, such as big cats and zebras.[61]

In addition to threatening the existence of animal populations worldwide, the breeding and trade of exotic animals for use as pets harms the individual animal and poses a risk to public health and safety. For example, Congress recognized the dangers posed by the exotic big cat trade when considering the "Big Cat Public Safety Act" in 2022. That act, discussed in more detail in chapter 9, prohibits the breeding, sale, and private possession of big cats and bars exhibitors from allowing direct contact with cubs. In enacting this landmark legislation, the sponsor of the law, U.S. Representative Quigley of Illinois noted that it would "not only help end the cruel and inhumane cub petting industry, it will also make our communities safer."[62]

Although Congress has acted to protect big cats, federal law remains silent on the breeding and private ownership of other types of exotic animals—leaving these issues to be addressed by the states. Some state and local governments have chosen to prohibit a broad list of exotic animals. For example, Hawaii has one of the most restrictive exotic pet laws, banning nearly all exotic pets with limited exceptions for certain small animals such as guinea pigs and parakeets.[63] New York also has prohibited a broad list of exotic animals and, in addition to state law, New York City recently enacted a ban on the sale of guinea pigs.[64] Other states allow exotic pets without limitation or with a few restrictions, such as requiring a permit to own an exotic animal. For example, in Wyoming, although wolves, wolf hybrids, big or trophy game, black bears, grizzly bears, mountain lions, and gray wolves are prohibited, nearly every other animal may be kept as a pet.[65] Texas also has a narrow list of prohibited pets but requires a permit to own "dangerous wild animals," which range from coyotes to great apes.[66]

Trap, Neuter, Return

While most state and local laws governing companion animals relate to animal ownership, community cats often pose complicated issues for law and policy-

60. Jani Hall, *Exotic Pet Trade, Explained*, NAT'L GEOG. (Feb. 20, 2019), https://www.nationalgeographic.com/animals/article/exotic-pet-trade.

61. *Id.*

62. Press Release, Mike Quigley, House of Representatives, *Quigley Big Cat Legislation Becomes Law* (Dec. 20, 2022), https://quigley.house.gov/media-center/press-releases/quigley-big-cat-legislation-becomes-law.

63. HAW. ADMIN. RULES § 4-71-3-6.5 (2001).

64. N.Y. ENV'T CONSERV. LAW §§ 11-0103, 11-0511, 11-0512, 11-0917 (2020); ADMINISTRATIVE CODE OF THE CITY OF NEW YORK § 17-1702 (2023).

65. WYO. STAT. § 23-1-101-103 (2017).

66. TEX. HEALTH & SAFETY CODE § 822.101-116 (2021).

makers. "Community cat" populations generally consist of a mixture of feral cats, semi-socialized cats, and lost or abandoned cats.[67] Community cats are found in all areas of the country and tend to gather in colonies. It is not known how many community cats live in the United States, but estimates are in the tens of millions.[68] Some local communities have adopted humane, lawful, and effective strategies for managing community cat populations, including programs involving trap-neuter-return-monitor (TNRM), return to field (RTF) or, as a last resort, community cat relocation (CCR) (collectively community cat programs). TNRM programs entail proactively trapping, scanning community cats for the presence of a microchip, vaccination, sterilization, ear "tipping,"[69] returning the cat to its original location, and then monitoring and caring for the cat and the colony to ensure that the cats receive adequate food, water, and shelter. Under RTF programs, community cats who have been admitted to an animal shelter and have been determined to be unowned or ineligible for adoption can be returned to the location where they were found so long as they appear to be thriving in this location without known threats to their safety.[70] CCR is a last resort program of relocating cats to a new territory due to a known risk to their survival and a lack of other available community cat programs or options.[71]

Community cat programs not only provide lifesaving options for cats—who might otherwise be euthanized if admitted to a shelter—but can also stabilize, and even reduce over time, the population of community cat colonies.[72] Nonetheless, community cat programs may inadvertently run afoul of existing law or face challenges from interest groups opposed to the presence of free-roaming cats. For example, a court enjoined the City of Los Angeles from

67. *Position Statement on Community Cats and Community Cat Programs*, ASPCA, https://www.aspca.org/about-us/aspca-policy-and-position-statements/position-statement-community-cats-and-community-cat [hereinafter, "ASPCA Community Cats"]. The term "feral" has often been used interchangeably with "community cat." "Feral" is a well-defined term in biology and behavioral ecology, referring to a domesticated animal who is now living wild or free and is not socialized to humans. By contrast, in animal sheltering, "feral" is a term used to describe a cat exhibiting certain behaviors. Unaccustomed to close contact with people, if taken to an animal shelter, such cats may not be good candidates for adoption into a home as a pet. But feral behavior can mask the social history of the cat. For example, a frightened cat may demonstrate feral behavior one day but, with time to acclimate, will no longer demonstrate such behavior. The kittens of feral-presenting cats can typically be acclimated to humans, particularly (but not exclusively) before eight weeks of age. *Id.*

68. *Id.*

69. Ear tipping is the surgical removal of the distal one-quarter of a cat's left ear when the cat is spayed or neutered to visibly signal that the cat has been sterilized. *Id.*

70. TNRM programs are generally preferred over RTF programs because (1) services are provided to the cat without involving admission to an animal shelter, which increases stress for the cat and potential for exposure to disease, and (2) the involvement of a caregiver increases the likelihood of success of the community cat population, by supporting the wellbeing and safety of cats, and provides a point of contact for the community if issues or complaints arise. *Id.*

71. *Id.*

72. Christine M. Budke & Margaret R. Slater, *Utilization of Matrix Population Models to Assess a 3-Year Single Treatment Nonsurgical Contraception Program Versus Surgical Sterilization in Feral Cat Populations*, 12 J. Applied Animal Welfare Sci., 277–292 (2009); Philip S. Miller et al., *Simulating Free-Roaming Cat Population Management Options in Open Demographic Environments*, PLOS One (2014).

carrying out its TNRM program on the basis that the city had failed to perform an environmental impact report as required by state law.[73]

Local laws pertaining to companion animals may not have been written with feral cats in mind, which may lead to complicated legal consequences.[74] The most common legal issue relates to ownership. While the legal definition of animal ownership varies, many local laws define ownership, in part, based on whether someone keeps, harbors, or provides food and water to an animal. While this definition may have the positive effect of conveying ownership of an abused or neglected cat to a caregiver, the definition could also have the negative impact of holding a colony caregiver or feeder responsible for the behavior of every cat in the colony.[75] For example, the City of Belton, Missouri defines an owner as "[a]ny person owning, keeping or harboring an animal or any person who possesses or allows any animal to habitually remain or to be lodged or fed within his or her house, yard or property for five days or more."[76] If ownership has been established, such laws may require a person to shelter and provide veterinary care to free-roaming or feral cats. Moreover, in places where all cats are required to be licensed, the colony caregiver or feeder may be required to claim ownership—potentially subjecting a person to liability for violations of a host of other laws, such as laws against abandonment, laws prohibiting free-roaming animals, laws limiting pet ownership, and laws requiring rabies vaccination and microchips for pets.[77]

It is therefore critical that those who implement community cat programs review existing law to ensure compliance. Animal organizations seeking to promote community cat programs through legislation should ensure that laws are drafted carefully and amended as needed to ensure that the specific needs of the community can be met. This may require attention to variables such as geography, climate, the presence of other animals (including predators and endangered species), past and current community cat programming, and cultural norms.

Under laws that encourage or protect community cats and their caregivers, owners should be those who self-identify as being the sole or primary caregiver

73. Urban Wildlands Group v. City of L.A., No. B222696 (Cal. Ct. App. Dec. 6, 2010).

74. Generally, state laws that define feral cats enable local governments to adopt their own solutions, such as community cat programs. Animal Legal and Historical Center, Brief Summary of Feral Cat Legal Issues, Michigan State University, https://www.animallaw.info/intro/feral-cat-legal-issues.

75. "Caregiver" is a term used to describe someone who provides food, water, sterilization, monitoring, and sometimes shelter and other care for community cats on an ongoing basis, whether regularly or intermittently. "Feeder," by contrast, describes someone who provides food, water, or shelter but does not provide sterilization or other care or monitoring. ASPCA Community Cats, *supra* note 67.

76. City of Belton, Mo., Mun. Code § 4-1(2011).

77. For example, the caregiver of a community cat that destroys a neighbor's property could be held liable for the damage if the law identifies that caregiver as the owner of the cat. In another example, every state prohibits abandoning animals in their animal cruelty statute. In community cat colonies, this becomes an issue when the cat is returned to the colony after being spayed or neutered. Caregivers argue that they are not abandoning the cats, but rather returning them to the same place where they came from and providing sustenance and support for them after the spay or neuter. However, as the "owner" of these animals, there are also requirements for what must be provided for the cats—usually adequate food, water, shelter, and medical care. *Feral Cat Legal Issues*, Animal Legal & Historical Center, https://www.animallaw.info/intro/feral-cat-legal-issues.

and decision-maker regarding a cat's care and wellbeing. Such laws should also include, at a minimum, definitions of key terms such as community cats and community cat caregivers. "Caregivers" should not be defined as the owner of the cat but rather as the person who is authorized to trap, alter, vaccinate, and provide food, shelter, and medical care.[78] Further, these laws can define how a community cat should be cared for and how one can be identified in the field, such as by ear-tipping. For example, California law clearly defines feral cats and recognizes that someone who cares for a feral cat in a cat colony may not be the cat's owner.[79] The California statute further provides direction for animal shelters in dealing with feral cats, allowing the caregiver to reclaim the cat without being the owner. The statute also implies that local animal control may recognize ear-tipping as an indication that the cat is cared for and part of a managed colony. Clarifying these definitions may enable law enforcement and the public to more easily distinguish cats that may be part of a managed colony, are vaccinated, and have been spayed or neutered from those who may require intake and adoption.

Shelter, Rescue, and Foster Home Laws and Regulations

In addition to community cats, lawmakers have sought to address the issues presented by other homeless pets. Every year in the United States, millions of companion animals enter animal shelters.[80] Shelters typically serve as animal control and take in stray animals as well as those who are surrendered by their owners.[81] By contrast, rescue organizations ("rescues") remove animals from shelters to adopt through their organizations and generally do not operate as animal control for a given area. Rescues typically help animal shelters and the communities they serve by making space at shelters for new animals to be held. Although both shelters and rescues share the goal of finding permanent placement for animals, they may have different legal obligations under state and local law.

State and local regulation of shelters and rescues is far from uniform. Some state and local governments have imposed minimum requirements on shelters, such as requiring stray hold periods, microchipping, spaying or neutering, and vaccination before adoption.[82] Many state and local governments also place limitations on the circumstances in which animals in the care of shelters may be euthanized. Such measures may, for example, include reporting requirements and specific mandated protocols for euthanasia decisions, such as that shelters may only consider euthanasia as a last resort.

---

78. *See* Baltimore City, Md., Health Code § 10-101 (2016).

79. Cal. Food & Agric. Code § 31572.5 (2019).

80. *Pet Statistics,* ASPCA, https://www.aspca.org/helping-people-pets/shelter-intake-and-surrender/pet-statistics.

81. Shelters may be operated and funded by the local government or be independently operated non-profits that contract with a local government to operate as animal control. *Detailed Discussion of the Laws Regulating Rescue and Foster Care Programs for Companion Animals,* Animal Legal & Historical Center, https://www.animallaw.info/article/detailed-discussion-laws-regulating-rescue-and-foster-care-programs-companion-animals.

82. Stray hold periods are the length of time an animal must be held by animal control before it may be placed for adoption or euthanized. These periods vary across jurisdictions.

Recently, more state governments have considered additional regulation of shelters and rescues. For example, the New York legislature recently enacted comprehensive legislation setting standards for shelters, rescues, and foster homes. Included in the new standards are requirements for personnel training, record keeping, and written protocols for animal handlings, behavioral assessment, enrichment and stress reduction, managements of bite/scratch cases, and sanitation.[83] The law also includes requirements that shelters have written agreements with foster homes and provide the foster care provider with veterinary records regarding the animal.[84] Maryland also recently adopted minimum standards of care for municipal shelters and shelters that receive grant money from the state's Spay and Neuter Grant Program, including relating to sanitation practices, enclosure standards, and record keeping, which rely heavily on the Association of Shelter Veterinarians' *Guidelines for Standards of Care in Animal Shelters.*[85]

Many rescues and shelters utilize foster homes to help care for animals. Foster arrangements are when individuals volunteer to shelter and care for an animal in their home as a temporary placement until the animal can be permanently adopted. The use of foster homes helps control shelter populations and allows animals to avoid the stress of a shelter environment.[86] Some states have regulated foster homes by requiring them to be licensed and meet certain requirements. Laws governing foster homes and their use often include requirements for written agreements between the foster home and the shelter, welfare standards, limits on the number of animals that can be fostered by one household, and documentation retention requirements.[87] For example, in Illinois, the number of animals in a foster home may not "exceed four foster animals or two litters under eight weeks of age at any given time."[88] While oversight of foster homes is generally left to the shelter or rescue, some states—including Iowa, Illinois, and Kansas—permit the Department of Agriculture to inspect foster homes based on a filed complaint.[89]

Pet Limits and Other Ownership Restrictions

Pet Limits and Responsible Ownership Laws

Courts have held that local governments may impose limitations on the number of animals an individual may possess. Some jurisdictions have considered or

83. S.B. S6870B, 2021–2022 Legis. Sess., New York State Senate, https://www.nysenate.gov/legislation/bills/2021/S6870.

84. *Id.*; *see also* Colo. Rev. Stat. § 35-80-101 (2018).

85. Md. Code Agric. § 2-1075 (2017); *Guidelines for Standards of Care in Animal Shelters,* Shelter Vet (Oct. 14, 2011), https://www.sheltervet.org/assets/docs/shelter-standards-oct2011-wforward.pdf.

86. *Laws Regulating Rescue and Foster Care Programs for Companion Animals,* Animal Legal & Historical Center, http://animallaw.info/intro/laws-regulating-rescue-and-foster-care-programs-companion-animals.

87. *Id.*

88. 225 ILCS 605/2 (2022).

89. *See generally* Iowa Code § 162 (2016); Kan. Admin. Regs. § 9-18-28 (2017).

imposed such limits in response to hoarding or animal fighting cases. For example, in 2017, Los Angeles County seized more than 7,000 birds—one of the largest animal-fighting seizures in U.S. history. In response, the next year, the county adopted legislation limiting the number of roosters that may be kept based on the size of a given property.[90] In another example, in 2014, a Grand Rapids, Michigan resident pled guilty to animal cruelty after the city found thirty-seven dogs on her property in poor condition. The resident was sentenced to five years' probation and was permanently prohibited from owning animals. That same year, a city commissioner introduced a pet limit ordinance to prevent similar incidences in the future. The proposal was withdrawn after animal advocates argued that pet limits would not address issues of hoarding and neglect.[91]

To avoid running afoul of constitutional issues, pet limit laws must be substantially related to a legitimate government purpose.[92] For instance, in enacting these laws, a local government may claim an interest in reducing noise from excessive barking, odor, or pollution, or may cite concerns associated with free-roaming animals, such as disease spread and safety. Given the deference the law affords to local government decision-making, legal challenges to pet limit laws may not be successful. Despite the lack of successful legal challenges, members of the public have been successful in appealing directly to their local officials to amend or repeal pet limits. For example, in 2004, residents and animal advocates in San Jose, California successfully lobbied the city council to raise its pet limit law from two per resident to "no more than three adult dogs, or more than five adult cats, or more than a combined total of five adult dogs and cats" and to exclude animal rescues from pet limits.[93]

Local governments may express interest in pet limit laws in response to cruelty, hoarding, or irresponsible breeding cases that generate public discord and debate. However, each case may present unique challenges and, in addition to animal welfare concerns, may involve other issues of interest such as mental healthcare, equity, public health and safety, and in some instances, business and personal rights. As with other laws applicable to pet ownership, animal organizations seeking to address pet ownership should consider responsible pet ownership and a person's ability to provide care.

As an alternative to pet limit laws, some local governments have adopted ordinances that are neutral as to the number of animals a person can own. These laws permit ownership of any number of animals—provided that the animals are maintained and cared for. For example, an ordinance in Larimer County, Colorado provides, "[I]n no event shall any person keep at his or her premises more animals than can be properly maintained in a healthy condition

90. Melissa Palmer & Courtney Friel, *7,000 Roosters Found in Remote Val Verde Canyon in Largest Cockfighting Seizure in U.S. History: LASD*, KTLA (May 16, 2017), https://ktla.com/news/local-news/7000-roosters-found-in-remote-val-verde-canyon-in-largest-cockfighting-seizure-in-u-s-history-lasd/.

91. Bob Brenzing, *City Drops Proposal of Limiting Number of Cats and Dogs in Grand Rapids' Households*, FOX 17 (Mar. 15, 2017), https://www.fox17online.com/2017/03/15/city-drops-proposal-of-limiting-number-of-cats-and-dogs-in-grand-rapids-households.

92. *E.g.*, Commonwealth v. Creighton, 163 Pa. Commw. 68, 639 A.2d 1296 (1994).

93. City of San Jose, Cal., Mun. Code, § 7.08.595 (2000).

without presenting a safety hazard to the owner, keeper or others and without constituting a nuisance to the occupants or neighboring property."[94]

Nuisance Laws

Nuisance laws are another way local governments legislate the keeping of animals as well as their conduct and management. Established under common law, state constitutional authority, or by delegation from state legislatures to local government, local governments have broad authority to protect public health, safety, and welfare. Pursuant to this authority, local governments may, for example, establish laws prohibiting excessive barking, failing to curb a dog, or limiting the number of animals or the type of animal a resident can own. Nuisance laws pertaining to animals may be enforced by local law enforcement, animal control, and/or third parties contracted to act on behalf of the local government (such as societies for the prevention of cruelty to animals or humane societies).

An animal-related nuisance may be considered a public nuisance, a private nuisance, or both. A public nuisance occurs when a person unreasonably interferes with a right that the public shares in common. By contrast, a private nuisance occurs when a person's use and enjoyment of their land is interfered with substantially and unreasonably through a thing or activity.[95] For example, in *McKiver v. Murphy-Brown*, plaintiff neighbors of Murphy-Brown's hog production facilities filed suit against the company, seeking relief under state nuisance law from odors, pests, and noises they attributed to Murphy-Brown's practices at industrial scale pig farms. The Fourth Circuit Court of Appeals upheld the lower court's ruling, finding Murphy-Brown liable under state nuisance law and awarding punitive damages.[96]

Enforcement of nuisance laws can be difficult due to the temporal nature of alleged violations. For example, in *People v. Donato*, the defendant was charged with multiple violations of a local ordinance that prohibited "unnecessary animal noise."[97] In response to neighbors' complaints about a barking dog, the responding law enforcement officer "sat about 250 feet away from the garage in the street in front of the house for about 15 to 20 minutes, during which time he heard the dog barking continuously."[98] The defendant testified that the complaining neighbors' property was located where the neighbor could not identify from where the barking was coming. He also asserted that his dog only barks when someone approaches it, for example, the law enforcement officer who had sat outside the property, timing the barking. The City Court of New Rochelle, New York held that the ordinance was void for vagueness, in part because it

94. Larimer County, Colo. Mun. Code, § 6-81 (2002).

95. Legal Information Institute, *Wex Legal Dictionary*, Cornell Law School, https://www.law.cornell.edu/wex/nuisance#:text=A%20public%20nuisance%20is%20when,through%20a%20thing%20or%20activity.

96. McKiver v. Murphy-Brown, LLC, 980 F.3d 937 (4th Cir. 2020).

97. City of New Rochelle, N.Y. Mun. Code § 213–5(E) (2015).

98. People v. Donato, 684 N.Y.S.2d 394, 395 (N.Y.C. Ct. 1998).

failed to provide an objective standard by which to determine the volume or intensity of noise that would constitute a violation.[99]

Inhumane treatment of animals may also present opportunities for enforcement of nuisance rules. For example, in *Kuehl v. Sellner*, defendants owned a federally licensed zoo with more than 200 types of exotic animals. Four visitors to the zoo filed a lawsuit, claiming that the zoo was a public nuisance and seeking an order to remove the animals from the zoo. The district court ultimately granted relief to the visitors, finding the zoo to be a public nuisance under both statute and common law. Specifically, the district court ruled that the zoo was "injurious to the health of the animals and potentially to the invitees due to the poor care and living conditions of the animals" and that was "unreasonably offensive to the senses in the inhumane manner of living of the animals."[100]

Zoning Laws

Like nuisance laws, zoning laws are another way local governments may limit or restrict the number and type of animals that an individual may keep. Generally, there are four types of zoning categories (sometimes referred to as "districts") that can be relevant to the ownership or care of animals: residential, agricultural, industrial, and commercial. Within each of these categories, municipalities may have subcategories with specific restrictions, for example, areas required to have similarly sized residential structures or where certain types of agricultural endeavors are prohibited.

Residential zoning districts are intended for family homes and apartments. These areas might have specific restrictions about the species and number of animals or prohibit the operation of businesses or kennels. For example, in *Larsen v. McDonald*, the Supreme Court of Iowa enjoined an animal shelter that had housed up to forty stray dogs, finding that the operation of an animal shelter was entirely inconsistent with the nature of the residential neighborhood.[101] In another example, a Pennsylvania court held that operation of a nonprofit animal rescue out of a home did not meet the definition of a kennel (which were prohibited in the residential area at issue) because the rescue was not operated for compensation.[102]

Agricultural zoning areas are generally intended for raising agricultural crops and livestock. While this zoning category typically places few animal-related restrictions on property, the raising of dogs and the operation of certain types of businesses may be prohibited. For example, an Idaho court held that a property owner who had twenty dog kennel pens and fifty to sixty dogs was not

---

99. *Id.* at 398.

100. *Kuehl v. Sellner*, 965 N.W.2d 926 (Iowa Ct. App. 2021).

101. *Larsen v. McDonald*, 212 N.W.2d 505 (Iowa 1973); *see also* Animal Shelter League of Ozarks, Inc. v. Christian Cnty. Bd. of Adjustment, 995 S.W.2d 533 (Mo. Ct. App. S.D. 1999);Tucker v. Mecklenburg Cnty. Zoning Bd. of Adjustment, 557 S.E.2d 631 (2001); Ruley v. West Nantmeal Twp. Zoning Hearing Bd., 948 A.2d 265 (Pa. Commw. Ct. 2008).

102. *Ruley v. West Nantmeal Tp. Zoning Hearing Bd.*, 948 A.2d 265 (Pa. Commw. Ct. 2008).

raising household pets but rather was operating a commercial kennel that was not permitted in an agricultural zone.[103]

Industrial areas are intended for heavy industry such as large factories and noisy facilities. This zoning category may permit kennels or other types of animal facilities with certain limitations. In one example of an animal case relating to industrial zoning, where a zoning ordinance did not specifically provide for animal shelters in any district, a Connecticut court ruled that it was not unreasonable for the municipality to determine that a nonprofit animal shelter was a permitted use in an industrial area.[104]

Commercial areas are intended for businesses, such as offices, malls, and hotels, and generally permit animal hospitals or shelters. However, certain restrictions and requirements may apply. For example, Montgomery County, Maryland's commercial zoning ordinance requires animal service businesses (such as boarding facilities) to soundproof certain areas of their buildings, maintain minimum lot sizes, and meet setback minimum distances from adjoining properties.[105]

Some zoning laws may allow for special use permits that exempt elements of their operation, while others may strictly enforce zoning laws. In addition to zoning laws, homeowner and condominium associations may limit the size, number, breed, and species of animals permitted in their community. Even where such restrictions are generally prohibited by law, community associations may be allowed to enforce such limitations. Pet ownership restrictions in community associations are typically found in the community's governing covenants, conditions, and restrictions.[106]

Breed-Specific Legislation

In addition to legislation aimed at addressing health and safety concerns related to a certain species or quantity of animals, state and local lawmakers have exercised their legislative authority to restrict or prohibit ownership of certain breeds of dogs. Breed-specific legislation (BSL) is the blanket term for laws that either regulate or ban certain dog breeds, ostensibly to decrease dog attacks on humans and other animals.[107] These laws are often enacted by local governments in response to particularly violent individual dog attacks or, as some hypothesize, are the result of stereotypes and negative media coverage relating to particular breeds.[108]

103. Wyckoff v. Board of Cnty. Comm'rs of Ada Cnty., 607 P.2d 1066 (1980).

104. Westchester Cnty. Soc. for Prevention of Cruelty to Animals v. Mengel, 54 N.E.2d 329 (1944).

105. Montgomery County, Md., Mun. Code § 59-3.5.1–3.5.2.

106. *HOA Dog Rules and Policies Every Dog Owner Should Know About,* HOA Management, https://www.hoamanagement.com/hoa-dog-rules/.

107. *What Is Breed-Specific Legislation*, ASPCA, https://www.aspca.org/improving-laws-animals/public-policy/what-breed-specific-legislation#::text=Breed%2Dspecific%20legislation%20(BSL),on%20humans%20and%20other%20animals.

108. *Id.*

Opponents of BSL have also argued that such bans may be motivated by racism and classism.[109]

BSL relies on the false theory that some breeds bite more often and cause more damage, and therefore that laws targeting these breeds will decrease bite incidence and severity.[110] Although proponents of BSL argue that such legislation improves community safety, this argument remains largely unsupported. Moreover, in a study of fatal dog attacks, the Centers for Disease Control and Prevention strongly recommends against BSL, noting that data collection related to bites by breed is fraught with potential sources of error.[111] Specifically, the authors of that and other studies cite the inherent difficulties in breed identification (especially of mixed-breed dogs) and in calculating a breed's bite rate given the lack of consistent data on breed population and the actual number of bites occurring in a community. Supporting the concern regarding identification, another study noted a significant discrepancy between visual determination of breed and DNA determination of breed.[112]

BSL can cause hardship to responsible owners of properly supervised, friendly, well-socialized dogs.[113] Many breed-specific laws require that owners of regulated dogs comply with unreasonable ownership restrictions or surrender their pet. These laws may force responsible owners of banned dogs to make the difficult decision of moving to another jurisdiction to keep their pet.[114] Considering these hardships and the lack of credible evidence that BSL makes communities safer for people or other companion animals, at least twenty-one states have passed laws prohibiting local governments from enacting BSL.[115]

Although BSL is an ineffective and overreaching "solution," dangerous dogs may be a community problem that may require legislation. Carefully crafted breed-neutral laws that hold reckless dog owners accountable for their dogs' behavior address the risks related to dog bites, attacks, and roaming, and have been shown to have positive effects. For example, New York state law establishes a process for designating a dog "dangerous" and assessing penalties

---

109. *See generally* Ann Linder, *The Black Man's Dog: The Social Context of Breed Specific Legislation*, 25 Animal L. 51 (2018); Rachel Chasen, *Advocates Say Pit-Bull Bans Are Racist and Ineffective. This Md. Suburb Supports Them*, Wash. Post (Oct. 4, 2019), https://www.washingtonpost.com/local/md-politics/national-debate-over-pit-bull-bans-moves-to-prince-georges-county/2019/10/04/509d5016-e3c3-11e9-a6e8-8759c5c7f608_story.html.

110. *Position Statement on Breed-Specific Legislation*, ASPCA, https://www.aspca.org/about-us/aspca-policy-and-position-statements/position-statement-breed-specific-legislation. [hereinafter "ASPCA Breed-Specific Legislation"].

111. *Id.* (citing J.J. Sacks et al., *Breeds of Dogs Involved in Fatal Human Attacks in the United States Between 1979 and 1998*, 217 J. Am. Veterinary Med. Assoc. 836–840 (2000)).

112. ASPCA Breed-Specific Legislation, *supra* note 110 (citing Victoria L. Voith et al., *Comparison of Adoption Agency Identification and DNA Breed Identification of Dogs*, 12 J. Applied Animal Welfare Sci., 253–262 (2009)).

113. ASPCA Breed-Specific Legislation, *supra* note 110.

114. *E.g.*, Scott v. City of Lakewood, No. 2017CVE01691 (Lakewood Mun. Ct. Feb. 12, 2018).

115. ASPCA Breed-Specific Legislation, *supra* note 110. Although many breed-specific laws have been challenged on vagueness, notice, due process, and equal protection grounds, to date, BSL has often been upheld by courts as within the scope of local government authority. As of the date of this publication, a case challenging Prince George's County's breed ban law is pending adjudication. Venero v. Prince George's Cnty. Md., No. 8:2022cv1805 (D. Md. July 22, 2022).

as appropriate on a case-by-case basis.[116] Other examples of breed-neutral laws include, but are not limited to, enhanced enforcement of dog license and leash/dog-at-large laws, laws that mandate the sterilization of shelter animals, laws that prohibit chaining or tethering, and laws that hold dog owners financially accountable for failure to adhere to animal control laws, as well as civilly and criminally liable for unjustified injuries or damage caused by their dogs.

Many local governments have opted to repeal their breed-specific laws and replace them with breed-neutral laws that specifically address the risks posed by dangerous dogs.[117] Local governments seeking to enact breed-neutral legislation must be mindful of the legal status of dogs as property, as penalties for violating both breed-specific and breed-neutral laws may be viewed by courts as improperly restricting or revoking property rights. It is, therefore, critical that breed-neutral laws provide the owner with sufficient due process before their dog is classified as "dangerous" (or another similar designation).

To date, most breed-neutral laws have not been drafted with due process in mind, leaving these laws susceptible to legal challenge on that basis as well. For example, in county of *Pasco v. Riehl*, a Florida district court affirmed an order permanently enjoining the county from enforcing a dangerous dog classification. The court found that a pre-deprivation hearing had to take place before a dog could be declared dangerous and, since the law did not provide for such a hearing, the statute was unconstitutional.[118]

There is substantial variation within the universe of breed-neutral laws enacted to address dangerous dogs. The following drafting considerations are offered for consideration to assist in ensuring robust breed-neutral legislation addressing dangerous dogs:

- The classification of the dog as "dangerous" (or similar designation) should not occur until after a judicial hearing.
- The judicial hearing should be prompted by a citation from law enforcement based on observations by law enforcement or a verified witness complaint.
- The right to a judicial hearing should be automatic. Owners should not be required to request a hearing.
- Notice of the judicial hearing should be given via a delivery method that requires receipt confirmation.
- Notice of the judicial hearing should provide sufficient lead time for response.
- Impoundment of the dog pending the hearing should not be mandatory. Impoundment may be permissible in cases in which law enforcement

---

116. N.Y. Agric. & Mkts. Law § 123 (2021).

117. Such laws are sometimes known as "dangerous dog" or "responsible owner" laws. *E.g., Lakewood Pit Bull Ban Ends, Replaces with Dangerous Dog Ordinance*, Cleveland 19 (Apr. 2, 2018), https://www.cleveland19.com/story/37814099/lakewood-pit-bull-ban-ends-replaced-with-dangerous-dog-ordinance/; *see also* Scott v. City of Lakewood, No. 2017CVE01691 (Lakewood Mun. Ct. Feb. 12, 2018).

118. County of Pasco v. Riehl, 620 So. 2d 229 (Fla. Dist. Ct. App. 1993).

reasonably believes that the dog may pose an imminent threat to public safety.

- The judicial hearing should occur promptly after citation, and mutually agreed upon adjournments should be permissible.
- The burden of proof should be on the petitioner and/or law enforcement to prove by clear and convincing evidence that the dog should be classified.
- The classification of the dog should be subject to appeal in a court of appropriate jurisdiction.
- Euthanasia and mandated spay/neuter orders should be stayed pending appeal.
- Euthanasia should be reserved for the most severe cases.
- An owner should be entitled to another hearing when it is alleged that the owner of a classified dog has not complied with court-ordered ownership restrictions.

Laws addressing dangerous dogs should also ensure that, at a hearing, the court has discretion to order an evaluation of the dog by a certified applied behaviorist, a board-certified veterinary behaviorist, or another recognized expert, and to consider such testimony before classifying a dog. Furthermore, classification as dangerous should be prohibited when a court determines that the dog's conduct was justified, for example, where: the threat, injury, or damage was sustained by a person who at the time was committing a crime or offense upon the owner of the dog or upon their property; the injured, threatened, or killed person was tormenting, abusing, assaulting, or physically threatening the dog, its offspring, or another companion animal or has done so in the past; the dog was responding to pain or injury; or the dog was protecting itself, its owner, custodian, or a member of its household, its kennels, its offspring, or another companion animal.

Laws addressing dangerous dogs should also authorize courts to apply appropriate penalties on a case-by-case basis. Such penalties may include the secure humane confinement of the dog for a period of time and in a manner deemed appropriate by the court (not to include tying or chaining), restraint of the dog on a leash by an adult capable of controlling the dog whenever the dog is on public premises, muzzling of the dog whenever it is on a public premises in a manner that will prevent the dog from biting any person or animal, but does not injure the dog or interfere with its vision or respiration, or maintain a liability insurance policy in the amount determined by the court.

Farmed Animals

"Factory farm" is a term commonly used to describe an industrial facility that raises large numbers of farmed animals, such as pigs, chickens, or cows in intensive confinement with their movements and ability to engage in natural behaviors extremely inhibited. There are nearly 10 billion land-based animals slaughtered for food each year in the United States, the vast majority of whom live their short lives in industrial settings.[119] Yet, there is no federal law that prohibits inhumane practices on farms during the lives of the animals—despite the fact that, as discussed above, these practices are often exempted from state cruelty laws.[120]

Ag-gag

Over the course of the last decade, the animal agriculture industry has pushed for the introduction of so-called ag-gag bills in more than half of all state legislatures across the country.[121] These bills have been designed to silence whistleblowers who investigate the activities of factory farms and reveal animal abuses. For example, Montana's ag-gag law criminalizes "entering an animal facility with the intent to commit a prohibited act, entering an animal facility to take pictures by photograph, video camera, or other means with the intent to commit criminal defamation, and entering an animal facility if the person knows entry is forbidden."[122]

In general, ag-gag laws fall into one of three categories (and may include a combination of these approaches).[123] "Agricultural interference" laws prohibit the recording of images or sounds at farming operations without the owner's consent. "Agricultural fraud" laws prohibit entering or applying for employment at farming operations under false pretenses.[124] "Rapid-reporting" laws require anyone who records an image or sound on a farm that captures animal abuse to provide the images or sound to law enforcement within a specified amount of time, typically not to exceed twenty-four to forty-eight hours.[125] Rapid-reporting laws are problematic because they can require whistleblowers to report problems (thereby revealing themselves) before they have been able to document the larger patterns of abuse needed to support prosecution and to expose systemic abuses.[126] Despite these general similarities, ag-gag laws and their penalties (which can be both civil and criminal) vary quite widely.

---

119. *Revealing the Problem with Factory Farming*, ASPCA, https://www.aspca.org/protecting-farm-animals/problem-factory-farming.

120. *E.g.*, Joyce Tischler, *Foreword: Symposium on Animal Law*, 67 Syracuse Law Rev. 2–3 (2017); David J. Wolfson & Mariann Sullivan, *Foxes in the Hen House: Animals, Agribusiness, and the Law: A Modern American Fable* 205–233, *in* Animal Rights: Current Debates and New Directions (Martha Nussbaum & Cass Sunstein eds. 2005).

121. *What Is Ag-Gag Legislation*, ASPCA, https://www.aspca.org/improving-laws-animals/public-policy/what-ag-gag-legislation. The first ag-gag laws were passed between 1990 and 1991 in Kansas, Montana, and North Dakota, but did not catch the attention of other state legislatures until the last decade. Caitlin A. Ceryes & Christopher D. Heaney, *"Ag-Gag" Laws: Evolution, Resurgence, and Public Health Implications*, 28 Sage Js. (Nov. 19, 2018), https://journals.sagepub.com/doi/10.1177/1048291118808788?url_ver=Z39.88-2003&rfr_id=ori:rid:crossref.org&rfr_dat=cr_pub%20%200pubmed.

122. Mo. Rev. Stat. § 578.013 (2022).

123. Animal Legal & Historical Center, *Brief Summary of Ag-Gag Laws*, Michigan State University, https://www.animallaw.info/article/brief-summary-ag-gag-laws.

124. *Id.*

125. *Id.*

126. Samantha Hawkins, *Iowa's Latest "Ag-Gag" Law Violates First Amendment, Court Rules*, Bloomberg Law (Sept. 27, 2022), https://news.bloomberglaw.com/us-law-week/iowas-latest-ag-gag-law-violates-first-amendment-court-rules.

Although many states have introduced ag-gag legislation, where these laws have been adopted, they have been successfully challenged and repeatedly struck down for violating the First and Fourteenth Amendments of the U.S. Constitution.[127] For example, Idaho, Utah, Wyoming, North Carolina, and Iowa passed ag-gag laws that were immediately challenged and ultimately declared unconstitutional. Utah's ag-gag law made it a crime to obtain access to an agricultural facility under false pretenses, record an agricultural facility without the owner's consent, or apply for employment at an agricultural facility with the intent to record an image of, or sound from, the facility.[128] In 2014, a group of animal welfare organizations, journalists, scholars, news publications, and Amy Meyer (the first individual ever charged under an ag-gag law) brought suit challenging Utah's ag-gag law as unconstitutional content and viewpoint-based discrimination in violation of the Equal Protection Clause.[129] The plaintiffs also alleged that the law was overbroad and criminalized speech that was protected by the First Amendment.[130] The Utah District Court granted plaintiff's motion for summary judgment, finding that the misrepresentation and recording provisions of Utah's ag-gag law violated the First Amendment.[131]

Anti-Confinement Laws

Starting with Florida in 2002, fourteen states have taken steps to protect farm animals by passing laws that ban the use of battery cages for laying hens, gestation crates for sows, and/or veal crates for calves.[132] For example, in 2008, California passed a ballot measure phasing out battery cages, gestation crates, and veal crates. In 2010, California went further, banning the in-state sale of eggs from hens housed in battery cages.[133] Then, in 2018, California voters approved another ballot measure, known as Proposition 12 (Prop 12), which strengthened cage- and crate-free standards for laying hens, mother pigs, and veal calves, and expanded the in-state sales ban to also include pork and veal products.[134]

Prop 12 was the subject of a recent landmark decision by the U.S. Supreme Court, which rejected a legal challenge to Prop 12's statewide ban on the sale of pork from pigs housed in extreme confinement.[135] The National Pork Producers Council and American Farm Bureau Federation filed the lawsuit, seeking to

127. Animal Legal & Historical Center, *Detailed Discussion of Ag-Gag Laws,* MICHIGAN STATE UNIVERSITY, https://www.animallaw.info/article/detailed-discussion-ag-gag-laws.

128. Chip Gibbons, *Ag-Gag Across America: Corporate-Backed Attacks on Activists and Whistleblowers,* CENTER FOR CONSTITUTIONAL RIGHTS, https://ccrjustice.org/sites/default/files/attach/2017/09/Ag-GagAcross America.pdf.

129. Animal Legal Def. Fund, People for the Ethical Treatment of Animals, and Amy Meyer v. Gary R. Herbert and Sean D. Reyes, (D. Utah 2017).

130. *Id.*

131. *Id.*

132. *Farm Animal Confinement Bans by State,* ASPCA, https://www.aspca.org/improving-laws-animals/public-policy/farm-animal-confinement-bans.

133. *Id.*

134. *Id.*

135. National Pork Producers Council v. Ross, 143 S.Ct. 1142 (2023).

invalidate Prop 12 on the grounds that it violated the dormant Commerce Clause of the U.S. Constitution by "burdening" out-of-state pork producers. In its decision affirming the Ninth Circuit's prior decision, the Supreme Court upheld the law, recognizing that states "have long enacted laws aimed at protecting animal welfare."[136]

Wildlife

Where not preempted by federal law (discussed in chapter 9), wildlife management is predominantly governed by state law. While not always explicitly set out in state constitutions, wildlife is considered held by government in the public trust, as part of the natural resources that states have authority to regulate for the common good.

State restrictions on hunting, fishing, and trapping are typically found in regulations authorized by law. In some instances, hunting, fishing, and trapping is limited in the number of permits issued or number of animals captured per year, and the eligibility of applicants for permits.[137] A state may also keep track of the activities of hunters through issuing tags or stamps that are applied to animal once captured and through self-reporting requirements.[138] For example, Connecticut imposes daily limits as well as seasonal limits based on the species of animal being hunted.[139]

Every state has restrictions on the methods of hunting, fishing, and trapping, with some prohibiting the use of spotlights, poisons, dogs, traps, and vehicles in certain circumstances. Some states also limit the types of traps that may be permitted.[140] For example, in 2021, New Mexico banned the use of traps, snares, and poison on public land because of the impact on the Mexican gray wolf, an endangered species, and the unintended trapping, snaring, and poisoning of companion animals.[141] Limitations may also be imposed based on the geography and human population of the area being hunted.[142] In addition, states may limit the type of gun or crossbow that can be used. For example, in Pennsylvania, it is unlawful to "cast rays of artificial light of any kind on any game or wildlife or in an attempt to locate any game or wildlife while on foot, in any vehicle or its attachments, or any watercraft or any airborne craft while in

136. *Id.* at 1150.

137. National Research Council (US) and Committee on Agricultural Land Use and Wildlife Resources, *Legislation and Administration*, *in* Land Use and Wildlife Resources (National Library of Medicine, 1970).

138. *Id.*

139. Conn. Gen. Stat. § 26-66 (2012). *See generally Hunting Laws and Regulations*, https://portal.ct.gov/DEEP/Hunting/2023-Connecticut-Hunting-and-Trapping-Guide/Hunting-Laws-and-Regulations.

140. Association of Fish & Wildlife Agencies, *State Fish and Wildlife Agency: Trapping Regulations Survey & Best Management Practices, State Fish and Wildlife Agency: Trapping Regulations Survey & Best Management Practices* (Mar. 6, 2018), https://www.fishwildlife.org/application/files/5215/2123/4829/Trapping-Regulations-Survey-FINAL-03-06-18_reduced.pdf.

141. N.M. Stat. § 17-11-1; Susan Montoya Bryan, *Trapping Ban to Take Effect on Public Lands in New Mexico*, AP News (Mar. 31, 2021), https://apnews.com/article/environment-new-mexico-animals-wildlife-134e7f2c74a9b7c1e160f644fd08a677.

142. *E.g.*, Alaska Admin. Code § 92.106 (1998).

possession of a firearm of any kind, or a bow or arrow, or any implement or device with which any game or wildlife could be killed or taken even though no game or wildlife is shot at, injured or killed."[143]

Proponents of such hunting laws often argue that they advance the state's interest in ensuring that wildlife is not overhunted, and its population not diminished to the point where it would have a wide-ranging ecological impact.[144] Some critics of hunting for sport argue that it is immoral because hunters cause animals to suffer and intentionally kill the largest and strongest of the herd while putting themselves and others in danger.[145]

In addition to hunting, state and local laws may address how property owners are permitted to remove wildlife from their property. Wildlife that is injured or disruptive may be removed, relocated, or rehabilitated.[146] For example, in New York, if a raccoon takes up residence in an attic, the homeowner cannot remove the animal themselves and must engage a licensed trapper.[147] Similarly, if an owl is injured in a homeowner's yard, the homeowner cannot rehabilitate the animal themselves, but a licensed wildlife rehabilitator is allowed to remove the animal and provide it necessary veterinary care.[148]

Transportation Laws

Animals may be transported within and between states for a myriad of reasons, including for adoption, sale, slaughter, and entertainment and sport. Many state governments require the issuance of a Certificate of Veterinary Inspection (CVI) before certain animals may be transported across state lines. A CVI, also known as a health certificate, is an official document issued by a federal, state, tribal, or accredited veterinarian certifying that the animal identified on the document has been inspected and found to be healthy and compliant with any applicable transport rules.[149] For example, Virginia requires "any pet animal, including dogs, cats, monkeys, or other animals . . . wild or tame under domestication or in custody, or any poultry not intended for commercial use that by its nature is fit for use only as a pet" be accompanied by a CVI issued by the state of origin, dated "no more than 10 days before shipment."[150] Similarly,

143. 34 Pa. Stat. C.S. § 2310 (2010).

144. David Favre, *American Wildlife Law—An Introduction*, Animal Law Web Center (2003), https://www.animallaw.info/article/american-wildlife-law-introduction.

145. Richard L. Worsnop, *Hunting Controversy; Friends and Foes of Hunting Are Locked in a Bitter Public Debate*, CQ Researcher (Jan. 24, 1992), https://library.cqpress.com/cqresearcher/document.php?id=cqresrre1992012400.

146. *E.g.*, 58 Pa. Code § 141.3(1979); Ala. Admin. Code § 220-2-27 (2016); Iowa Admin. Code § 571-114.1 (2006); Wash. Admin. Code § 220-440-050 (2017).

147. N.Y. Env't. Conserv. Law § 11-0524 (2012).

148. Md. Code Regs. § 08.03.12.04 (2022).

149. American Veterinary Med. Ass'n, *Animal Travel and Transport*, https://www.avma.org/resources-tools/pet-owners/petcare/cvi.

150. Va. Code § 3.2-5902 (2008).

Georgia requires all livestock and poultry entering the state to be accompanied by a CVI.[151]

Some states have established requirements for pet transporters. Colorado's Pet Animal Care and Facilities Act and its associated regulations define "pet transporter" as "any firm, person, or corporation that accepts pet animals for transportation or relocation for the purpose of adoption, rescue, selling, harboring, sheltering, trading, or otherwise transferring from one location to another."[152] A pet transporter is required to be licensed by the Department of Agriculture and meet the regulatory standards. For example, animals must be secured by a "seatbelt harness or an enclosure that is secured in the vehicle," and enclosures must be "secured, water resistant, well-constructed of cleanable material, designed to protect the health and ensure the safety of the animal," and "have appropriate heating, cooling, and ventilation."[153] Enclosures are further required to have emergency access and permit the animal to "turn around, stand and lie down." The regulations also require exercise after a certain amount of time, and documentation of the animals in transport must be kept with the transporter.[154]

Many states place restrictions on the method of transport for companion animals. For example, Maine prohibits the transport of a dog "in the open portion of [a vehicle] on a public way unless the dog is protected in a manner that prevents the dog from falling or jumping or being thrown from the vehicle."[155] Massachusetts prohibits "an animal in the back of a motor vehicle in a space intended for a load on a public way unless such space is enclosed or has side tail racks to a height of at least 46 inches extending vertically from the floor, the animal is cross tethered to the vehicle, the animal is protected by a secured container or cage or the animal is otherwise protected in a manner which will prevent the animal from being thrown or from falling or jumping from the vehicle."[156]

Conclusion

The state and local legal landscape affecting animals will continue to grow as social perceptions of animals evolve. Animal protection organizations should monitor lawmaking and policy proposals in areas in which they operate, not only to ensure compliance with applicable laws, but also to identify changes in the field that may impact the organization's strategies and goals. To the extent possible, animal protection organizations should also stay apprised of animal welfare legislation enacted in other states as these laws may signal future trends. When appropriate, animal protection organizations should work with other stakeholders to help ensure robust legislation and positive outcomes for animals.

151. Ga. Comp. R. & Regs. 40-13-2-04 (2011).
152. Colo. Rev. Stat. § 35-80-101 *et seq.* (2018).
153. *Id.*
154. *Id.*
155. Me. Stat. tit. 29-A § 2087 (1998).
156. Mass. Gen. Laws ch. 90, § 22H (2021).

CHAPTER 9

Federal Law

Akela Baldwin and Jamie McLaughlin

Federal Laws

There are a number of federal laws of great relevance to animals and animal advocates. This chapter provides general information on these federal laws, with a focus on the most important for the majority of animal advocates and lawyers representing animal protection organizations. Some well-known pieces of federal legislation relating to animals include the Animal Welfare Act and the Endangered Species Act, but there are many others. To give a sense of the development of the legal terrain, the federal laws are described in chronological order. This chapter also briefly describes key environmental laws relevant to protecting animals. Finally, this chapter introduces the Administrative Procedure Act, an important law for advocates engaging with federal administrative agencies.

In the United States, animals do not have legal standing to be represented as plaintiffs in lawsuits. Attorneys working on behalf of animals or animal protection organizations therefore must overcome the challenge of establishing standing for their clients, with the specific requirements varying depending on which law is being applied and what type of action is being brought. In general, standing to bring a civil action in federal court (often referred to as "Article III standing," in reference to the Constitution's grant of jurisdiction to federal courts to hear "cases" and "controversies") requires the plaintiff to meet the three-part test established under *Lujan v. Defenders of Wildlife.*[1] To have standing, a person must suffer an "injury-in-fact" that is concrete and particularized, and actual or imminent; the injury must be the result of the unlawful conduct of the defendant; and there must be "redressability"—that is, if the court decides in favor of the plaintiff, the injury will be redressed.

1. 504 U.S. 555 (1992).

The most notable federal statute that relates directly to animals and that grants an explicit right to citizens to bring a lawsuit is the Endangered Species Act.[2] Select environmental laws also allow for citizen suits, including the Clean Air Act, the Clean Water Act, the Resource Conservation and Recovery Act, Comprehensive Environmental Response, Compensation, and Liability Act, the Surface Mining Control and Reclamation Act, and the National Environmental Policy Act.

Another federal statute (which does not relate directly to animals or the environment and therefore is not discussed below) that merits brief mention here is the False Claims Act (FCA).[3] The FCA has been used by animal advocates to challenge fraudulent practices used to obtain federal funds through transactions with the government relating to animals or animal products.[4] A private person or organization can bring a civil action under the FCA, known as a *qui tam* lawsuit, essentially standing in the shoes of the government.[5]

Citizen suits aside, when federal laws are violated, it is usually the responsibility of government agencies to determine whether to take legal action to correct harms to animals. When agencies do not exercise that power or have not followed required administrative procedures, the Administrative Procedure Act (APA) allows a private citizen or organization to file suit.[6] This makes the APA a highly relevant tool for organizations wishing to prevent or reduce animal harms. Many federal regulatory agencies enforce animal-related laws and enact regulations of relevance to animals and the organizations that work on their behalf. Examples include: Bureau of Land Management, Center for Disease Control and Prevention, Environmental Protection Agency, Fish and Wildlife Service, Food and Drug Administration, Forest Service, Department of Agriculture and its Food Safety Inspection Service, Securities and Exchange Commission, and others. This list is not exhaustive. The APA is further discussed at the end of this chapter.

Key Federal Legislation Relating to Animals

The Twenty-Eight Hour Law

The Twenty-Eight Hour Law[7] was enacted in 1873 to regulate the transportation of live farmed animals within the United States. When the Twenty-Eight Hour Law was

2. 16 U.S.C. § 1540(g).

3. 31 U.S.C. §§ 3729–3733.

4. *See* United States *ex rel.* Humane Soc'y of U.S. v. Hallmark Meat Packing Co., No. EDCV 08-00221-VAP, 2013 WL 5753784 (C.D. Cal. Apr. 30, 2013) (successful FCA claim against Hallmark for fraudulently providing meat to the National School Lunch Program in contravention of humane treatment of animal rules required by their government contracts); *see also* Complaint of Plaintiff-Relator in *United States ex rel. Compassion Over Killing v. Transhumance Holding Co., Inc.*, No. 2-17-cv-00210-MCE-CKD (E.D. Cal. 2017) (a case that settled after the government intervened regarding lamb processor Superior Farms' failure to conform to the Humane Methods of Slaughter Act in supplying meat under government contracts).

5. 31 U.S.C. § 3730.

6. 5 U.S.C. §§ 551–559.

7. 49 U.S.C. § 80502.

first enacted, farmed animals were sent to slaughter in railroad stock cars, often over long distances. Today, they are primarily transported by truck, but still over long distances to slaughterhouses. The law does not apply to transport by air or water.[8]

The purpose of the law is to ensure that farmed animals are given a break during transport exceeding twenty-eight hours. The Twenty-Eight Hour Law mandates that livestock must be "unloaded in a humane way into pens equipped for feeding, water, and rest for at least five consecutive hours" following a twenty-eight-hour period of transport.[9] According to the law's current definitions, "livestock" does not include poultry,[10] so chickens, turkeys, and other birds can be transported long distances with no respite. Chickens are the most common farmed animal in the United States, accounting for 9.35 billion of the 9.76 land animals slaughtered for food in the United States in 2020.[11] Furthermore, the rule does not apply when livestock "are transported in a vehicle or vessel in which the animals have food, water, space, and an opportunity for rest."[12] There are three other exceptions to the law. When a twenty-eight-hour transport period of sheep ends at night, the sheep can be confined for an additional eight hours.[13] Animals are not required to be unloaded if it is impossible due to an unavoidable cause or accident.[14] Finally, if the person in custody of the animals, or their owner, submits a written request for an extension, the twenty-eight-hour period can be extended to thirty-six hours.[15]

Three agencies have enforcement authority for the law: Department of Justice (DOJ), Department of Transportation (DOT), and U.S. Department of Agriculture (USDA). While the USDA has promulgated regulations to enforce the law,[16] neither the DOJ nor the DOT have done so. Unfortunately, the purpose of the law is largely unachieved: livestock truck transport is usually unmonitored for violations of the Twenty-Eight Hour law, and USDA enforcement of violations is lax.[17]

Lacey Act

The Lacey Act, first passed in 1900, is the oldest federal law regulating wildlife.[18] The original purpose of the act was to protect America's wild animals by

8. 49 U.S.C. § 80502(a)(1).

9. 49 U.S.C. § 80502(b).

10. *E.g.*, 29 C.F.R. § 780.328 states, "The term 'livestock' includes cattle, sheep, horses, goats, and other domestic animals ordinarily raised or used on the farm. This is further discussed in § 780.120. Turkeys or domesticated fowl are considered poultry and not livestock within the meaning of this exemption." Equine transport is governed under 9 C.F.R. Part 88.

11. *U.S Animal Kill Clock*, https://animalclock.org/ (based on data from the U.S. Department of Agriculture).

12. 49 U.S.C. § 80502(c).

13. 49 U.S.C. § 80502(a)(2).

14. 49 U.S.C. § 80502(a)(2)(A).

15. 49 U.S.C. § 80502(a)(2)(B).

16. 9 C.F.R. § 89.

17. *See* Animal Welfare Institute Farm Animal Program, *Animals in Transport Languish as Twenty-Eight Hour Law Goes Off the Rails*, 25 J. Animal L., no. 1, 2018, at 1.

18. 16 U.S.C. §§ 3371–3378.

preventing illegal poaching of wild species and then transporting the animal across state lines for sale. A 2008 amendment to the Lacey Act prohibits trade in wildlife, including fish and plants, that are harvested in violation of any state, federal, tribal, or foreign law.[19] To be in violation of the Lacey Act, there must be (1) a violation of a law, and (2) a related commercial activity. The act authorizes law enforcement to investigate and prosecute cases of illegal trade in plants and wildlife.[20] Today, the act prevents the introduction of invasive species that can harm native ecosystems and threaten biodiversity by prohibiting both domestic and international wildlife trafficking.

Penalties for violating the Lacey Act vary in severity based on the violator's level of knowledge of the illegal origin of the wildlife product. Violators who trade wildlife that they know were illegally harvested are subject to felony criminal penalties, including fines and imprisonment. By contrast, individuals or companies that fail to exercise "due care" to determine whether the wildlife that they are trading was legally harvested are subject to misdemeanor criminal or civil penalties.[21] Depending on the severity of the violation, the Secretary of the Interior or the Secretary of Commerce "may also suspend, modify, or cancel any Federal hunting or fishing license, permit, or stamp, or any license or permit authorizing a person to import or export fish or wildlife or plants."[22]

A unique aspect of the Lacey Act is that, in addition to potential state and federal violations, an individual or company is subject to penalties and sentencing for violating foreign laws in effect in the wildlife's country of origin. For example, in *United States v. McNab*,[23] Honduran fisherman David Henson McNab was indicted for violating the act because he exported Caribbean spiny lobster from Honduras into the United States in violation of a Honduran law. On February 3, 1999, the National Marine Fisheries Service (NMFS) received an anonymous fax, notifying the agency that McNab's cargo transport vessel would arrive in a port in Bayou La Batre, Alabama, with a shipment containing "undersized (3 & 4 oz) lobster tails, [in] violation of Honduran law."[24] NMFS agents seized that lobster shipment, and McNab was sentenced to ninety-seven months in prison. Assessing the statutory language, the court concluded that the phrase "any foreign law" encompasses regulations and other legally binding provisions that foreign governments may promulgate to protect wildlife.[25]

Migratory Bird Treaty Act

The Migratory Bird Treaty Act (MBTA) of 1918[26] prohibits the taking, or possessing, of birds or bird parts as well as the killing of birds without prior

19. 16 U.C.C. § 3372(a).

20. *See Prosecution of Federal Wildlife Crimes*, U.S. Dept. Justice, https://www.justice.gov/enrd/prosecution-federal-wildlife-crimes (accessed June 9, 2023).

21. 16 U.S.C. §§ 3373(a)(1).

22. 16 U.S.C. § 3373(e).

23. 331 F.3d 1228 (2003).

24. *Id.* at 1233.

25. *Id.*

26. 16 U.S.C. §§ 703–712.

authorization from the Department of the Interior's Fish and Wildlife Service. Further, the MBTA prohibits any person from using bait to take migratory birds, or hunting in areas that one knows or reasonably should know are baited. The MBTA was passed to combat overhunting and poaching of migratory birds for feathers to adorn women's hats, which resulted in the rapid decimation of bird populations. While the Act was originally based on a single treaty between the United States and Great Britain (on behalf of Canada), the MBTA later became an amalgamation of conservation treaties with Mexico in 1936, Japan in 1972, and Russia in 1976.[27] Thus, protection for the birds covered in those subsequent international treaties was added to the MBTA. The MBTA now protects over 1,000 native migratory bird species. Any person, association, partnership, or corporation that violates the MBTA or its regulations may be found guilty of a Class B misdemeanor and subject to a fine or imprisonment, or both. In addition, any person who knowingly takes a migratory bird with commercial intent may be found guilty of a felony and subjected to a fine or imprisonment, or both.

The Migratory Bird Treaty Reform Act of 2004 (MBTRA) amended the MBTA by stating that the MBTA applies only to migratory bird species that are native to the United States or U.S. territories, and that a native migratory bird species is one that is present as a result of natural biological or ecological processes. The MBTRA was primarily the result of a case, *Hill v. Norton*,[28] in which the plaintiff, Joyce Hill, alleged that the Secretary of the Interior had violated the MBTA by excluding mute swans (a non-native bird) from the List of Migratory Birds.[29] This exclusion had allowed for the killing and egg destruction of mute swans, and—as successfully argued by Hill—the injuring of those who derive aesthetic and cultural value from the presence of mute swans in the environment. The court found that the secretary had pointed to nothing in the statute, applicable treaties, or the administrative record that justified the exclusion of mute swans from the List of Migratory Birds. The MBTRA was passed in response

Humane Methods of Slaughter Act

The Humane Methods of Slaughter Act (HMSA) was enacted in 1958 to reduce suffering of farmed animals who are slaughtered for human consumption.[30] Farmed animals slaughtered in foreign countries and then imported to the United States are also subject to the HMSA under an amendment.[31] The 2002 Farm Bill added the requirement that the USDA must track and report HMSA violations.[32]

27. The underlying treaties are discussed in the subsequent chapter on international law.
28. 275 F.3d 98 (D.C. Cir. 2001).
29. 50 C.F.R. § 10.13 (2000).
30. 7 U.S.C. §§ 1901–1906.
31. 21 U.S.C. § 620.
32. Pub. L. No. 107–171.

The purpose of the HMSA is to decrease the pain and suffering of farmed animals by slaughtering them using more humane methods. The HMSA aims to "prevent needless suffering," provide "safer and better working conditions" for slaughterhouse employees, improve "products and economies in slaughtering operations," and "to expedite an orderly flow of livestock and livestock products" in commerce.[33]

The HMSA lists two methods of humane slaughter. The first method requires that animals must be "rendered insensible to pain" prior to slaughter.[34] Under this method, animals must be made unconscious through an approved stunning process before they are killed and hoisted for dismemberment. The second method allows animals to be slaughtered "in accordance with ritual requirements."[35] Under this provision, animals slaughtered for religious purposes can be killed based on the slaughter rules of a religion, as long as it is done through a "method of slaughter whereby the animal suffers loss of consciousness by anemia of the brain caused by the simultaneous and instantaneous severance of the carotid arteries with a sharp instrument and handling in connection with such slaughtering."[36] Thus, under the religious slaughter exception, animals are not required to be rendered unconscious before they are killed.

Unfortunately, the HMSA is inadequately enforced.[37] Moreover, while the act applies to cattle, calves, sheep, pigs, horses and mules, and other livestock,[38] the USDA has interpreted it to exclude poultry.[39] As mentioned above, poultry are by far the most common farmed animal in the United States.

The USDA's Food Safety and Inspection Service (FSIS) is responsible for enforcing agency regulations promulgated under the HMSA. There is no private right of action under the HMSA. In *Levine v. Conner*, plaintiffs used the APA to challenge the USDA's interpretation of the HMSA exempting poultry from stunning prior to slaughter, but the court deferred to USDA's interpretation.[40] On appeal, the court held that plaintiffs could not meet the redressability prong of Article III standing.[41]

33. 7 U.S.C. § 1901(a)(2)(A)–(D).

34. 7 U.S.C. § 1902(a).

35. 7 U.S.C. § 1902(b).

36. *Id.*

37. *See* U.S. Gov't Accountability Off., GAO-10-487T, Humane Methods of Slaughter Act: Weaknesses in USDA Enforcement (2010), https://www.gao.gov/assets/gao-10-487t.pdf.

38. 7 U.S.C. § 1902(a). While horses are covered under the HMSA, horse slaughter is currently prohibited in the United States. During the 2005–2006 legislative session, H.R. 2744-45 Sec. 794 was used to block federal funding for USDA inspection of horse slaughter facilities, effectively ending horse slaughter. The last horse slaughterhouses were closed in 2007. However, if such budget blocking language is omitted by a future Congress, horse slaughter could legally resume. The proposed Save America's Forgotten Equines Act (SAFE), reintroduced in 2021, would ban horse, burro, and mule slaughter in the United States, and also ban export of equines for foreign slaughter.

39. *Notice of Treatment of Live Poultry Before Slaughter*, 70 Fed. Reg. 56,624 (Sept. 28, 2005). ("The HMSA . . . requires that humane methods be used for handling and slaughtering livestock but does not include comparable provisions concerning the handling and slaughter of poultry.").

40. 540 F. Supp. 2d 113 (N.D. Cal. 2008).

41. Levine v. Vilsack, 587 F.3d 986 (9th Cir 2009).

Animal Welfare Act

In 1966, in response to increasing public outcry over stolen pets being sold and used for research, Congress enacted the Laboratory Animal Welfare Act, which was the first federal law regulating the care, treatment, and transportation of animals used in research. In 1970, Congress amended that act, expanding its coverage to all warm-blooded animals in laboratories as well as to animals used in exhibitions. This amendment also required the licensing of all animal dealers and the use of anesthetics or other appropriate tranquilizers in certain circumstances. That 1970 amendment, known as the Animal Welfare Act (AWA), remains today the primary federal law regulating the treatment of animals used for research and exhibition to ensure that the animals are provided minimum standards care. The AWA sets minimum standards for animal housing, feeding, handling, and medical treatment, in addition to requirements to provide animals with food, water, and proper ventilation during transport.[42] There have been numerous amendments to the AWA since 1970. A 2019 amendment prohibits animal fighting in U.S. territories, including in Guam, Puerto Rico, and the U.S. Virgin Islands, where local laws had previously allowed it.[43]

Despite the AWA's successes in protecting animals, the most notable shortfall of the AWA is its limited scope. It does not cover all animals. The AWA currently defines "animal" as "any live or dead dog, cat, monkey (non-human primate mammal), guinea pig, hamster, rabbit, or such other warm-blooded animal, as the Secretary may determine is being used, or is intended for use, for research, testing, experimentation, or exhibition purposes, or as a pet," and protects only those listed animals.[44] The AWA expressly excludes farmed animals used for food and fiber, amphibians, reptiles, horses not used for research purposes, fish, and invertebrates.

Critically, a 2002 amendment further limited the definition of "animal" by excluding "birds, rats of the genus Rattus, and mice of the genus Mus, bred for use in research."[45] Ultimately, since the AWA does not protect the mice and rats—which account for approximately 95 percent of research animals—or the billions of farmed animals who are slaughtered for food, the vast majority of animals used by humans receive no protection under the AWA.

The USDA Animal Care unit ("Animal Care") within the Animal and Plant Health Inspection Service enforces the AWA by issuing licenses that authorize the use of animals, imposing penalties for violations of the law, and conducting inspections of facilities that use animals. Animal Care conducts two main types of inspections: pre-licensing inspections and unannounced compliance inspections.[46] Pre-licensing inspections are not required under the AWA, but facilities may request one. During unannounced compliance inspections at AWA-licensed and registered facilities, Animal Care inspectors review the

42. 7 U.S.C. §§ 2131–2159.

43. 7 U.S.C. § 2156.

44. *Id.*

45. 7 U.S.C. § 2132(g).

46. *Animal Welfare Act Inspections*, U.S. Dep't of Agric. (Nov. 18, 2020), https://www.aphis.usda.gov/aphis/ourfocus/animalwelfare/awa/ct_awa_inspections.

premises, husbandry practices, program of veterinary care, records, and animal handling procedures.

Lawsuits relating to the AWA have highlighted the need for continued and enhanced enforcement in various arenas, such as research laboratories, puppy mills, and zoos. For example, in *Salzer v. King Kong Zoo*,[47] the court issued a permanent injunction of King Kong Zoo, an AWA-licensed exhibitor of wild and domestic animals in North Carolina. Over the course of several years, state and federal regulators, including the USDA, had conducted inspections and repeatedly cited the zoo's cruel treatment of the animals in violation of North Carolina's animal cruelty laws and the AWA. These inspections noted inadequate veterinary care, unsanitary living spaces, and failure to provide animals with proper food, water, and shelter to meet their biological needs. A key issue in the case was whether the AWA "expressly preempts any State regulation of animal welfare."[48] The court found that the AWA did not preempt the state's animal cruelty law because Congress empowered individual states to work in conjunction with the AWA.

Because there is no private right of action under the AWA, an individual or organization cannot directly file suit against those responsible for poor animal welfare. Instead, the APA can be utilized to claim injury due to government agency action or inaction in regulating the entity or person responsible. It is not required that the injury be economic in nature: an aesthetic injury can also create standing for an individual or organizational APA claim challenging agency action under the AWA. In *Animal Legal Defense Fund v. Glickman*, the court determined that the plaintiff had Article III standing because he had suffered "aesthetic and emotional" injury caused by witnessing the inhumane treatment of primates at Long Island Game Farm Park and Zoo.[49] Plaintiff's experience and training as a wildlife rehabilitator informed his observations that primates living in isolation with no enrichment were being kept in inhumane conditions, and his repeated visits to view the primates and subsequent requests for agency intervention lead to no changes in the circumstances under which the animals were kept. The court found that repeatedly observing the isolated primates under these conditions caused him aesthetic injury. As exemplified in *Glickman*, animal protection groups and regular viewers of animal exhibitions can have standing to bring APA claims alleging AWA violations where adequate agency action is lacking.

Wild Free-Roaming Horses and Burros Act

The Wild Free-Roaming Horses and Burros Act (WHBA) of 1971 was an expansion of a 1959 law that had prohibited the taking of wild horses from rangelands for commercial purposes.[50] Prior to these laws, wild horses and

47. 773 S.E.2d 548 (N.C. Ct. App. 2015).
48. *Id.*
49. 154 F.3d 426 (1998).
50. 16 U.S.C. §§ 1331–1340.

burros were subject to capture and slaughter, and exploitation by mustangers and encroachment of ranch lands had led to a significant decline in wild horse and burro populations.[51]

Although wild horses and burros are not native to North America, having been introduced by Spanish colonizers in the late 1400s, these animals are considered an integral part of the ecosystem on public lands in the western United States. In the WHBA, Congress declared "that wild-free roaming horses and burros are living symbols of the historic and pioneer spirit of the West . . . [that] contribute to the diversity of life forms within the Nation and enrich the lives of the American people."[52] Wild free-roaming horses and burros include "all unbranded and unclaimed horses and burros on public lands of the United States."[53] The purpose of the WHBA is to protect and manage wild horses and burros on public lands, while maintaining ecological balance and preserving them for future generations. The agencies do this by identifying the locations of horses and burros, counting their numbers, and managing herd sizes.

Wild horses and burros are under the jurisdiction of the Secretary of the Interior (through the Bureau of Land Management (BLM)) and the Secretary of Agriculture (through U. S. Forest Service (USFS)). These two administrative agencies are responsible for wild horses and burros on public lands within specified territories, including twenty-four active wild horse and burro territories managed jointly by USFS and the BLM.[54] The BLM and USFS appoint an advisory board of experts, interest organization members, and advocates who are responsible for advising the agencies on matters concerning wild horses and burros.[55]

The WHBA makes it illegal to subject wild horses and burros to "capture, branding, harassment, or death."[56] Agencies use birth control, culling, and gathers to remove animals deemed excess. The WHBA defines excess animals as those "removed from an area by the Secretary pursuant to applicable law," or those removed "in order to preserve and maintain a thriving natural ecological balance and multiple-use relationship in that area."[57]

Animals who stray onto private land may remain there as long as they were not lured or illegally brought to the property, are kept free of harassment, and provided that the landowner notifies the agency of the approximate number of

51. Kleppe v. New Mexico, 426 U.S. 529 (1976).

52. 16 U.S.C. § 1331.

53. 16 U.S.C. § 1332(b).

54. *Wild Horse and Burro Territories*, U.S. Forest Serv., https://www.fs.usda.gov/wild-horse-burro/territories/index.shtml (accessed Feb. 25, 2023).

55. 16 U.S.C. § 1337. Advisory board meeting information is published in the *National Register*.

56. 16 U.S.C. § 1331.

57. 16 U.S.C. § 1332(f)(1)–(2). Different removal methods are assigned a priority order. 16 U.S.C. § 1333(b)(2). First, old, sick, or lame animals may be humanely destroyed. 16 U.S.C. § 1333(b)(2)(A). Next, horses and burros may be removed from rangelands through humane gathering, and then adopted out to qualified individuals. 43 C.F.R. § 4700.0-5(e); 16 U.S.C. § 1333(b)(2)(B). Finally, excess animals for whom there are no qualified adopters may be "destroyed in the most humane and cost-efficient manner possible." 16 U.S.C. § 1333(b)(2)(C). "Humane treatment means handling compatible with animal husbandry practices accepted in the veterinary community, without causing unnecessary stress or suffering to a wild horse or burro." 43 C.F.R. § 4700.005(e).

animals on the private land.[58] Landowners wishing to remove wild horses and burros from private land must inform the appropriate agency or local federal marshal, who will arrange for removal. The WHBA prohibits removing a covered animal from public lands without authority, converting animals to private use, maliciously causing death or harassment to an animal, processing an animal into products without a permit, or other willful violation of the act.[59] Criminal penalties include a fine of $2,000, up to one-year imprisonment, or both.[60] There is no private right of action under the WHBA.

Disputes arise regarding agency management, removal, and adoption of excess animals. Public lands are used for multiple purposes, and ranchers compete with wild horses and burros for livestock grazing on public rangelands. When healthy animals are removed, BLM must determine what to do with them. In 2004, the Burns Amendment modified the WHBA by adding a section that allows for unlimited sale of excess horses and burros taken from rangelands.[61]

High numbers of wild horses and burros have been gathered and are permanently maintained by government agencies, leading to management budgetary pressures.[62] Fertility control, adoptions, sales, and permanent off-range holding are proposed solutions which have been evaluated based on cost.[63] The BLM has implemented a controversial 2019 adoption program which awards $1,000 per untrained animal taken by qualified adopters.[64] Qualified individuals may adopt up to four animals per year, and title to the animals is granted after a one-year holding period.[65] Incentivized adoptions have led to concerns that many animals are ending up at slaughterhouses following the waiting period.[66]

Marine Mammal Protection Act

The Marine Mammal Protection Act (MMPA) was enacted by Congress in 1972.[67] Unsustainable hunting, bycatch, and removal of animals from the wild has caused the threat of extinction for many marine mammal species. The MMPA seeks to protect marine mammals by preventing populations from diminishing "beyond the point at which they cease to be a significant functioning element in the ecosystem."[68]

58. 16 U.S.C. § 1334.

59. 16 U.S. Code § 1338(a).

60. 16 U.S. Code § 1338(a)(6).

61. 16 U.S.C. § 1333(e). *See* Pub. L. No. 108-447.

62. *Id.*

63. *Id.*

64. *Id.*

65. 16 U.S.C. § 1333(c).

66. Dave Philipps, *Wild Horses Adopted Under a Federal Program Are Going to Slaughter*, N.Y. Times (July 20, 2021), https://www.nytimes.com/2021/05/15/us/wild-horses-adoptions-slaughter.html.

67. 16 U.S.C. §§ 1361–1423.

68. 16 U.S.C. § 1361(2).

The MMPA prohibits the taking of marine mammals,[69] as well as the importation of marine mammals who are pregnant or nursing, members of a depleted species, or have been subjected inhumane taking.[70] The act defines "taking" to include harassing, hunting, capturing, killing, or attempting to do any of those things to a marine mammal.[71] Note that some animals protected under the MMPA may also be protected under the Endangered Species Act (discussed below) and/or the Convention on International Trade in Endangered Species of Wild Fauna and Flora (discussed in the following chapter).

Administration of the MMPA is the responsibility of both the Department of Commerce and the Department of the Interior. Under the Department of Commerce, the National Oceanic and Atmospheric Administration's NMFS administers the MMPA for the majority of marine mammals, including whales, dolphins, porpoises, seals, and sea lions. NMFS also has the authority to require observers to be present on commercial fishing vessels. Information collected by an observer can be used in proceedings against MMPA violators. Under the Department of the Interior, Fish and Wildlife Services (FWS) is responsible for management of polar bears, sea otters, walruses, dugongs, and manatees. In addition to these agencies, the independent Marine Mammal Commission provides scientific oversight of agency action as well as analyzing domestic and international policy. While it has no enforcement authority, the commission produces congressional briefings, testifies before Congress, and funds studies for marine mammal research.

The MMPA can be enforced against persons or vessels subject to domestic or extraterritorial US jurisdiction.[72] Agencies may impose fines for violations and may seize of cargo.[73] There is no private right of action under the MMPA.

Not all takes are prohibited under the MMPA. Exceptions exist under domestic treaties entered into prior to the MMPA and under international treaties. Both the NMFS and FWS have regulatory authority and permitting authority to allow marine mammal takes, and they may grant permits for exceptions.[74] For example, there is a broad exception for marine mammal takes by indigenous Alaskans as long as those takes are for traditional purposes and are not wasteful.[75] Additionally, incidental takes are allowed for commercial fishing activity if the fishery has a permit.[76] Animal protection organizations

69. 16 U.S.C. § 1372(a).

70. 16 U.S.C. § 1372(b).

71. 16 U.S.C. § 1362(13). Taking by harassment is broken into two categories. 16 U.S.C. § 1362(18)(A). Harassment includes "pursuit, torment, or annoyance" that may potentially injure wild marine mammals. 16 U.S.C. § 1362(18)(A)(i). In addition, acts that potentially disturb wild marine mammals by disrupting their "migration, breathing, nursing, breeding, feeding, . . . sheltering" or other natural behaviors are considered harassment. 16 U.S.C. § 1362(18)(A)(ii).

72. 16 U.S.C. § 1372.

73. 16 U.S.C. § 1375.

74. 16 U.S.C. § 1374.

75. 16 U.S.C. § 1371(b).

76. 16 U.S.C. §§ 1374, 1387. *See Marine Mammal Authorization Program*, NOAA, https://www.fisheries.noaa.gov/national/marine-mammal-protection/marine-mammal-authorization-program#reporting-a-death-or-injury-of-a-marine-mammal-during-commercial-fishing-operations. Category 1 and II licensed fisheries with a state or federal fishing licenses are automatically registered for a Marine Mammal Authorization Certificate. As

that work with marine mammals (e.g., such as providing veterinary care and relocation to animals stranded on beaches) must take care to comply with the MMPA and obtain required government permissions.

Geographic considerations add an additional level of complexity. The MMPA applies in cases where marine mammals are unlawfully taken outside of U.S. territories and then imported into the United States. For example, importation of seal skins from a seal hunt in South Africa was found to have violated the MMPA.[77] However, where a U.S. citizen hunted dolphins outside of U.S. territories but did not attempt to import the catch into United States, no MMPA violation was found.[78]

Endangered Species Act

The Endangered Species Act (ESA) of 1973 protects endangered and threatened species and their habitats with the goal of preserving biodiversity.[79] The ESA is intended "to provide a means whereby the ecosystems upon which endangered species and threatened species depend may be conserved, [and] to provide a program for the conservation of such endangered species and threatened species."[80] Further, the "plain intent of Congress in enacting this statute was to halt and reverse the trend toward species extinction, whatever the cost."[81]

The ESA defines "endangered species" as "any species which is in danger of extinction throughout all or a significant portion of its range . . . ,"[82] and defines "threatened species" as "any species which is likely to become an endangered species within the foreseeable future throughout all or a significant portion of its range. . . . "[83] The ESA also protects the "critical habitat for a threatened or endangered species."[84]

Under the ESA, the Secretary of the Interior and the Secretary of Commerce split the responsibility of listing endangered and threatened species, with the Secretary of the Interior delegating its authority to FWS and the Secretary of Commerce delegating its authority to the NMFS. Unlike FWS, the NMFS has limited discretion in making listing determinations because NMFS decisions to remove a species from the threatened or endangered lists or to demote a species' listing classification from "endangered" to "threatened" must be approved by

long as their license is current, the Certificate is automatically renewed. However, fisheries must report marine mammal injury or death to NOAA Fisheries on the require form.

77. Animal Welfare Inst. v. Kreps, 561 F.2d 1002 (D.C. Cir. 1977).

78. United States v. Mitchell, 553, F.2d 995 (5th Cir. 1977).

79. 16 U.S.C. § 1531 *et seq.*

80. 16 U.S.C. § 1531(b).

81. Defenders of Wildlife v. Babbitt, 130 F. Supp. 2d 121, 124 (D.D.C. 2001).

82. 16 U.S.C. § 1532(6).

83. 16 U.S.C. § 1532(20).

84. The ESA defines "critical habitat" as: "(i) the specific areas within the geographical area occupied by the species, at the time it is listed . . . on which are found those physical or biological features (I) essential to the conservation of the species and (II) which may require special management considerations or protection; and (ii) specific areas outside the geographical area occupied by the species . . . upon a determination . . . that such areas are essential for the conservation of the species." 16 U.S.C. § 1532(5)(A).

the Secretary of the Interior.[85] NMFS decisions to upgrade a species' classification from "threatened" to "endangered" are not subject to such review.

Once a species is listed as an "endangered" or "threatened" species under the ESA, the killing, harming, or harassing of that species, or the damaging or destroying of the species' habitat, is strictly prohibited, with violations punishable by criminal and civil penalties. Animal protection organizations, such as sanctuaries, that work with endangered species must take care to comply with the ESA and obtain required government permissions.

The ESA further enforces compliance by creating special obligations for federal agencies regarding listed species. One such obligation is for each federal agency to consult with the Secretary of the Interior to "insure that any action authorized, funded, or carried out by such agency is not likely to jeopardize the continued existence of any endangered or threatened species."[86] The Supreme Court has described the ESA as "the most comprehensive legislation for the preservation of endangered species ever enacted by any nation."[87]

One of the most legally important cases involving the ESA is *Lujan v. Defenders of Wildlife*, in which the Supreme Court established heightened standing elements under Article III of the Constitution.[88] The issue in *Lujan* was whether the plaintiffs, wildlife conservation organizations, had standing to file an action under the ESA. Plaintiffs challenged a 1986 revision of the ESA that limited the geographic applicability of the act to actions within the United States or on the high seas, and excluded actions taken in foreign nations.[89] Plaintiffs brought a citizen-suit seeking an injunction requiring the Secretary of the Interior to restore the earlier ESA interpretation and geographic scope to include actions in foreign nations. The plaintiffs' alleged injury was that the lack of consultation for certain government-funded activities abroad (including restoration of the Aswan High Dam in Egypt and the Mahaweli Project, a reservoir in Sri Lanka) that would increase "the rate of extinction of endangered and threatened species."[90] The plaintiffs argued that they had standing because they desired to view the species in their wild habitat and therefore faced potential aesthetic injury. The Court ruled that the plaintiffs lacked standing, finding that they had failed to show an injury in fact that was actual or imminent: previous attempts to view animals did not constitute an injury, and plaintiffs had no imminent plans to return to the region. Moreover, the Court found that the injury was not concrete or particularized (because a similar claim could be brought by any number of people desiring to study or view animals in the wild), and the injury was purely speculative.

Although the ESA has been successful in preventing the extinction of many endangered and threatened species, ambiguities in its statutory language can

85. 16 U.S.C. § 1533(a)(2).

86. 16 U.S.C. § 1536(a)(2).

87. *See* Tennessee Valley Auth. v. Hill, 437 U.S. 153, 180 (1978).

88. 504 U.S. 444 (1992). "Standing" refers to the determination of whether a party has the right to bring a lawsuit.

89. *Id.* at 551. Plaintiffs challenged the amendments to § 7(a)(2) of the ESA.

90. *Id.*at 562.

weaken its enforcement and have led to court challenges. For example, in *Weyerhaeuser Co. v. U.S. Fish & Wildlife Service*, the Supreme Court considered the question of when unoccupied habitat may be designated "critical habitat."[91] The Supreme Court acknowledged that, for an area of land to be eligible for designation as critical habitat under the ESA, it is not required that the species currently exist in that habitat. However, the Court remanded to the 5th Circuit for determination of whether an uninhabitable area that can reasonably be modified to support a species can be defined as critical habitat. Following this case, in 2020, the Departments of Interior and Commerce enacted a rule to define "habitat" to include both occupied and unoccupied areas "that currently or periodically contain[] the resources and conditions necessary to support one or more life processes of a species."[92]

The Animal Enterprise Terrorism Act

The Animal Enterprise Terrorism Act of 2006 is an expansion of the 1992 Animal Enterprise Protection Act (AEPA).[93] The 1992 AEPA was enacted as a mechanism for prosecuting persons engaging in physical disruption of animal enterprises involving interstate or foreign commerce, creating penalties for crimes that, until 1992, had been considered to be primarily property crimes. The 1992 AEPA was modified when special interest groups, who would benefit from enhanced penalties against animal and environmental activists engaging in disruptive activities, pushed for an expansion of the AEPA. At the time, animal and environmental activists were receiving what many observers perceived as levels of inordinate attention from law enforcement, in light of the relative threat posed to society.[94] The proposed enhanced penalties were supported by federal law enforcement. In 2005, FBI Deputy Assistant Director John Lewis stated that "[t]he No. 1 domestic terrorism threat is the eco-terrorism, animal-rights movement."[95] In 2006, the Animal Enterprise Terrorism Act (AETA) was signed into law, expanding the AEPA in notable ways that impact both animal and environmental activism.

Like the AEPA, the AETA not only protects the property of animal enterprises but also extends protection to "real or personal property of a person or entity having a connection to, relationship with, or transaction with an animal enterprise."[96] The AETA also expands injury beyond the physical disruption of an animal enterprise and causing serious bodily harm, by criminalizing placing a person "in reasonable fear of the death of, or serious bodily

91. 139 S. Ct. 361 (2018).
92. 50 C.F.R. § 424 (2021).
93. 18 U.S.C. § 43.
94. *E.g.*, Will Potter, Green Is the New Red: An Insider's Account of a Social Movement Under Siege (2011).
95. Henry Schuster, *Domestic Terror: Who's Most Dangerous?*, CNN (2005), https://www.cnn.com/2005/US/08/24/schuster.column/. *See also* John E. Lewis, *Testimony Before the Senate Judiciary Committee*, FBI (May 18, 2004), https://archives.fbi.gov/archives/news/testimony/animal-rights-extremism-and-ecoterrorism.
96. 18 U.S.C. § 43(2)(A).

injury to that person, a member of the immediate family, . . . spouse or intimate partner of that person by a course of conduct involving threats, acts of vandalism, property damage, criminal trespass, harassment, or intimidation."[97] A reasonableness standard is referenced to determine fear of serious bodily injury or death, which may be applied differently in different jurisdictions.[98]

The AETA lists three broad categories of animal enterprises and leaves room for interpretation. Enterprises engaging in commercial and academic uses, agriculture, research and testing, and educational use of animals are included under the act.[99] The AETA also covers animals used in entertainment, such as zoos, aquaria, pet stores, circuses and rodeos,[100] and events "intended to advance agricultural arts and sciences."[101]

Criminal penalties were also increased under the AETA. The 1992 AEPA had imposed penalties of fines, or up to one year in prison, or both; when serious bodily injury occurred, up to ten years in prison, and life imprisonment if violations of the AEPA caused a human death. The AETA has a tiered fine and penalty structure depending on the amount of damage caused by the criminal act.[102] In cases where no bodily injury occurred, but the economic damage caused ranged between $10,000-$100,000, the penalty includes a fine and up to five years imprisonment or both.[103] When property damage exceeds $100,000 or an "offense results in substantial bodily injury to another individual," penalties of fines, imprisonment up to ten years, or both may be imposed.[104] The final penalty tier addresses property damage exceeding $1,000,000 and offenses resulting in serious bodily injury of an individual. In these cases, the penalties include fines, imprisonment for up to twenty years, or both.[105] The AETA also allows for life imprisonment where an offense has caused death,[106] and restitution to pay for repeating interrupted animal experiments, loss of food production, or other economic damage caused by the offense.[107] Federal criminal sentencing guidelines[108] provide a framework based on the basic offense level, but a judge may depart from the guidelines, depending on the severity of the damage caused to person or property. Furthermore, the Mandatory Victims Restitution Act applies to the AETA, and the court can order restitution for the victim or victim's estate. Economic damages resulting from protected activities—such as lawful boycotts—are not subject to the AETA.[109]

97. 18 U.S.C. § 43(a)(2)(B).

98. Nicole K. Drumhillera & Jason Roesler, *Perceptions of Fear Among Targets of Radical Animal Rights Extremism*, 44:3 Stud. Conflict & Terrorism 248, (2021), https://doi.org/10.1080/1057610X.2018.1538143.

99. 18 U.S.C. § 43(d)(1)(a).

100. 18 U.S.C. § 43(d)(1)(b)

101. 18 U.S.C. § 43(d)(1)(c).

102. 18 U.S.C. § 43(b).

103. 18 U.S.C. § 43(b)(2)(A).

104. 18 U.S.C. § 43(b)(3)(A)–(B).

105. *Id.*

106. 18 U.S.C. § 43(b)(5).

107. 18 U.S.C. § 43(c)(1)–(3).

108. U.S. Sentencing Guidelines Manual § 2B1.1 (2021).

109. 18 U.S.C. § 43(d)(3)(B).

Both the Department of Homeland Security and the FBI are responsible for preventing and investigating terrorist activities within the United States, including federal crimes under the AETA.[110] The DOJ has authority to prosecute alleged AETA violators. To prove an AETA violation, the offense must involve interstate or foreign commerce, which includes travel as well as mail and use of the Internet.

Many legal observers and advocates have criticized the act for its vagueness, but pre-enforcement challenges to the act have encountered Article III standing problems. In *Blum v. Holder*, animal activists were found to lack standing on the basis that they had failed to show that they faced imminent injury because their proposed activities would have been lawful under the AETA.[111] While many animal advocates are concerned that the act could be used to prosecute constitutionally protected activity, First Amendment defenses claiming that the AETA is overbroad and vague have likewise failed. In *United States v. Fullmer*, defendants were charged with conspiracy to violate the AEPA.[112] Activist group Stop Huntingdon Animal Cruelty (SHAC) protested the practices of Huntingdon Life Sciences ("Huntingdon") after undercover investigators exposed beagles being shaken and punched during lab experiments.[113] SHAC ran a website encouraging direct action against Huntingdon, including public protesting, which is constitutionally protected. However, the website also urged other actions such as crashing company websites to disrupt business activity, removing animals from the lab, and threatening people linked to Huntington—all of which the court found to be unlawful. Although the defendants did not directly engage in all of these activities, they were convicted of conspiracy. The court noted that while legal protest activities are exempted from the act, SHAC had fair warning of what type of conduct is prohibited. The court found that circumstantial evidence indicated SHAC defendants were aware of their risk of prosecution because they took precautions to encrypt devices, hide their identities, and other covert actions. The court held that the illegal activity and true threats encouraged by SHAC are not protected by the First Amendment and rejected the argument that the act was void for vagueness.

Others have argued that the use of the word "terrorism" in the title of the act violates defendants' substantive due process rights. In *United States v. Johnson*, defendants were charged under the AETA for property damage occurring when they vandalized farm equipment and released minks from a fur

---

110. Under the National Defense Authorization Act, the FBI and DHS are required to issue an annual strategic intelligence assessment on domestic terrorism. The assessments report statistics and incidents of domestic terror activity, including violations defined under the AETA, committed by alleged animal and environmental activists. *See Strategic Intelligence Assessment and Data on Domestic Terrorism—2022*, FBI (Oct. 22, 2022), https://www.justice.gov/hatecrimes/resource/strategic-intelligence-assessment-and-data-domestic-terrorism-2022.

111. 744 F.3d 790 (1st Cir. 2014), *cert. denied*, 135 S. Ct. 477 (2014).

112. United States v. Fullmer, 584 F.3d 132 (2009). Note that in *Fullmer*, defendants were charged under the 1992 AEPA because their alleged crimes occurred prior to the 2006 amendment and renaming of AEPA as the AETA.

113. 584 F.3d 132 (3d Cir. 2009).

farm in Illinois.[114] Defendants claimed violation of their substantive due process rights on the basis that, if convicted under the AETA, a government counterterrorism employee would review their case for incarceration placement purposes. The court noted that such review does not automatically result in assignment to high security prison units, finding that there is no fundamental right to not be labeled as a terrorist under the AETA, thus no liberty interest is at stake.

Pets Evacuation and Transportation Standards Act

The Pets Evacuation and Transportation Standards (PETS) Act of 2006 is a federal law that seeks to protect pets and service animals, as well as their owners, when they evacuate their homes and seek temporary shelter due to a major disaster or emergency.[115] The PETS Act was introduced in response to the Hurricane Katrina disaster in 2005, which highlighted the need for emergency preparedness for pets and service animals. Because existing disaster and emergency assistance regulations at that time did not expressly cover emergency assistance for service or companion animals,[116] many people were separated from their animals when forced to relocate to shelters, and others refused to leave. According to one poll, nearly half of the people who did not evacuate made that decision because they were not willing to leave their pets. People and animals died as a result.[117]

Under the PETS Act, state and local emergency preparedness operational plans must provide for "the needs of individuals with household pets and service animals following a major disaster or emergency."[118] If a state or local government fails to comply with the PETS Act, Federal Emergency Management Agency (FEMA) may withhold disaster relief funding from that state or local government until it demonstrates that it has taken steps to comply. In this way, federal disaster funding is conditioned on PETS Act compliance. Local emergency preparedness operational plans must cover the evacuation, sheltering, and transport of pets and service animals, as well as ensuring that emergency shelters and other facilities are equipped to accommodate the animals.

Further, the PETS Act authorizes FEMA to provide assistance, through funding and reimbursement, to states and localities in providing shelter and veterinary care for pets and service animals during and following major disasters and emergencies. Under FEMA's "Eligible Costs Related to Pet Evacuations and Sheltering" policy, specific guidelines determine which expenses are reimbursable. Note that the PETS Act applies to state and local governments: hotels are not required to accept pets during a major disaster or emergency.

114. 875 F.3d 360 (7th Cir. 2017).

115. Pub. L. No.109-308.

116. The PETS Act amends the Stafford Disaster Relief and Emergency Assistance Act of 1988.

117. Louisiana SPCA, *Hurricane Katrina Animal Rescue Facts*, https://www.louisianaspca.org/about-us/hurricane-katrina/animal-rescue-facts/; *see also* Animal Welfare Institute, *Katrina's Lessons Learned: Animals No Longer Excluded from Storm Evacuations*, AWI Quarterly (Winter 2017).

118. Pub. L. No. 109-308.

Preventing Animal Cruelty and Torture Act

The Preventing Animal Cruelty and Torture (PACT) Act of 2019 is a federal ban on certain types of animal cruelty.[119] This law replaces the Animal Crush Video Prohibition Act of 1999, which the Supreme Court ruled unconstitutional in 2010 on the grounds that the language was so broad that it could have applied to activities protected by the First Amendment.[120] Under the PACT Act, it is a federal crime, punishable by severe fines and imprisonment of up to seven years, to engage in certain types of animal cruelty and torture, including bestiality, crushing, burning, drowning, suffocating, impaling, or otherwise subjecting animals to serious bodily harm. The law also prohibits creating and distributing "animal crush videos," in which a person purposely subjects small animals to serious bodily injury.[121] The PACT Act is enforced by the FBI and the DOJ. The law provides for criminal penalties, including fines and imprisonment, for individuals who engage in animal cruelty or torture on federal property or in interstate commerce.

The act applies to "living non-human mammals, birds, reptiles, or amphibians."[122] Although the act is a step forward in protecting animals by preventing and punishing animal cruelty at the federal level, the act is not without several concerning limitations, such as only protecting certain types of animals. For example, the act expressly excludes the slaughter of animals for food, the use of animals in medical and scientific research, and sporting activities such as hunting, fishing, and trapping.

Puppies Assisting Wounded Servicemembers Act

U.S. military veteran access to service dogs is governed by the Department of Veterans Affairs (VA). Prior to the 2021 Puppies Assisting Wounded Servicemembers (PAWS) Act, veterans' service dog benefits were limited to those veterans diagnosed by the VA as having "a visual, hearing, or substantial mobility impairment."[123] The PAWS Act expands veteran access to service animals by allowing VA clinically diagnosed veterans with post-traumatic stress disorder (PTSD) to train and potentially adopt service dogs.[124]

While the VA can authorize use of a service dog, the VA does not provide service dogs to veterans. Instead, veterans who are diagnosed with visual, hearing, or mobility impairments are authorized by the VA to receive a service dog from an approved nonprofit.[125] The VA then provides benefits, including special equipment and pet health insurance, to allow the veteran to utilize the

119. Pub. L. No. 116-72.

120. Pub. L. No. 106-152.

121. Pub. L. No. 116-72.

122. 18 U.S.C. § 48(f)(1).

123. 38 C.F.R. § 17.148(b).

124. Pub. L. No. 117-37.

125. The VA approves dogs from specific nonprofits including Assistance Dogs International and the International Guide Dog Federation.

service dog and to maintain the dog's health.[126] This is considered to be part of the veteran's own health care.

The PAWS Act is currently operating as a five-year pilot program. Admitted PTSD-diagnosed veterans[127] work in groups under the guidance of a nonprofit organization to teach basic obedience and specialized skills to dogs. The dogs will either become a service dog for another veteran, or the participating veteran may be offered the opportunity to adopt the dog. The PAWS Act directs the VA to study the effectiveness of service dogs in treating mental health conditions among PTSD-diagnosed veterans. The pilot program study will evaluate the impact of service dogs on the mental health and quality of life of veterans, as well as the cost-effectiveness of using service dogs as an option for treating veterans with mental health conditions.

Big Cat Public Safety Act

There are an estimated 20,000 privately owned lions, tigers, cheetahs, and other big cats within the United States.[128] The Big Cat Public Safety Act (BCPSA) of 2022 aims to address the public safety and animal welfare concerns associated with the private ownership of big cats.[129] These concerns were the result of the lack of federal oversight because there was no reliable method of tracking the trade of big cats as pets. Further, given big cats' natural instinct to hunt and attack, combined with the inability for humans to domesticate them, there have been numerous injurious and fatal incidents involving captive big cats, highlighting the need for a federal solution to protect public safety. In one tragic incident, an Ohio man released fifty-six privately owned exotic animals before committing suicide.[130] Local authorities shot and killed forty-nine of the animals, including tigers and lions, to protect the public.[131] Many injuries and fatalities have occurred where the public is allowed to interact with big cats, or when individuals caring for big cats come in contact with them.[132]

The BCPSA amends the Lacey Act, with a stated goal of furthering the conservation of wildlife by prohibiting the private possession of lions, tigers, leopards, cheetahs, jaguars, cougars, or any hybrid of those species. In addition, the BCPSA restricts direct contact between the public and big cats while exempting zoos, sanctuaries, and universities. Under the BCPSA, current pet big

---

126. *Service Dog Veterinary Health Insurance Benefit (VHIB) Rules*, U.S. Dep't Veterans Aff., https://www.prosthetics.va.gov/factsheet/PSAS-FactSheet-ServiceDogs.pdf.

127. To participate in the pilot and benefit from the act, a veteran must meet three threshold conditions: (1) enrollment in the VA health care system; (2) diagnosis with PTSD; and (3) recommendation from a VA mental health care provider or VA clinical team. *See* Implementation of the PAWS for Veterans Therapy Act, 87 FR 18481 (Mar. 30, 2022).

128. *June 18 Deadline for Compliance with Big Cat Public Safety Act*, U.S. Fish & Wildlife Serv. (Apr. 18, 2023), https://www.fws.gov/press-release/2023-04/big-cat-owners-must-register-june-18.

129. Pub. L. No. 117-243.

130. Timothy Williams, *Preserve Owner Was Bitten by Big Cat, Authorities Say*, N.Y. Times (Oct. 20, 2011), https://www.nytimes.com/2011/10/21/us/preserve-owner-was-bitten-by-big-cat-authorities-say.html.

131. *Id.*

132. *Big-Cat Incidents in the U.S.*, P.E.T.A. (2021), https://www.peta.org/wp-content/uploads/2021/06/BigCatIncidentList.pdf, (accessed June 20, 2023).

cat owners are grandfathered in and are only required to register their cats to ensure that first responders and animal control officers are aware of the cats' presence and location. Violations of the act in any district in which the defendant may have taken or been in possession of the prohibited wildlife species are punishable by fines or imprisonment, or both.[133]

Federal Environmental Laws of Particular Relevance to Animals[134]

National Environmental Policy Act

The National Environmental Policy Act (NEPA) of 1970 is a federal law that requires federal agencies to consider the environmental impacts of proposed projects and to involve the public in the decision-making process.[135] More specifically, NEPA requires federal agencies to prepare an Environmental Impact Statement (EIS) for any major federal action that could have a significant impact on the environment. The EIS must evaluate the potential environmental impacts of the proposed action and any alternatives, as well as identify ways to mitigate any adverse impacts. NEPA involves the public in the decision-making process by providing opportunities for public comment and review.

Although NEPA does not directly protect on animals, it places procedural requirements on government agencies that plan to engage in activities that could impact the environment in which both humans and animals live. Litigants often use NEPA to defend the interests of animals because NEPA extends a critical procedural protection to animals and habitats relating to actions by federal agencies.

As one example, in *Natural Resources Defense Council v. National Marine Fisheries Service*, leading environmental protection groups sued the federal government to prevent seismic air gun blasting in the Atlantic Ocean.[136] The plaintiffs, which included Natural Resources Defense Council and Center for Biological Diversity among others, claimed that the NMFS violated the MMPA, ESA, and NEPA by permitting loud sounds from seismic blasting that would harm marine mammals, including whales and dolphins, by disrupting their feeding and communication behaviors. The court ruled in favor of plaintiffs, ordering NMFS to reconsider its decision in light of the potential impacts on marine mammals.

---

133. Pub. L. No. 117-243.

134. The Clean Air Act (CAA), 42 U.S.C. §§ 7401–7671, an environmental statute that could be relevant to animals if it were applied to emissions from animal farming, is not covered in this chapter. Despite long efforts of environmental and animal advocates, industrial animal agriculture operations have consistently been exempted from the CAA. *E.g.*, Ryan Levandowski, *Polluting 'Til the Cows Come Home: How Agricultural Exceptionalism Allows CAFOs Free Range for Climate Harm*, 33 Geo. Envtl. L. Rev. 151, (2020).

135. Pub. L. No. 91-190.

136. National Res. Def. Council v. Nat'l Marine Fisheries Serv., 409 F.Supp.2d 379 (S.D.N.Y. 2006).

Clean Water Act

The Clean Water Act (CWA) of 1977 prohibits the discharge of any pollutant from a point source, such as a pipe or a factory, into navigable waters of the United States without a permit.[137] Enforced by the Environmental Protection Agency (EPA) and the states, the CWA is designed to protect and improve the quality of the nation's waterways. The CWA establishes water quality standards for surface waters and sets limits on the number of pollutants that can be discharged into them. Further, the CWA includes provisions to protect wetlands, which are important for filtering pollutants and providing animal habitats.

The CWA is relevant to industrial animal agriculture operations, including "concentrated animal feeding operations" or "CAFOs,"[138] because they create enormous amounts of liquid and solid animal waste. The EPA has maintained authority to regulate CAFO discharges for CWA compliance since the mid-1970s.[139] The EPA classifies CAFOs as "point sources"[140] of pollution that are subject to permitting requirements if they discharge or have the potential to discharge pollutants. Nonetheless, CAFOs that violate the CWA through inadequate waste management systems or insufficient permitting are rarely subjected to strict enforcement measures.[141]

As an example of litigation in this area relating to animals, in *Food & Water Watch v. U.S. Environmental Protection Agency*, environmental organizations challenged the EPA's issuance of a National Pollutant Discharge Elimination System (NPDES) permit for Idaho CAFOs.[142] Plaintiffs claimed that the permit lacked sufficient monitoring provisions to ensure compliance and therefore violated the CWA.[143] The court agreed with plaintiffs, finding that the NPDES permit had no monitoring provisions for dry weather discharges from land-application areas even though records indicated that such discharges can occur during irrigation of fertilized fields. The court ultimately granted the petition and remanded the NPDES permit to the EPA for further proceedings consistent with the opinion.

---

137. 33 U.S.C. §§ 1251–1387.

138. The definition of CAFO varies depending on species and number of animals held. For example, facilities with at least 700 dairy cattle, or 82,000 laying hens, constitute CAFOs and therefore may be subject to the CWA. 40 C.F.R § 122.23(b)(4).

139. Claudia Copeland, Cong. Rsch. Serv, *Animal Waste and Water Quality: EPA's Response to the Waterkeeper Alliance Court Decision on Regulation of CAFOs*, RL33656, June 1, 2016, https://crsreports.congress.gov/product/pdf/RL/RL33656/27.

140. 33 U.S.C. § 1362(14).

141. U.S. Gov't Accountability Off., GAO-21-290, Clean Water Act Enforcement 16 (2021), https://www.gao.gov/assets/gao-21-290.pdf; *see also* D. Lee Miller & Gregory Muren, *CAFOs: What We Don't Know Is Hurting Us*, Nat'l Res. Def. Couns. (Sept. 2019), https://www.nrdc.org/sites/default/files/cafos-dont-know-hurting-us-report.pdf.

142. Food & Water Watch v. Env't Prot. Agency, No. 20-71554 (9th Cir. 2021).

143. *Id.*

Resource Conservation and Recovery Act

The Resource Conservation and Recovery Act (RCRA) of 1976 is a federal law that protects public health and the environment by regulating the generation, transportation, treatment, storage, and disposal of hazardous wastes.[144] Under RCRA, hazardous waste is any waste that is potentially dangerous or harmful to human health or the environment.[145] RCRA requires generators of hazardous waste to manage their waste in a way that is safe for human health and the environment, and to properly label and store hazardous waste until it can be transported and disposed of in a safe and responsible manner. Open dumping of solid waste is prohibited.[146] RCRA also requires permits for facilities that treat, store, or dispose of hazardous waste, setting standards for the design, construction, and operation of these facilities. Under RCRA, hazardous waste is tracked from the time it is generated to when it is disposed. Individuals and organizations may bring lawsuits under RCRA's citizen suit provision.

In *Community Association for Restoration of the Environment, Inc. v. Cow Palace*, plaintiffs C.A.R.E. and the Center for Food Safety brought suit under RCRA, challenging a dairy's mismanagement and improper disposal of waste.[147] The dairy generated over 100 million gallons of waste annually, including manure and manure laden water used to wash cattle. Waste was stored in onsite manure lagoons and sprayed onto fields as fertilizer. However, the dairy regularly over-sprayed the fields in excess of state dairy nutrient management plan rules, causing nitrogen and other substances to contaminate surface and drinking water, and threatening public health. On summary judgment, the court determined that overapplication of waste from the dairy cattle constituted solid waste under RCRA's definition, and that over spraying the waste onto fields was open dumping.

Administrative Procedure Act

As many federal laws lack a citizen suit provision, the APA plays an important role in protecting animals. Advocates and organizations can use the APA to challenge federal agency actions that negatively impact animals. Where an agency fails to follow proper administrative procedures, a plaintiff may sue based on procedural injury, asserting a defect in an agency's action and requesting that the agency take corrective action.

---

144. 42 U.S.C. §§ 6901–6992k.

145. 42 U.S.C. § 6903(5)(A)–(B).

146. 42 U.S.C. § 6945(a).

147. 80 F. Supp. 3d 1180 (E.D. Wash. 2015). This case settled, with the defendants consenting to double line the manure lagoons, submit to inspections by the EPA and plaintiff designees and other remediation to protect the ground water. *See also* Water Keeper All. v. Smithfield Foods, 2001 WL 1715730 (E.D.N.C. 2001). (Motion to dismiss denied. Under RCRA, manure over sprayed on crops is no longer considered fertilizer and instead meets the definition of solid waste when it is overapplied in amounts that cannot be absorbed by the soil.)

The APA is purely procedural. It lays out the steps that an agency must take during rulemaking and adjudication.[148] Rulemaking is the process of creating a new agency regulation. This is most commonly done when an agency proposes a new rule, which is published in the Federal Register with adequate time for public notice and comment by interested parties. In contrast, administrative adjudication involves a petition challenging an agency action or inaction when a statute entitles an interested party to a hearing in front of the administrative body. In addition to rulemaking and adjudication, the APA governs procedures for agencies that issue and regulate licenses or permits. The APA applies to all federal executive departments, many of which are highly relevant to animals—such as the Department of Interior and the USDA. It also applies to independent federal agencies such as the EPA and the Securities and Exchange Commission.

The APA establishes both formal and informal processes for rulemaking, but provides only formal adjudication procedures. Informal rulemaking,[149] also called "notice and comment" rulemaking, requires a public comment period on the proposed rule. The comment period allows individuals, groups, businesses, or any interested parties to submit a statement about the draft rule. Their comments could be for or against the rule, indicate potential benefits of or concerns about its language, and/or suggest additional considerations or changes that should be made. The agency must allow for a comment period of no less than thirty days. Written comments may be submitted online, and will be considered by the agency during rulemaking. When the agency formulates a final rule, the rule is published in the Federal Register.

APA formal rulemaking is used less frequently than informal rulemaking. In contrast to informal rulemaking, the formal rulemaking process requires a formal hearing,[150] and is only available when an enabling statute expressly indicates that "on the record" rulemaking is required. Where a statute requires formal rulemaking, the APA dictates how an administrative judge will be appointed, how the public may provide input, and how the process and regulation will become the final rule.

Unlike APA rulemaking—which is forward-looking and will generally impact the future actions of many—APA adjudication is backward looking and is applied to specific circumstances that typically impact individuals. Adjudication by an administrative agency is often conducted through an administrative hearing, which is presided over by an administrative law judge, a board, or a hearing officer of the agency. Formal adjudication is required when an enabling statute requires "on the record" adjudication. Informal adjudication processes are not defined by the APA and instead are guided by other laws.[151]

---

148. 5 U.S.C. §§ 551–559.

149. 5 U.S.C.§ 553.

150. 5 U.S.C.§§ 553(a), (b), (d), (e), 556, and 557.

151. Informal procedures can be defined within agency regulations, under a statute, or by application of the Due Process Clause in the Fifth and Fourteenth Amendments of the U.S. Constitution. There is a range of informal adjudication procedures, with some requirements being trial-like, and others being procedurally minimal.

Conclusion

The federal laws described in this chapter are not an exhaustive list. Although current federal statutes provide limited protections for some animals, and fully exclude others, creative application of federal laws can provide opportunities for strategic litigation on behalf of animals. There is increasing public interest in the humane treatment of companion, captive, farmed, and wild animals. When cruel practices are brought to light, the public can take action. California's Proposition 12[152] (passed via a ballot measure) was recently upheld by the Supreme Court,[153] which has the potential to ignite renewed efforts and debate around the need for a federal law providing standard and more humane treatment of farmed animals during their lives on farms. Looking forward, another potentially significant development is the Recovering America's Wildlife Act,[154] which was recently reintroduced in Congress and has gained bipartisan support. If passed, it would be the most substantial protection for American wildlife since the ESA was passed fifty years ago. While existing federal laws leave much room for improvement, increased public awareness of the plight of animals, and growing advocacy to make change on their behalf, signal a brighter future.

152. Among other things, Proposition 12 prevents the sale of certain animal products in California that were produced from a farmed animal who was confined in a cruel manner. This requires producers to provide covered farmed animals with enough room to stand, stretch, and fully turn around. H.S.C. §§ 25990–25994. Veal, pork, and eggs sold in California must be sourced from farmed animals kept under minimum welfare standards as designated by 3 C.C.R. §§ 1320–1327.3.

153. National Pork Producers v. Ross, 598 U.S. __ (2023), https://www.supremecourt.gov/opinions/22pdf/21-468_5if6.pdf.

154. Recovering America's Wildlife Act, S.1149, 118th Cong. (2023), https://www.congress.gov/bill/118th-congress/senate-bill/1149.

CHAPTER 10

International Law

Rajesh K. Reddy

Calls for international law to safeguard the interests of animals have grown over the last century,[1] with numerous countries, otherwise referred to as "states" in international law, having entered into treaties to give rise to their protection.[2] As this chapter illustrates, together these agreements attest to the need for cooperation among states and international organizations to meet the unique, extraterritorial challenges of protecting animals. Animals are treated as commodities in an increasingly interconnected global marketplace, migrate across borders, reside in international waters, serve as hosts and intermediaries of zoonotic disease pathogens, provide vital ecosystem functions, face species-level threats of extinction, and are increasingly the subject of public moral concern.[3] As distinct from private international law, which focuses on relations between private individuals, public international law, which concerns relations among states or international organizations, holds inherent promise in elevating the interests of animals globally. That said, some of the agreements discussed in this chapter show that treaties that institute flawed or unambitious standards can forestall progress and leave states with little incentive to expand upon their commitments.

Against this backdrop, this chapter provides an overview of the background, structure, and limitations of treaties, to contextualize international protections afforded to animals today. From here, the chapter scrutinizes the context and conditions that gave rise to one of the world's first animal protection agreements, the Fur Seal Treaty of 1911,[4] which was negotiated to

1. Guillaume Futhazar, *Biodiversity, Species Protection, and Animal Welfare Under International Law*, *in* Studies in Global Animal L., 95, 105–106 (Anne Peters ed., 2020).

2. *Infra* Part III.

3. *Infra* Parts II & III; Miyun Park & Peter Singer, *The Globalization of Animal Welfare: More Food Does Not Require More Suffering*, 91.2 Foreign Affairs 122, 122–33 (2012) ("[N]ational governments and the global community have increasingly voiced concern for farm animals, no matter where they may be raised.").

4. Convention between the United States and Other Powers Providing for the Preservation and Protection of Fur Seals, July 7, 1911, 104 BFSP 175 [hereinafter FST].

preserve seal populations to allow for their continued exploitation. This chapter then delves into more modern agreements that directly or indirectly advance the interests of animals. In doing so, it illustrates how certain animal treaties have grown more progressive over time and speaks to how more modern perspectives on animals, as well as a deeper appreciation of how their well-being inures to the benefit of humankind, have helped to start to raise consideration of their interests on the world stage. While this chapter focuses on international frameworks—calling attention to how global instruments inform and complement one another—it also illustrates how international developments impact the domestic animal laws of individual states and vice versa. Attorneys with a firm grasp of international law will arguably prove better equipped to serve the animal protection organizations they represent, by utilizing these global frameworks to advance and expand their efforts, and by being cognizant of the impact—both intended and unintended—that their strategies may have on animals in other jurisdictions. In charting the current landscape of international animal law, this chapter also explores contemporary proposals to address some of the most pressing issues that animals face and advances a view of international law as a productive and necessary path to realizing meaningful gains for animals.

An Overview of International Law

The Vienna Convention on the Law of Treaties

One of the inherent complexities of international law is that states, by their very nature, are deemed sovereigns on the world stage—meaning that they are subject to no law save by their own consent.[5] By entering into a treaty, then, a state voluntarily sacrifices aspects of its sovereignty in agreeing to be bound. Historically, such agreements between or among states were governed by what is known as international customary law, or quite literally "international custom, as evidence of a general practice accepted as law."[6] Given the confusion over treaty law during and after World War II, the need to codify international customary law became readily apparent.[7] This decades-long effort concluded in May 1969 with the Vienna Convention on the Law of Treaties (Vienna),[8] which is widely hailed as "the treaty on treaties,"[9] or the authoritative source on international law.[10] Given its widespread adoption,[11] Vienna affords advocates

5. Ronald A. Brand, *Sovereignty: The State, the Individual, and the International Legal System in the Twenty First Century*, 25 Hastings Int'l & Comp. L. Rev. 279, 284 (2002).

6. Statute of the International Court of Justice, art. 38(b), June 26, 1945, 1055.

7. Daniel N. Hylton, *Default Breakdown: The Vienna Convention on the Law of Treaties' Inadequate Framework on Reservations*, 27.2 Vanderbilt J. of Transnational L., 419, 424 (1994).

8. Vienna Convention on the Law of Treaties, May 23, 1969, 1155 U.N.T.S. 331 [hereinafter VCLT].

9. Richard D. Kearney & Robert E. Dalton, *The Treaty on Treaties*, 64 Am. J. Int'l L., 495 (1970).

10. *Law of Treaties*, United Nations Treaty Collection, https://treaties.un.org/pages/ViewDetailsIII.aspx?src=TREATY&mtdsg_no=XXIII-1&chapter=23&Temp=mtdsg3&clang=_en (last visited Oct. 1 2022).

11. *Id.*

working on global animal law issues a critical lens through which to appreciate the elements, context, enforceability, and more of animal protection agreements.

Before turning to Vienna, however, it is important for animal protection lawyers to note that states may have an internal, constitutionally informed definition of what constitutes a 'treaty' that differs from how the term is conceived under Vienna. The United States stands as an excellent example in this regard. Under Article II of its Constitution, a treaty can be entered into only by the president upon receiving the advice and consent of two-thirds of the Senate.[12] Yet the United States is party to many international agreements that constitute treaties under Vienna that have not gone through this formal process and are thus not deemed treaties under domestic law.[13]

Vienna identifies three requisite elements for a treaty: it must be in "written form," whether contained in one or over multiple instruments; constitute "an international agreement concluded between States;" and be governed by international law.[14] Seemingly straightforward, this definition leaves much to unpack. While treaties may be contained within a single instrument, or text, they may also be constructed across a series of exchanges, such as letters between states.[15] Notably, Vienna applies to agreements between and among states but not to international organizations[16]—such as the World Trade Organization (WTO) and the World Organisation for Animal Health (WOAH)[17]—which were created *by* treaties and can even be signatories *to* treaties.[18] Similarly, outside Vienna's purview are self-governing, quasi-sovereign entities, such as tribal nations in the United States that have entered into treaties with the United States but are not themselves recognized as states internationally.[19] Lastly, the requirement that treaties must be governed by international law ensures that the instrument in question imposes obligations that are enforceable. This element distinguishes treaties from declarations, which are generally understood to be statements of principle,[20] and other instruments that may have signatory states but are not binding. Furthermore, Vienna does not require that a treaty be called a "treaty"[21]; rather, as long as the instrument(s) contains these requisite elements, Vienna deems it a treaty even if

12. U.S. Const. art. II.

13. *About Treaties*, U.S. Senate, https://www.senate.gov/about/powers-procedures/treaties.htm (last visited Oct. 1, 2022).

14. VCLT, art. 1, ¶ a.

15. *See Glossary*, United Nations Treaty Collection, https://treaties.un.org/pages/overview.aspx?path=overview/glossary/page1_en.xml (referencing VCLT art. 13).

16. *See* VCLT, art. 1, ¶ a (defining treaties under VCLT as being concluded between states).

17. *Infra* Part III.

18. *Infra* Part III.

19. Annika Tahvanainen, *The Treaty-Making Capacity of Indigenous Peoples*, 12:4 Int'l J. on Minority & Group Rights, 397, 399 (2005) (observing that it is "doubtful whether one could consider that indigenous peoples constitute subjects of international law").

20. *See Definitions*, United Nations Treaty Collection, https://treaties.un.org/Pages/overview.aspx?path=overview/definition/page1_en.xml (last visited Oct. 1 2022) ("The term 'declaration' is used for various international instruments. . . . The term is often deliberately chosen to indicate that the parties do not intend to create binding obligations but merely want to declare certain aspirations.").

21. *See* VCLT, art. 1, ¶ a (noting that as long as the elements are met, an instrument will constitute a treaty, "whatever its particular designation").

it is known by a corollary term, such as international agreement, pact, protocol, accord, exchange of letters, convention, and so on.[22] As long as these three criteria are met, agreements with states that have ratified Vienna are treaties.

Another of the complexities of international law concerns how states express their consent to be bound. Generally speaking, states express their intent by ratifying a treaty.[23] What ratification looks like and the name it takes, however, takes on different forms depending on the stage the instrument is in, the stipulations of the treaty itself,[24] as well as each state's rules that govern how treaties may be entered into. Generally, a proposed treaty will state a requisite number or even list specific states that must ratify it in order for it to go into effect.[25] Once a treaty has crossed the threshold of having been negotiated and signed by states, other states may ratify it through the act of "accession,"[26] though the distinction makes no difference as to their obligations.[27]

But what does a state consent to do when ratifying a treaty? Although their obligations run to other contracting parties, states must pass domestic legislation to effectuate their treaty obligations.[28] Put differently, international obligations are fulfilled through domestic law. Usually, domestic laws that fulfill a state's treaty obligations are deposited with a secretariat identified in the treaty, with the secretariat then making each party's instrument available to all other parties.[29]

Treaty Elements and Structure

While Vienna identifies necessary elements, it does not stipulate the structure treaties must take. That said, treaties generally adhere to a standard format. Many treaties open with a series of preambular statements declaring contracting parties' rationale for entering into the agreement, as well as the treaty's object and purpose.[30] Although the preamble offers guidance as to how the text of the treaty is to be constructed and thereby has legal influence,[31] it does not create obligations in and of itself. Rather, treaty obligations are found in other provisions, which identify requirements that contracting parties must abide by to effectuate the treaty's purpose.[32] Of note is that some treaties lead to the

22. *See* Tashmayee Sarkhel, *Vienna Convention on the Law of Treaties*, Law Insider (Aug. 3, 2022) https://www.lawinsider.in/columns/vienna-convention-on-the-law-of-treaties (observing that a "[t]reaty can be called a convention, a protocol, a pact, an accord, and many more" and that the "content of . . . [an] agreement[] decides whether it is a treaty or not.").

23. VCLT, art. I, ¶ b.

24. *Glossary*, *supra* note 15.

25. *Definitions*, *supra* note 20.

26. VCLT, art. 2, ¶ 1, cl. b; VCLT, art. 15.

27. *Glossary*, *supra* note 15.

28. *Id.* ("The institution of ratification grants states the necessary time-frame to seek the required approval for the treaty on the domestic level and to enact the necessary legislation to give domestic effect to that treaty.")

29. VCLT arts. 16, 76, 77.

30. Max H. Hulme, *Preambles in Treaty Interpretation*, 164 Univ. of Penn. L. Rev., 1281, 1288 (2016).

31. *Id.* at 1290 (noting that "preambles serve only to clarify ambiguous text in the 'actual' act, a non-trivial but nevertheless severely limited role").

32. *Id.* at 1283–1284.

creation of intergovernmental bodies to carry out the functions of the treaty, such as the International Whaling Commission (IWC) under the International Convention for the Regulation of Whaling (ICRW).[33] If applicable, a treaty may also address whether contracting parties are to reconvene. For example, the Conference of the Parties in the Convention on International Trade in Endangered Species of Wild Fauna and Flora (CITES)[34] meets at least every two years to determine which species are to be protected and what level of protections they should enjoy.[35] CITES is also an example of a treaty that employs appendices,[36] or lists that can be updated as a means to allow the treaty to readily adapt to threats that animals face. Some treaties also provide for protocols, or sub-treaties to which contracting parties may agree to craft additional rights and obligations.[37]

Treaties also feature important procedural provisions, such as rules on how to ratify or accede, whether reservations are permitted, if and how the treaty may be amended, denounced, or exited, and what enforcement mechanisms exist, such as negotiation, arbitration, or submission of disputes to an international tribunal.[38] Although Vienna does not apply retrospectively—meaning it does not govern treaties entered into before a state ratified Vienna—as a codification of international customary law,[39] Vienna nevertheless proves a helpful tool to analyze all treaties.

The Advent of the Animal Protection Treaty

Negotiated over a century ago, the Fur Seal Treaty of 1911 (FST) exemplifies the historical need for cooperation among states to protect animals to prevent the extinction of heavily commodified species,[40] a peril many still face today. Broadly, the FST concerned dwindling seal populations due to unregulated hunting by Russia, Japan, and Canada around the Pribilof Islands, which the United States acquired from Russia as part of the Alaska Purchase.[41] With the seals' rookeries, or nesting grounds, under its sole jurisdiction, the United States

33. International Convention for the Regulation of Whaling, Dec. 2, 1946, 161 U.N.T.S. 72, art. III [hereinafter ICRW].

34. Convention on International Trade in Endangered Species of Wild Fauna and Flora, Mar. 3, 1973, 27 U.S.T. 1087 [hereinafter CITES].

35. *Id.*art. XI.

36. *Id.* arts. II–IV.

37. *See Glossary*, *supra* note 15 ("An Optional Protocol to a Treaty is an instrument that establishes additional rights and obligations to a treaty. . . . Such protocols enable certain parties of the treaty to establish among themselves a framework of obligations which reach further than the general treaty and to which not all parties of the general treaty consent. . . .").

38. VCLT, arts. 14, 19–23, 39, 44, 66.

39. VCLT, art. 4; *Vienna Convention on the Law of Treaties*, U.S. Dep't of State, https://2009-2017.state.gov/s/l/treaty/faqs/70139.htm (last visited Oct. 1, 2022).

40. Amanda L. Shirnina, *The Fur Seals of Early American Alaska*, Nat'l Park Service, https://www.nps.gov/articles/000/aps-20-2-9.htm.

41. *Id.*

attempted to engage in on-shore resource management;[42] however, the fact that the seals migrated through "open," or extraterritorial waters, which lie outside the control of any nation, meant that other states could hunt them with impunity.[43] As a result, seal populations dropped dramatically, from 4.5 million in 1884 to 200,000 in 1909.[44] This extraterritorial resource management predicament implicated by seals' migratory nature constituted a proverbial zero-sum game, such that each state was incentivized to hunt as many seals as it could, with any measures to stop doing so to allow numbers to rebound inuring to the benefit of their counterparts—unless those states followed suit as well. Yet unlike a zero-sum game, seals constituted an exhaustible natural resource. As such, if an agreement was not struck to rein in their exploitation, each player on the international stage would stand to lose entirely.

What the FST achieved by facilitating cooperation among states was nothing short of remarkable. First, the states instituted a moratorium on pelagic seal hunting,[45] with each required to pass domestic legislation banning such hunts by its nationals.[46] The treaty then dictated that seal hunts would only be conducted on shore by the United States,[47] the party best able to manage seal numbers. In exchange, Canada, Russia, and Japan would receive direct payments from the United States.[48] The treaty also provided for the interests of nonparties by carving out exceptions for indigenous hunting,[49] which had historically been carried out for subsistence as opposed to commercial purposes —a key distinction that many modern animal protection treaties and regulations account for as well.[50]

The FST was noteworthy as a novel solution to the extraterritorial problem of animal protection and thus proves instructive on numerous levels. First and foremost, it demonstrates the need for all affected parties to enter into negotiations in order to protect animals. Further, the exception carved out for indigenous hunting demonstrates an understanding that subsistence hunts by groups who were not responsible for the overexploitation of animals are different from commercial activities. The treaty also demonstrates that states are often incentivized to protect animals out of financial, rather than moral, concern, with the viability of entire animal-use industries hanging in the balance. Although the FST was entered into for the purpose of protecting animals in order to continue their exploitation, it is likely that the seals would have gone extinct without that animating rationale.[51]

---

42. *Id.*

43. Alton Y. Roppel & Stuart P. Davey, *Evolution of Fur Seal Management on the Pribilof Islands*, 29:3 J. OF WILDLIFE MANAGEMENT, 448, 455 (1965); Helen Cowie, *Seals, Science and Nations*, BRITISH LIBRARY (Aug. 25, 2015), https://blogs.bl.uk/science/2015/08/seals-science-and-nations-.html.

44. *Id.*

45. FST, arts. I–IV; Shirnina, *supra* note 4.

46. FST, art. I.

47. FST, art. X.

48. FST, arts. X–IVX.

49. FST, art. IV.

50. *See infra* note 148 (showcasing an example of an exception for subsistence hunting in the context of whale conservation agreements).

51. Roppel & Davey, *supra* note 43, at 448.

Modern Animal Protection Treaties

Avian-Related Treaties and the Migratory Bird Treaty of 1916

On the heels of the success of the FST, a treaty was negotiated between the United States and Canada (with Great Britain acting on the latter's behalf) to address yet another extraterritorial animal protection issue: the hunting of migratory bird species for sport and fashion, uses that were driving them to near extinction.[52] As with the seals, both powers could control the killing of migratory birds within their respective territories through domestic law, but such measures could go only so far to bring their populations back from the brink of extinction without the other's cooperation.

The ensuing agreement, the Migratory Bird Treaty of 1916 (MBT),[53] articulates in its preamble the "great value" birds offer as food and a natural pest control to the benefit of agriculture.[54] With their economic "useful[ness]" affirmed, the MBT divides migratory species into three categories: game; nongame; and insectivorous.[55] It bans hunting game birds during "closed" seasons, as well as the hunting of insectivorous birds year-round.[56] The hunting of nongame birds was allowed only by Indians and Eskimos for noncommercial food and clothing purposes.[57] Domesticated by Canada as the Migratory Birds Convention Act in 1917 and by the United States as the Migratory Bird Treaty Act of 1918,[58] the MBT has proved a critical success. Indeed, the treaty has been credited with saving billions of birds, with many having been brought back from the edge of extinction.[59] Notably, its success encouraged Mexico, Japan, and Russia to enter into similar agreements with the United States,[60] and numerous other states have since entered into other migratory bird treaties agreements around the world.[61]

---

52. Rachelle House, *The Origins and Evolution of the Migratory Bird Treaty Act of 1918*, AUDUBON (Aug. 9, 2017) https://ca.audubon.org/news/origins-and-evolution-migratory-bird-treaty-act-1918.

53. Convention between the United States and Great Britain for the Protection of Migratory Birds, 39 Stat. 1702 (Aug. 16, 1916) (ratified Dec. 7, 1916) [hereinafter MBT].

54. *Id.* at Preamble.

55. *Id.* art. I, ¶ 1–3.

56. *Id.*art. II.

57. *Id.*

58. House, *supra* note 52; *Birds Protected Under the Migratory Birds Convention Act*, GOVERNMENT OF CANADA, https://www.canada.ca/en/environment-climate-change/services/migratory-birds-legal-protection/convention-act.html (last visited Oct. 1 2022).

59. Jesse Greenspan, *The History and Evolution of the Migratory Bird Treaty Act*, AUDUBON (May 22, 2015) https://www.audubon.org/news/the-history-and-evolution-migratory-bird-treaty-act.

60. *Id.*

61. Mitsuhiko A. Takahashi, *Migratory Bird Treaties' Issues and Potentials: Are They Valuable Tools or Just Curios in the Box?*, 24.2 ENV'L L., 609, 611 (2012).

Territorial and Open Seas: Fisheries and Whaling

The United Nations Convention on the Law of the Sea

The question of state sovereignty over the seas is directly relevant to the conservation, if not protection, of animals. Historically, claiming wide swaths of the seas became the norm during and after World War II,[62] with some states extending their maritime claims to their continental shelf and triggering other states to do the same.[63] At this time, states were beginning to mine the outer shores and seabed.[64] The United States was one of the first to do so, with then-President Truman unilaterally extending U.S. jurisdiction over natural resources on its continental shelf in pursuit of oil, gas, and minerals in 1945.[65] Others followed suit.[66]

The ownership of the seas had implications for resources above the seabed, including living resources. There was a rush to plunder the world's richest fisheries, directly targeting animals themselves and threatening the livelihoods of workers in coastal states who had long managed those same fishing stocks.[67] During this period, states like Iceland claimed sovereignty over nearby waters only to see British ships refuse to acknowledge the claim, with the two powers seizing and rescuing fishing vessels in what would become known as the "Cod Wars."[68]

To address these and other problems, the United Nations held its first Conference on the Law of the Sea in 1956.[69] The meetings resulted in four treaties in 1958—the first three with a geographic focus and the fourth concerning fishing and conservation of living resources.[70] Collectively, these treaties offered general, if unclear, rules for the seas; moreover, they were ineffective in important ways, including because they failed to address the core issue of where a state's territorial seas ended and international waters began.[71] By 1960, many states had asserted a three-mile claim, while other claims reached as far as twelve, thirty, and even two hundred miles from the shore.[72] Looking to address this fundamental question and foster uniformity, the third U.N. Conference on the Law of the Sea combined the existing four treaties into one: the United

62. Bo Johnson Theutenberg, *Mare Clausum et Mare Liberum*, 37:4 Arctic, 481, 490 (1984); *The United Nations Convention on the Law of the Sea (A Historical Perspective)*, United Nations, https://www.un.org/depts/los/convention_agreements/convention_historical_perspective.htm.

63. *Id.*

64. *Id.*

65. *Id.*

66. *E.g.*, Argentina, Peru, Chile, and others extended their coastal claims two hundred nautical miles into the sea. *Id.*

67. *Id.*

68. *Id.*

69. *What Is The Law of The Sea?*, Nat'l Oceanic and Atmospheric Admin. (updated July 13, 2021) https://oceanservice.noaa.gov/facts/lawofsea.html.

70. *The United Nations Convention on the Law of the Sea*, *supra* note 62.

71. *Id.*

72. *Id.*

Nations Convention on the Law of the Sea (UNCLOS) which was adopted in 1982 and entering into force in 1994.[73]

UNCLOS is relevant to the conservation of living resources because it creates a maritime delimitation framework for coastal states. UNCLOS sets a state's territorial waters, which are recognized as extensions of a state's sovereign territory, at twelve nautical miles from its coastal baseline.[74] UNCLOS next establishes a state's "contiguous zone," extending twelve miles beyond and including a state's territorial waters.[75] Within this band, states are empowered to prevent the violation of certain laws, such as those concerning immigration, customs, sanitation regulations, and more.[76] UNCLOS also defines each coastal state's Exclusive Economic Zone (EEZ), which extends up to two hundred nautical miles from its coastline.[77] Within the EEZ, states enjoy a sovereign right over all living and nonliving resources, with the former including fishes and other marine life and the latter concerning minerals, oil, and more.[78] Notably, UNCLOS also contemplates states' interest in their continental shelf and gives them rights over their seabed (including minerals) but not anything above it.[79]

Against this backdrop, UNCLOS addresses the conservation of living resources. States are required to ensure the proper conservation and management of living resources to prevent endangering stocks through overexploitation.[80] States are also required to maintain species within their EEZ to produce a "maximum sustainable yield."[81] Further, UNCLOS requires states to "optimally utilize" the living resources in their EEZ, meaning states must allow use of those species that are not required to be conserved.[82] To this end, UNCLOS requires states to determine total allowable catch sizes for their EEZ using the best science.[83] If a state is unable or unwilling to optimally exploit its living resources, it is required to provide access to geographically disempowered states, or those states that may be landlocked or have little shoreline.[84] Pragmatically, the underlying rationale can be seen as a means to entice geographically disempowered states to ratify a treaty that otherwise does little to benefit them.

UNCLOS also ensures that nearby coastal states work together to promote conservation.[85] For example, for stocks or species outside of a state's EEZ, that state must work with other states to ensure that their numbers—both EEZ and

73. *Id.*; U.N. Convention on the Law of the Sea, Dec. 10, 1982, 1833 U.N.T.S. 397 (entered into force Nov. 16, 1994) art. 311, ¶ 1 [hereinafter UNCLOS].

74. *Id.* pt. II, art. 3.

75. *Id.* art. 33.

76. *Id.*

77. *Id.* art. 57.

78. *Id.* art. 55.

79. *Id.* art. 61.

80. *Id.*

81. *Id.*

82. *Id.* art. 62.

83. *Id.*

84. *Id.* arts. 62, 69, 70.

85. *Id.* art. 63.

non-EEZ stocks—do not fall below an agreed-upon threshold.[86] A similar rule pertains to highly migratory species for which cooperation is needed to promote conservation.[87] In effect, these measure help ensure that a state's fishing practices do not affect other states.

Notably, UNCLOS distinguishes the treatment of marine mammals from other living resources. Beyond the general requirement to optimally utilize all living resources, marine mammals may be protected to any extent a state or states working through an international organization decide.[88] Going further, UNCLOS requires states to both cooperate to conserve marine mammals and "work through the *appropriate* international organizations for [the] conservation, management and study" of cetaceans.[89] As discussed below and as an example of how treaties can interrelate, this article in UNCLOS indirectly references the ICRW,[90] which affords contracting states a seat on the board of the IWC.[91]

Finally, UNCLOS also governs fishing in open waters, also known as the "high seas."[92] It requires that states regulate the fishing activities of their nationals on the high seas and uphold conservation measures.[93] States must also cooperate with other states that exploit resources in the same area to promote long-term conservation.[94] States must employ the best scientific evidence available to achieve a maximum sustainable yield.[95] Citing the carveout for marine mammal management of a state's EEZ, UNCLOS applies additional protections to marine mammals on the high seas.[96] Thus, UNCLOS attempts to negotiate the historically unfettered right of states to engage in fishing on the high seas based on the tacit recognition that fisheries are not limitless and thus demand cooperation among states, to prevent their depletion and ensure their optimal productivity.

Absent definitive guidance as to what constitutes a maximum sustainable yield, however, UNCLOS offers a framework but lacks concrete directives. Further complicating the matter, as a preeminent international maritime agreement with 168 members,[97] UNCLOS prohibits states from entering into agreements that conflict with its measures—which can be viewed as stymieing

86. *Id.*

87. *Id.*art. 64.

88. *Id.* art. 65. ("Nothing in this Part restricts the right of a coastal State or the competence of an international organization, as appropriate, to prohibit, limit or regulate the exploitation of marine mammals more strictly than provided for in this Part.")

89. *Id.* ("States shall cooperate with a view to the conservation of marine mammals and in the case of cetaceans shall in particular work through the appropriate international organizations for their conservation, management and study.") (emphasis added).

90. *Id.*

91. ICRW art. III.

92. UNCLOS art. 116.

93. *Id.* art. 117.

94. *Id.* art. 118.

95. *Id.* art. 119.

96. *Id.* art. 120 (applying the requirements of art. 65 to the high seas).

97. *United Nations Convention on the Law of the Sea*, United Nations Treaty Collections, https://treaties.un.org/pages/ViewDetailsIII.aspx?src=TREATY&mtdsg_no=XXI-6&chapter=21&Temp=mtdsg3&clang=_en (last visited Oct. 1 2022).

efforts of states to promote conversation.[98] With UNCLOS failing to address the precipitous declines in fish stocks that were apparent even before it entered into force in 1994,[99] states sharing this concern began negotiating a treaty that could promote conservation while not conflicting with their obligation under UNCLOS.

The United Nations Fish Stocks Agreement

To this end, states concluded the 1995 U.N. Fish Stocks Agreement (UNFSA), which came into force in 2001.[100] The focus of UNFSA, in the face of "overutiliz[ation]," is the long-term conservation of straddling and highly migratory fish stocks,[101] with the former being those species that move between or among EEZs and the latter being those residing in the high seas. To this end, UNFSA's preamble discusses the harms of unregulated fishing and excessive fleet sizes, inappropriate fishing equipment, and a dependence on unreliable science and databases.[102] The preamble also emphasizes the need to protect biodiversity, maintain ecosystems, prevent the irreversible effects of poor fisheries management, and provide technological assistance to party states.[103]

UNFSA defines "conservation and management measures" as in accordance with those conceived by UNCLOS and declares its objective to be the "effective implementation of [UNCLOS'] relevant provisions."[104] Thus, UNFSA frames itself not as an extension or expansion of UNCLOS's provisions but as a (more effective) example of them—one that states can choose to adopt as their own understanding of UNCLOS's framework. Under this conceit, UNFSA exists within—or at least avoids violating—UNCLOS.[105]

98. *See generally* P. Hoagland, J. Jacoby & M. E. Schumacher, *Law of the Sea*, *in* Encyclopedia of Ocean Sciences (2d ed. 2001), 432–43; *see also* UNCLOS art. 311 (allowing states to enter into separate agreements so as these agreements are not incompatible with UNCLOS' object and purpose and do not affect the rights of other UNCLOS party states).

99. JR Mack, *International Fisheries Management: How the U.N. Conference on Straddling and Highly Migratory Fish Stocks Changes the Law of Fishing on the High Seas*, 26 California Western Int'l Law J., 313, 314–21.

100. Agreement for the Implementation of the Provisions of the United Nations Convention on the Law of the Sea of 10 December 1982 Relating to the Conservation and Management of Straddling Fish Stocks and Highly Migratory Fish Stocks, Aug. 4 1995, U.N.T.S. 2167 [hereinafter UNFSA]; *Law of the Sea*, United Nations https://treaties.un.org/Pages/ViewDetails.aspx?src=IND&mtdsg_no=XXI-7&chapter=21&clang=_en.

101. *Id.* at Preamble.

102. *Id.*

103. *Id.*

104. *Id.* art. 2.

105. Indeed, the U.N. Fish Stocks Agreement takes care to emphasize this point: "Nothing in this Agreement shall prejudice the rights, jurisdiction and duties of States under the Convention. This Agreement shall be interpreted and applied in the context of and in a manner consistent with the Convention." *Id.* art. 4. Although UNFSA represents a standalone treaty, it can be helpful to consider it a protocol within UNCLOS, at least for those states that are party to UNCLOS. However, UNFSA being a standalone treaty readily allows for states that did or have not ratified UNCLOS to become party to UNFSA for fisheries management purposes, as is the case with the United States. Office of Treaty Affairs, *Multilateral (01-1211)—Agreement for the Implementation of the Provisions of the United Nations Convention on the Law of the Sea Relating to the Conservation and Management of Straddling Fish Stocks and Highly Migratory Fish Stocks*, U.S. Dep't. of State (Dec. 11, 2001), https://www.state.gov/01-1211.

As to how it represents an effective implementation of UNCLOS's conservation measures, UNFSA requires states to employ a "precautionary approach" and exercise caution in the face of uncertainty and lack of reliable data.[106] It also contemplates the creation of subregional fisheries agreements to hold states accountable for their nationals and to provide more robust dispute resolution procedures.[107] Notably, states that are members of UNFSA yet fail to join or cooperate with a regional fisheries management authority are prevented from allowing their nationals to fish straddling or highly migratory fish stocks.[108] Furthermore, whereas fishing vessels on the high seas could historically be boarded only by their flag (home) state, UNFSA gives all contracting parties to a regional fisheries agreement the ability to board a vessel of a state that has also ratified UNFSA.[109]

To date, several regional fisheries have been created under the framework of UNFSA to promote conservation beyond that called for by UNCLOS.[110] That said, while UNFSA may represent an improvement over UNCLOS, fishes around the world are still being overexploited, with many regional fisheries failing to adequately protect species.[111] In a bid to address the conservation and sustainable use of living resources on the high seas as part of a "whole-ocean" approach to addressing declining fish stocks, states convened in August 2022 to negotiate a new treaty; however, no agreement was reached, as talks stalled.[112] That said, in light of the biodiversity and other crises facing the world, advocates have witnessed some momentum to change the current paradigm,[113] with a new approach to marine animal conservation and protection having the potential to emulate the significant gains made to protect the world's whales (discussed below).

Biological Diversity Beyond National Jurisdiction

In March 2023, states finalized a draft agreement under the framework of UNCLOS to help provide for the conservation and sustainable use of biological diversity in international waters.[114] Commonly referred to as the "BBNJ" treaty,

106. UNFSA art. 6.

107. *Id.* art. 7, ¶ 7.

108. *Id.* art. 17, ¶ 2.

109. *Id.* art. 20, ¶ 6.

110. David A. Balton & Holly R. Koehler, *Reviewing the United Nations Fish Stocks Treaty*, 7 Sustainable Development Law & Policy, 5, 8 (2006).

111. Jessica F. Green, *Do We Really Need a New U.N. Oceans Treaty? Yes, and Here's Why*, Wash. Post (Apr. 25, 2016), https://www.washingtonpost.com/news/monkey-cage/wp/2016/04/25/do-we-really-need-a-new-maritime-treaty-for-biodiversity-yes-and-heres-why ("A handful of regional fisheries organizations [created under the U.N. Fish Stock Agreement] manage either individual species (notably tuna) or specific areas, but they have come under widespread criticism for failing to protect species.").

112. Claire Griffin, *Media Statement: Latest Round of UN High Seas Treaty Talks Ends Without Resolution in New York City*, The Nature Conservancy (Aug. 27, 2022), https://www.nature.org/en-us/newsroom/statement-on-igc-bbnj.

113. *Id.*

114. Karen McVeigh, *High Seas Treaty: Historic Deal to Protect International Waters Finally Reached at UN*, The Guardian (Mar. 4, 2023), https://www.theguardian.com/environment/2023/mar/05/high-seas-treaty-agreement-to-protect-international-waters-finally-reached-at-un.

the draft agreement under the United Nations Convention on the Law of the Sea on the Conservation and Sustainable Use of Marine Biological Diversity of Areas Beyond National Jurisdiction,[115] recognizes the impact of climate change on marine ecosystems and biodiversity, the need to conserve and sustainably use biological diversity, and equity concerns among states.[116]

The BBNJ draft agreement features four predominant themes. First, Marine Protected Areas are to be created using the best available science and indigenous knowledge to protect natural resources within their boundaries by limiting certain activities.[117] Second, contracting states must carry out Environmental Impact Statements if they determine that their activities may pollute or cause other environmental harms.[118] The third centers on the sharing of Marine Genetic Resources, and the fourth addresses the need for capacity-building and the transferring of marine technology, such that less developed and developing states can also share in the benefits of the conservation and sustainable use of marine biological diversity.[119] While the BBNJ draft agreement represents a major development to better protect marine life, its provisions will not be binding until 120 days after the 60th state ratifies it.[120]

The International Convention for the Regulation of Whaling

The 1946 ICRW represents one of the most successful animal protection treaties to date. The largest animals in the world,[121] whales had been hunted for their meat, bones, and oil for centuries.[122] With the advent of new technologies, however, hunts that were historically limited to coastal areas were able to be carried out deeper in international waters and at a scale never before seen.[123] A series of treaties were struck to prevent the total collapse of global whale stocks, yet these proved ineffective.[124] This harsh reality ultimately led to the development of the ICRW, the preamble of which underscores states' common interest in conserving "the great natural resources represented by the whale stocks" for future generations, the need to protect not just some but all of the world's oceans and species from overexploitation, how the proper regulation of whaling will allow whale populations to grow and lead to an increased bounty

115. Intergovernmental conference on an international legally binding instrument under the United Nations Convention on the Law of the Sea on the conservation and sustainable use of marine biological diversity of areas beyond national jurisdiction, *Draft Agreement Under the United Nations Convention on the Law of the Sea on the Conservation and Sustainable Use of Marine Biological Diversity of Areas Beyond National Jurisdiction* (New York: United Nations, Mar. 3, 2023).

116. *Id.* at Preamble.

117. *Id.* pt. III.

118. *Id.* pt. IV.

119. *Id.* pts. II, IV.

120. *Id.* art. 61.

121. *Meet the Biggest Animal in the World*, World Wildlife Foundation, https://www.worldwildlife.org/stories/meet-the-biggest-animal-in-the-world (last visited Oct. 1 2022).

122. Malgosia Fitzmaurice, *International Convention for the Regulation of Whaling*, United Nations Audiovisual Library of Int'l L., 1, 1 (2017).

123. *Id.*

124. *Id.*

for all, and that reaching this optimum level should be done quickly but without causing "economic or nutritional distress," among other considerations.[125] Also of note is the ICRW's listing of not just a threshold number of states that had to join the treaty for it to enter into force but also the identification of specific states,[126] a tacit recognition—as in so many global contexts relating to animals—that the agreement's object and purpose would be thwarted if any of the world's major whaling states continued to hunt whales at historic numbers.

Similar to the FST, the ICRW's primary purpose was to enable populations to rebound as a means to secure "sustain[able] exploitation."[127] Unlike its predecessors, however, the ICRW is noteworthy for its creation of an intergovernmental body, the IWC, to regulate whaling through the periodic amendment of a schedule.[128] Composed of members from each contracting party,[129] the IWC has the power to sponsor and organize studies on whaling, assess data, produce information related to how whale stocks can be sustained, if not increased, and make recommendations to contracting parties of the ICRW.[130] A significant aspect of the IWC's power lies in its ability to amend the schedule by regulating "protected and unprotected species; open and closed seasons; open and closed waters, including the designation of sanctuary areas; size limits for each species; time, methods, and intensity of whaling (including the maximum catch of whales to be taken in any one season); types and specifications of gear and apparatus and appliances which may be used; methods of measurement; and catch returns and other statistical and biological records."[131] In a nod to state sovereignty, the ICRW affords contracting parties a ninety-day window from when they are notified of the IWC's adoption of an amendment to lodge an objection and thus prevent the application of that amendment to their whaling activities.[132] Notably, party states also have the ability to withdraw their objection later, at which point the amendment becomes binding on them.[133]

Yet another critical facet of the ICRW is its allowance for contracting states to permit their nationals to kill whales for purposes of scientific research, with the limits of this provision proving the basis for arguably the most prominent animal law case brought before an international tribunal. This exception provides:

> Notwithstanding anything contained in this Convention any Contracting Government may grant to any of its nationals a special permit authorizing that national to kill, take and treat whales for purposes of scientific research subject to such restrictions as to number and subject to such other conditions as the Contracting Government thinks fit, and the killing, taking, and

125. ICRW, Preamble.
126. *Id.* art. X.
127. *Id.* arts. I, V.
128. *Id.* art. III.
129. *Id.*
130. *Id.* arts. IV, VI.
131. *Id.* art. V.
132. *Id.* art. 5(3).
133. *Id.*

> treating of whales in accordance with the provisions of this Article shall be exempt from the operation of this Convention.[134]

Here, the plain language of Article VIII allows a contracting state to authorize its nationals to engage in whaling subject to any restrictions the state, in its sole discretion, deems appropriate. In theory, and arguably in effect, Article VIII enables a contracting state to work outside any restrictions established by the schedule—so long as the whaling activity in question is conducted "for purposes of scientific research." While the data gleaned from the research must be presented to the IWC,[135] Article VIII also states that whales taken under the exception created by Article VIII "*shall* so far as practicable be processed," with the contracting state given sole discretion in dictating how the proceeds are directed.[136] By its very nature, then, Article VIII proved ripe for exploitation by a contracting state disinclined to act in good faith.

Such was the claim brought by Australia (with New Zealand as an intervening party) before the International Court of Justice (ICJ) in its assertion that Japan was exploiting the Article VIII exception to engage in whaling for commercial as opposed to scientific purposes. The ICJ found merit in this argument and revoked all the permits Japan had granted through its scientific research program, known as JARPA II.[137] That said, the ICJ recognized that if Japan developed a new research program that conformed with the requirements of Article VIII, it could authorize permits again.[138]

Japan sought to do just this, along with other steps to continue whaling. Just a year after the ICJ ruling, it announced its new scientific research program, NEWREP-A.[139] In response, the IWC pushed Japan to prove that its new program constituted scientific research.[140] Seemingly unable to do so, Japan petitioned the IWC in 2018 to allow it to resume commercial whaling in international waters and, upon being rebuffed, officially denounced the ICRW, unbinding itself from its former treaty obligations.[141] As discussed below, however, by importing sei whale meat from international waters for primarily commercial purposes, Japan was found to have violated its obligations under

134. *Id.* art. VIII, ¶ 1.

135. *Id.* art. VIII, ¶ 3. This information, then, is intended to support the IWC's power to oversee the collection, analysis, and dissemination of data regarding the maintenance and increase of whale stocks, as contemplated by art. IV. In this vein, the data gathered is viewed as "indispensable to the sound and constructive management of whale fisheries." *Id.* art. VIII, ¶¶ 3–4.

136. *Id.* art. VIII, ¶ 2 (emphasis added).

137. Whaling in the Antarctic (Australia v. Japan: New Zealand intervening) (2014), ICJ Reports 2014, ¶¶ 244–246.

138. *Id.*

139. Hilary Whiteman, *Japan Defies World as "Research" Ship Embarks on Minke Whale Kill*, CNN (Dec. 1, 2015), https://www.cnn.com/2015/11/30/asia/japan-whaling-research.

140. Agence France-Presse, *Japan Asked to Prove Its Whaling Is for Scientific Research*, The Guardian (June 19, 2015), https://www.theguardian.com/environment/2015/jun/19/japan-asked-to-prove-whaling-for-scientific-research.

141. Simon Denyer & Akiko Kashiwagi, *Japan to Leave International Whaling Commission, Resume Commercial Hunting*, Wash. Post (Dec. 26, 2018), https://www.washingtonpost.com/world/japan-to-leave-international-whaling-commission-resume-commercial-hunt/2018/12/26/2c32fb20-08c9-11e9-892d-3373d7422f60_story.html.

another treaty, CITES.[142] Since then, Japan has engaged in commercial whaling but has restricted its activities to its own EEZ.[143] Still, Japan is arguably in violation of its obligations under UNCLOS, which it joined in 1996 and which, as discussed above, requires that states "work through the *appropriate* international organizations for their conservation, management and study."[144]

While Japan may be the highest-profile state to have commercially whaled since the IWC's adoption of the global moratorium, it was not alone.[145] Indeed, both Norway and Iceland continued commercial whaling operations for decades.[146] With the decline in demand for whale meat in Iceland, however, the country has stated that it will cease all whaling activities in 2024.[147] In addition to these state-sponsored commercial hunts, the IWC provides for subsistence hunting by indigenous communities, such as those carried about by the Makah Tribe in the United States and others in Greenland, Russia, and Denmark.[148] Arguably outside the scope of the ICRW are smaller cetaceans, such as pilot whales, who are herded in large numbers to shore, where they are killed as part of the Faroe Islands' annual Grind Festival.[149]

Given the small number of states that have engaged in whaling since the moratorium was put in place, the IWC has expanded its focus. The same year that Japan denounced the ICRW, the IWC broadened its scope beyond conservation to contemplate welfare.[150] With the input of veterinarians, animal welfare specialists, and others, the IWC is in the process of developing a Cetacean Welfare Assessment Tool.[151] With it, the IWC hopes to address other issues that affect whales, such as ship strikes, pollution, strandings, and entanglements, alongside raising general awareness of how securing the interests of whales inures to the benefit of the environment and thus to humans.[152]

---

142. *Id.*

143. *Id.*

144. UNCLOS art. 65 (emphasis added); *United Nations Convention on the Law of the Sea*, *supra* note 97. Even though scholars point to the IWC as the appropriate entity, the question of which international organization or organizations are "appropriate" is not specified in UNCLOS itself. Chris Wold, *Legal Opinion concerning Japan's Duty to Cooperate with the International Whaling Commission with respect to Any Resumption of Commercial Whaling*, Intl Envl. Law Project (Apr. 26, 2019).

145. Keiko Hirata, *Why Japan Supports Whaling*, 8 J. Int'l Wildlife L. & Pol'y 129, 182 (2005).

146. *See Japan Leaves IWC to Resume Commercial Whaling*, NRDC (July 1, 2019), https://www.nrdc.org/media/2019/190701-0 (observing that both countries still engage in commercial whaling). Both lodged or registered an objection to the ban; Jemima Webber, *Whaling in the Faroe Islands: What You Need to Know About the Controversial Tradition*, Plant-Based News (July 10, 2021), https://plantbasednews.org/culture/ethics/faroe-islands-whaling-explained.

147. AFP in Reykjavik, *Iceland to End Whaling in 2024 as Demand Dwindles*, The Guardian (Feb. 3, 2022), https://www.theguardian.com/environment/2022/feb/04/iceland-to-end-whaling-in-2024-demand-dwindles.

148. *Aboriginal Subsistence Whaling*, International Whaling Commission, https://iwc.int/management-and-conservation/whaling/aboriginal (last visited Oct 1. 2022).

149. Webber, *supra* note 146.

150. *Welfare Issues*, International Whaling Commission, https://iwc.int/management-and-conservation/welfare (last visited Oct 1, 2022).

151. *Id.*

152. *Id.*; *IWC Workshop: The Value of Whales to the Ecosystem*, International Whaling Commission (Mar. 17, 2022), https://iwc.int/resources/media-resources/news/iwc-workshop-the-value-of-whales-to-the-ecosystem.

Protecting Animals Across Borders

The Convention on Migratory Species

Also known as the Bonn Convention due to its having been opened for signature in Bonn, Germany,[153] the Convention on the Conservation of Migratory Species of Wild Animals (CMS) addresses the need for cooperation among states to overcome the jurisdictional hurdles to protecting species that migrate across borders.[154] In doing so, CMS underscores the value of wild animals, who constitute an irreplaceable part of nature and ecosystems and are recognized as having diverse values, such as environmental, ecological, genetic, scientific, aesthetic, recreational, cultural, educational, social, and economic.[155] Notably, CMS echoes the view expressed in other treaties that the present generation owes a duty to conserve wildlife as a natural resource for future generations, as well as asserts that a state's sovereignty implies a duty to conserve and manage wildlife.[156] In light of this pronouncement, some may wonder why CMS applies only to transboundary migratory species. Again, the answer touches upon the view that, as sovereigns, states are naturally disinclined to voluntarily subject themselves to obligations and that they should enjoy near if not total control over those resources within their own territories. CMS offers a framework for states that desire yet lack the power to sufficiently protect wild animals due to their migratory nature.

But what constitutes a "migratory species," and how does CMS determine whether and to what extent a species merits protection? Here, CMS defines "migratory species" as the entire or a subset of a species or lower taxon whose members "cyclically and predictably" cross jurisdictional boundaries.[157] Notably, these conditions narrow the scope of the treaty to exclude species that may occasionally or irregularly cross borders, whether due to human intervention, natural disasters, or otherwise.

CMS provides for a biennial Conference of the Parties[158] at which contracting states determine which species qualify as migratory species, as well as which of the three conservation statuses apply to them (favorable, unfavorable, or endangered), with each status carrying implications for conservation and management.[159] For the status of a species to be favorable, four criteria must be met: it has to be able to maintain itself on a long-term basis as a viable component of an ecosystem; its range is not actually or predicted to be reduced in the long term; there is currently and a projected likelihood that it will have sufficient habitat for the long term; and its distribution and number meets near

153. Convention on the Conservation of Migratory Species of Wild Animals, June 23, 1979, 19 I.L.M. 15, 1651 U.N.T.S. 333, art. XV [hereinafter CMS].

154. *Id.* at Preamble.

155. *Id.*

156. *Id.*

157. *Id.*art. I, ¶ 1, cl. a.

158. *Id.*art. VII.

159. *See id.* arts. I, ¶ 1, cl. c, III–IV (laying out the three statuses a species may be listed as and the elements to be considered for their conservation status).

historic levels and coverage.[160] Absent any of these criteria, the status of the species will be deemed unfavorable, and it will be listed in Appendix II,[161] which requires that range states "endeavor to" enter into agreements with other range states to promote its conservation and management.[162] The "endangered" status is assigned to a species facing extinction "throughout all or a significant portion of its range."[163] For these species, which are listed on Appendix I of CMS, range states are required to prohibit takings, which include "hunting, fishing, capturing, harassing, deliberate killing, or attempting to engage in such conduct," although certain exemptions exist.[164] In addition, CMS requires that range states "endeavour" to take additional steps to protect Appendix I species, such as conserving and restoring their habitat, removing, compensating for, or minimizing adverse effects and obstacles that seriously impede migration, and addressing other factors that have or may further endanger them, including the controlling of exotic species.[165]

Again, while CMS requires that states endeavor to enter into agreements with other range states, these need not be formal treaties with binding obligations as conceived by Vienna.[166] Given that they are not binding, agreements such as memoranda of understanding, have the benefit of being easier to negotiate. Just a couple of examples of agreements crafted under the CMS framework include the Agreement on the Conservation of Gorillas and their Habitats,[167] which has seven contracting parties,[168] and the Agreement on the Conservation of Small Cetaceans of the Baltic, North East Atlantic, Irish and North Seas,[169] which has ten contracting parties.[170] Thus, the CMS framework empowers states to cooperate regionally, with the umbrella framework bringing conformity to the process of protecting migratory species.

While CMS does provide meaningful protections for migratory species in certain contexts, it does have shortfalls. Indeed, like other conservation-based treaties, CMS embraces an approach to animal protection that is concerned with animals only if their survival is in question and renders those that enjoy a favorable status out of its scope. If, conversely, the treaty encouraged contracting parties to enter into agreements to safeguard all migratory species, CMS could better ensure that all migratory species thrive, preventing parties from having to act only when there is a threat. Another hurdle to advancing the

160. *Id.* art. I, ¶ 1, cl. c.

161. *Id.* art. I, ¶ 1, cl. d.

162. *Id.* arts. I, ¶ 1, cl. f, II, ¶ 3, cl. c.

163. *Id.* art. I, ¶ 1, cl. e.

164. *Id.* arts. I, ¶ 1, cl. i, III, ¶ 5.

165. *Id.* art. III, ¶ 4.

166. *See Memoranda of Understanding*, Convention on the Conservation of Migratory Species of Wild Animals, https://www.cms.int/en/cms-instruments/mou (last visited Oct 1. 2022) (listing current MOUs created under the auspices of CMS).

167. *Gorilla Agreement*, Convention on the Conservation of Migratory Species of Wild Animals, https://www.cms.int/en/legalinstrument/gorilla-agreement (last visited Oct 1. 2022).

168. *Id.*

169. *Parties and Range States*, ASCOBANS, https://www.ascobans.org/en/parties-range-states (last visited Oct 1, 2022).

170. *Id.*

conservation goals of CMS arises in light of coastal states' obligations under UNCLOS, which addresses both catch limits and yield requirements for living resources in their EEZs. To address this, CMS states that it does not prejudice UNCLOS or affect any of the rights or obligations of contracting parties that have ratified treaties that may impose catch or animal-use requirements that would frustrate CMS's conservation objectives.[171]

Convention on International Trade in Endangered Species of Wild Fauna and Flora

Whereas CMS addresses the protection of migratory species that cross borders, CITES concerns the international trade in wild plant and animal species, whether dead or alive, and in their parts.[172] With an acknowledgment that international cooperation was needed to prevent the extinction of heavily trafficked species, negotiations for CITES began in the 1960s. The treaty opened for signature in Washington, DC, in 1973, and entered into force two years later.[173] Calling attention to the dire need to protect wildlife, CITES recognizes the beauty and diversity of animals and acknowledges their ever-growing value across multiple contexts: aesthetic, scientific, cultural, recreational, and economic.[174] In doing so, it underscores that states must act to combat species loss as a matter of utmost urgency.[175] That said, CITES observes that its purpose is not to prevent the exploitation of wild plants and animals altogether but rather their "over-exploitation," with negotiating states limiting the ability of the treaty to undermine their sovereignty. In this regard, CITES reaffirms the sovereignty of states, emphasizing that states are and should be the best protectors of the wildlife within their territories, with international cooperation necessary at certain times to aid in this global goal.[176] Given this framing, the self-imposed limitations of CITES become clear: it is only when covered species are transported across borders that its protections are implicated.

To appreciate how CITES combats the international trade in threatened wildlife, it is helpful to understand the bodies that carry out its provisions at the state level. In ratifying CITES, states are required to create two authorities: a Scientific Authority and a Management Authority.[177] The former is tasked with providing analyses and recommendations on matters involving the implementation of CITES.[178] This includes identifying, assessing, and recommending species for protection or changes in their listing status, monitoring trade and the status of the species in the wild, evaluating CITES documents and technical proposals, reviewing permit applications of listed species to determine if their

171. CMS, art. XII.

172. CITES art. 1, ¶ b.

173. *What Is CITES?*, CITES, https://cites.org/eng/disc/what.php (last visited Oct. 1, 2022).

174. CITES, Preamble.

175. *Id.*

176. *Id.*

177. *Id.* art. IX.

178. *Id.* arts. III–VII.

trade would be detrimental to their survival and, for live Appendix-I species, determining whether a recipient is equipped to house and care for that specimen, and more.[179] Complementing the work of the Scientific Authority, the Management Authority is charged with implementing the permitting program, monitoring trade, coordinating with inspection and enforcement officials, communicating on CITES issues with other contracting parties, and providing technical assistance to other contracting parties, among other responsibilities.[180] In carrying out these vital tasks, these authorities fulfill many of their state's CITES obligations. The matter of what level of protections are offered and which species receive them is determined by contracting parties at a biennial (or more frequent) Conference of the Parties, where at-risk species are listed in one of three appendices.[181]

Appendix I species are those threatened with extinction that are or may be affected by trade.[182] Commercial trade in wild-caught specimens of these Appendix I species is illegal, but exceptional circumstances allow for it if both import and export permits are authorized.[183] A permit from the exporting state is allowed only if it can be demonstrated that: the specimen was legally obtained; its trade will not be detrimental to the survival of the species; and, in the case of living specimens, its shipping will minimize risk of injury, cruelty, and health concerns.[184] In addition, for the importing state to authorize a permit, it must be shown that the specimen: will not be used for primarily commercial purposes, will be used for purposes not detrimental to the species' overall survival; and, in the case of live specimens, that the recipient is able to house and care for it.[185]

Appendix II lists species not necessarily threatened with extinction but whose trade must be controlled in order to "avoid utilization incompatible with their survival."[186] Appendix II also includes other species whose trade must be regulated to protect Appendix II species, such as if two species are mutually interdependent—an implicit recognition of the need to take biodiversity into account.[187] Notably, Appendix II also includes captive-bred Appendix I species,[188] with this provision enabling industries to engage in the commercial trade of animals in which they could not otherwise engage. For Appendix II species, the criteria for the exporting state to issue a permit are the same as for Appendix I: the specimen has to have been legally obtained; there has to be a nondetrimental finding; and appropriate measures must be taken to prevent injury in transport.[189] In contrast to the requirement for Appendix I species,

179. *Id.*
180. *Id.*
181. *Id.* art. XI.
182. *Id.* art. II.
183. *Id.* art. II.
184. *Id.* art. II.
185. *Id.* art. II.
186. *Id.* art. II, ¶ 2, cl. a.
187. *Id.* art. II, ¶ 2, cl. b.
188. *Id.* art. VII, ¶ 4.
189. *Id.* art. 4.

however, no import permit is required for species listed in Appendix II.[190] Ultimately, this permitting framework empowers states of origin to conserve potentially at-risk species, a nod to their sovereignty and the view that states are the best protectors of their own resources.

Finally, Appendix III contains species unilaterally listed by a contracting state, with trade controls in effect for that state only.[191] By listing a species in Appendix III, a contracting state expresses its desire for international aid to protect that species, which may not be threatened with extinction or may be at-risk only within its territory, as opposed to globally. Trade in these species is permitted only with an appropriate export permit and a certificate of origin from the state that listed it.[192] In this vein, other states can import Appendix III-listed species only with the state of origin's permission.[193]

While CITES does create numerous checks to control the international trade of at-risk species, it also contains numerous exceptions that limit its effectiveness. For example, specimens acquired before they were listed on an Appendix can be exempted from CITES trade controls.[194] Also exempt are "household effects," though some exclusions to this exemption apply.[195] Exemptions also exist for scientific research[196] for circus animals, if certain conditions are met, and in other instances.[197]

In addition to concerns that exemptions within CITES frustrate its purpose, some criticize its negative-listing approach to wildlife conservation: if a unlisted species were to be suddenly imperiled, it could go extinct before the next Conference of the Parties. Conversely, a positive-listing approach (i.e., listing only those species that could be traded) could provide more robust protections. In addition, CITES lacks a clear set of guidelines for what qualifies as a "non-detrimental" finding for Scientific Authorities to employ when making their determinations. Further complicating their work, findings require copious amounts of information that may or may not be accessible. As such, states can knowingly or unwittingly permit trade that violates the spirit of their obligations. Perhaps most glaringly, domestic trade remains unchecked under CITES, which is also silent as to the issue of habitat conservation—even though habitat loss is a key driver of species loss.[198]

Of course, an inherent limitation of CITES to protect animals as individuals is found in its extension of protections based upon the status of their species. As such, if a species listed under any of CITES's appendices subsequently thrives, it

190. *Id.*

191. *Id.* art II, ¶ 3.

192. *Id.* art. V.

193. *Id.*

194. *Id.* art. VII, ¶ 2.

195. *Id.* art. VIII.

196. *Id.* art. VII, ¶ 6.

197. *Id.* art. VII, ¶¶ 3, 7.

198. *Losing Their Homes Because of the Growing Needs of Humans*, WWF, https://wwf.panda.org/discover/our_focus/wildlife_practice/problems/habitat_loss_degradation (last visited Oct. 1, 2022). Note that while CMS does address habitat loss, partially helping to fill this void, it applies only to the habitat of migratory species, leaving other threatened habitats outside its purview.

is liable to be removed at a later Conference of the Parties, enabling it to be traded freely once more and thus potentially subjecting it to the same pressures that threatened its existence to begin with. A treaty that views animals as commodities can arguably go only so far to secure their protections.

The Convention on Biological Diversity

Developed at the 1992 Earth Summit in Rio de Janeiro, the Convention on Biological Diversity (CBD) was a core component of a comprehensive global plan to protect biological diversity while promoting sustainable development.[199] The CBD employs an ecosystem-wide approach to conservation, with its purview including plants and microorganisms in addition to animals.[200] Notably for purposes of this book, the CBD does not seek to protect individual animals for their own sake, but rather views them as integral parts of ecosystems. Chief among its goals are the conservation of biological diversity, the sustainable use of biological components, and the fair and equitable sharing of the benefits from the use of genetic resources.[201] In its preamble, the CBD acknowledges the anthropocentric as well as intrinsic value of biological diversity, which it frames as vital for evolution and life-supporting systems.[202] As with other treaties, the CBD acknowledges the sovereignty that states have over the resources in their jurisdiction, while also underscoring the collective need to prevent harms that extend beyond borders.[203]

As a first step in effectuating these goals, the CBD obligates parties to develop strategies, programs, and plans, and generally to provide for the conservation and sustainable use of biological diversity.[204] In doing so, parties are to identify and monitor the use of the "components" of biological diversity, distinguishing between those in critical need of conservation and those with the widest potential to be sustainably used.[205] To guide parties' identification and monitoring, the treaty features three categories to consider: the first concerns ecosystems and habitats, specifically those featuring significant diversity, large numbers of endemic or threatened species, and wilderness needed by migratory species; the second focuses on species and communities under threat, wild relatives of domesticated species, and those with medicinal, agricultural, economic, social, scientific, or cultural value; and the third focuses on genomes and genes of social, scientific, or economic importance.[206]

To promote the conservation of the components of biological diversity, the CBD requires parties to employ both in situ and ex situ conservation measures. With regard to the former, parties must advance measures to establish protected

199. *Sustaining Life on Earth*, Convention on Biological Diversity (Sept. 9, 2009), https://www.cbd.int/convention/guide/.

200. Convention on Biological Diversity, May 6, 1992, 1760 U.N.T.S. 79, art. II [hereinafter CBD].

201. *Id.* art. I.

202. *Id.* at Preamble.

203. *Id.*art. III.

204. *Id.*art. VI.

205. *Id.* art. VII.

206. *Id.*art.VII, Annex I.

areas, encourage the safeguarding of natural habitats and ecosystems, and support sustainable development practices around them.[207] In addition, parties must seek to rehabilitate degraded ecosystems and advance the recovery of threatened species.[208] With regard to ex situ measures, which the CBD frames as a means to "complement" in situ conservation,[209] parties are required to undertake measures to conserve biological diversity, preferably within their own borders, by developing conservation facilities and recovering and rehabilitating threatened species with the intent of restoring them in their natural habitat.[210]

At present, the CBD arguably represents the world's most significant agreement concerning biological conservation, with only the United States and the Holy See having failed to formally ratify it.[211] As with CITES and CMS, the CBD features a Conference of the Parties,[212] which negotiates and adopts decade-based target goals, with the most recently completed being the Aichi Biodiversity Targets, which ran from 2010 to 2020 and included goals around curbing deforestation, pollution, and more.[213] Upon the formal adoption of the decade-long targets, parties are expected to implement national programs and strategies to achieve them.[214] Notably, one of the criticisms of the CBD has been the failure of parties to meet these targets, with none of the twenty Aichi targets having been met globally, and few parties having fully implemented their programs within their jurisdictions.[215] As such, although the CBD offers a compelling framework to promote the conservation of biological diversity, including the prevention of species loss, it has not realized the impact that world leaders have hoped for.

Protecting Animals Through Trade Agreements

WTO

Whereas CITES employs only species-specific trade controls to protect wildlife from extinction, the WTO features more general international trade measures that states can use to protect not only endangered species but also individual animals, both wild and domestic. Containing multiple sub-agreements,[216] the WTO's main purpose is to remove barriers to trade, thereby bringing

207. *Id.* art. VIII.

208. *Id.*

209. *Id.*art. IX.

210. *Id.*

211. Benji Jones, *Why the US Won't Join the Single Most Important Treaty to Protect Nature*, VOX (May 20, 2021), https://www.vox.com/22434172/us-cbd-treaty-biological-diversity-nature-conservation.

212. CBD, art. XXIII.

213. Patrick Greenfield, *World Fails to Meet a Single Target to Stop Destruction of Nature—UN Report*, THE GUARDIAN (Sept. 15, 2020), https://www.reuters.com/business/environment/why-did-past-targets-protect-nature-fail-over-last-decade-2022-12-09.

214. *Id.*

215. *Id.*

216. *WTO Legal Texts*, WORLD TRADE ORGANIZATION, https://www.wto.org/english/docs_e/legal_e/legal_e.htm (last visited Oct. 1, 2022).

conformity to global trade.[217] The first and arguably the most important of these sub-agreements is the General Agreement on Tariffs and Trade (GATT).[218] The GATT features a pair of noteworthy principles that prevent states from creating discriminatory trade barriers with regard to "like products" in their domestic markets.[219] Enshrined in Article I, the Most Favored Nation principle requires that trade concessions that a member state extends to any other member state be extended to all other member states;[220] this measure helps ensure that states do not discriminate between like products imported from other member states, affording one less favorable treatment than another. Similar to the first and enshrined in Article III, the National Treatment principle prevents states from engaging in the same kind of discrimination between their domestically produced products and those imported from other member states.[221] The Technical Barriers to Trade Agreement (TBT) is a subagreement to the WTO that prevents states from employing technical measures, such as regulations and labeling standards, to skirt the GATT framework.[222]

While the Most Favored Nation and National Treatment principles inform the general rules of the GATT, the GATT also features key exceptions, under which member states may justify discrimination against like products in certain circumstances. Enshrined in Article XX,[223] these exceptions allow states to discriminate for the following reasons, among others: "if necessary to protect human, animal or plant life or health;" to "conserve exhaustible natural resources," so long as the state takes measures to restrict its own domestic production or consumption; and if necessary to protect public morals.[224] These exceptions are not whole-scale carveouts, and they may not be applied in ways that give rise to arbitrary or unjustifiable discrimination.[225]

The question of what constitutes a "like product" informs what is regarded as the "Process and Production Method" debate,[226] which implicates important animal protection issues. For example, what if an animal product—for example, tuna—is produced using capture methods that likely resulted in dolphin deaths? Would that product be similar to, or "like," a tuna product that was made using a method that avoided killing dolphins? With respect to its domestic market, should a state that requires its nationals to use the dolphin-safe method for tuna products be allowed to discriminate against imported tuna that allows for non-dolphin safe methods if the end product (the tuna itself) is technically the same?

217. *What We Stand For*, World Trade Organization, https://www.wto.org/english/thewto_e/whatis_e/what_stand_for_e.htm (last visited Oct. 1, 2022).

218. GATT 1994: General Agreement on Tariffs and Trade 1994, Apr. 15, 1994, Marrakesh Agreement Establishing the World Trade Organization, Annex 1A, 1867 U.N.T.S. 187 (1994) [hereinafter GATT].

219. GATT art. I, ¶ 1.

220. *Id.*

221. *Id.* art. III.

222. Agreement on Technical Barriers to Trade 1868 U.N.T.S. 120 [hereinafter TBT Agreement].

223. *Id.* art. XX.

224. *Id.* art. XX, ¶¶ a, g, b.

225. *Id.* art. XX.

226. *WTO Rules and Environmental Policies: Key GATT Disciplines*, World Trade Organization, https://www.wto.org/english/tratop_e/envir_e/envt_rules_gatt_e.htm (last visited Oct. 1, 2022).

If so, would that discrimination be justifiable under the GATT exception to protect animal life, even if that animal life lies outside a state's jurisdiction?

US-Tuna II

This particular question animated the US-Tuna II dispute addressed by the WTO appellate tribunal in 2017.[227] The case concerned a particular region of the Eastern Tropical Pacific, where dolphins and tuna were known to associate, with the presence of dolphins enabling the fishing industry to easily locate schools of tuna.[228] Fishing boats would employ a "setting-on," or purse seine, tuna capture method, which led to bycatch and dolphin mortality.[229] Following the outcry over dolphin deaths, the United States banned this capture method and created a labeling regulation that allowed tuna products sold in its domestic market to bear a "dolphin-safe" label if the purse-seine capture method was not used.[230] If the purse-seine capture method was used, however, no mention as to the safety of dolphins or other marine mammals could be made on the tuna product in question—even if no dolphins had actually been harmed in its production.[231]

Given that Mexico allowed for the purse-seine capture method, it argued that the U.S. labeling regulation constituted a technical barrier to trade under the TBT and resulted in unjustifiable discrimination.[232] To counter this argument, the United States initially argued that "dolphin-safe" and non-dolphin-safe tuna were not "like products," and so no discrimination analysis should have been conducted.[233] The tribunal, however, rejected this view, finding that the tuna products were the same and that only the method of production (or capture) distinguished them.[234] The core remaining issue concerned whether the United States was engaging in arbitrary or unjustifiable discrimination.[235] Noting that the United States imposed the unfavorable label if the purse-seine method was used regardless of whether dolphins had been actually harmed and allowed for use of the preferred label for other capture methods even if they resulted in dolphin deaths,[236] the tribunal found that the regulation misled consumers because it allowed a "dolphin-safe" label for products that actually did lead to dolphin deaths.[237] While the tribunal thus ruled against this attempt to protect animals, the United States later amended its dolphin-safe labeling regulations to ensure the label more accurately reflected whether the dolphins

227. Appellate Body Report, United States—Measures Concerning the Importation, Marketing and Sale of Tuna and Tuna Products, WTO Doc WT/DS381/AB/RW2 (adopted 2012) [hereinafter US-Tuna II].

228. *Id.* ¶¶ 5.1–5.25.

229. *Id.* ¶¶ 1.2–1.3, 5.8.

230. *Id.* ¶ 139.

231. *Id.*

232. *Id.* ¶ 145.

233. *Id.* ¶ 169.

234. *Id.* ¶ 187.

235. *Id.* ¶ 180.

236. *Id.* ¶ 208.

237. *Id.* ¶¶ 180, 264.

were actually harmed in the production of a tuna product.[238] In addition to leading to more accurate consumer information, *US-Tuna II* illustrates how the WTO framework can be leveraged to advance animal protections and hold states accountable, leading to animal protection regulations being not only recalibrated but also strengthened as a result.

EC-Seal Products

A more recent WTO dispute, *EC-Seal Products*,[239] is noteworthy for affirming that animal protection is an issue of public moral concern, on the basis of which states may discriminate against products. In 2010, the European Union banned the import of seal products under what the WTO referred to as the EU Seal Regime, which included three exceptions: products brought by travelers (who could not later sell them); products from marine resource management practices; and those obtained through indigenous community subsistence hunts, with Greenland's indigenous communities being the main beneficiaries.[240] In their complaints to the WTO, Canada and Norway argued that the regulation discriminated against both their commercial sealers and their indigenous populations.[241] Although the Appellate Body found the regulation violated the GATT framework because it did not adequately distinguish commercial from subsistence hunting and also failed to provide equitable access to Canada's indigenous communities,[242] it effectively affirmed that, under Article XX, states may discriminate against "like" animal products based upon the moral views of their citizens. What is particularly compelling about this decision is its potential to empower stakeholders in higher-welfare states to affirm that animal welfare is an important moral issue, with resulting regulations in such states having the power to persuade companies abroad to follow suit or lose access to those markets.

Animal Health and Disease Prevention

Three-quarters of diseases that afflict humans originate in animals.[243] Thus, securing the health of animals to protect that of people has been the focus of global efforts for roughly a century. When a rinderpest outbreak emerged in

238. *Dolphin-Safe*, Nat'l Oceanic and Atmospheric Administration, https://www.fisheries.noaa.gov/national/marine-mammal-protection/dolphin-safe (last visited Oct. 1, 2022).

239. Appellate Body Report, World Trade Organization, European Communities—Measures Prohibiting the Importation and Marketing of Seal Products, WT Doc. WT/DS400/DS401/AB/R (adopted June 18, 2014) [hereinafter EC-Seal].

240. *Id.* ¶¶ 1.2–1.4.

241. *Id.* ¶¶ 1.2–1.4, 2.4

242. *Id.* ¶ 5.338–39.

243. Rajeshwari Sinha, *75% Emerging Infectious Diseases Zoonotic: UN Report*, DownToEarth (July 7, 2020), https://www.downtoearth.org.in/news/health/75-emerging-infectious-diseases-zoonotic-un-report-72173.

cows being transported from India to Brazil in 1920,[244] states called for the creation of a global organization to combat the spread of zoonotic diseases, or those that can spill over from animals to humans.[245] WOAH, previously known as the Office International des Epizooties (OIE), was formed to carry out this directive in 1924.[246] WOAH's efforts have improved global animal veterinary health. For example, the last documented case of rinderpest having been reported in 2001.[247]

Recognizing the interdependence among human, animal, and environmental health, WOAH employs a One Health approach to carry out its core mission to eradicate disease.[248] Other aspects of its global initiatives include the combating of antimicrobial resistance and biological threats, as well as improving food safety.[249] Recognizing the interconnectedness of animal health and welfare, WOAH has created terrestrial and aquatic animal health and welfare codes and standards.[250] While these standards are not binding and do not obligate member states to carry out animal welfare improvements,[251] they nevertheless inform the international trade of animals and animal products. In particular, the Sanitary and Phyto-Sanitary (SPS) Agreement, another subagreement of the WTO framework that was negotiated in 1998,[252] incorporates WOAH's guidelines as a global standard for animal health.[253] As the SPS Agreement makes clear, its standards do not constitute a ceiling for animal health,[254] and states may create stricter standards so long as the specific health risk is identified and they do not engage in unjustifiable or arbitrary discrimination.[255] With the COVID-19 pandemic having drawn the world's attention to zoonotic disease risks,[256] states and world leaders are arguably more

---

244. *Multiple Species*, World Organization for Animal Health, https://www.woah.org/en/animal/multiple-species (last visited Oct. 1, 2022).

245. *Id.*

246. *Id.*

247. *Rinderpest*, World Organization for Animal Health, https://www.woah.org/en/disease/rinderpest/ (last visited Oct. 1, 2022).

248. *One Health*, World Organization for Animal Health, https://www.woah.org/en/what-we-do/global-initiatives/one-health (last visited Oct. 1, 2022).

249. *What We Do*, World Organization for Animal Health, https://www.woah.org/en/what-we-do (last visited Oct. 1, 2022).

250. *Animal Welfare*, World Organization for Animal Health, https://www.woah.org/en/what-we-do/animal-health-and-welfare/animal-welfare/#ui-id-2 (last visited Oct. 1, 2022).

251. *Development of Animal Welfare Standards*, World Organization for Animal Health, https://www.woah.org/en/what-we-do/animal-health-and-welfare/animal-welfare/development-of-animal-welfare-standards (last visited Oct. 1, 2022).

252. *World Organisation for Animal Health* (WOAH, founded as OIE), European Commission, https://food.ec.europa.eu/horizontal-topics/international-affairs/international-standards/woah_en (last visited Oct. 1, 2022).

253. *Understanding the WTO Agreement on Sanitary and Phytosanitary Measures*, World Trade Organization, https://www.wto.org/english/tratop_e/sps_e/spsund_e.htm (last visited Oct. 1, 2022).

254. *Id.*

255. *See id.* (observing how "governments which do not base their national requirements on international standards may be required to justify their higher standard if this difference gives rise to a trade dispute" and that "[s]uch justification must be based on an analysis of scientific evidence and the risks involved").

256. Rajesh K Reddy & Joan Schaffner, *The Convention on Animal Protection: The Missing Link in a One Health Global Strategy for Pandemic Prevention*, 10 Global J. of Animal L.1 (2022).

conscious of the need to take animals' basic welfare interests into account, if only as a means to better protect human health.[257]

From Past to Present and Margins to Center

As exemplified by the near-global end of commercial whaling, the call to better conserve fishes on the high seas, and the creation of trade bans that seek to improve the lives and welfare of animals, advocates have successfully leveraged international agreements to realize meaningful change for animals not just in their home countries but also across the world. In driving this change, advocates have encouraged states to adopt more enlightened views as to *who* rather than *what* animals are, and why they merit protection—even if states largely still consider animals to fall in the category of property. In this vein, animal-related treaties are arguably evolving from viewing animals as merely the *objects* of international animal protections to being their *beneficiaries*. Against this backdrop, advocates have also advanced declarations and treaty proposals to establish a global foundation on which animals' interests as individuals can be advanced.

A handful of animal welfare-focused global initiatives have been proposed, though none have yet been adopted. One is the Universal Declaration for Animal Rights, first presented at the United Nations Educational, Scientific and Cultural Organization in 1978.[258] Another is the Universal Declaration on Animal Welfare, drafted in 2005.[259] Each lays out foundational principles regarding animal rights and welfare. As declarations, however, they do not create binding obligations and are thus distinct from treaties in terms of their potential impact. That said, declarations signal state interest in creating national legislation inspired by their principles, and even a willingness to engage in treaty talks.

As the first proposed framework that would legally obligate states if adopted, the International Convention on the Protection of Animals (ICPA) was drafted in 1988.[260] Employing an umbrella approach, ICPA includes general animal protection principles and would allow for protocols to be negotiated and adopted to address context-specific welfare issues, such as the taking of wild animals, the welfare of exhibited wildlife, and the international transportation of animals.[261] To be a party to ICPA, states would have to adopt both its framework and at least one of its protocols.[262] While ICPA has not been adopted by

257. *COVID-19 Shows Why United Action Is Needed for More Robust International Health Architecture*, World Health Organization (Mar. 30, 2021), https://www.who.int/news-room/commentaries/detail/op-ed—covid-19-shows-why-united-action-is-needed-for-more-robust-international-health-architecture.

258. Jean Marc Neumann, *The Universal Declaration of Animal Rights or the Creation of a New Equilibrium Between Species*, 19 Animal L. 91, 94–95 (2012).

259. Miah Gibson, *The Universal Declaration of Animal Welfare*, 16 Deakin L. Rev. 539, 541 (2011).

260. David Favre, *An International Treaty for Animal Welfare Symposium Article*, 18 Animal L. 237, 246 (2012).

261. *Id.* at 259.

262. *Id.* at 255.

any state,[263] it nevertheless represents a framework capable of advancing the myriad interests of animals. Other treaty proposals have since been developed, such as the United Nations Convention on Animal Health and Protection (UNCAHP) in 2019,[264] followed by the Convention on Animal Protection for Animal Well-Being, Public Health, and the Environment ("CAP") a year later.[265] Developed around the COVID-19 pandemic, the UNCAHP and CAP are both grounded in the connection between animal welfare and health, as well as the links between the health of animals, humans, and the environment.[266] Such proposals evidence a desire to move beyond both past and present frameworks and to center animals in animal protection treaties, which have historically situated their interests at the margins.

263. *Id.* at 262.

264. Global Animal Law Association, UN Convention on Animal Health and Protection (2019) (available at www.globalanimallaw.org/gal/projects/uncahp.html).

265. Reddy & Schaffner, *supra* note 256, at 1.

266. *Id.*; Global Animal Law Association, *supra* note 264.

Conclusion

Laws and policies change with global events, scientific advances, and society's ever-shifting attitudes. Thus, the laws and policies in this book reflect a moment in time when animals are generally still considered property and institutional cruelty continues, largely unchecked, around the world.

On behalf of our authors and the many advocates and lawyers who work tirelessly to change the laws, spread compassion, and protect animals, we hope the next edition of this book will herald a fundamental change in how we view nonhuman animals, both for their own sakes and in light of their unquestionable contributions to human well-being.

Index

About the Editors

Daina Bray is a clinical lecturer and senior research scholar in Law with the Law, Ethics & Animals Program at Yale Law School, where she leads the Climate Change & Animal Agriculture Litigation Initiative. Daina previously served as general counsel of the nonprofits Mercy For Animals and the International Fund for Animal Welfare, and practiced with major international law firms in the areas of litigation and international arbitration. Daina is a past chair of the ABA International Animal Law Committee, the ABA TIPS Animal Law Committee, and the Tennessee Bar Association Animal Law Section. Daina received a JD from Stanford Law School with pro bono distinction, a BA in international studies from the University of North Carolina at Chapel Hill as a Morehead Scholar, a Fulbright scholarship for research in environmental education, and the 2021 ABA Excellence in the Advancement of Animal Law Award.

Yolanda Eisenstein is an attorney with experience in animal, wildlife, and nonprofit law. She is president of the Animal Law Commission of Paris-based *Union Internationale des Avocats* (UIA), where she focuses on international wildlife issues and represents the UIA at the United Nations in New York. She is vice chair of the ABA International Law Section Animal Law Committee. In 2018, Eisenstein received the ABA Excellence in the Advancement of Animal Law Award in recognition of her work to advance the humane treatment of animals through the law. She developed and taught the first animal law and wildlife courses at SMU Dedman School of Law. Eisenstein's books include *Careers in Animal Law, The American Bar Association Guide to Dog Laws*, and *Wildlife Law and Ethics* (co-editor with Bruce Wagman). She was a contributor to *Animal Cruelty: A Multidisciplinary Approach to Understanding.*

About the Authors

Akela Baldwin is a JD candidate at Lewis & Clark Law School in Portland, Oregon. She is focused on using the law to advance animal interests. Akela holds a BA in Environmental Anthropology from Hamilton College in Clinton, New York. She advocates for animal rights and welfare through her involvement with organizations, including Anonymous for the Voiceless, Farm Sanctuary, and Humane Voters Oregon.

Meredith Beach is legislative counsel, Legal Advocacy and Investigations at the American Society for the Prevention of Cruelty to Animals (ASPCA) where she analyzes federal, state, and local legislation impacting animal welfare. Prior to joining the ASPCA, Meredith worked in state and local politics in Maryland and the Congressional Research Service at the Library of Congress.

Akisha Townsend Eaton began her animal law career in 2009 as an animal welfare fellow in the U.S. Senate. She has since served as a legislative attorney, policy advisor, and managing attorney at a variety of national and international animal protection and lifesaving organizations. She currently serves as chief of policy, Environmental Justice Division at Companions and Animals for Reform and Equity, a human and animal well-being organization. Akisha received her law degree from Georgetown University Law Center and her bachelor's degree from Stanford University where she graduated with distinction.

Tamara Feliciano is senior legislative counsel, Legal Advocacy and Investigations, at the ASPCA where she advises on matters of law and policy, manages the organization's legislative counsel practice, and handles agency litigation. Before joining the ASPCA, Tamara worked in private practice handling pro bono animal welfare cases, including complex civil, criminal, and legislative matters.

Robert Hensley is senior counsel, Legal Advocacy and Investigations for the American Society for the ASPCA where he advises on matters of law and policy and oversees the ASPCA's civil litigation and legislative practice as well as the organization's Puppy Mill Initiative. Prior to joining the ASPCA, Robert practiced law with Kilpatrick, Townsend & Stockton, LLP, in Raleigh, North Carolina, where he represented an array of clients, from Fortune 100 Companies to small nonprofit organizations in both state and federal courts.

Rebecca J. Huss joined Best Friends Animal Society as General Counsel in July 2019 and is a Professor Emerita from Valparaiso University Law School. Professor Huss was the 2011 recipient of the ABA TIPS' Animal Law Committee's Excellence in the Advancement of Animal Law Award and the 2019 recipient of the Excellence in Animal Law Award from the Association of American Law Schools Animal Law Section. Professor Huss has a Master of Laws in International and Comparative Law from the University of Iowa College of Law and graduated magna cum laude from the University of Richmond School of Law.

Abbey Jay is the assistant general counsel of Programs at Mercy For Animals. After graduating from NYU School of Law and practicing corporate law in New York, Abbey entered the field of animal law five years ago by joining the Mercy For Animals legal team. She is passionate about legal advocacy and animal welfare, and she is grateful for the opportunity to combine both passions into a career in animal law. She also enjoys writing, mentoring others, volunteering, and spending time with her companion animals.

Beverly J. Jones is senior vice president and chief legal officer of the ASPCA, providing support on a range of programmatic and operational areas, including contracts, tax, employment, litigation, lobbying and political activity, and animal law. Prior to joining the ASPCA, Jones served as in-house counsel at the Vera Institute of Justice and in the Tax-Exempt Organizations practice group of Preston Gates & Ellis, LLP (now K&L Gates). Before law school, Jones conducted fieldwork and lobbying workshops for youth on LGBTIA+ civil rights issues with the Human Rights Campaign.

Cheryl Leahy is executive director of Animal Outlook, a national nonprofit animal protection organization. She is responsible for development and oversight of investigations, litigation and policy, and effecting mainstream corporate and cultural change to shift away from animal products. Cheryl developed and taught one of the nation's first courses on animals in agriculture and the law at UCLA Law. She earned her JD from UCLA School of Law and her BA from the University of Chicago in Environmental Studies. She is a member of the bar in the District of Columbia, Maryland, and California, and is based in Los Angeles.

Lauren Martin is the vice president, deputy general counsel at the ASPCA where she provides legal counsel for ASPCA programs and infrastructure teams. Martin was an adjunct assistant professor of Animal Law in the Veterinary Forensics program at the University of Florida and an adjunct professor at St. John's University School of Law, where she taught animal law to second- and third-year law students. Prior to joining the ASPCA, Martin worked at Willkie Farr & Gallagher where her legal work focused on hedge funds and commodity pools.

Jamie McLaughlin is an animal and environmental lawyer. Her focus is the intersection of industrial animal agriculture, social justice, and the environment.

Jamie received her JD with a Public Interest Law Certificate from DePaul University College of Law in Chicago, Illinois. She holds an LLM in Animal Law (cum laude) from Lewis & Clark Law School in Portland, Oregon and is currently working toward an Environmental Law LLM. Jamie serves as animal law commission working group vice president of the *Union Internationale des Avocats.*

Russ Mead lectures on professional responsibility to bar associations across the country. Mead is the Shared Earth Foundation visiting professor at Lewis & Clark Law School. His prior experience includes general counsel for Best Friends Animal Society, general counsel for Farm Sanctuary, and Farm Sanctuary interim executive director. Mead is the author of *Trial Advocacy in Animal Law, Nonprofit Animal Law,* and *Put These Seeds in Your Pocket: The Ukrainian People Fight Russia with Sunflower Seeds* (Amazon) and *Grass Roots Animal Legislation* and *Farm Animal Law Readings and Materials* (Smashwords).

Dr. Rajesh K. Reddy directs the Animal Law Program at the Center for Animal Law Studies at Lewis & Clark Law School, where he also serves as an assistant professor of Law, teaching Animal Legal Philosophy, International Animal Law, Introduction to U.S. Legal Studies, and Emerging Topics in Animal Law, among others. Outside of Lewis & Clark, he sits on the boards of Minding Animals International and the International Coalition for Animal Protection, as well as co-chairs the International subcommittee of the Animal Law Committee of the American Bar Association.

Margaret Robinson is a staff attorney at the Humane Society of the United States and has taught at George Mason University Antonin Scalia Law School. Her current practice focuses on protecting wildlife both in the wild and in captivity, including countering cruel trophy hunting practices, advocating for former research chimpanzees, and defending fur sales bans.

John Seber is the general counsel of the Animal Legal Defense Fund, directing the legal affairs of the organization and serving as a member of the organization's senior executive team. Prior to joining the Animal Legal Defense Fund, John was the senior vice president of Advocacy at Mercy For Animals. He graduated cum laude from the University of Michigan Law School and magna cum laude from Georgetown University. Prior to joining the animal protection movement, he was an associate at the law firm of Eimer Stahl LLP in Chicago, Illinois.

Michael Swistara is an animal protection lawyer, advocate, and independent scholar. His practice focuses on litigating to improve the lives of farmed animals and animals in captivity. His academic work addresses the intersection of animal law with other areas of social justice, and it has been published in numerous animal studies and legal journals around the world. He earned his JD and MPP with a focus in Environmental Law and Policy from The George Washington University, his MA in Economics from Columbia University, and his BA from McGill University. He is a member of the state bar in Illinois and is currently based in Chicago.

Bruce Wagman has been using his legal education and well-honed skills to help animals in all sectors of society for almost three decades. He litigates, drafts animal-friendly legislation, oversees rescue operations, and advises clients who care for and protect animals. He has published two major works, the leading casebook for law schools nationwide—*Animal Law: Cases and Materials*—and a global survey of animal laws, *A Worldview of Animal Law*. Bruce also founded Project Chimps, a chimpanzee sanctuary that is home to chimpanzees retired from a research laboratory.